TO Aaro
Electrons
        P
So comes knowledge, is
   it power
      or
   Love ?
        J Slyde

BLOCKCHAIN FAITH

BLOCKCHAIN FAITH

*A Guidebook to The Future of Promises, Relationships
and Conflict Resolution in The Post-Digital Age*

Jonny Stryder

Eggseed Press
Monrovia, California
First Edition
2018

To my mother Lorna, who taught me
all people have equal rights
and freedom fulfills itself by love.

ISBN No. 978-1-948956-00-0 (6x9 Print)
Library of Congress Control Number: 2018940918
ISBN No. 978-1-948956-01-7 (eBook)

AUTHOR'S PREFACE

While Bitcoin was increasing in value from a few dollars to over $10,000 per coin, I occupied myself with an odd idea I called "voluntary law." By that I meant a social order in which no one is forced to obey rules they oppose. Not so much by consensus, more by accepting diversity. Everybody obeys a code of honor they personally accept, a bit like the promises taught to children in the Boy Scouts and Girl Scouts. I wanted to learn how people might extend social promises to broader society, with no leadership in charge of what the promises say. Everybody picks their own social promises expressing their personal code of honor for social conduct and publishes their social promises in an encrypted public ledger. Each adult's honor and reputation depend on what their promises say, how they keep their promises and how they resolve differences with others. All participants can resolve their disputes based on social promises without looking to the state.

My friends were skeptical of my ideas about voluntary law. Looking back, resistance was less about the ideas and more about my difficulty in overcoming communication barriers. I learned to express unconventional ideas in ways that people could understand, by connecting the ideas to familiar, positive concepts. Talking about social promises instead of voluntary laws was a big help.

Speaking and writing about voluntary law led me to an unpleasant discovery. For those abused by state-run systems or vengeful vigilantes, words like "justice" and "law" trigger unpleasant emotions. Too many people are scarred by violence and oppression in the name of authoritarian shibboleths. Here I use the words "law" and "justice" in a non-authoritarian sense that contradicts abuse meted out under privilege of state monopolies. In this book, "law" is the set of social obligations that each self sovereign accepts and takes responsibility for, without coercion or fraud. "Justice" is what happens when self-sovereigns fulfill the social obligations they have made, and none are coerced to do more than promised. Justice includes enabling those who have dishonored themselves by violating their own promises restore their honor by making amends. It means conflict resolution is fair and free of any bias.

Too many words mean the opposite of what they should. Take "rule of law" for example. It should mean that the community doesn't let the strong dominate the weak. Abusers suffer consequences of their bad behavior and everyone receives rewards for cooperative behavior, from an early age. How powerful you are doesn't determine whether you are right. But nowadays, many believe the opposite. When they hear "rule of law," they think of powerful police that none dare disobey. If the power of the police comes from their superior capacity for violence, that's tyranny, not rule of law. Many see the world in that upside-down way, confusing tyranny with rule of law. That's a fact we must accept, and tailor the message around.

"Faith" means reasonable trust in strangers. "Blockchain" is a less emotionally laden word but is mysterious for many. It's used here to refer to secure distributed public ledgers kept as community assets, whatever the technical details. In this book, "ledger" means any organized set of records, regardless of the information contained. It encompasses all indexed data structures. Methods for decentralized order taught here depend on distributed public ledgers for success at scale. You will not find technical details of public ledger architectures or protocols here. Instead you will learn how people can use encrypted public ledgers to leverage social promises into new and healthier forms of social order, including fair and effective conflict resolution. Using the principles and methods laid out in this Guidebook, our children and successors can find better ways to organize their society, celebrate the beauty and freedom of life, and thrive all the way to the stars.

At root, methods for using social promises as explained here are for building relationship networks offering ethical conflict resolution outside of the courtroom. People can resolve their disputes without resorting to judges, lawyers or police under laws imposed by politicians and special interests. Radically alternative conflict resolution comes before and supersedes action involving the state. It eliminates the need to "take it to the man." When social promises succeed, individuals have a basis for building interpersonal trust outside of state or corporate institutions.

Ethical conduct is honorable, and the most precious asset is honor. Instead of provoking fear and enmity by casting slings and arrows at the state, this Guidebook would help build alternatives that enable relationship building and conflict resolution within a decentralized, stateless community. The community emerges as violence by the state lessens.

I began my exploration of social promising in public ledgers by blogging at The Voluntary Law Development Association (www.vlda.org). This First Edition is loosely based on those posts with much new material added. After the blogging had gone far enough I felt the subject matter deserved to be refined and organized in a book. Refining and analyzing is slow and iterative work, so I took it offline. Out of a literary allusion to nuts, organization took the form of 12 chapters each including two or three sections:

1. First Look
2. Kernel
3. Basket of Nuts (sometimes omitted)

The First Look is a basic overview of the chapter. The Kernel provides more detail but in summary form, more than enough for any cocktail conversation. If you have appetite for more, open the Basket of Nuts and munch away. You will understand the philosophical foundations of social promise community, grasp its revolutionary implications, and be equipped to lend a hand in its development.

I am grateful for all the people who helped and encouraged me along the way of writing this book. Activists from libertarian and anarchist groups led me to be curious about the topic and taught me many things. Among those lessons was the realization that free people will never agree on every rule of social conduct. We can't achieve ethical consensus by suppressing dissent or even by civil debate. If we would build free community, we must make space for diversity in lifestyles and beliefs limited only by consideration for the equal rights of others.

My wife Josi deserves special thanks. This book would not have been written without her quiet support and patience for my long work without pay. David Sperling helped with proof reading and Matthew Barnes was an outstanding sounding board and contributor of ideas. So many of my friends endured my Power Point presentations about voluntary law, later social promise community, and encouraged me to continue. I have too many clients, friends, family and supporters to name here. Thank you all from the bottom of my heart. You are my lucky stars.

Publishing a vision of how encrypted public ledgers and social promises can revolutionize law and justice is risky. How so? The vision might be just a foolish dream that no one is likely to notice; an eccentric form of folk art; a quaint but unproductive hobby. Worse, a massive book exposing unconventional perspectives might be an embarrassing monument to pure folly, a proof of professional incompetence. What a burden that would be! But the most dramatic risk is this: once coders turn ideas like those this book into useful applications, blockchain faith spreads like Bitcoin. Big Brother finds the spread disturbing and suppresses it with violence and terrorism. Agents of the state punish supporters of social promise community. Going out on a limb exposes the climber to many risks. Is the reward worth it?

The prize is vast for humanity and the risk of failure in the short span of one human lifetime is tolerable. What makes publishing this Guidebook not so daring? Only you! You carry the egg of future life encapsulated, the irrepressible seed of truth and freedom. To be human is to be both self-sovereign and social. Social promising fulfills both natures, perfecting both cooperation and freedom.

No utopia awaits us. The furnace of our desire and vanity will still cause pain. But we can pursue any imaginable happiness in a society ordered by social promises. The sum of those free but conscientious pursuits will cause a great outpouring of profound and sustainable wealth for every member. I want a taste of that outpouring. Do you?

-Jonny Stryder

Los Angeles, California, April 20, 2018

CONTENTS

Emancipate yourselves from mental slavery
None but ourselves can free our minds[1]

---

[1] Bob Marley, *Redemption Song* (1980), borrowed from Marcus Garvey, *Black Man* magazine, Vol. 3, no. 10 (July 1938), pp. 7–11.

INTRODUCTION: The Nut

Blockchain is a hot topic, thanks to Bitcoin and its crypto-ledger progeny. For good reason. Public crypto-ledgers are an unprecedented tool for empowering the masses, cutting out the middle men, and breaking monopolies. We have only begun to explore possibilities for their use. This Guidebook explores a use case for public crypto-ledgers: building social trust, and achieving self-organized social order using social promises within a multicultural community of sovereign entities. It explores how far the concept might reach, identifies issues and solutions, and presents a road map for getting to a new decentralized yet orderly paradigm. "Blockchain faith" does not express faith in any certain set of cryptographic protocols. It expresses faith in strangers and fellow society members made possible by blockchain technology and honor.

This is not a technical survey, an academic study, or a book of algorithms. It's a non-technical introduction to social promising in encrypted public ledgers written for hackers and non-hackers alike, an investigation of novel use cases in preparation for new technical designs. You need not know anything about blockchain, cryptocurrency, the philosophy of law or social philosophy to learn new ideas here. All you need is curiosity, an open mind and an ability to reason.

Whatever your level of knowledge, this book will be worth your while. It breaks new ground in applications for distributed ledgers in ethical social order without rulers. If you're already knowledgeable in distributed autonomous networks or stateless governance, reading this book will change your view of how to use secure public ledgers for self-governance, illuminate the challenges ahead, and inspire you to new solutions. If you're new to the topic, you'll have fun reading about how social promises work and how you can take part. The coming social promise communities will welcome everybody, and everybody can contribute to making them better.

The root issues of new social orders are ethical and practical. Coders of cryptocurrency networks consider both in their designs. Game theory and ethics underlies networks like Bitcoin and Ethereum. Evolution is iterative.

Richard Stallman, Linus Torvalds and other open-source pioneers laid the groundwork for this Guidebook. Torvalds released Linux 1.0 in 1994. By the time the mysterious Satoshi Nakamoto published the Bitcoin whitepaper in 2009, open-source applications and platforms were well established. Open-source made it possible to build applications in public and gave operators the tools and confidence needed for serving public networks. Digital currency came along around the same time as Linux, with David Chaum introducing Digicash in 1990. E-gold was introduced in 1996 and Liberty Reserve in 2006. All these currencies failed; the latter two because of violent shutdowns by Federal agents.

The purpose of Bitcoin as stated in Nakamoto's original whitepaper was to build a distributed ledger resistant to raids and server takedowns. Bitcoin succeeded spectacularly in its purpose and in public acceptance. Later crypto-ledger designs extended the capabilities of blockchain networks beyond tracking the spending of electronic tokens. Current designs such as Ethereum are capable but have limitations that make them less than ideal for the social promise and reputation ledgers described here.[2] Despite present limitations, distributed public ledgers are the right tool and are improving all the time. Privacy, identity, and providing a more efficient and fairer means of security are the main challenges ahead.

---

[2] See Chapter 12, "Medium of Exchange" and "Infrastructure Design."

Despite the advances already made in crypto-ledger technology, implementing useful ledgers for social promises and reputation feedback is not a trivial exercise. Before we get to security challenges like privacy and identity, we need to figure out what the system needs to do. It would be pointless to design a network for duplicating existing institutions. We will do better with a design that preserves the best of the past while reforming governance for a decentralized network and society. Nodes are not people, and network design is not social design. We must design the network for the social use case: ethical conflict resolution without introducing central authority or imposing overly exclusive conditions. For that we must deconstruct law to its roots and construct a more ethical framework for rights and obligations that is both feasible and free of bias against any self-sovereign perspective.

This Guidebook teaches order by social promises and rejects all sovereignties except over the self. We work outside the box; outside the box of central authority and outside old ideologies on the left and the right. If order by social promises seem idealistic and improbable, read on. Once you've considered some of the Guidebook's hypotheticals, you'll perceive a harder edge. Social promise community has strong bones and sharp teeth. Criminals and frauds will find the community inhospitable and look for easier targets elsewhere. This Guidebook proposes practical solutions, not fantasies.

Sometimes imagined solutions seem impossible, you might say "nutty." Inventive nuts contradict truths "everyone" assumes are true. Let's recall a few old tropes now debunked: the sun and stars revolve around the Earth, machines heavier than air can't fly, personal computers are useless for ordinary people, nobody will shop over the Internet, nobody will write useful open-source public-licensed software, distributed databases aren't secure, and cryptocurrency isn't worth anything. Still, failure and embarrassment often go with challenging old assumptions. Experiments fail before they succeed, making caution in experimental design prudent. Poking out too conspicuously may attract hammer blows. Don't be nutty for the fun of it; don't run in front of raging bulls for the thrill of it. Be nutty with purpose and determination and change the world!

The Guidebook aspires to be a nutty in another sense, like an acorn is nutty by encapsulating the essence of the oak tree and the first substance of a seedling's life. Given the right conditions, and the passage of time, the acorn sprouts. The sprout grows, extends leaves and roots, extracts energy from the sun and directs the energy and matter it absorbs into an oak tree. The ideas in this book may sprout and grow. But instead of growing in soil, these ideas may, given the proper conditions, grow in your mind. Fed by your life energy and experience, the ideas may grow into massive and surprising forms, evolving your worldview and your reality. As these ideas spread from mind to mind, a towering forest may gradually arise, forever transforming your world. No boasting here; we have no guarantee the nut will even sprout. But the Guidebook is without a doubt a nut.

A third nut cinches everything together. New social possibilities are in a branch of endeavor called social engineering. In social engineering, fantasies are forbidden. Ethical engineers must work in the realm of the possible without initiating aggression or violating natural or economic laws. Instead of forcing people to obey legislatures and officials, engineers must persuade by building designs and messages that are socially aware and attuned to the emotions of others. They must market new and better ways of providing social trust and dispute resolution to people who have never heard or considered other possibilities. The third nut turns by the social engineer.

Nuts aside, the Guidebook is a journey. Strap in, and let's go for a ride!

Chapter 1: Blockchain Faith and Social Promises

First Look

Order can exist without rulers. Each can rule their own selves, and most do in their daily lives. Rules imposed on others against their will do not deserve to be called "law." But we have no other word to describe rules for determining which rights and obligations should apply when people cannot agree, or when actions have harmed a victim. Without some way to resolve conflicts honorably, all that remains is "might makes right." Civil order becomes an illusion hiding control by the powerful.

Phrases like "voluntary law" distinguish between decrees imposed by rulers and civil order without rulers. This Guidebook will avoid using "law" unless preceding it with "voluntary." But to be clearer that this Guidebook is not about law as made by states or others claiming authority to rule, it will use words and phrases like "social promises" and "blockchain faith" except when needing to make a philosophical point.

When law is voluntary, each is sovereign over themselves. Social promises express rights that each self-sovereign offers to reciprocal promisors. Collective organizations can make rules that all members accept as valid, such as conditions of membership or later changes by consensus. Whether by individual social promises or collective consensus, a voluntary law is any rule with a moral force that all will obey without threat or fraud.

Voluntary law is ancient. It claims no authority except mutual, uncoerced consensus among individuals. Blockchain faith describes a mental state allied with a network hosting a secure indexed database. The state of mind is for spreading voluntary order by securing social promises and keeping reliable records regarding their breach or fulfillment in encrypted public ledgers. An emergent social movement enabled by new methods for using and securing data leads to mutual, uncoerced consensus about rules with a moral force within a community – a social promise community whose most valuable assets are mutual trust and honor.

Reaching the mental state of "blockchain faith" involves discovering and teaching methods for coping with differences in moral views without resorting to violent condemnation. The Guidebook promotes consensus only at the most fundamental levels, leaving all the details within the graces of equal self-sovereigns. Justice in social promise community includes providing neutral guidance as to the rights and obligations of parties to a dispute, requiring none of the parties to submit to a rule they have not accepted. Enforcement includes letting others know about wrongs proved by due process, and empowering all to act on their knowledge, at first by quiet avoidance or vocal shaming of wrongdoers. So voluntary society begins, and once learned expands to fill every facet of social order. Nothing good we do by empire and the authority of power cannot be done better by unforced cooperation.

Kernel

Our forebears have understood law as something imposed by a higher or more powerful authority on the rest of us. Whether the authority for law comes from God, old traditions, priests, monarchs, emperors, legislatures, electoral majorities, legal experts, judges, lawyers, special committees, or a combination of such things, we have not learned that law is subject to individual consent. Instead, we are learned that law is inviolable, and must be obeyed no matter how stupid or cruel. Sadly, victims of imprudent and vain authority have learned to hate the word "law" for good cause.

Voluntary social order can exist without imposed rules. It can prevail and spread! Large numbers of people can and will cooperate to solve common problems, out of honor free of threats and abuse. Even more compelling: voluntary arrangements for social order can coexist with imposed laws tainted by coercion, and after enough social evolution has occurred, eliminate the coercion and the imposition.

We can make order and cooperation voluntary in different ways. For example, any group of persons can follow a rule or set of rules by consensus, as done in sports leagues, games, theme parks, churches, clubs and other limited venues. Relying on unanimous consent has its limits, though. Either the genuineness of the consent becomes questionable, or the size and scope of the group remain limited. When it comes to general rules for everybody, people have many worldviews, moral beliefs, cultures, experiences, and personal desires. Diversity is a good and useful thing, but it makes universal consent to a single rule of law impossible.

Another approach, described by science fiction writer Robert Heinlein,[3] is for society members to submit their disputes to a mutually acceptable independent judge. Independent judges make the law and attract clients by their reputations for being fair and efficient. With this approach, any two people can learn which rules will be applied between them by agreeing in advance to use a certain judge or group of judges. Others will not know what rules will be applied when a dispute arises, unless every judge follows the same rules. Diversity among judges, however, makes unanimous consent about rules impossible. In addition, there will always be those holding minority views who can find no judge to apply their preferred rules. Although free selection of judges (like human

---

[3] The Moon Is A Harsh Mistress (1966).

diversity) is a good and useful thing, it fails to provide predictability in multicultural communities.

This Guidebook explores a way to reach social promise community, where a universal but personalized order applies for everyone willing to participate, and none submit to the rule of another. The method works for everybody who will make three initial commitments. The system is underlain by three foundational rules we will later express more succinctly as social promises:

1. Each member is honor bound to keep their own promises, and nothing more. No right is enforceable unless granted by a social promise of another. The social promise must be made without coercion or fraud, and not withdrawn prior to the events out of which the right arose.

2. Each member publishes their social promises. No member will enforce an unpublished promise without consent. This rule makes the system stable, practical, and social. The identity of each person who is party to a claim, the social promises made by each and the times when made are known to the parties. For example, the social promises are recorded in a blockchain ledger. The recorded social promises make up the rule of the case.

3. No member will ask more from another, than what the member grants to others in similar circumstances. Social promising is based on reciprocity. Reciprocity enables predictable results when members make different promises and enables sovereigns with different promises to coexist and interact under a rule of honor agreed between themselves. Reciprocity may be expressed as "The Rule Of The WEaker Tool," (TROTWET), discussed later.

To bind their honorable selves in respect for this three-part framework, self-sovereigns make Three Promises. That blockchain faith will create social promise community out of the recorded promises of equal self-sovereigns is the conceit that the Guidebook unfolds.

Three Promise systems do not result in the same rule for everybody. Instead, Three Promise systems provide a predictable rule between any two members, based on their social promises. Three Promise systems are universal in applicability, and capable of serving groups of unlimited size. The systems are non-territorial, and do not depend on universally accepted property rights regarding land or other subjects. They have no jurisdictional limits, can resolve any dispute, and order all manner of rights and responsibilities. Any group of people using the Three Promises for resolution of all their disputes and questions of social responsibility can escape need for other justice systems. The Guidebook provides a practical path to finding your own stateless society. Whether or how you walk that path is up to you.

The Three Promise system's simple foundation can support complex and surprising results. The journey involves unexpected twists and turns. This Guidebook can only explore a few of them, enough so social engineers understand the major wrinkles and can get to work on the blockchain part. No matter how convoluted the hypotheticals get, the Three Promises are a touchstone. The Guidebook may express the Promises differently without changing their essence.

In a well-developed social promise community, the rules observed may approach each sovereign's personal code of honor. In a less developed society, rules may be dimly understood by some members. Casual members may make promises more for convenience, and less for expressing personal codes of honor. Maybe everybody will make lighter promises for unserious uses. Regardless, those with the best reputations will understand and live by their codes of honor, guided by personal integrity. Either way, if a society complies with the rules ascribed above, the society is a social promise community.

Moral societies will reject the imposition of any substantive law on any person, without prior knowledge and consent. Imposed diktats are unworthy of being considered "law," are barbarous evil by nature if not always in effect. We who will prove that self-sovereign governance works better can no longer regard imposition of law by force as a necessary evil. Only by demonstrating effective alternatives can we prove that law by force is unnecessary and destructive. Whether this new morality spreads will depend on the success of your experiments to prove voluntary cooperation works better than imposed laws. This Guidebook will pique your interest, grow your understanding, and encourage you to help build blockchain faith yourself.

Basket of Nuts

How can people participate in open, *ad hoc* communities with effective channels for dispute resolution and reputation discovery? One approach is to foster a self-organizing trust network, the "social promise community," using information technology. To prevent dominance by any entity, the technology should use a peer-to-peer, open source network. Data regarding promises and events reflecting on personal honor should be held in distributed data structures in the public domain, with privacy under the control of each user. Useful networks can be constructed differently, but before building these networks, a set of specifications and protocols would be helpful. In addition, after networks become available, consumers must distinguish trustworthy networks for social promise communities from untrustworthy ones. People must also learn the basics of social promise communities, and guidance in how to make useful social promises consistent with their moral beliefs.

The author founded the uRULEu Institute (www.uruleu.org) as a non-profit, public benefit corporation supporting social promise communities by offering consumer education and trust certification. The Institute will help "you rule you," and certify social promise members and components with its name. If the Institute succeeds, many people will learn the techniques in this Guidebook for ethical conflict resolution without taking their dispute to court. uRULEu will become a trusted mark of honor for those rightly bearing its name.

Social promises are "voluntary laws" in a philosophical sense but the two phrases have different connotations. To speak of promises instead of laws makes the subject more approachable, and its operation more understandable. It avoids using the emotional trigger word "law" in an unconventional way that some may find confusing or disturbing. "Law" has included rules that slave masters made for their plantations, and corporate governance systems imposed on their subjects, often to great harm. This book will sometimes use the terminology of voluntary law but will more often use the promise terminology.

Speaking of promises instead of laws points out a difference in frame of reference. A law is objective: "whoever does 'A' shall suffer 'B.'" The condition 'A' precedes the consequence 'B.' A social promise is subjective: "if I do 'A' I shall do 'B'" expresses the same condition and the same consequence but reminds everyone that self-sovereigns bind only themselves. In Three Promise systems, either formulation results in the same consequence applying in the same circumstances.

Let's be more succinct. A social promise community is a self-organized borderless set of people who interact by choice, each of whom have made these three social promises:

The First Promise: I'll take responsibility for my own promises and stake my honor on keeping them.

The Second Promise: I'll disclose my promises to everyone for whom I intend them. My secret promises will carry no weight.

The Third Promise: I'll demand no burden greater than I have promised to carry. I'll accept whichever fulfillment is least burdensome: of the other's promise, or mine.

A secure public network enables discovery of social promises made by each member of the network. Disclosure is controlled by the member who has made the promise. The network also collects and distributes information about reputations of members under each member's control.

Under social promises, one can only make rules for oneself, as commitments to other members. To create rules binding on others, members make promises that are no more burdensome than the promises of other members. The Third Promise ensures that all carry the lessor of their own promises or their fellow's. The set of all member promises defines the rules for every relationship. Every member accepts the duty to disclose their own promises if they intend others to respect the promises. Every member can discover the published social promises of others. Knowing those social promises, the member can learn how to avoid and resolve conflicts with every other member.

A social promise system should create incentives for members to publish their promises and transactions wherever the potential benefits of publication outweighs the risks. In addition, the system should create incentive for users to record high-quality, useful content in community ledgers, and discourage poor quality, useless or destructive content. Networks might discard or flag content intended to attack or subvert the network. There are few limitations on operating social promise networks. Operational details can vary based on a system designer's preferences and insights.

Nothing limits social promising to the Three Promise system described here. That is one "door" to a social promise society, but other doors in the sense of threshold promises may exist. To the extent these doors can exist without self-contradiction, the societies they support will be distinct and incompatible. For example, a "Vulcan" social promise society might use different threshold promises from a "Klingon" social promise society. Regardless, for the society to be voluntary people must be free to leave it as they please.

Activism for social promising may include participating in electoral politics. For example, activists may advocate for state legal systems to include more voluntary elements, and to recognize the freedom of all to make and keep social promises. Ample evidence exists to show that voluntary forms of social organization are more beneficial, more moral, or both more beneficial and more moral, than compulsory forms of organization.

Other tracks of development are outside of electoral politics. The uRULEu Institute, for example, will focus on teaching ordinary people how to take part in and use the Three Promises to achieve their goals. Many other ways exist to promote voluntary cooperation and decrease use of compulsion, beginning with our day-to-day relationships with others. But social promise activism can't happen until hackers build a network that will support a thriving social promise community. Hackers must lead the way!

Authority for social promises is not granted by privileged authority. Authority derives from people choosing, without coercion or fraud, to accept a rule for social behavior. Promisors can obligate only themselves, and never another. Those who will not obligate themselves are either absent from the ledger, or their failure to make any certain promise is evident there. Either way, others can treat them with appropriate caution.

Well-designed social promise systems may evolve towards more perfect expressions of natural law. But immutable perfection of "natural law" is a chimera. Although law will always be in flux, law discoverable by reason is that most consistent with our natures as entities sovereign over no more than ourselves. Social promising will achieve better ends than the traditional forms that vex us today; it will be more stable and less subject to political whims. It cannot be worse because it is voluntary.

Social promising rests on a few key concepts. "Promisor" is a key concept, as is "consent." Later pages will delve into meanings of these terms. Non-aggression is baked into social promising, by way of the limitation to voluntary action. Those who adhere to the non-aggression principle will find much to like about social promising.

People who esteem civil rights and fear too much accumulation of private property by a few will also find much to like about social promising. Property rights are not an essential feature. Voluntary forms of public property rights and mutual aid can thrive where conflicts are resolved by social promising.

Instead of imposing concepts of property rights, social promising allows for different definitions of property rights. The moral principle that each person is sovereign over themselves alone governs these rights. All property rights depend on individual acceptance before being enforceable.

Individuals alone choose the conditions for ownership of property, and what rights will go with ownership. Property rights arise by and between different definitions of property adopted by different persons. No person can enforce property rights against another, without prior acceptance by the other. None can amass property that confers an unacceptable degree of forcible control over the lives of others. Different property rights coexist and evolve. Bloody revolutions to correct injustice in distributing property rights are no longer needed when those who hold social power embrace the Three Promise system.

Social promising does not belong on the left or the right of the political spectrum. The left is skeptical of private property rights and favors allocation of property according to some theory of greatest common good. The right favors private property rights and is skeptical of property being held or redistributed by anything other than voluntary consent of rightful owners. Three Promise systems transcend the left-right dialectic, imposing self-sovereignty alone with no single definition of property. Self-sovereignty allows private property rights, if any two people will honor those rights in their own dealings.

Under social promising, nobody can force another to obey any rule. Everybody is in control of their own social promises. No person can force a definition of property on another. Members enforce honorable behavior by reputation.

That's the nut of it!

Chapter 2: Why Bother?

First Look

Theories about the mechanics of flight are most interesting to those who build flying machines. Theories about social promising are most interesting to those who want to live in social promise communities. If you are not interested in being a developer or member of social promise communities, you may get little out of these pages. If the Guidebook interests you, it may be because you can hear the call to become a developer or user of social promising.

Every person who joins a Three Promise community is helping social promising progress, just by publishing their own promises. Most who join will be followers, except for making and choosing their own social promises. Leaders in development of social promising will influence system design, set examples of social promises that others choose to follow, and teach people how to make and use social promises.

Once established, online promise communities will enable personal trust networks to develop, such as the world has never seen. These networks will open opportunities we can only dream of today. They will create peaceful political pressure for positive social change that will transcend national boundaries. There can be no guarantee that social promise communities will succeed, but there is a vision for success. Explore the vision by reading on.

Kernel

If this book seems impractical, you might be more of a practical than a philosophical person. As a practical person, know that social promising is not yet (as of 2018) a household word. It is still in an early development stage. We can't bring social promising into the mainstream ready for use by practical people without work. It will take time, dedication, and patience.

So, here's a tip for you practical folks: skim most pages, until you get to Chapter 12. Then read every word until the end. Skim by reading the First Look and the Kernel of each chapter and skip most of the rest. Once you've read the material from Chapter 12 to the end, you can circle back and fill in any details you find interesting.

Chapters 3 to 11 of this book wrestle with basic issues raised by restructuring of society and law based on individual sovereignty and equality. Digging the foundations for a new social order is unglamorous, risky for one's social status, and sometimes lonely. This Guidebook is for those nutty folks who believe it is possible to engineer fundamental changes in human society by non-threatening persuasion. Everybody can be a little nutty, at least sometimes.

If you are one of those usually not-nutty people, here's a few practical things for you to consider. Not everybody has the time or inclination to change the world, but what if you could pursue your goals more effectively by taking part in social promise community? Just by joining, you can contribute in your own way to achieving voluntary society without thinking much about all the philosophical stuff. Join and build relationships with the coworkers and friends who will help you reach and expand your goals.

Once put into practice, blockchain faith will provide practical products and services for improving the quality of all human life. Practical offshoots will include social promise clubs or promise networks, also called social promise communities or societies. Imagine you can join a social promise club that provides you with big discounts on your insurance and legal bills. Membership in the club not only saves you money; it also helps you resolve serious disputes with other club members faster.

There is much more to imagine. Membership in the club is free in perpetuity. The tremendous value of the reputation information that the club generates funds all operational costs. To join, you agree to resolve all your disputes with other members of the club according to a simple, easy-to-understand rule book personal to you. Your social promises won't change until you want them to. You enter friendly relations with others by revealing promises to one another. You can quit the club when you wish, but then you will lose the benefits of membership.

People with the same or compatible social promises form a decentralized, self-organizing social promise club. The set of all members' social promises provides the rule book, but your social promises are your own. Nobody but you can change your promises, which determine how others perceive your reputation, and your obligations to other members. The club is massive and influential yet has no dues or no officers. The club's design ensures nobody can ever own or control it. Club members live and do business with each other all over the world, in just about every country. No matter where you go, you can always find members who will happily interact with you, expecting no more from you but fulfillment of your own social promises.

Because membership and status of members in this club is for most a matter of public record, being a member of this club also provides you with access to a reliable friend finder service. You can find other members of your club in every city, all over the world, using a computer search. You can also see reputation information for every member of the club. The reputation information paints a complete and correct picture of each member's character and conduct; at least, for members with good reputations. The reputation information grows out of each member's social promises, how well each member has kept their promises, and how the member has settled complaints.

You can find reputation information more easily by paying a small fee to a reputation service, or by using a free advertising-supported service. You can use the available information services to find new friends, customers, suppliers and service providers around the world. By building a reputation as a trustworthy club member, you can attract customers and supporters for your endeavors. If your reputation is good, new customers or business partners will be attracted, providing abundant opportunities for you. A good reputation as a club member is better than gold.

The social promise club includes many tribes organized around different social promises. A group of members who chose the same promise set make up a tribe. Every member controls their own promises, but many find it convenient to make most of the same promises as their friends, sometimes adding a few unique ones. Shared promises make it easier to find compatible members, reducing risk and inconvenience for everybody. Many sets of social promises are available, for different occupations, cultures, and preferences, to name just a few possibilities. A smorgasbord of standard promise sets exists for every conceivable purpose. You may pick more than one set if you please. For example, you might pick one set for business, and another for personal matters. A group of members who chose the same promise set make up a tribe.

The many tribes make up a self-organized freedom tree. All the tribes use compatible information systems, so interacting with members of different tribes is easy. Some tribes have well-known promise sets and millions of members; others have small memberships. Members of tribes can be local or distributed over any geographic region. Conservative tribes seldom or never revise their promise set. More progressive tribes may change their promise sets occasionally, causing splits in their membership, because not all members adopt the revised sets. Tribal boundaries can be fuzzy, as individuals in full control of their own social promises coalesce around certain principles of social order.

Your children or grandchildren learn about the major tribes and the differences in their rules before they are twelve years old.

They rely on the information they learn as a child about the major branches of the "freedom tree" throughout their lives, because the social promise sets do not need frequent updating. Translations of the promise sets of all the major tribes exist in every major world language. You may change tribe membership as your views or life situation changes, or to start a new tribe by creating a variation on an existing promise set. If you are talented and dedicated, you can write a whole new promise set for a new tribe.

Imagine that global growth of the club and its diverse tribes creates a new basis for mutual acceptance of different viewpoints, both inside of political boundaries, and across them. Members of all the tribes recognize and respect the legitimacy of members of other tribes, in a manner resembling respect for citizens of other nations. Fair rules exist for resolving disputes between members of different clubs, based on the promise sets adopted by the people in the dispute. Everybody in the club knows and follows these short and simple rules. People of different religions and beliefs use the rules to live according to their own beliefs, while doing business, if they choose, with members of other tribes that hold to different beliefs.

Since members control their own tribe promise sets, the sets are stable and succinct. Contrast that to other forms of government, in which politicians often enact new rules, regulations and laws to serve the self-interests of influential players. The stability and succinctness of club rules makes it easy to assess the risks of transactions between members of the same tribe, and even between members of different tribes. Programmers develop artificially-intelligent relationship counselling systems that are available online. You can consult an automated oracle about your rights and obligations in relation to any other member, avoiding the need to hire an expensive lawyer.

The social promise club slowly grows larger and larger. Over time, the social promise club becomes so large and indispensable that almost everybody joins. Once membership in the club becomes massive, wars between nations and terrorism become politically infeasible. Most politicians, soldiers and civil military contractors are club members. These members are unwilling to ruin their reputations by killing or injuring other club members without proper justification and are politically powerful enough to prevent wars from starting. Once war is no longer possible, governments of the world evolve into voluntary organizations serving the public.

Practical enough for you? The social promise club helps make your life experience richer, deeper, safer, and more prosperous. If the design succeeds, membership will enable and protect your personal empowerment within a community of equally empowered persons. It will make you better off while making no one else worse off.

Perhaps only some of these imagined outcomes are possible. The more distant, pie-in-the-sky outcomes need not happen, to make social promising worth investing in now. Great outcomes are possible but are not inevitable. Even if social promise clubs do not grow large enough to provide the greatest possible benefits, they can still benefit those who invest their time and energy to participate.

This Guidebook is for social engineers. Like an engineering plan, these pages straddle the practical and the theoretical; they are both plan and advocacy for social engineering. The author owes an intellectual debt to greater minds in economics, non-aggression, anarchy and law, and so forth — great moral philosophers, economists, activists and visionaries like Lysander Spooner, Benjamin Tucker, Emma Goldman, Ludwig Von Mises, Murray Rothbard, Richard Stallman, and others. Despite their inspiration, the arguments here stand on their own. You need not consult earlier writers or know the history of ideas to understand this book.

There will be other pieces of future social promise societies that work with the pieces described here. You need not believe the business models of Amazon or eBay are better than others in every respect, to shop at their stores. You do not have to believe social promising will come to dominate the world, to participate in a social promise club. It is enough that your participation provides a benefit justifying your time and attention spent.

Changes in human society depend both on new technologies and new ideas about what is possible. Consider the history of the airplane. Heavier-than-air flight did not happen without prior technological breakthroughs. Before airplanes could fly, engine technology had to advance. Engineers needed to invent new techniques to do formerly impossible things. Powered flight required both advances in enabling technologies, and new ways of thinking about airflow and airfoils. Similarly, social promise clubs were impossible before recent advancements in distributed public ledgers, and new ways of thinking about fair and effective conflict resolution.

These advancements include open-source public registries (e.g., blockchains), popularized by the mysterious Satoshi Nakamoto and the release of the Bitcoin application. This technology enabled decentralized trading networks centered on exchange of an electronic currency, by making it infeasible for governments or other powerful actors to shut down the public registry. Cryptocurrencies such as Bitcoin represent but one application of blockchain technology. Already, this technology is being applied in ingenious ways in other applications. One such application, released in 2014, is named Bitnation (now Bitnation 2.0)[4]. Bitnation is directed towards dispute resolution services within a voluntary network. Bitnation uses existing state-made laws

---

[4] https://tse.bitnation.co/

but is compatible with using social promises. When social promises become available and are of acceptable quality, perhaps networks such as Bitnation will use them. Others have focused on writing laws for stateless societies, the Creative Common Law Project[5] being an example. Social promise frameworks like uRULEu will allow people to use whatever laws they please and teach them to treat laws as social promises.

Social networks like Bitnation focus on providing an infrastructure for providing dispute resolution, enforcement and insurance services based on any law chosen by disputants. This book focuses on a different goal: development of new and superior operating procedures for ethical ordering of the voluntary networks of tomorrow. As you read this book, you may learn why new rules are necessary for voluntary dispute resolution networks. Existing laws developed by and for state-based legal systems are not well-suited for dispute resolution in voluntary societies, although they may lend helpful basic building blocks. You may realize that social promise systems are the best way to build voluntary society under ethical rules.

New social orders need robust and coherent conceptual foundations. The author would build up those foundations, by engaging you in a dialog about order in human society. Your positive engagement with this dialog will lead to a growing understanding about how to make social promise clubs work. This growing understanding will lead members to create and promote robust sets of social promises for social promise clubs. As more people join and make social promises, social promise clubs will become a practical reality capable of providing new freedoms, paths to happiness and peace for all people.

---

[5] https://creativecommonlaw.com/

Chapter 3: Engineering a More Voluntary Society

First Look

You may read this because you love freedom and long to live in a more voluntary world. When possible, you want to resolve social problems by voluntary cooperation, not by force. You believe initiating force, fear, or fraud to the detriment of others is wrong. If many people share these hopes and beliefs, why does society so often fall short of them?

Whatever the answers, before we can find better solutions we must overcome our own ignorance and confusion. We must learn to crawl before we walk, and to run before we fly. We who would build new social systems must master the basics, before going to work. Like any good engineer or politician, we must understand the environment we work in, and concern ourselves with what is possible. Otherwise, we will waste our efforts, and our designs will fail.

The conceptual fundamentals of social promising cover who can be a self-sovereign promise keeper, free will, and publication. Read on to grow your understanding. Explore how the meanings of force, fear, fraud, enforcement, and morality intertwine with self-sovereign order.

Kernel

Society is a natural phenomenon, that emerges from aggregate behavior of the society's individual members. Society implies relationships with order. Social behavior follows a discernable pattern. From the pattern, we can deduce that rules of behavior exist. By influencing those rules, we can change the society. People can engineer societies. Engineering of human societies has been going on for millennia. For most of that time, privileged players were manipulating the rules of member behavior for self-serving motives. The resulting societies are flawed and diminish the long-term survival prospects of our species. We can hope to do better.

Open any engineering textbook in a technical field, and you will find in its earlier chapters the field's fundamental concepts and quantities. These basic principles are the tools of the trade, designed for reaching the goals the technical field exists to serve. Whether the aim is an airplane, a rocket, or a cure for cancer, the quest begins by envisioning the goal. The Guidebook aims to inspire engineers building a voluntary society under social promises. The goal provides direction but does not tell us how to build a social promise society any more than imagining an airplane without any experimentation teaches us how to make it fly.

The fundamentals of engineering exist only in the minds of engineers, who direct their search for essential elements to those most useful. In choosing their basic tools, engineers watch and describe nature using abstractions made for a purpose. For example, in aeronautical engineering, static pressure and ram air pressure are useful for determining an object's airspeed and altitude. It would be difficult or impossible to design or fly an airplane without using these abstract quantities. Being elementary and essential, the concepts are fundamental in the field.

Social engineering is as much art as science, because it operates on the will. The will is unpredictable, being creative, rational and irrational. Despite its fluidity, art possesses essential principles as logic does. But making use of artistic principles sometimes means we must set aside reason to forge new mental connections. We express art using a different language than reason. The language of art releases emotions and feeds our intuitive senses. Reason can seldom exercise these powers and energizes only a minority.

Engineering a voluntary society melds the emotional and intuitive language of art with the logic of reason and the scientific method. In a hybrid of art and science, engineer-philosophers express essences using a hybrid language hard for rational thinkers to understand and for intuitive thinkers to find interesting. The essence of our goal is an increase in order without imposed authority.

Our goal is to increase the ordering of society by rules acceptable to everyone. We cannot achieve perfection — the condition of all members applying all acceptable rules whenever proper — but aiming towards an increase in morality is our constant direction. To move in our preferred direction, we must convince people to accept moral rules for interpersonal behavior. Persuading is the first task, which we must do without violating our own morality. For example, our moral beliefs forbid us from using the tools of coercion, theft or fraud to further our objectives. Before we worry about regulating our campaigning, we must know the target audience.

We can identify our audience by asking a single question: who can accept a moral rule? Suppose we define any individual who can as an "honorable self-sovereign." Only people can accept moral rules, so what qualifies an individual to be an honorable self-sovereign is fundamental. To say an honorable self-sovereign is someone who can accept a moral rule is a tautology. To help you see the equivalence, here's another tautology posing as a definition: a mail carrier is someone who carries mail.

Who qualifies to carry mail? A tautology cannot tell us. We must look to the contexts in which mail carriers do their carrying. By doing so, we discover mail carriers must have legs, hands, eyes and a brain. Likewise, to find those qualified to accept moral rules we must look to the contexts in which people accept moral rules. Those contexts are social contexts.

Different social contexts can exist. The present-day context is a global apex single-species society. Single-species simplifies the analysis, by dropping issues of inter-species law. Within a species, the gene pool does not separate into strands; genes from any two individuals of opposite gender can mingle. In single-species societies, there's no rational basis for discrimination in basic rights.

In voluntary society, equal rights mean every self-sovereign must have equal sovereign power. If none can have greater autonomy than another, no one can demand that others recognize fictional persons. Enforcement of such demands would violate the individual self-sovereignty of those who would not recognize those fictions. Only natural persons remain as self-sovereigns entitled to respect for their sovereignty and social promises. Our quest for fundamentals leads us to understand what it means to be a self-sovereign person honor bound to keep their social promises.

Just to avoid any doubt, arbitrary distinctions such as ancestry, ethnicity, place of birth, parentage, and so forth, have no place in status as a self-sovereign member of society. People are living individuals possessing reason, morality, free will, and a capacity to act. People need these qualities to follow a rule for morality's sake.

What does it mean for an act to be voluntary? An act is voluntary when motivated by the free will of the doer unbent by fear, force or fraud applied with intent by another. The meaning of free will (also called volition) is fundamental, and intertwined with the meanings of fear, force and fraud. "Voluntary" means conscious acceptance, with knowledge of the thing assented to, free of coercion and fraud.

A third fundamental principle — publication — fulfills a responsibility to declare one's code of honor. Those with an obligation to honor a social promise must be able to understand it beforehand. If there's no way to learn the rules before the action, the rules may as well be coin flips. Territorial sovereign systems rely on written legal codes, without which there can be no rule of law in complex societies of strangers. Publication of each member's social promises enables order and a basis for deciding hard cases under defined rules while preserving maximal autonomy for all.

Publication serves a second purpose. It strips each person naked and exposes freely chosen moral preferences. To enable self-sovereignty, people must accept their responsibilities to expose their moral code to others. Where each is responsible for their own code of honor, the law provides no moral cloak for anyone's evil actions.

What is a moral rule? Forget about morality for a second and focus on rules. Rules are logical statements capable of being expressed with symbols. Social rules set remedies for actions that affect others, and the circumstances that justify those remedies. Secret rules cannot fairly apply to those who could not have learned of the rules in time. To achieve justice, every member must publish their social promises to other members of the society, before the promises can have any effect. What qualifies as publication is fundamental.

Moral rules aim to teach good conduct, by distinguishing between right and wrong. Those distinctions vary from person to person. Morality exists, but opinions on morality often differ. Instead of imposing a single moral opinion, social promises operate in part by exposing the morality of every member. Each member publishes their own social promises, obligating themselves. None requires others to follow social promises that the others have not adopted in public. Enforcement means submitting disagreements to voluntary due process, while conforming outcomes of disagreements to the published social promises of the people.

These basic principles of self-sovereign promise keeper, volition and publication will start us. The Basket of Nuts digs deeper, because we want to spot every issue large enough to spoil our plans. In places we get exacting, but perfect exactness is impossible. Many interesting problems in social promise community stem from differences of opinion over application of principles to difficult cases.

Differences of opinion about fundamental definitions do not make social promising any less practical or useful than other systems for civil order. Every system for social order, dealing as it must with the abstract notions and emotions of people, involves differences in opinion. People disagree about basic morality, the rules that apply, and their meaning. Social promises are no less subject to differences of opinion but are designed for bridging differences in moral preferences without imposing rules on anybody. Responsibility for ambiguity rests with the promisor.

The fundamentals of self-sovereign capacity to make and keep social promises, voluntariness, and publication distinguish boundaries of voluntary Three Promise societies. In brief, Three Promise societies are made up of natural people who live by their public social promises. The outcome of disputes does not depend on arbitrary qualities such as ethnicity, nationality, or gender. Arbitrary distinctions between persons deny the fundamental equality on which social promising is founded. To achieve voluntary society, each must extend to others the basic rights each would claim as their own. Equal reciprocity sustains equal rights.

Basket of Nuts

Boundaries can be fuzzy. We can disagree about how to apply principles we agree on. Issues like who (or what) belongs in voluntary society, how promises are published, and what constitutes consent may divide us. Fracturing of voluntary society is inevitable, but unlike squabbling over power does not divide the people. Social promisors spread morality by example, not by coercion. Everybody has an equal right to follow their own conscience. Each prospers by earning respect from peers, which comes with less effort by learning and respecting the moral positions of others.

A distinction exists between those who are inside of voluntary society and those who are not. These boundaries of voluntary society should be wide enough to admit every willing member that can fit through the gate. Civil society needs ideological walls and gates to exclude both attackers and unwilling subjects. The gates should close to any not entering of their own free will or who will not grant reciprocal freedom to other members. Those who can fit through the gate to social promise community are self-sovereigns.

The Self-Sovereign Promise Keeper

Being human is not enough to be a self-sovereign promisor. For example, infants or people with severe mental disabilities cannot make or understand social promises. Whether or not non-human persons exist, no human can be a self-sovereign promisor all the time. Every human must fall unconscious during sleep and lose for a period any ability to do voluntary acts or to reason. Every human spends a significant fraction of life sleeping, and another significant fraction as a child. Some humans never in their life gain the ability to reason. We must look to criteria other than being human, to understand who can belong.

Making and keeping social promises requires an ability to choose, or to refuse. It must be possible to reject any promise and make instead a different promise, to preserve choice. What kind of actor can judge actions based on morality? What kind of actor can divide alternatives into separate categories of "acceptable" or "right," and "punishable" or "wrong," while retaining a capacity to do actions in either category? Every actor will need certain necessary abilities, enabling them to distinguish between moral and immoral actions.

A. The Self-Sovereign Abilities

Self-sovereign power requires a set of mental abilities. There are many mental abilities, but not all are necessary to be a self-sovereign promise keeper. To give a simple example, some people have photographic memory, but nobody needs an amazing memory to adopt, publish, keep or enforce social promises. The abilities of the self-sovereign person are those that everybody needs to understand and make social promises.

1) The first self-sovereign ability is <u>apparent free will</u>. Apparent free will is the ability to act with purposeful unpredictability. This includes the ability to choose between alternatives, but more than that, to create new alternative sets of purposeful actions even when faced with the same stimuli. Free will directs action to a purpose without becoming predictable. A being cannot be a person subject to justice unless capable of performing a volitional act. Apparent free will is a prerequisite not only for social promise, but for any system that assigns fault.

We need not get stuck on the philosophical question of whether humans or other beings have free will. It is enough that the actor appears to an impartial observer to be acting freely. If the being in question has no free will, it is a machine, incapable of voluntary action. Being incapable of volition, it cannot participate in a justice system that requires it to make voluntary choices. Apparent free will is a necessary ability for status as a sovereign person.

2) Another self-sovereign ability is <u>awareness of self and others</u>. A being may have apparent free will but may fail to recognize its own independence. Infants and young children, for example, lack this mental ability. Self-awareness intertwines with the ability to reason and speak,

so this ability is seldom lacking in natural persons. Deterministic machines can also use language, and yet lack any apparent sense of self-awareness. Without enough self-awareness to recognize a social environment and one's place in it, a person cannot recognize the rights and obligations of itself or others and is incapable of governing its actions.

3) To communicate social promises, self-sovereign people need <u>language and memory</u>. They must be able to communicate using symbols, and to remember. Without these abilities, an otherwise free and rational person cannot comply with or enforce any social promise or code of justice.

4) Someone without the <u>ability of reason</u> cannot speak with others based on reason. An irrational person cannot understand the effect of any social promise, or how others will understand social promises. Every conflict resolution system involves a logical scheme. Someone incapable of following logic cannot take part in a logical scheme for fairly resolving disputes.

People sometimes experience their emotions causing irrational thoughts or actions. Some may always be irrational about specific things, such as being deathly afraid of spiders. Episodes of irrationality exclude no one from making social promises, so long as the person can reason once calmed.

Minors and the mentally disabled may have all the other mental abilities and qualities of a person and yet cannot act rationally. Meaning not "without emotion," but meaning "acting in a way capable of being explained with reason," such as "I hit her because I was mad she took my apple." People lacking the ability to reason will make irrational social promises or will be silent. It is unfair for others to judge them as if they were acting as reasonable adults.

5) Besides reason, self sovereigns need an emotional ability too: to <u>desire justice</u>. A thirst for justice underlies all systems for conflict resolution. The desire exists in any natural person who possesses all the other abilities of a self-sovereign actor, except for someone in the grip of a rare mental illness. Almost everybody feels that evil should have its price and recognizes that others may expect them to pay recompense for their own wrongdoing. Although the thirst for justice is ubiquitous, other motives can move people to join social promise communities. They won't stay if the communities cannot provide justice.

An otherwise capable self-sovereign actor, perhaps of a non-human sort, might lack a desire for justice. Such a being experiences no emotional distress over wrongs committed against it and cannot comprehend that others feel anger or negative emotions when abused. We might imagine a self-aware android with no ego and no fear of death. Such a being if it can exist will not desire justice, nor need a system for achieving it.

A dependent person lacks one or more of the self-sovereign abilities, and so is not self-sovereign. Human dependents still enjoy human rights. Dependent people may enjoy any protected status that the laws of their community afford them. Social promise communities may protect any other living or non-living being, without granting such beings status as self-sovereigns capable of making binding social promises and fairly being held accountable to others based on those promises. Many other legal systems also recognize rights of dependent or minor persons apart from self-sovereign actors, so we are not breaking new ground with this distinction. More detailed discussion of the rights of dependents is in Chapter 9.

B. The Disabilities

Just as a person must have certain abilities to qualify as an honorable self sovereign capable of making their own binding social promises, self sovereigns must *lack* certain powers or capabilities. Entities lacking the characteristic *dis*abilities of natural persons can't be included without breaking the reciprocity on which equal self sovereignty depends. The characteristic disabilities of natural persons include mortality and corporeality (limitation to a physical body). Other disabilities are not shared by all. For example, not all people fear spiders. In leveling the playing field for natural persons, we should realize that non-universal qualities such as unshared disabilities can't be a basis for excluding people.

When a natural person refuses to recognize entities that lack the disabilities of equal sovereigns, nobody is being treated unfairly. Nobody is treating others differently than they ask others to treat them. Reciprocity exists. But when we force a natural person to accept the equal sovereignty of entities that are not natural persons, we violate the self-sovereignty of the natural person. We destroy reciprocity, causing the system to contradict itself and fail. Some disabilities are necessary.

The necessary disabilities are those impossible for natural people, possible for other entities having the self-sovereign abilities, and that break reciprocity if any members are forced to recognize a like sovereign status of an unlike entity.

1) The prominent necessary disability is <u>corporeality</u>, meaning the limitation of living in a physical body. Humans all over the world have long believed in spirits, ghosts, gods and other forms of disembodied minds. Whether such beliefs could be true, consider the theoretical possibility of a

disembodied mind. Such a mind might have all the necessary mental abilities yet lack the need for a specific physical body. A disembodied mind maintains an identity, a power to act in the material world, and sense of self, but exists as pure energy, or as an abstract idea.

This requirement that the person have a physical body does not lack practical application. Far from it! There is at least one kind of incorporeal person recognized by most modern legal systems: the corporate or collective person, and similar fictional entities. States and nations themselves fall into this category. Corporations and other collectives seem capable of acting in the material world and having the mental capabilities of a person. Suppose we put a natural person and a group of persons organized as a corporation into separate black boxes and ask questions. Absent direct admissions it will not be possible to tell which box contains the corporation, and which the natural person. Despite its abilities, the corporation is nothing more than an abstract idea, existing only in the mind.

Collectives and other fictional persons can coexist with natural self-sovereign promisors, and can serve their stakeholders and customers, but are not on an equal footing with natural persons. But why is this? Why shouldn't fictional persons have the same rights and obligations as natural persons, in a system based on the sovereignty of the individual? The question answers itself. A system of order based on the sovereignty of the individual must deny sovereignty to other entities, fictional or not, that break the reciprocity of the system.

One of the moral foundations of rule by social promises is reciprocity: every qualified self-sovereign promisor is in the same circumstance as every other. If we grant collectives and other fictional persons equal sovereign status with natural persons, then we destroy reciprocity. We burden natural persons with corporeality while forcing them to play on a level field with actors that do not share their grave and characteristic disability. A fictional entity cannot, in any social system founded in individual sovereignty and equality have all the rights and powers of real, corporeal persons embodied in physical bodies.

States grant sovereignty to fictional persons while also claiming a right of monopoly on force in a territory. Such is the legal landscape of today. Were we to abolish the territorial right of monopoly but keep the sovereign rights of fictional persons, will we have made any real improvement? If we put corporations on the same playing field as individuals, we set up a corporatist world. In that world, collectives hold superior bargaining rights over the individual in every claim. Only collective entities can exploit being incorporeal and having collective resources. The collective still dominates the individual. Individual rights suffer.

Fictional entities need not participate in a system of justice designed for persons limited to physical bodies, and natural persons cannot admit them as equal players without risking their own sovereignty. These incorporeal entities may use their own system of justice among themselves. Unlike social promise community, these corporate systems cannot rest on individual sovereignty as a theoretical basis. Most states run corporate justice systems based on territorial sovereignty. These systems serve neither corporations and individuals well and might be improved by transitioning to justice based on reciprocal commitments (e.g., social promises) among collective entities instead of territory. So long as fictional entities can accept the absence of mandatory recognition, they can adapt to social promise community without difficulty. Fictional entities might be better off without states that mandate their conditions of existence, even at the cost of becoming second-class citizens that cannot demand others acknowledge their existence.

Members of voluntary societies can recognize or form corporations, trusts, estates and other fictional constructs if they wish, but only for themselves. None can force others to recognize a fictional entity. This Guidebook will take a more detailed look at collectives and other fictions within social promise community in Chapter 9.

2) In a community of self-sovereign mortals, <u>mortality</u> is a necessary disability. Immortal beings cannot be self-sovereigns of equal status with mortals, for the same reason as incorporeal persons. An immortal person cannot die and cannot engage with mortals in a reciprocal system of obligations.

Mortals have a finite time to live, and a life to lose, existing under constraints that do not exist for immortal beings. When performing any action, for example bringing a claim against another, a mortal sacrifices the possibility of other actions it might do instead. An immortal being escapes this scarcity of time. Whatever it cannot do now, it can always do later. If an entity cannot die, what needs does it have, and what penalty would deter it from predatory conduct? Fifty years of toil and slavery to pay for murder is a much heavier burden for a mortal expected to live seventy years, than for an immortal who cannot die.

Immortality is not a practical bar to be a self-sovereign promise keeper, separate from corporeality. Although incorporeal fictions such as nations and corporations may endure for indefinite periods of time, immortality for people with bodies is unproven if not impossible even in theory. A social promise system designed for immortal natural persons is possible, but not worth thinking about for engineering social promise communities. In a universe in which every known natural and corporeal person is mortal, exclusion of immortal persons reflects nature.

Being Voluntary

By way of reminder, "voluntary" means conscious acceptance, with knowledge of the thing accepted, free of coercion and fraud.

Conscious Acceptance.

Knowledge of the act or transaction involved is a well-recognized condition for an act of free will. The actor must know the act performed, or it is not a voluntary act. You cannot sleep walk your way into being bound by a social promise, or accidentally find yourself there.

When person makes a public record adopting a social promise, most will presume the act was voluntary. Absent evidence of coercion or fraud, neutrals will presume those making social promises could have fairly read and considered their promises in advance and are under no compulsion. Sometimes, a social promisor might overcome a presumption of voluntary action. For example, the promise maker might prove she suffered from some mental disability depriving her of awareness of her promise. Or she might prove coercion or fraud caused her to make a promise against her will.

Voluntary promise making does not require knowledge of every detail of the social promise. It is enough for the promisor to have prior access to the text of the promise he will be making. Others cannot deprive or defraud him of the opportunity to study the text before making the promise. Not everybody wants to be a scholar, or even to read a set of social promises about circumstances not of current interest. Once social promise communities become popular, many will make social promises based on the recommendations of trusted leaders without careful study.

Following leaders might go a step further. A member may delegate her power to make social promises, based on trust in the good intentions and judgment of a lead promisor who accepts the power. A group of people appointed by multiple members might resemble a traditional council of legislators but would have no power to bind anybody who does not grant them power. In addition, the person granting the power retains the power to retract it. A promisor might delegate her promise-making power by publishing an appointment: "My social promises shall be those Group X publishes." She can later retract the appointment by publishing a retraction.

Most members will avoid appointing anyone else to make social promises on their behalf. A few exceptions might arise. Somebody expecting to be out of touch for a period might appoint a proxy promisor as a hedge against unforeseeable changes. Legal environments and customs change. An absentee owner might delegate the power of promising so the promises that concern the owner's property can evolve with the times. But if the absentee owner can communicate, there would be no reason to grant such power. Appointments are contrary to one of the main advantages of social promises: stability of rule sets, with full control over modifications retained in the sovereign person. Specialists might draft social promises, but such drafts would have no enforceable effect until individuals make them their own.

In exceptional cases, neutrals may impute a social promise to achieve a fair result. For example, a neutral might find that an orphaned minor child or mentally disabled person has made a social promise by implication, for example a promise shared by the parent or guardian, or by the child's natural community. The requirement that promises be voluntary should serve society, not to bind it with chains that hinder fairness. Exceptions might evolve in different communities, in justifiable circumstances that do not subvert the general rule: no valid social promise can be made under compulsion or fraud.

Freedom from Coercion and Fraud

Coercion means force or the threat of force against a person or property. If directed against property, coercion includes simple theft. Although a thief can part property from its owner without using violence, none can steal without exerting force. If a member of society compels a social promise from another, the compulsion destroys validity of the act of promising. If the promising is invalid, the member may break the resulting promises without dishonor. But she must disavow the unintended promises once she knows of them.

Coercion by non-members, for example by acts of nature, cannot taint social promises even if fear of dire consequences impels action. The waste howling wilderness may impel hard labor, but coercion involves a purposeful act to bring about the fear in another. To taint anyone's making of a social promise, a member of the voluntary society must cause the coercing. Coercion by non-promisors resembles fear caused by inarticulate nature but differs in that an articulate aggressor can set specific conditions. So fear of non-promisors may have weight in determining whether one's social promises are voluntary, depending on the circumstances. Fraud means providing false information or withholding information material to the action, with intent to deceive. Like coercion, fraud directed for causing a member to make or change specific social promises undermines the validity of those promises.

Some examples demonstrate these premises. Suppose a space faring adventurer builds a craft and launches for Titan, one of Saturn's moons. On the way, her craft suffers an accidental misfortune and she must choose between safe harbor at a human-colonized asteroid or drifting through space with no hope of rescue while her life-support systems fail. The asteroid's inhabitants resolve all their disputes using social promises and refuse to render services to anyone who has not made social promises compatible with community standards. Every person controlling a point of entry to the habitat offers the same choice: make social promises acceptable to us, or we will not open the door. Having no hope of survival drifting through space, the adventurer publishes social promises to enter the doors of the community. Have the asteroid's doorkeepers coerced her? No, because they have done nothing to put the adventurer in the predicament in which she finds herself, and don't owe her any duty absent reciprocal promises.

We reach the opposite conclusion by changing the hypothetical. Suppose an inhabitant of the asteroid detects the passing spacecraft and dispatches an intelligent robot to disable it, knowing this will force the traveler to seek refuge at the asteroid. This is coercion, and it taints all resulting actions taken by the traveler to recover from the attack, whether the traveler is aware she has been the victim of an attack or not. When she arrives at the asteroid habitat doors and makes her social promises to save her life, the attack has tainted her promising. When she learns someone waylaid her ship, she can retract her social promises without penalty. Or if she prefers, she can confirm her social promises despite the attack. The good inhabitants of the asteroid should not deprive her of this choice because of the evil actions of others.

Suppose that instead of attacking the spacecraft, a member of the asteroid society bribes her to pay a visit. If the bribe does not involve deception or theft, it taints nothing. The astronaut's social promises are enforceable. But if the bribe is stolen from non-promisors or otherwise uninvolved members, does the theft taint the astronaut's promising? Does it matter if she knows the bribe is stolen?

Before the astronaut makes her social promises, she is a non-promisor to the asteroid's people. She can accept a stolen bribe without breaking her promises, and members can enforce the promises she makes to enter the gate. If the bribe giver fails to disclose the theft, she is a victim of fraud. In her ignorance, entering the asteroid is riskier. Victims of the theft may discover she possesses stolen property and demand its return. In that case, members should excuse the astronaut and allow her to go on her way. If she goes away as a non-promisor, the asteroid society will not protect her from efforts by the victims of the theft to recover their property. If she confirms her social promises and remains a member of the asteroid's voluntary society, the parties involved can settle any disputes over the stolen property by voluntary due process.

This result does not change if the bribe is stolen from non-promisors. Nor does the result change if the person offering the bribe is a non-promisor, except for the process used to settle any dispute with the one who bribed.

A variation on the space faring hypothetical illustrates another effect of fraud. Suppose that the adventurer requests navigational guidance from the asteroid colony. Nobody in the colony answers the request, and the traveler receives either silence or an affirmative refusal to help, such as "I will not answer." As a result, the traveler's craft encounters a debris field known to the inhabitants of the asteroid and suffers its mishap. Has fraud or aggression occurred? No, because no one purported to offer advice or help. Suppose that she asks: "is my trajectory clear?" And the answer is: "I don't know," or "yes." If the person answering knows or should know the debris field is ahead and answers so to cause the traveler to underestimate the risk, the answer is negligent or fraudulent. If the answer is fraudulent, the fraud excuses its victim from her social promises if causing her visit to the asteroid. As with coercion, the traveler retains her option to excuse the fraud once she discovers it and to confirm her social promises despite it. If the answer is negligent, then the consequence will depend the social promises of the inattentive person, assuming the traveler elects to enter asteroid society rather than perish. Living in the vacuum of space will be dangerous and depend on diligence. The negligence standards will be high.

Pressure to make social promises to gain access to some desired product or service is not wrong. If social promising is ever to spread among the masses, it may be by commercial pressure. For example, suppose a doctor develops new life extension technology, and refuses to offer it to anyone who does not make acceptable social promises. The doctor is not forcing people who make social promises to get the desired services. But working to make others dependent on you is coercive. For example, addicting others to drugs or making them dependent on a resource you control are coercion. Where coercion or fraud causes a promisor to make social promises, the beneficiaries of those promises should excuse the promisor from fulfillment.

Distinctions between coerced promises and voluntary promises may sometimes be unclear without being any less meaningful. Theories of governance based in territorial sovereign powers (e.g., statism) provide an example of fuzzy boundaries, although in a different context. For example, does imposing a set of laws on everyone within a set of territorial boundaries result in coercive imposition of law? Although this question arises only under a statist legal system, contrast how social promises systems handle the problem with the statist approach. If within a statist paradigm a person may leave the territory, the person accepts state law if she remains. But as the alternatives to remaining in the territory become less feasible, the extent to which the choice is voluntary diminishes. There is no clear bright line distinguishing the voluntary maintaining of residence within a territory and being forced to stay in a place blighted by rule of tyrants. If leaving a jurisdiction entails sacrifice to the refugee or does not afford escape from imposed laws, the territorial enforcement of law is coercive.

We can avoid fuzzy boundaries by basing law in personal sovereignty. A simple example illustrates why. Suppose a person named "Monarch" has a valid property claim to a territory under reciprocal social promises. May Monarch enforce a rule that anyone found in territory must make his chosen social promises? No, because such a condition requires any person who would enter Monarch's territory to recognize his territorial sovereignty. Suppose a guest named Immigrant who rejects Monarch's territorial claims visits a relative living in the kingdom. Unless Immigrant accepts Monarch's territorial claim, Monarch cannot enforce his conditions against Immigrant merely because Immigrant is inside territory that Monarch claims.

Suppose that the Immigrant follows a social promise under which Monarch's territorial claim is valid. May Monarch require that Immigrant make any social promise as a condition of entry? Yes, because Immigrant accepts Monarch's right to control access to his territory. Monarch is unlikely to require Immigrant to make social promises of unlimited geographic reach. Immigrant poses no threat Monarch's claim; instead, Immigrant's acceptance of the claim helps confirm it. Monarch will be more concerned about protecting the property claim from those who do not recognize it. If Monarch wants to apply a uniform standard within his property, he may require those who respect his property claims to agree that the standard will apply to actions and events on the property. It is unnecessary to require entrants who respect Monarch's territory to make social promises that do not pertain to the property. Nor could Monarch prevent guests from renouncing his imposed social promises after the guests leave. Rational actors will avoid making such demands.

Clash of property rights is an interesting topic in social promise community and a stumbling block for some. Chapter 5 treats the topic in greater detail. For now, recognize that social promises do not permit imposition of rules based on a rejected claim of territorial sovereignty. Social promise community permits no sovereign but that of the person. Sovereignty over the self does not exist where people are not free to make the social promises of their liking.

Publishing Your Promises

By the Second Promise introduced in Chapter 1, a person's social promises are not effective or enforceable until published. Four parts are needed for publication: identification of the person making the promises and time when made, a definite social promise, means for authenticating the record of publication, and an accessible record.

Identification of the Person and Time of Publication

Records of social promises must identify who made them, or the records are not useful. A social promise applies only to the one who makes it. If others cannot learn who made the social promise, it is meaningless. In addition, records that identify promisors must be reliable. To maintain reliability, promise records should enable verification of the identities of the promisors and the values of timestamps.

Making a social promise is an event and happens at a definite time. Social promises are only valid after being made. The usefulness of a social promise to resolve conflicts or measure honor depends on when the promise maker first published it. Record keepers will include the time of first publication in the promise record as a secure timestamp.

The certainty carried by a personal identification and timestamp varies. Certainty is a question of evidence and often depends on reliability of record keepers. There are many ways to provide reliability. Solutions may vary depending on the environment in which people make social promises. For example, a close-knit and homogenous social promise society does not need formal promise records. Everyone shares their promise profiles through speech, ceremony, and symbolism, without formal written records. In a less homogenous, more scattered community, members will need technical solutions to secure reliable promise records.

Such technical solutions will include electronic registries, which can be in various forms. There is no authority with which a promise maker must register her choice of promises. Promise communities can discover optimal ways to preserve promise records by enabling free exchange and experiment. Promise makers may use any desired form of publication that other members can verify. They might use skywriting, for example, but may find that skywriting is expensive, difficult to authenticate, and limits the publication to a specific area and time. Most promise makers will use a registration service, centralized or decentralized. Registration services will compete on their reputations for credibility, reliability, and efficiency. Decentralized crowd-hosted public ledgers using blockchain or other encryption technologies are the most secure option. Free people will provide efficient and effective solutions, in time.

A Definite Social Promise

Promisors who publish definite social promises build their reputations. Those who promise gibberish hurt only themselves. Not that social promises must address every conceivable detail; that is impossible. But each social promise must have a single meaning without self-negation or ambiguity or be useless. For example, promises to break promises or to do nothing are self-negating and invalid.

Social promises are subjective, expressing what a promisor will do. Voluntary laws are objective, expressing a preference for what all should do. But both social promises and voluntary laws state a condition and an associated consequence. Sometimes, the condition implies an associated consequence. For example, a child might promise "I will not raid the cookie jar," stating a condition with no consequence. The child implies that the consequences of breaking that promise are up to Mom. A more complete formulation is "I will not raid the cookie jar, but if I do, I will pay for any cookies I took." You will make social promises to inform others what consequences you will accept for breaking your promise. So show others those consequences. State your conditions in definite terms.

The promisor cannot make a social promise by reference to an ambiguous source. For example, a promise to "keep British Common Law" fails the need for a definite statement, unless referring to a specific writing that defines British Common Law. Although the term has meaning in legal history, British Common Law has been changing for centuries. The statement makes no reference to a specific publication, so fails to specify the law as it existed at a point in time. British Common Law has another problem. It is mashed with civil codes made by Parliament. The extent of its Common Law part is vague, even if tied to a publication made at a certain time. To be definite, state the whole social promise, or refer to a record that does.

A definite statement may be simple. For example, you might pronounce as an entire set of social promises "I will not aggress, except in self-defense, and will pay restitution for my unjustified aggression." If so, you will let the neutral decide the restitution you should pay and cannot complain about the amount if heavier than expected. Many will prefer more detail in their promise statements. Social promising will not be popular until concise and elegant social promises are available and tested. Writers of promise sets must offer choices to accommodate different moral preferences.

A promisor can amend social promises, creating no implication that a prior social promise is indefinite. For example, suppose Mr. Taciturn makes a simple promise to not aggress without defensive justification. He later promises more specific obligations. That he has added to his earlier statement does not mean the earlier statement lacked definiteness. If he wishes, Mr. Taciturn can confirm his earlier promise when adding to it. If he makes a second promise without confirming an earlier promise, the second promise replaces or supplements the first, depending on what both promises say.

A definite social promise need not cover the entire field. For example, a person might make promises pertaining only to family law, or to contracts, and avoid promise making in other areas. Others cannot expect him to use social promises for issues in areas he avoids. Social promising must be voluntary. If any do not wish to adopt a personal code of conduct in a subject area, they may be silent. Others cannot complain but can consider whether and how they will do business with the silent ones.

For things not covered by a published social promise, the promisor is a non-promisor. To illustrate, suppose Maggie Partial makes social promises regarding family matters only, and disclaims social promising in all other subject areas. Ms. Partial then marries Sally Wholeheart, who has made social promises covering all areas of life. Ms. Wholeheart sues Ms. Partial for divorce, and both will go ahead according to their respective social promises.

Now suppose an issue not covered by family law comes up. For example, suppose one accuses the other of stealing. Then neither of them can resolve the matter using social promises without the consent of the other. If Ms. Wholeheart wants to recover from Ms. Partial for theft, she cannot do so under social promises unless Ms. Partial consents. Because she has made no relevant social promise, Ms. Partial is outside of voluntary jurisdiction. If Ms. Partial would bring a claim for theft against Ms. Wholeheart, a No-Hypocrisy rule — the Third Promise — prevents her from proceeding under social promising unless Ms. Wholeheart consents.

Either party may seek their remedy outside of social promising in areas where at least one party is a non-promisor, with no stain on their reputations in social promise community. This Guidebook calls the ability to exclude topics from one's social promises "modularity." Modularity is useful for harmonizing conflicts between social promises and non-voluntary (e.g., state) laws. Read more about this in Chapter 4.

Transparency and Privacy

When you make your social promises available to others, you give your words meaning and promote transparency. Community is transparent when every member can see what their fellows believe. With modern technology, anyone can provide records for little cost. If you withhold your promises from members who interact with you, you are keeping them in the dark just when your social promises would be most meaningful for them. You cannot expect them to consider your social promises in their interactions with you, making your promises meaningless to them. The fewer records you publish, the less visible you become to other members of your society. You become increasingly opaque. But by making your beliefs transparent, you can expand social progress. When all your neighbors can see your promises and you can see theirs, your community can evolve by grassroots political pressure. Your neighbors will not apply this pressure by voting to impose rules on you. Instead, they will nudge you through social forces such as admiration, fashion, free association, and shame.

Transparency is desirable for social progress and new opportunities but is not compulsory. It may be unwise if taken to extremes. Keep some of your social promises private, sometimes. You might wish to withhold your social promises from adversaries or others, for specific reasons. Privacy can shield you from unwanted political pressure or persecution by your enemies. You may sometimes need to conceal your social promises to protect confidential information from competitors, predators, parasites, or unwanted salespeople. Sometimes, you might need to use a hidden registry to avoid persecution. But unnecessary privacy will deprive you of opportunities, making you invisible to other members. Strangers cannot find you by searching for people with compatible promises, or good reputations.

Each member decides how to balance privacy and opportunity, based on their personal circumstances. Some might find partial privacy preferable to complete transparency. They will publish most of their promises and related reputation feedback but will keep sensitive information private. Others may make no use of social promising systems without control over who can discover they are members. These members may need to keep their membership secret from most people. Whatever the desired balance, unpublished social promises do not exist for those unable to access them and have no effect.

Most members will make their core social promises public as soon as possible, for several reasons. These reasons include to preserve a right to make a claim, to protect against litigation under state laws, and to protect against enforcement outside of promise community rules. Non-promisors have no right to enforce social promises against members. Nor can outsiders pressure members to resolve any dispute using voluntary due process. If you cannot prove that you published a relevant social promise before a claim arose, you lose all your defenses in social promise community and are a non-promisor. For example, a thief belonging to your voluntary society may disregard your promise to not steal, unless you publish your promise before the thief steals from you. If you have not, you will be a non-promisor and must find your remedy outside social promise community or by agreement with the thief.

Some examples will illustrate these points. Suppose Xavier does not recognize copyright as property and long ago published social promises stating his position. He runs a business cracking copy protection schemes. Zyla is a movie producer and has published her social promises recognizing copyright. She investigates Xavier's business and determines that he is liable to her for copyright infringement by state law and would be liable had he made social promises like hers. If she can find no public record that Xavier was a member of a social promise community (i.e., had published his Three Promises) when he performed his infringing acts, she may sue him under state law without any loss of honor. But Xavier has been a member of the community with published copyright-less promises for longer than Zyla has been producing movies. So Zyla cannot sue him or take enforcement into her own hands without risking loss of her reputation for violating her own Three Promises. But Zyla can recognize Xavier as a copyright risk based on his published promises. She can use technological measures to prevent him from gaining access to her protected content.

To vary the example, suppose Xavier lives in a territory ruled by morally obtuse politicians who imprison anybody who dares publish social promises. Being ruled by evil clods gives Xavier a legitimate reason to register his declaration of self-sovereignty in a private register. Or he wishes to avoid junk mail. For whatever reason, he registers his social promises in an encrypted registry, protected by a cryptographic key he controls. Whoever Xavier provides the key to can verify the social promises he has made, and when he made them. If Zyla threatens to enforce copyright against him, he can give her his key. This will create pressure for her to bring her complaint in social promise community, if she values her reputation. Before doing business with Xavier, Zyla can request access to his social promises and refuse to do business unless he provides the key. If she does not know Xavier's promise profile, she can avoid dealing with him. If Xavier damages Zyla despite her care, she is no worse off than had he published all his social promises. Either way, she cannot enforce her own social promises against him. Meanwhile, Xavier sacrifices opportunity to maintain secrecy. Other community members who share his skepticism of copyrights cannot find him, without his access key. His secrecy will limit his business opportunities and his ability to attract paying customers for cracking copy protection schemes.

We'll change the story for a last time. Suppose Xavier first publishes promises respecting copyright, and on that basis receives access to Zyla's protected content. Later, Xavier retracts his earlier promise and publishes a different promise that does not respect copyright, in a private record. Perhaps he has a legitimate reason for so doing, or perhaps not. Either way, he must take care to avoid using the earlier registration to mislead others into actions they would not otherwise do. As a practical matter, this means providing notice to anyone who transacted with him based on the earlier registration, or risking liability for claims based in fraud or negligent failure to inform. If Zyla first accepted Xavier as a customer while he promised to respect copyrights and continues to do so after Xavier secretly retracted his promise, Xavier cannot use his secret social promises for defense.

Suppose Xavier is a decent person and does his secret change in good faith. He may still be liable for his negligence or fraud if he neglects to inform Zyla of his changes. Xavier might make a social promise he hopes will excuse him from liability for evil actions. But every odious promise risks blowback, as we will explore in Chapter 4 on conflict of promises. First, he cannot recover from others who victimize him by the same fraud his promise excuses. Second, sooner or later someone will reveal his evil promise, destroying his reputation. Third, a neutral might refuse to enforce his evil promise, or pronounce him fair game for retribution without due process. Members have many ways to punish those who use social promises to prey on others.

The foregoing examples illustrate why most promises will be transparent within voluntary society. Members should limit access to social promise records only for good reasons. When members withhold their social promises, they should remember that no secret promise has meaning.

Promises to Follow State Laws

Promising to follow the law of a state is possible but pointless. State courts will not expand or shrink their jurisdiction based on anyone's social promise. Instead, state courts will act where they can and apply their own laws, regardless of anyone's social promises. If two Chinese citizens promise to follow Swiss law, neither the Swiss nor Chinese courts will respect their promises unless made in a valid contract under Chinese law. The state determines jurisdiction, not those entering the contract. The two citizens can bring their dispute to a neutral and ask for application of Swiss law. Choice of law provisions are commonplace in contracts enforced under state laws. We don't need social promise systems to use state law in such contracts. We cannot choose state laws out of the context of state-recognized contracts, unless we are under the jurisdiction of the chosen state anyway. If we wish to settle a dispute under the law of the state that claims jurisdiction, we have no need for social promises. But if state laws contain concepts we find useful, we can borrow the good parts and express them in promise form.

Sometimes we may acknowledge state laws in our social promises to help us coexist with people who want to impose state laws on us. You can read more about coexistence with state law in Chapter 6. For now, forget about promising to follow the law of a state, because such notions will blind and confuse you. Social promising operates by publishing each member's moral beliefs about social obligations, for which state laws are useless. Politicians and judges don't write state laws to express anyone's personal moral beliefs about social behavior. They write laws to impose them on everybody under the jurisdiction of the state, regardless of beliefs.

Moral Discovery

Ancient stories revealing human psychology have long treated social shame. Consider the Book of Genesis: Then the eyes of both of them opened, and they knew they were naked; so they sewed fig leaves together and made coverings for themselves. Genesis 3:7 (NET Bible). But lasting shame does not arise from exposing our physical bodies to strangers or to divine spirits, but from exposing our misdeeds and evil thoughts. Whatever one's views on the Torah, Bible, or other sacred writings, covering the shame of nakedness with fig leaves is like justifying shameful behavior with laws. After humans made moral judgments and first felt shame, they sought to justify aggression by cloaking it under the sanctity of authority.

Little has changed since this development in human social evolution. Authorities justify their own aggression while condemning identical aggression by commoners. The law often plays the role of the fig leaves, woven together. Too often, the perpetrators of cruel and malicious deeds excuse themselves by saying "it's the law." Backed by libraries full of laws, and authorized by votes of millions, they do so much evil in the name of greater good.

If authorities who do evil have pangs of conscience, they mollify themselves with the laws they swear to follow and replace their own morality with rules made by politicians. No individual person accepts moral responsibility for the law itself, and few have the power to influence its making. Ordinary individuals do not make law. Only special collectives control the law, and everyone else must obey. Law that excuses shame by a claim of authority is not law. Imposed rules too often do the will of the most powerful political actors, or failing that, inject evil into human society for no reason.

Willing subjects of the state have been behaving badly for millennia. Despite this dismal record, when challenged with the possibility of social promising, some react by saying "Who is to prevent people from adopting immoral, evil promises?" The good judgment of their neighbors! In a word, shame, meaning fear of righteous examination, answers the question best. Self-sovereignty strips away the fig leaves and excuses of laws imposed by others. It leaves individuals nothing to cover moral choices that might expose them to rejection by other members. Instead of seeking cover for moral ugliness, self-sovereigns can follow those moral leaders, past or present, who best guide them in their chosen paths of righteousness. They will work to make their nakedness beautiful.

Social promising is both public and personal. No member of voluntary society can hide behind a law of a collective or claim a higher authority. No collective or authority can adopt or impose laws; only individuals can, and only for their own selves by making social promises. Each publishes their social promises, to the extent they want others to know the social obligations they accept. Every member displays their chosen obligations for the entire world to see; or at least, for all fellow followers of social promising who care to look. And all who see the promise assume its maker made it voluntarily. No one else makes ugly choices for you. Each person must take care that their moral nakedness is not repellant to other members.

If a social promise is evil, the promisor prefers evil, or has chosen an evil promise by ignorance or mistake. Knowing the extent to which others will judge their own choices, few will dare to adopt social promises most around them will regard as evil. Few will fail to make popular promises. Nobody desires the sting of righteous judgment from every person around them. To err is human, and their neighbors may forgive temporary lapses of evil, with an apology and payment of compensation. For someone who chooses a damnable law, forgiveness requires repentance. Until then, such a person has chosen evil, and bears the risk of their open choice.

Under social promising, no employee of a collective can use the law of the collective as an excuse or shield. No police action can claim an excuse under the law of a state, nor can employee seek an excuse under the law of his employer. Each person chooses their own moral code, to which they promise obedience. Each person agrees that neutrals will resolve disputes based on the social promises of the disputants. Wrongdoers cannot hide behind a duty or law imposed by a higher authority. No human agency can offer an authority higher than the self-sovereign person.

What happens when the population is evil, or deluded? Where no controversy over social promises exists, how can the promises be evil? Sometimes, harsh choices are adaptations to a harsh environment. Hard rules may be a necessary evil when living in hard places. Moral differences are a necessary feature of life in any sophisticated society and are better treated openly than suppressed and denied. Although the Three Promises lack direct levers for attacking the promises or lifestyle choices of others where no unwilling victims exist, the Three Promises enable members to apply social pressure where most effective. Chapter 11 explores means and ends of applying social pressure to enact changes in moral views and behaviors of others, without infringing the self-sovereignty of fellow members.

Some moral divisions, such as divisions over the rights of children or animals incapable of choosing a law for themselves, may lead to conflicts without due process. For example, a division between those who tolerate infanticide and those who prohibit it may lead to attacks against people who have advertised a different moral preference. Such instances should be rare, because any who attack must bear the full responsibility for their deeds. The next chapter analyses clashes over the rights of those unable to articulate their own social promises. Deep moral divisions may sometimes lead to tragic outcomes, but outcomes under social promising will be less tragic than outcomes under imposed laws in similar circumstances. The flexibility and lack of central authority characteristic of social promising will reduce violent or aggressive clashes in favor of multiple modes of social pressure. A free society will generate frequent reminders that fair treatment entails thinking through the consequences of your own actions.

What about the intransigent? A few negative persons may always exist to make odious social promises intending to offend. Must voluntary society tolerate these troglodytes? For those who accept the Three Promises, harm from odious promises falls on their makers. Self-hating troglodytes adhering to the Three Promises cannot force others to follow their promises. All are better off for having the troglodytes show themselves. Troglodytes who do not accept the constraints of the Three Promises are non-promisors, outside the realm of social promising. Rule by those who would impose their will on others is the realm of the present day, the realm of imposition of law by force, the realm of the state and the fall of humankind.

In a system that enhances and rewards moral discovery, shame is an effective moderating force on social promises and private behavior. Shame urges abominable moral preferences out. Reciprocity is another moderating force. To benefit from obligations made by others, each must oblige themselves to those others. Reciprocity allows each to live by their published social obligations while preventing any from imposing obligations or denials of any obligation on others. Each member lives as much as possible within their own moral framework. Between shame and reciprocity, self-governing social promise societies will be more regulated and well-ordered than societies under authoritarian systems of law. Ascendance of respect for equal self-sovereignty over central authority will bring a more ordered society, not a more disordered one.

Chapter 4: Resolving Conflicts of Promises

First Look

Conflicts between people holding to different social promises will happen. Mismatched obligations can create resentment. Claimants can despise lighter obligations promised by those who have wronged them. Defendants can chafe under that scorn. The Three Promises leads them both to a rule both are honor bound to apply in their controversy. The Third Promise supplies the rule; the First Promise creates the bond of honor.

Conflict between rules is not unique to self-sovereign society. Dealing with conflicting laws from conflicting authorities is a routine branch of legal systems today, sometimes called "conflict of law" or "choice of law." Traditionally, judges resolve these conflicts based on which country is sovereign over the territory. Where in conflict with self-sovereignty, claims over territory have no force in voluntary society. Nor need we look to territorial claims to resolve conflicts in social promises. We have the Third Promise instead. Every member makes it, and it applies to every conflict. This chapter considers consequences of resolving conflicts between social promises based on the Third Promise: that promise to accept performance of the least burdensome social obligation, when promised obligations differ.

A fair rule for resolving conflict between social obligations promised by self-sovereigns must rest on the promised obligations alone. No other approach honors the sovereignty of each person. But we naturally stop short of rewarding hypocrisy. Only a hypocrite would insist you keep your social promise to them, while refusing to make the same promise to you. Toleration of hypocrisy corrodes fair treatment and interpersonal trust. Keepers of the Third

Promise cannot demand obligations from another greater than the rights they promise to grant under the same circumstances.

Another view angle exists. Suppose we call the less burdensome obligation "weaker," because it has less power to burden others. We'll then apply the weakest of conflicting rules to achieve a just result. We might sometimes call the Third Promise "The Rule Of The WEakest Tool," (TROTWET). Whether we call it the Third Promise, the "No Hypocrisy Principle," or TROTWET, the phrases boil down to the same essence.

An ordinary ten-year-old can understand the elements of TROTWET, but when applied to real social tensions it is subtle and surprising enough to busy a professor for a lifetime. When unfolded, it has an amazing power to smash cultural notions about unanimity to bits and open the door to intriguing new forms of society. For example, the Third Promise enables layered, interlocking systems of different property rights that make old notions of property obsolete. Without the Third Promise, social promising could never be more than a curiosity, observed only within homogenous groups, and dependent on unanimous consent. Your support for social promising as an experiment worth doing depends on your understanding of the Third Promise, why it is indispensable, how it achieves justice, and the wonderful uses it has. Understand before moving on.

For a more detailed discussion of TROTWET, read the Kernel. For application of TROTWET to different problems in conflict resolution and illustrative examples, read the Basket of Nuts.

Kernel

People by nature hold different moral preferences. For example, people have differing religious beliefs, sometimes leading to persecution and war. People have different beliefs about the morality of various kinds of victimless behavior, and the morality of actions with victims. Some regard sex outside of marriage, or sex for purposes other than procreation to be immoral. Others believe all sex between consenting adults is virtuous when practiced with loving care, even when partly motivated by other voluntary exchange. Some put those who use or sell mind-altering substances for recreational, medicinal or religious purposes in prison, while others explore the potential social and medical benefits that responsible use of mind-altering substances brings and believe imprisonment for self-exploration, self-medication or recreation is immoral. Violent disagreements sometime erupt over the morality of abortion or euthanasia, while civil debate is helpless to bridge these divides. People disagree about moral uses of political power, which wars are just, and the just limits to defense of borders and property. We even disagree about what kinds of property we should recognize as proper. Many more deep divisions exist. All difficult moral questions create social fractures that run deep, and that will not heal until the moral dilemmas that energize these divides pass away.

It is a mistake to regard moral disagreement by itself as a negative thing, or to stamp it out. Diversity of opinion and belief is indispensable for healthy society, just as genetic diversity is indispensable to genomes. We should not force our moral differences to disappear. We can't! Each of us is sovereign over our own mind alone. We have no control over the thoughts of others. Each of us is a product of our unique cellular makeup and personal experiences. Our beliefs will differ, by nature! We progress by exploring our differences peacefully and learning to respect one another.

No rule is moral unless accepted by the person on whom enforced, and opinions on morality differ. People of different beliefs and customs must coexist or there can be no social order based in liberty. The Three Promises provide a means for equal coexistence between people holding to different moral codes. Social promise communities have no physical borders to keep people with different beliefs apart, so ordinary disputes between people holding to conflicting social promises are inevitable.

People can practice social promising with no universal conflict of law principles, by making the first two of the Three Promises, and limiting the Third to the special case of identical reciprocity (exchanging identical promises). Doing so restricts the rule of law to those limited circumstances in which the people involved have made the same social promises. Self-organizing society cannot use force to impose one set of rules. Without voluntary principles for resolving moral differences, natural moral fractures will prevent self-organizing society from growing beyond a limited size. The Third Promise bridges those fractures and walls, predictably settling conflicts between different social promises. This Guidebook explains how the Third Promise works, and argues it is the optimal approach for a universal voluntary society. If any two people accept the Third Promise as understood here, they can coexist in the same social promise community despite living by different social promises.

Members of voluntary communities can resolve conflicts in their promises without resorting to state law. Besides conflicts between social promises, conflicts may arise between social promises and state laws. Conflict between state law and social promises pertains to coexistence with state systems, a different topic treated in a different chapter.[6]

Can any rule for resolving differences between social promises hold every promise enforceable while also respecting self-

---

[6] See "Coexisting With State Legal Systems" in Chapter 6.

sovereignty? No. We must choose. Either we allow people to break their social promises sometimes or allow hypocrites to hold others to a higher standard than they hold themselves. Which is worse? Hypocrisy is more corrosive to society than forgiveness. If you think that position is unfair or unworkable, hold your skepticism in check for a little while. Consider that grace may guide you to excuse your friend, when holding her to all her promises is unfair.

If you can demand obligations you are unwilling to reciprocate, you have no reason to make promises of your own. Promise society cannot not exist. Anyone foolish enough to make a social promise becomes subject to claims from everyone with no right to claim back. Rights and obligations become unfair and unequal. But if you must reciprocate promises before you can demand that others keep them, promise society can exist. It forms naturally when people make their social promises public. When you ask less of others than they have promised, nobody is surprised or taken advantage of. When you promise less, you can fairly demand performance of the lesser promise. Rights and obligations become equal and fair. In promise community, no one must do more than they have promised others, or more than the other has promised.

Our journey to social promises for justice started by jettisoning law as something imposed by higher authority. By rejecting authority, we open the door to diversity in social obligations. We then need an approach that provides definite outcomes in disputes involving conflicting social promises. The approach of the Third Promise appeals to intuition, but can it work in practice? To answer the question, we'll analyze the interaction of social promises as an exercise in noncooperative game theory. We won't apply game theory using symbols or expert jargon. We'll just notice what consequences self-interested or just plain evil people will experience when trying to outsmart the Third Promise. We'll consider whether people of good conscience are punished for good behavior.

Let's run some thought experiments to better understand the Third Promise. Examples will show how applying the Third Promise creates incentives for reciprocal treatment of others, penalizes hypocrisy, and provides predictability. If they will keep all the Three Promises, even self-interested people can practice social promising. Beyond that, the Three Promises provide a system capable of preventing self-interest from destroying sustainable voluntary society. If you don't want to strain your brain, don't worry about all the intricate details. Just know that in Social Promise community, you cannot rightly expect your fellow members to carry any social burden for you greater than you have promised to carry for them.

Keep Your Promises and I'll Keep Mine

Justice requires reciprocity, meaning that all receive what they will give. That what a person metes out, others mete back. Social promise communities can enforce reciprocity because everybody promises to keep their own promises and to not ask for more than they promise to others.

The opposite of reciprocity is hypocrisy. Hypocrites apply different rules to the conduct of others than they apply to their own conduct, denying equality under the law. Instead of dispensing equal rights, hypocrites hold others to a higher standard than they hold themselves. Authoritarians often assume or pretend everybody follows same law. But authoritarian solutions reach for impractical ideals. Those in power are too often exempted from the laws they impose on others, either by making laws they know will never apply to themselves, by corruption, or both. We should not fantasize that rulers will enforce the same law on themselves and on those they rule. Such error will lead astray.

70

To build a voluntary society, we must jettison the idealistic fantasy of equal justice under one optimal law. We limit universal law to its most inclusive form: the Three Promises, which offer a way to resolves disputes between persons who have made conflicting social promises, without violating self sovereignty. Self sovereignty requires equal respect for the social promises of all parties and for every member's moral code. Respecting the promises of others is the First Promise in action: "I'll keep my promises." One defending against a claim — the defendant — can honorably refuse if she has not promised what the claimant requests. Whenever a complaint about a broken promise exists, there is always a defendant. The First Promise applies first to the defendant (the obligor), so we'll call the principle "Defendant's Promise." The claimant has no right to expect that others must perform his promises, but only that the defendant should fulfil the promises she has made for herself.

Holding a defendant to nothing more than her own promise opens the door to opportunistic adoption of law in pursuit of hypocritical ends. Since social promises must be voluntary, it must be possible to withdraw them. Withdrawal of a prior promise is not itself hypocritical but basing your social promises on your temporary personal circumstances can lead to hypocrisy if you change your social promises to disadvantage others.

To remove incentives for opportunistic making of social promises, neutrals should apply the most burdensome promise adopted by the defendant since just before the complaint arose. Defendant cannot choose her promise with a certain claim in mind, unless the claimant consents. Instead, the defendant's chosen promise is the last she made before the earliest event supporting the claim against her.

For example, suppose Natalia changes one of her social promises to recognize real property, after refusing to recognize real property for several years. By changing her promise, Natalia opens herself to claims based on her new social promise and related promises. Those new claims may reach back in time. If Natalia is prudent, she will avoid infringing the rights she plans to recognize for a while before changing her promises. What qualifies as enough time might not be under Natalia's control, and may reach back farther than she appreciates. The less sincere Natalia's change appears to neutrals, the more likely they will hold her responsible for fraud. For example, suppose Natalia squatted on Alexey's land while saving money to buy her own house, relying on her social promises to resist eviction. She only changed promises after she was ready to buy a house of her own. A neutral hearing a complaint by Alexey might decide that Natalia's change in promises is fraudulent and hold her responsible for back rent, assuming Natalia has promised to not defraud others. By holding the defendant to her most burdensome promise, we discourage people from hiding weak and insincere promises behind socially acceptable promises for nefarious purposes.

Potential for unfairness or abuse remains, however. People adopting more burdensome promises can be liable to those who have shielded themselves by adopting less burdensome promises. When claimants can hold others to more stringent standards than they hold themselves, everyone feels pressure to make promises relieving themselves of fair obligations. Rewarding hypocrisy ruins the value of social promises for defining suitable remedies for wrongs, and for incentivizing settlement by due process under agreed rules instead of retribution without due process. The Third Promise prevents the ruination of self-sovereign order.

Don't Be A Hypocrite

By the "No-Hypocrisy" rule of the Third Promise, members promise to enforce no obligation greater than they promise. A rule against hypocrisy prevents people from exploiting obligations they are unwilling to bear for others. This is a simple concept with profound implications.

When working together, the "Defendant's Most Burdensome Promise" and "No-Hypocrisy" rules produce almost the same result as applying the least burdensome of the parties' promises. That which is least burdensome we might also call "lightest" or "weakest." We can describe selecting the lightest promise as "The Rule of The Weakest Tool" (TROTWET). "Tool" sounds odd but fits from the viewpoint of the neutral whose task is to resolve disagreements. In social promise communities, each member's social promises are the primary tools for honorable conflict resolution. Each party's social promise can affect the outcome, because neutral process must consider the promises and assertions of both sides.

In every conflict, someone seeks a neutral opinion on an issue of social consequence. Otherwise, no real controversy exists; the parties settle their affairs by agreement. Matters of social consequence that need neutral process do not always involve opposition. For example, uncontested adoptions or property claims can use a neutral to confirm actions no one opposes. We'll consider uncontested actions in a later chapter. But the main use of neutral opinions is to resolve conflicts between opposing parties.

Before we consider more examples, let's review terminology. One who asks for a neutral opinion is a "claimant," because this person desires to validate a claim. The claimant brings the claim. One who defends against a claim is a "defendant." The claimant and defendant together are the "parties," and as unspecified individuals "each party." Promises that enable others to bring claims are "positive" promises. Social promises can be made in another, negative form. Negative promises nullify positive promises under specific circumstances. Lawyers will recognize negative promises as "affirmative defenses" because negations are defenses excusing otherwise culpable conduct. Affirmative defenses specify conditions relieving promisors from obligations. For example, a member might promise to pay restorative and punitive damages if convicted of theft, unless to preserve life. The promise to pay damages creates a positive right, and the exception "unless to preserve life" creates an affirmative defense against accusations of theft.

By the First Promise, claims must rest on social promises made by defendants. By the Third Promise, no claim can exist unless the claimant has made a reciprocal social promise. By "reciprocal," we mean a promise that would oblige the claimant to the defendant, were the circumstances of the claim reversed. Each party to the dispute must have made a reciprocal social promise bestowing positive rights under the circumstances, or the claim is not justiciable. If the claim is not justiciable, the defendant can ignore the claimant without risk of dishonor.

Conflict resolution often involves a struggle, due to our animal natures. As any parent knows, the ego begins its battle of wills no later than infancy. Although no analogy is perfect, we can analogize conflict resolution to a contest waged using tools. To that contest, each party brings their social promises containing two classes of rights: offensive tools (positive rights) and sometimes defensive tools (affirmative defenses). The neutral decides which tool in each class is weakest, and the weakest tools govern the outcome.

Positive rights and affirmative defenses that the parties have promised make up the "promise pool" of each issue. The neutral first excludes all promises except defendant's strongest positive promise and weakest affirmative defense, with claimant's weakest positive promise and strongest affirmative defense. On most issues, the parties will not bring multiple promises and the neutral has less excluding to do. For example, when both parties bring a single promise, the pool at first contains all the promises from each party.

Second, the neutral picks one positive right and one affirmative defense (if any) from the pool using the rules we discussed earlier. The positive right and affirmative defense the neutral selects are the rule for the issue at hand. For many issues, none but the weakest promises stay, so the weakest tools prevail.

More rarely, a party has multiple identities holding different social promises, or makes different promises at different times without canceling their earlier promises. In those cases, the neutral examines the different promises of each party, and excludes every promise but claimant's lightest and defendant's heaviest from the pool. If (1) claimant's lightest promise is weightier than the defendant's heaviest promise and (2) the defendant has made at least two applicable but different promises, then the neutral will not choose the lightest. Instead, the neutral will keep the heaviest of defendant's applicable promises, which the neutral will apply if not more burdensome than claimant's lightest promise.

Measuring weakness differs based on the class of right. Neutrals will assess the weakness of affirmative defenses using a different method than for positive rights. For positive obligations, the weaker promise is the one that when applied to the facts results in a smaller burden for the defendant. For affirmative defenses, the weaker promise results in greater *liability* for the defendant. The weaker defense is the weaker shield; the strength of the tool depends on its intended function. For positive promises, strength increases with the burden to defendant, and for affirmative defenses, strength increases with the protection enjoyed by the defendant. The reason for the different measurement methods is best illustrated by examples, which you can find in the following Basket of Nuts. As explained in the Basket of Nuts, it is always possible to identify the weaker tool by testing the preferences of the parties, even when burdens are incomparable.

Since all social promises are of equal power, defendants can make social promises that disavow rights, or can abstain from making social promises that recognize the rights. Members may sometime refuse to recognize a right by silence. For example, a promise to respect tangible property with silence regarding other property rights provides a similar but more general exclusion than a promise to respect all property of labor paired with a promise to attach no property right to information of any kind. Either promise set will negate obligations of intellectual property for the one who makes it.

Under TROTWET, all parties have a reason to make promises that spell out reasonable remedies for infringement of the rights they recognize. When people promise to pay reasonable penalties, they provide an incentive for those they have wronged to seek remedies consistent with the parties' social promises instead of retribution without due process. Reciprocity in social promises provides many benefits.

How Three Promise Systems Deter Evil

Everybody can spot people who openly refuse to take responsibility for their actions, before they act. It is much harder to spot people who promise to take responsibility but deny it when they can. These hidden evil doers can escape payment when doing evil to those who, by their social promises, refuse to take responsibility for doing the same.

Consider the example of Candy Cane and Abel Lyful. Ms. Cane makes no promise that penalizes murder. Mr. Lyful promises to give up his own life for murdering another. Suppose both are members of a large voluntary society and are strangers to one another. Secretly, Abel enjoys murdering people if he can get away with it. He can easily find Candy and murder her without penalty, under protection of her published promise. Candy has no way to find Abel in advance because he promises to pay the ultimate penalty for murder.

Unless Candy is suicidal or a professional assassin, she should make a social promise accepting a heavy penalty for murder. When consequences are lighter, she may not mind being a person who will not accept penalties. For example, if Candy does not depend on inventing for her livelihood, she can with little risk refuse to accept penalties for using the inventions of others without their consent. The worst that can happen is that inventors refuse to do business with her.

For more examples, read the Basket of Nuts.

Basket of Nuts

More examples will help illustrate the Third Promise and TROTWET in operation. Let's begin by continuing the example of Ms. Cane and Mr. Lyful. Except this time, Candy is tipped off and proactively murders Abel. Abel's heirs cannot recover from Candy in a voluntary forum, because Candy has not promised to pay any penalty for murder. So Candy and her heirs cannot claim any damages for her murder. Suppose Candy's killing motivates Abel's heirs to kill her. Her omission of penalties for murder frees them to avenge his blood with hers, without penalty. Once again, only a suicidal person or a professional assassin would fail to promise payment of heavy penalties for murder.

But what if Candy is a professional assassin? She lives in an underground fortress protected by superior defenses. Her expeditions are secret or surrounded by overwhelming firepower. None can kill her without imperiling themselves, their families and their most loyal allies. She is practically immune from being murdered. As a professional assassin with remarkable powers, in theory Candy could be a member of voluntary society who makes no promise to pay penalties for killing others. In practicality, she faces two enormous hurdles. First, making herself invulnerable to motivated avengers is expensive and risky. Second, her refusal to promise penalties for murder reveals herself as a dangerous or foolhardy person.

Acquiring immunity from murder is impossible except for militant fictions like states, and even governments can crumble from inside or be defeated in war. But immunity from money damages is easy. All you need is poverty, to be bereft of transferable assets or earnings power. When an aggressor is practically immune to retribution, the "Impossible Reciprocity Problem" is at work. The Impossible Reciprocity Problem often comes up in property claims, and more rarely in claims for bodily or personal harms. Impossibility of reciprocity may be a problem for personal safety where state or state-like (e.g., organized crime) powers grant practical immunity from retribution with or without due process. But gangs of thugs exist by aggression and are non-promisors. The misconduct of non-promisors provides no evidence of defect in voluntary principles. It is enough for members of voluntary society to recognize non-promisors, and to exclude them from society to any extent desired. Those in voluntary society will seldom find any dilemma in applying the weaker tool.

With Negative Promises, Reverse The Sign

An affirmative defense is an excuse for evil actions, an exception to an obligation, a promise that subtracts, a negative promise. For example, self-defense or defense of others can be an affirmative defense to battery or murder. Necessity can be an affirmative defense to trespass. One can avoid obligations by not making promises that create duties, shaping positive law. Another way to avoid duties is by promising to respect conditions that excuse performance of a duty, creating an affirmative defense. You can express the same obligation by a single positive promise, or by combining a positive promise with a negative. The distinction between promises depends on phrasing, on the way the promise operates. Learn to distinguish between positive and negative promises. When dealing with a negative promise, reverse the sign. The weakest negative promise is that which excuses least. The weakest positive promise is that which obligates least.

If we can express the same obligation with a single positive promise, or by combining a positive and a negative promise, why should the manner of expression matter? Why shouldn't the weakest rule always be that which results in the least obligation to the one accused? Reciprocity is the answer. With a positive promise, we cannot expect to receive more than we have promised to others. With a negative promise, we open exceptions for others, not for ourselves. We cannot excuse ourselves by making a social promise. If we could, if everybody could excuse themselves from evil in circumstances of their own choosing, there could be no social order. Natural impatience and selfishness might drive some to resolve social tensions by doing evil, for which they would then excuse themselves using a negative promise. Others would see social promises failing and feel compelled to follow aggressive examples. After a short while all would realize that their social promises offer no protection. If nothing prevents members from using negative promises as a shield to prey on victims, promise community will abort itself at inception.

We can avoid a travesty of voluntary order by recognizing a simple principle of comparison: a negative promise that excuses more is stronger than one that excuses less, despite the greater net obligation left by the latter. Neutrals should evaluate the strength or weakness of a rule from the viewpoint of the party who suffers the rule's consequences. Doing so prevents defendants from using promised exceptions to escape liability and limits them to the weakest negative promise in every case. In mathematical terms, we measure the strength of a positive or negative promise by its absolute value. In engineering terms, process control requires a feedback mechanism that reduces undesired effects. For those who think in practical terms, the best way to understand why defendants cannot be free to pick their own affirmative defenses is by considering examples. Suppose, for the sake of argument, neutrals award defendants their affirmative defenses no matter how strong. The two following counter-examples show the consequences.

A first counter-example, Violent Defense of the Unborn: Fanatic makes social promises that justify as defense of others any harm committed to prevent abortion. Then, he hides in an abortion clinic and attempts to murder Hook, an abortion doctor, just as Dr. Hook is aborting a fetus as its mother requested. Fanatic maims and disables Doctor Hook, who seeks compensation for his injuries. Prior to the attack, the doctor made social promises that permit abortions requested by the mother. Fanatic raises his intended defense under the rule of Defendant's Promise for affirmative defenses, and the doctor cannot recover for his injuries. Fanatic gets off scot-free. Feeling encouraged, Fanatic continues his rampaging against anyone he disagrees with, while encouraging others to join him. Soon, social promising becomes meaningless, and voluntary society devolves into brutish, violent chaos.

A second counter-example, Violent Defense of Property: Luckless owns almost nothing. He adopts a law permitting poverty as a defense against continuing trespass. Then, he moves into Rich Brother's spare vacation house. Rich has never recognized poverty as an affirmative defense to trespass. Instead, Rich has promised that defense of property always justifies eviction, no matter how forceful. Rich Brother cannot evict or claim any damages from Luckless under voluntary due process if Luckless raises poverty as affirmative defense to the claim of trespass. Under Luckless' rule, poverty is a complete defense depriving the property owner of any remedy for the trespass under social promises. Encouraged by his successful possession of Rich's home, Luckless builds a career teaching others "How to Live in The Home of Your Dream — For Free!" Soon, many others follow Luckless' example, upsetting and disgusting Rich. In anger, Rich contemplates adopting an affirmative defense of hatred, leaving Rich free to kill or maim anyone he hates. He decides not to, realizing his brother may hate him. Instead, Rich realizes he may evict Luckless however he wants, in defense of his property. Social promises fail to restrain aggressive behavior when we forget to enforce the Third Promise.

Let's alter the second counter-example. Suppose Luckless does not recognize rights in real property. If we apply the weakest positive law, Rich's trespass claim fails. Rich's property right in the vacation home is not valid under Luckless' weaker positive promise. Once again, Rich has no remedy under social promises, but this time due to Luckless' weaker positive promise. Rich's only choice besides tolerating Luckless is to remove him without due process. Rich can plead defense of property if Luckless brings a claim for damages based on the removal action because (under our counter-hypothetical) all affirmative defenses must be respected. Rich can use any method he likes to carry out the eviction, so long as he has made a social promise in which defense of property excuses all use of force. For example, if Rich Brother shoots Luckless in both legs and throws him out the third-floor window, it's just tough luck for Luckless. If Luckless brings a claim for the violent removal, Rich Brother as the defendant enjoys his positive property promise and his affirmative defense and escapes all liability. Luckless recognizing no property right cannot raise a claim for possession. If claiming personal injuries, Luckless cannot overcome Rich Brother's affirmative defense. Instead of encouraging peaceful settlement of disputes, the parties' negative promises create incentives to retaliate for evil with more evil. Chaos and destruction!

These counter-examples show the Impossible Reciprocity Problem at work, creating obvious injustice and providing incentives for predators or parasites. Fanatic will abort no fetus. He has no concern about the fetal defense excuse ever being raised against a claim he might make. Luckless owns no property. He will adopt poverty as a defense to claims based in property. Rich will adopt property as a defense to personal injury during evictions, so long as he never expects to trespass on the property of others. All will excuse themselves from aggression under conditions they know others cannot use against them. When we allow evil doers to choose their own excuses, we undermine everyone's ability to predict the effect of positive promises. We make the outcome of every case depend on whatever defense the defendant chooses and transform due process into an unbreakable shield for evil doers. Allowing defendants to always apply their own defenses is unworkable and would be disastrous for voluntary society.

Achieving a Balance

Defendants control their affirmative defenses by making exceptions to their own social promises. Any promisor can craft an exception that excuses them from aggressive conduct every time. Promises that always excuse the promisor make retribution impossible. To use a trivial example, I could take responsibility for any harm caused by my aggression against others, unless my eyes are blue. My eyes are blue in their natural state, or else why would I create the exception? Anyone I have wronged knows my positive promises are illusory, and in reality, I have promised them nothing. If I may have my affirmative defense, none can make a claim that will stick against me. Their only choice for recovering is to take what they feel I should pay by force. They may take retribution or restitution in their own hands by making illusory promises with unreasonable affirmative defenses and helping themselves. Putting the power to excuse breaking of their own promises in the hands of defendants is like demolishing the foundation of the building. Once people realize they are in complete control of creating exceptions to evil conduct, fear drives a race to lawlessness and the pure exercise of might over right. Any possibility for a balanced voluntary society operating on reciprocal promises vaporizes. Poof!

A simple solution to the problem exists: assess the strength of an affirmative defense based on its defensive purpose. For negative promises, the weaker promise is that which defends less. As always, apply the weaker promise. Prevent defendants from using stronger defenses than promised by their victims. Does the proposal work? What happens when we apply the least burdensome positive promise with the least protective negative promise? Consider these examples:

First Example, <u>Defense of Children from Their Caregivers</u>: Defender makes a social promise stating he will pay restitution for harm, unless committed to prevent abusive injury to a child. Defender learns that Abuser has imprisoned his own children and is beating them bloody every day. Defendant executes a daring rescue, freeing the children, but injuring Abuser and destroying part of his home. Abuser seeks brings a claim under social promises for the attack, having long adopted a promise that excludes defense against parental abuse as a valid defense. Because his own preferred defense would excuse behavior that claimants would not, Defender cannot rely on it. He must rely on Abuser's defense, instead. Abuser has no such defense, so Defender must pay Abuser for his injuries and property damage. In addition, Defender cannot recover from Abuser for any injuries inflicted by Abuser in reasonable self-defense, assuming the promises of both parties excuse reasonable self-defense.

If this result feels unsatisfactory, consider the alternative. Abuser deserves little sympathy, but what if Defender mutilated everybody who raised their voice to their children? When Defender knows she is entitled only to Abuser's defense, she has a reason to exercise care while rescuing children even from those who are undeserving in her eyes. The alternative would allow zealots to appoint themselves judge, jury and executioner upon the public, leading to lawlessness. Social promise systems should prohibit no one from defending others or doing other good deeds but should encourage everybody to act with care while doing good.

Abuser cannot claim a right to abuse anyone against their will, even when he is a parent or caregiver of the victim. Such an exception disregards the independent personhood of victims and is outside the bounds of social promising. No one can own another, even parents cannot own their children. Abuser will be liable under claims brought on behalf of his freed children, where his conduct violates community norms.[7] Merits of the children's claims against Abuser are not the question presented by the hypothetical. The question presented is whether a scoundrel like Abuser can deprive Defender of her affirmative defense when she seeks to defend Abuser's children. He can, but undeserved respect cannot be worse than unmitigated predation or fury.

Suppose we turn the tables and apply the same rule for affirmative defenses: Abuser attacks to defend Defender's children (assuming Defender has become an abuser). Can Abuser gain the benefit of Defender's affirmative defense? The No-Hypocrisy Rule says no. Because Abuser has adopted a law with greater liability, Abuser cannot receive the benefit of Defender's affirmative defense with less liability, if Defender brings a claim. Neutrals should judge Abuser by the same affirmative defense he allows for those he makes claims against unless doing so lets the claimant enjoy greater benefits than provided by claimant's own law. When raising an

---

[7] See Chapter 9, "Children and Other Dependents."

affirmative defense, defendant must do so under claimant's law, unless defendant's own law provides a weaker affirmative defense than claimant's.

Let's consider the effects of our balancing plan. We'll revisit the second counter-example, Violent Defense of Property starring Rich Brother and Luckless, but change it to show how applying TROTWET as the Guidebook proposes balances social tensions. Suppose Rich Brother brings a claim against Luckless for eviction. Luckless recognizes Rich Brother's property right to his spare home but has adopted poverty as an affirmative defense. By TROTWET, Luckless can only plead Rich Brother's promised affirmative defenses, but Rich has not promised to respect poverty as a defense to trespass. Rich presents his complaint to a neutral. The neutral looks up both parties' social promises and discovers that Luckless has promised to respect real property but Rich has not promised to respect poverty as a defense to trespass. Based on these promises and the facts, the neutral issues an unbiased opinion that excuses Rich for evicting Luckless from the vacation home.

Suppose Luckless has not promised to respect real property. In that case, Rich cannot get a neutral opinion justifying forcible eviction. Luckless cannot get a property title or other right to possess Rich's vacation home, because Luckless disclaims any right to own real property. Rich knows he cannot get a neutral to condone eviction because of Luckless' disclaimer. So Rich evicts Luckless on his own, without a neutral's opinion. After consulting with a removal specialist, he mixes a sleeping drug into cheesy nachos, one of Luckless' favorite foods. Luckless eats the nachos and falls into a deep sleep. Rich rents a room elsewhere, places Luckless inside, and then changes the locks on the vacation home. If Luckless brings a claim against Rich Brother for kidnapping and coercive drugging, Rich Brother cannot raise defense of property as an excuse, because Luckless made no reciprocal promise. Luckless has not promised to respect defense of property as a valid excuse for kidnapping. So Luckless will recover penalties from Rich Brother for his method of removal. These penalties may include damages for any physical or emotional trauma suffered by Luckless but will exclude any award of a claim of ownership or tenancy to this property, based on the parties' promises respecting property. Next time, Rich Brother will be cleverer about how he gets Luckless to leave, to limit his exposure to a claim for damages.

Suppose Luckless then changes his positive promise to recognize real property only for "personal residences that the owner lives in for at least 50% of the time since first possession." Rich Brother cannot meet this test for his vacation home, so Luckless brings a claim seeking title or a right to occupy the home. For reasons considered in Chapter 5 on voluntary property, neutrals will consider Luckless' property claim less valid than Rich Brother's. Luckless' complaint will so fail. If Luckless gains possession of the vacation home despite the failure, Rich Brother can evict in the same way as he did when Luckless recognized no real property, with care to do no harm.

These examples show how the Rule of The Weakest tool creates incentives for reasonable behavior. In the first hypothetical (the counter-example), both Rich and Luckless could make any excuse they pleased for breaking their social promise. Each could choose his own defense. Both chose excuses that could not be turned against them, converting due process into a contest of power. In the second example, we held both Rich and Luckless to the weakest defense in their collective promises. We recognized that the weaker defense is that which defends least. In the words of the Third Promise, we held that the least burdensome defense excuses least. We drew a contrast to positive promises, noting that the least burdensome positive promise is that which obligates the promisor least. We noted how TROTWET gives both Rich and Luckless a reason to decrease harm when resolving their conflict.

Analysis of motives aside, using the language of social promises makes it easy to remember how to balance the competing claims and defenses of society members. Each member of voluntary society can only bind themselves. Each can promise only to respect the rights or defenses of others. None can compel others to promise any measure of reciprocal respect. Under TROTWET, we have reason to make meaningful promises because we cannot receive more than we have promised to give. We must each promise what we hope to receive, or always receive less than our right measure.

Distinguishing Negative from Positive Promises

It is always possible to express an affirmative defense as a positive promise. "I will not kill, except in self-defense" accomplishes the same result under due process as "I will not kill, and I will excuse murder for killings necessary in self-defense." The first self-defense promise is negative, and the second is positive. In both cases, so long as the killer has made an equivalent or stronger promise, self-defense excuses killing. So how can we distinguish between them, calling one negative and one positive?

In the first case the promisor can trigger the exception by killing in self-defense. The promisor can choose victims who have made similar social promises. In the second case, the promise is to not enforce claims against people who kill in self-defense. The promisor cannot trigger this obligation, unless by killing somebody who has made the same positive promise. Self-sovereigns can always choose their victims. We'll just measure the weakness of a promise differently depending on whether it is positive or negative. The weakest positive promise obligates least. The weakest negative promise excuses least.

The mode of measurement is all that makes the distinction meaningful, in the end.

Variations on The Weaker Tool Rule

Diverse social promises can combine in an infinite number of different combinations. Limitless possibilities cannot be catalogued, but we can foresee larger issues. For example, perhaps neutrals will have difficulty determining the "weaker" tool when the remedies afforded by different promises are different in kind, i.e., of different types difficult to compare. We will consider one way around this difficulty in the next essay. Although derived from the Third Promise, The Rule of The Weakest Tool (TROTWET) is not the final word, nor does it foreclose debate on the question of how to harmonize conflicting social promises fairly. But the Rule of the Weakest Tool may represent an idealized optimal solution to the problem of finding a fair and stable balance between the rights of claimant and defendant, based solely on the social promises made by each party. The solution avoids consideration of imposed territorial boundaries in choice of law.

Are alternatives to resolving conflict of laws limited to a choice of either defendant's or claimants promise? What about combining claimant's and defendant's promises, or choosing a third rule? Other conceivable solutions, for example averaging of damages from different promises or random selection, fail to provide the same incentives for decent and reasonable behavior afforded by the Rule of The Weakest Tool, and contradict the Third Promise. Parties to a dispute are always free to agree on some other way to resolve differences between social promises they have made. People might alter the Third Promise to adopt conflict of promise rules different from TROTWET. Where all parties accept an alternative rule, they don't need TROTWET. If all parties to a dispute cannot agree to use the same conflict of law rules, a default rule provides the only option for resolving the dispute without forsaking social promising. Universal conflict of law rules must be neutral, fair and workable enough to gain widespread acceptance as the conflict resolution rule of last if not first resort for any person living by their own social promises.

Variations in the default rule for choice of law can work if confined to boundaries naturally hard to pass. For example, dispute resolution services on the Moon might apply different conflict of law rules than similar services on Earth. Such differences could exist without injecting uncertainty into interpersonal relations, depending on the difficulty of Earth-Moon travel. So long as constraints on travel between the Moon and Earth (a) make it easy for Moon people to avoid contact with Earth people, and vice versa, and (b) make the probable forum for resolving disputes between Moon people and Earth people predictable, then different customs for fulfilling the Third Promise might coexist comfortably. Without separation between neutral forums that apply different default conflict of promise rules, the practical effect of making a social promise will become unpredictable, discouraging social promising.

Without universal rules accepted by all parties, options for resolving different promises are limited to negotiating an agreement, acting without due process, or appealing to a non-voluntarist authority. These options leave members without a common instrument for bridging divides. Without universal conflict of law principles, the self-directed, atomistic nature of social promising will lead to division. Difficult disagreements will arise over which promises to apply in disputes between members holding to different social promises. These differences may become every bit as bitter and divisive as political fights over moral preferences in statist institutions. Instead of encouraging peaceful acceptance and commerce despite differences in worldviews, social promises would drive people with different beliefs apart. Fortunately, we have the Third Promise and all it implies to avoid those social wedges.

If you think applying the weaker promise is unfair, you can easily opt yourself out of it. For example, you can make a promise you will always perform the greater obligation or will always honor the promised obligations of claimants. To avoid being victimized by opportunistic claimants, you might limit your promise to cases where the claimant's promised obligation is genuine, such as by actual prior performance of the promisor. You can control only your own obligations, however. Outside of specific contracts, you will likely discover that the risks of promising more than TROTWET requires entails taking on risk without compensatory benefits.

At this nascent stage, nothing is better suited for resolving differences between social promises than the Rule of The Weakest Tool. This Rule fosters mutual respect and understanding between people of different beliefs, without requiring that any person bow to authority higher than their own sincere moral lights. TROTWET is remarkable, for that.

Determining the Lesser Penalty

Those arguing over which social promise is weaker might often disagree, whenever the damages are not specified strictly by comparable quantitative measures. A kilogram of gold is indisputably more valuable than a gram, but what is the monetary value of non-monetary penalties? Sometimes, we can assess value by the relative cost of the obligation to the one on whom it would be enforced. For claims based on conflicting promises, the weaker obligation is the one in which the promised cost to be paid is least. "Least cost" can be determined by monetizing non-monetary costs using reason and by reducing monetary costs to present value based on prevailing interest rates and applicable parameters (e.g., payment schedules and risk ratings). If the costs to be compared concern acts or properties for which a free market exists, cost should be determined by the current market price.

But some penalties can't be exchanged for money. Many remedies are not monetary, or can't be reduced to comparable (e.g., quantitative) measures. For example, the cost of a death penalty cannot be monetized in the general case, because no natural market in death can exist. Death and other forms of bodily injury or impairment are not fungible. Each can die only one death and live only one life: their own. Other forms of bodily impairment are also not fungible. For example, most would not consider a sentence of life imprisonment satisfied, if the person convicted of the sentence hired another to be imprisoned. A dilemma of incomparable costs occurs if one promise requires a non-fungible remedy and the other requires a fungible remedy (e.g., monetary damages).

How can neutrals determine which of incomparable obligations is weaker? For example, suppose the claimant has promised one month of indentured servitude for theft, while the defendant has promised to cut off a digit. If the defendant is convicted of theft, should she be expected to cut off one of her digits, or to work for a month as an indentured servant? We cannot answer the question by attempting to compare incomparable things. We might accept arbitrary judgments by neutrals on the question, but arbitrary judgments undermine predictability and fairness.

Fortunately, neutrals need not identify the lesser of incomparable burdens, an impossible task. Instead, following the example of King Solomon,[8] they can employ a simple test based on measuring the preferences of the parties. The test will always show

---

[8] Faced with the dilemma of discerning the true mother of an infant, King Solomon tested the parties' preferences by ordering that the child be divided in two and shared. When only one of the parties expressed a strong preference that the child's life be spared even if it meant losing her parental rights, King Solomon awarded custody of the child to her, "for she is the mother thereof."

which promise is weaker. The answer might not be the same in different cases involving different parties but will always be fair and unambiguous where applied.

Let us first suppose that dilemma of incomparable obligations can be fairly resolved without ambiguity by asking the claimant to choose a preferred remedy from those available by the promises of the parties and proceeding based on the defendant's reaction.[9] For example, suppose that a defendant is accused of murder by the heir of a deceased person. The deceased person whose claim the heir prosecutes promised to accept a penalty of death if convicted of murder. The defendant promised a lifetime of involuntary servitude for the same offense. If the claimant is unwilling to accept the lifetime of involuntary servitude promised by the defendant, the claimant is admitting that the death penalty is the greater burden. The defendant has promised the lesser obligation, which will be the just remedy applied. If the claimant lies and says the involuntary servitude is acceptable while hoping for a sentence of death, then there is no dispute about applying defendant's promise. If the defendant objects to involuntary servitude because death is the lighter penalty and must be applied, the claimant will agree to the death penalty because that is claimant's true preference. Again, involuntary servitude will be the just remedy under either choice made by the claimant, unless both the claimant and defendant prefer a penalty of death.

If the claimant prefers defendant's promised remedy while defendant prefers claimant's, the result differs but the parties' preferences still point to the correct choice. Recall that the victim promised to accept a penalty of death while the defendant promised involuntary servitude. If the claimant prefers involuntary servitude,

---

[9] We will reconsider this supposition after following it to a logical conclusion.

the defendant can be asked if she will accept involuntary servitude instead of death. If the defendant accepts involuntary servitude, then both agree on the just penalty for the case. If the defendant rejects involuntary servitude, she can fulfill her own promise by committing suicide. But suppose the claimant prefers to keep the defendant alive in a padded cell as a form of involuntary servitude, for the defendant a fate worse than death. By stating a preference for servitude in the face of defendant's preference for death, the claimant is admitting that death is the lesser obligation. The neutral will opine that death is the lighter penalty, so the claimant cannot imprison the defendant in a padded cell without breaking his own Third Promise. To preserve his reputation as a faithful promisor, the claimant must either kill the defendant or let her go.

Just to be sure the logic is sound, suppose the victim promised involuntary servitude while the defendant promised a penalty of death. The claimant prefers a lifetime of involuntary servitude or lies and says so hoping for a death sentence. If the defendant agrees, the problem is solved: servitude is the just remedy. If the defendant prefers death, then claimant's stated preference is an admission that death is the lighter remedy. A neutral's determination of the lesser of incomparable burdens depends on the preferences of both parties. If both parties agree on the penalty, there is no dispute. If the parties disagree, the defendant chooses the penalty.

If we start by supposing that the remedy least preferred by the claimant is weightier, the defendant will control which remedy applies. Why is that a good premise? If we posit the remedy least preferred by defendant to be weightier, we will obtain the opposite result: the claimant will choose the remedy where the options are incomparable. It is a sturdy premise because claimants choose their defendants and create claims. Claimants cannot be allowed to control which of incomparable remedies applies, without creating incentives for professional, judgment-proof claimants to enforce unnaturally heavy obligations for self-immunized offenses. This danger does not exist for defendants, who do not bring claims.

For example, suppose Arum never prepares food for anyone, and makes a social promise he will submit to ten years of involuntary servitude for anyone that suffers from food he prepares. Suppose food preparers customarily promise restitution for medical expenses, under similar circumstances. Knowing he will choose his remedy, Arum eats out a lot and presses claims whenever he contracts mild food poisoning, choosing his remedy of servitude. He either ruins the reputations of honest food preparers who are unwilling to serve ten years for slightly contaminated tacos or achieves mastery over many indentured servants for no good reason. If you think ten years of servitude can be easily quantified and compared, consider the hypothetical if Arum promised to accept a penalty of death or maiming.

Defendants can choose their victims, but not who to press claims against. They can make promises with unnaturally light obligations if they wish. Doing so increases the risk they will be victimized by their victims or by like-minded predators, as we have noted. This risk balances the impulse to get a free pass for bad behavior. Defendants may seek to avoid the risk of being victimized by their own tactics, such as by acquiring strong physical defenses. But immunity from victimhood is much harder to achieve than immunity from claims. One can become judgment proof against some claims merely by abstaining from certain actions, as Arum did by avoiding the preparation of food. Shielding oneself from aggressive attack requires a great deal of skill, dedication, and assets. Few can achieve it. For cases in which neutrals cannot persuasively identify the lesser obligation, allowing the defendant to choose the lighter obligation is most consistent with social order under the Three Promises, and least likely to create perverse incentives. Preference testing can be reduced to logical expression and implemented by a protocol, as summarized in Fig. 1 below. The protocol determines the lesser obligation in every case, without ambiguity. FIG. 1:

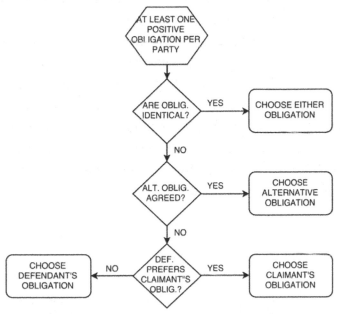

The less burdensome of any two promised obligations is always determinable, by using a logical protocol that rests on the obligation most preferred by the defendant. This protocol upholds the principle that no defendant must do more than promised. We need not be troubled by uncertainty over which obligation is less, when obligations are not easily comparable.

We can extend the protocol to determine the weaker of any two affirmative defenses, by uncovering the defense that is most preferred by the claimant. Fig. 1 works for affirmative defenses by exchanging "claimant" and "defendant," and "affirmative defense" for "positive obligation." For example, in the last decision block, ask whether the claimant prefers that the neutral apply the affirmative defense of the defendant. The claimant's preference controls for incomparable affirmative defenses.

Sven, a blue-eyed Swede, promises to do no harm unless he is a blue-eyed Swede. Othello, a black-eyed African, promises to do no harm unless in self-defense. Sven attacks Othello without provocation. Sven can't use his negative promise in defense, without Othello's consent. Othello can hold Sven to his own more limited exception based on self-defense. If Othello attacks Sven and Sven brings a claim, Sven can pick being a blue-eyed Swede as Othello's only defense. Othello can't defend for self-defense against a claim by Sven, but he can bring a counterclaim against Sven if Sven made an improper attack on him. Suppose Othello and Sven make positive promises instead. Sven promises to excuse claims against blue-eyed Swedes, and Othello promises to excuse claims against self-defenders. These are non-overlapping positive promises, and neither will apply as between Sven and Othello.

Letting defendants choose positive obligations and claimants negative obligations can remove the need to measure and compare different obligations from an objective standpoint. Awareness of relative burdens can still provide insight if parties choose obligations or exceptions against self-interest. Neutrals should intervene to make sure that the party making an election against interest understands the consequences of their choice.

The Justiciable Claim

Let's walk back a few steps. After considering approaches for resolving differences between promised obligations, consider what happens when there is a mismatch between conditions that cause a promised obligation. Every promised obligation is made subject to a condition: "If condition 'A' occurs (e.g., if I wrong another) I am obliged to do 'B' (e.g., make restitution). Suppose a person ("First") makes a promise stating a condition 'A_1' for an obligation. A different person ("Second") states a condition 'A_2.' Suppose $A_1 \neq A_2$. Second cannot rightly complain about what First has not promised, and vice-versa. In that new sense, any pair of promises made by different people are "not justiciable," i.e., provides no basis for complaint, if either of the pair specifies conditions unreciprocated by the other. The honor of the self-sovereign cannot fairly be questioned where the conditions of the sovereign's obligation are not met.

You might be wondering, "What if the other dude has the social graces of a turd?" If this business about "no promise, no complaint" feels like a muzzle on prosecution of just grievances, take a deep breath and reconsider. Actual or would-be offenders who fail to make the usual promises wear virtual badges, signaling their lack of social sense to the world. You may criticize them openly, generally or by name, shun them for being too risky to engage, and do to them what they would do to others without loss of honor. You can even win a neutral hearing for your complaint, subject to their consent on the conditions for liability and the measure of damages. Where one accused has done obvious damage to a victim, many accused will prefer a fair hearing to a reputation as an evil-doer. They will be naturally disposed to accept if not request a fair hearing, regardless of their state of promises. Those who care little about their own reputations will suffer the natural consequences of their carelessness.

A promise pair can be justiciable when a broadly-written positive social promise of one party matches up to more particular promises of another. Which of these more particular promises should the neutral select as the promise to compare? There is no dilemma under TROTWET if the meaning of the promises is not disputed. If the claimant's social promises are broader, the neutral should consider the subject area of defendant's promise that is most applicable to the facts. The claimant's broader promise will apply only if it results in liability less than defendant's promise, under the facts. Conversely, if the defendant's promise is broader, the neutral should apply one of claimant's more particular promises only if resulting in liability less than defendant's promise. If promises made by the same party in different subject areas equally apply to the case and result in the same liability, it makes no difference which is applied. The same analysis applies for affirmative defenses, the only differences being that the most applicable one of claimant's more particular social promises will govern the choice of affirmative defense when the claimant holds more particular promises. As between claimant's and defendant's promises, the affirmative defense that results in the greatest liability for the defendant is the default rule.

Sometimes, there will be gray areas. It will not always be clear whether a claim is justiciable. Sometimes whether a more general offense encompasses a more specific condition will be debatable. For example, suppose Gentificus promises to pay restitution for "tangible harm to another caused by my aggression or gross negligence." Specificus makes no similar general promise, instead publishing a litany of specific conditional obligations. Among these is Specificus' promise to pay restitution for "intentional infliction of emotional distress." Neutrals may differ on whether "emotional distress" is a "tangible harm" or conditions under which inflicting it constitutes aggression. If Gentificus and Specificus hold irreconcilable views on these questions, their promise pair is not justiciable without a rule for reconciling differences.

In other cases, there can be little debate about whether a more specific condition is included in a more general statement. For example, simple assault is a lesser included offense in "assault with a deadly weapon," because assault with a deadly weapon cannot be done without also doing simple assault. The "lesser included" offense is broader than the offense that includes it, because the lesser included offense applies in a greater number of circumstances. Think of a set made up of all the circumstances that a condition encompasses. The set for the more specific offense is a subset of the set for the broader, "lesser included" offense. Sets of circumstances work equally well for social promises. Any pair of social promises is justiciable so long as the intersection of the promise condition sets (A_1, A_2) is not empty ($A_1 \cap A_2 \neq null$). If what claimant has promised is included in what defendant has promised, it is just for claimant to hold defendant liable for what claimant has promised, but not more.

People can disagree about which circumstances make up any pair of promise condition sets (A_1, A_2). They can also disagree about the content of intersection $A_1 \cap A_2$, which determines whether the claim is justiciable. As in the case of Gentificus and Specificus, irreconcilable opinions on justiciability reduce the usefulness of social promises. But we overcame a similar problem with determining the lesser obligation, by leaving the choice of penalty to the one accused, and the choice of defense to the one bringing the complaint.[10] It is worth considering whether we can find a similar process to eliminate or reduce irreconcilable disagreements over justiciability.

To find a similar solution for justiciability, we'll consider whether it can rest on the preference of a definite party to the action. Can a preference protocol *Pr*(CL, DF) capable of resolving disagreement over justiciability of different promises exist? If we allow the claimant to have the final word, the answer to disagreements will always be that the claim is justiciable. We will reach the opposite result if the defendant has the last word. In both cases, interpreting promise statements is at issue.

Let's try another approach. What if we give the last word to the party making the broadest promise? When the broadest

---

[10] The choice being limited, of course, to the pre-existing promises of both parties or to what both agree is right.

promisor is the defendant, we let the defendant specify the meaning of their promise for the present case and the future. If the defendant makes unreasonable exceptions to their general promise to escape due process, their unreasonableness will be visible to others and binding on them in future cases. If they make a principled distinction, they will have added to the meaning of their own social promises. Most will welcome opportunities to clarify the meaning of their general promise. Letting defendants specify the meaning of their own general promises seems fair and reasonable, so long as they hold to consistent positions. It is unavoidable, if we will respect the self-sovereignty of the defendant.

What happens when the claimant holds the broadest promise? The claimant cannot bring a complaint unless the more general promise intersects the more specific promise of the defendant. The claimant declares that the general includes the specific by making a complaint. The claimant will be held to that declaration in future cases, just as defendant is. Letting the broadest promisor clarify the meaning of their own words is the only approach that respects self-sovereignty. In addition, the rule neatly removes all possibility of promises with indefinite meanings leading to irreconcilable differences over the meaning of words.

If social promises are expressed using consistent semantics, machines will have no difficulty in determining whether a justiciable claim exists, and which obligation or affirmative defense should apply. But in every case with or without the help of machines, the preference of a definite party to the action controls the answer to all these questions. Preferences are choices; definite by nature. Likewise, so is any pair of social promises applied with respect for the equal self-sovereignty of both parties.

The Principled Non-Promisor

Every sincere social promise is rooted in individual preferences, beliefs, and biases. Human diversity leads to mutually respected diversity in social promises. Many will promise nothing on subjects others regard as essential. No matter how careful the promisor is to cover every conceivable subject, there will always be subjects beyond the imagination or will. The conscientious promisor will avoid making promises about subjects not well understood. Whenever the community reflects a diversity of beliefs and experiences (as it nearly always will) principled members will be both promisors and non-promisors. Every promisor abstains from social promises designed for unknown circumstances and will be ignorant about different things. But not every principled abstention will arise from ignorance.

Principled non-promisors will refrain from obligations they know of but do not want others to reciprocate. For example, some may promise to pay for offending others with rude speech. Others will not want to be paid for mere rudeness and will abstain from this promise or specifically exclude it. Promises bind only the promisor but stand as invitations for others to reciprocate. Everybody can develop their own personalized lists of obligations they do not want to be owed, leading over millions of members and billions of transactions to a fine-grained and sophisticated modularity that fills every conceivable need in diverse and surprising ways. Detailed modularity can bring efficient moral character discovery and conflict resolution to many unique promise sets. Each combination of promise sets provides a predictable outcome, and the number of different combinations is limitless. Scale is not a problem; it's a virtue!

Suppose a million strains of social promise are in use by a billion persons speaking a hundred languages. A neutral might practice dispute resolution for a lifetime without ever hearing a dispute involving the same combinations of promises. As voluntary society expands, each member's social promises will form a shrinking part of the society's total body of unique social promises.

Promise semantics will explode into countless pieces in some groups while coalescing into major threads in others. Social forces of expansion and gravity will push and pull expectations of voluntary society into complex and efficient patterns. Perfect efficiency is impossible because errors in judgment are unavoidable consequences of free will. But ways of interpreting and using complex combinations of promise sets will tends towards efficiency by the power of choice. Less efficient social promises will cost more for the same result, and so become less preferred. The semantic pieces of the social promise corpus will fit together as modules well-ordered by a plan. Social promises will be modular, to avoid ambiguity and deliver answers more effectively.

What is this modularity? We can divide our social promises, like laws, into non-overlapping subject areas or "modules" for convenience and efficient communication. States make laws in different subject areas, for property and tort, for vessels on the high seas, and so forth. Likewise, social promises will have topics of varying scope. As the topics narrow, the number of social promise modules multiples. By compartmentalizing our promises, we enable others to focus on areas of greater concern. Neutrals and other service providers can specialize in their favored subject areas, harnessing division of labor to resolve social questions. Members can divide social promises into as many subject areas and levels of generality as desired. For example, a promise to restore damages of any sort is broader than a promise to pay only for negligent or intentional damage. Social promises will branch like trees, from trunks to boughs to branches to twigs. Each promise will have its scope. Modularity means that social promises have defined scopes, that can be compared and distinguished. Forks will divide promises into sub-promises. Academics will map the resulting set of forks. Well-crafted promises will fit easily into the organic, fluid scheme. Promises that fit awkwardly will be disfavored. Shared economic desires will drive modularization, without imposition by authority.

Self-organizing communities of social promisors will learn the benefits of modular promises and will prefer what brings greater benefits.

Can neutrals be expert when social promises have unlimited diversity? Wouldn't complexity make use of social promises inefficient and expensive? Not when each promisor bears their own cost, in the sense of being responsible for and accepting the consequences of one's own promises. We are on the verge if not well past having the ability to translate and correlate promise sets in different languages using artificial intelligence. It will become trivial to translate millions of different social promises into a uniform logical language. Expressed in one language the social promises can be compared without ambiguity. The parties can understand how to apply the Third Promise with confidence, and often with no outside help. Expensive experts will not be needed often.

To handle factual disputes, the parties may hire a neutral to give an opinion on the facts that are true. The parties can also use a neutral to opine on clashing interpretations of social promises. The neutral's job is to be neutral and diligent, interpreting the application of the parties' social promises to the circumstances at hand. Effective neutrals will be intelligent, perceptive and fair, but will not need to be experts in Byzantine laws. A competent neutral will guide the parties into a complete understanding of the moral and practical implications of their preferences and help them interpret their proposals and actions under the Three Promise schema.

Some social promises will stand alone. For example, social promises made by members of Amazonian jungle tribes might include concepts not understood elsewhere. Promises in a unique subject will cause every person not adopting a relevant promise to be a non-promisor in that subject. To avoid becoming an accidental non-promisor, a prudent traveler might prepare for a journey by researching local social promises commonly found along the planned trail and making suitable promises of their own beforehand. Some won't bother with such precautions, knowing they can always agree to resolution of a dispute under a customary rule instead of taking chances on enforcement in a strange location. Prudent travelers will consult their travel guides to learn any conflicting or critical social promises prevalent at their destination.

Most will be non-promisors regarding unconventional social promises unless a promise gains traction in a community. Suppose "Jester" adopts an odd promise that if he directs any vulgar word at another, he must pay a fine to the "victim." It is easy for Jester to find non-promisors in vulgarity. He can be vulgar to these non-promisors with impunity. He might encourage non-promisors to adopt a promise like his, by unleashing an astonishing barrage of unmentionables at them. Some non-promisors will become promisors just to escape Jester's vulgar taunts. Others will recognize a flip side: promisors are no less likely than non-promisors to be targeted by the likes of Jester. For any social promise easily broken and enforced, opportunists will provoke slip-ups hoping to recover fines. By interacting with people like Jester, members will learn to recognize consequences of making social promises, and of being a principled non-promisor. They will learn to take responsibility for their own promises without judging others for making different choices. Principled non-promising will be socially acceptable, as an unavoidable outcome of liberty, diversity, and social evolution. As social consciousness evolves, promises thought to be odd may grow in popularity to become customary, and customary social promises may grow to be odd.

Modularity in social promising will enable efficient conflict resolution among adopted promises, despite great diversity. The need to harmonize social promises will encourage members to express their promises in ways that can be accurately translated to a universal logical language, and so to become modular. Online services will help members with promise expression, by providing abundant choices between different popular expressions. Enterprising authors will publish tribal promise books to influence and encourage social promising for members of different cultural groups. Members will learn to accept principled non-promising as a necessary feature of social promising. They will learn to appreciate how principled non-promising facilitates social experimentation, giving each member the freedom to define new expressions and applications for social promises and to phase out archaic or less optimal expressions. We cannot predict how social promising will evolve. We can hope that personal freedom to be a principled non-promisor and to forge new social promises will bring amazing new solutions to social problems and outshine centralized justice systems of the present day.

Chapter 5: Weaker Property Prevails

First Look

Property, in the sense of a right to exclude, is not absolute in social promise societies. Sovereignty of the self is the only absolute possession, but it cannot be "property" because it concerns only that non-fungible unit the embodied person, under the control of one nervous system. The right to exclude others from one's own body and mind is inalienable: it can't be bought or sold. Self-possession needs no status of "owner" to exist; it is self-fulfilling. Being self-sufficient and non-transferable, self-possession cannot be property.

All other rights to exclude exist only because others in society respect such rights, which can pass from person to person. Such rights to exclude are "property." Every form of property amounts to a social privilege, even voluntary property. The privilege of voluntary property comes from the mutual consent of self-sovereign individuals, and not by the diktats of a ruling class. In social promising, logic parallel to that which determines the weaker promise determines the weaker property right. Many types of property coexist. Each successful type of property exists because it proves useful for fairly and efficiently allocating a resource among a community of users. A subset of the society recognizes and deals in each property type, and by doing so supports existence of that type. If ever property rights conflict, the weaker right prevails. As between any two property rights, members can rightly enforce only the weaker right.

Kernel

What on Earth could this mumbo-jumbo about weaker property mean, in a practical sense? Nothing in social promising is more unfamiliar than its notions of property. If you feel baffled, be patient. Once you have understood the basis for analyzing voluntary property claims, and seen it at work in a few examples, you will have a much better idea how voluntary property works. You will understand how and why to apply the weaker tool principle to property claims. The concept of the "Weaker Property Prevails" is easy. It parallels The Rule of The Weaker Tool, but with a twist because of the different nature of property claims.

Voluntary property is new. It's not something you have experienced nor have any reason to understand before reading this book. Voluntary property is only difficult because it is alien to our cultural expectations. It is simple to understand in principle. For cultural comfort, we can see traces of voluntary forms in traditional property. For example, we are familiar with overlapping coexisting claims in the same property. States claim a right to collect property taxes (rent) coupled with a right of eminent domain and land use regulation, titleholders claim a right of occupation and use, landlords hold title while tenants hold occupancy rights, and the public holds a right of easement. We do not think it strange when different property rights attach to the same asset and are held by different owners in traditional property rights. Similar diversities under voluntary property are likewise not bizarre.

We can find another present-day example in intangible property. Intangible ownership claims (e.g., copyright) are often unenforceable against end users, because infringers are too numerous and (as a group) too poor to practically sue. Despite this, many practical people respect copyrights as a matter of convenience, often paying for access to myriad types of content even when there is no penalty for non-compliance. Copyright holders seldom bother to enforce their rights against those who ignore copyrights in small ways. We live with what is voluntary property in all but name already.

We can analyze voluntary property law like any other claim, with adaptations we will explore in this chapter. Everyone must adopt their own rules for property claims and live by them. If this approach seems too complex to lead to anything but chaos and disharmony, suspend your judgment for a while longer. In the Basket of Nuts, we will explore examples that show how voluntary property balances competing social interests over control of resources using a simple, predictable set of rules. These new rules create incentives for constructive social behavior and discourage attempts to use property rights as a tool for domination over others or other anti-social purposes.

Basket of Nuts

Property the Social Sword

Voluntary property flexibly solves age-old conflicts rooted in property claims. Those fights have been many and brutal. Many social conflicts have been powered by a struggle between the haves and the have nots. Wars over territory are massive exercises in extending dominion by violence, claiming territory and the right to rule those within it. In less dramatic times, privileged classes quietly impose their property rules on a compliant underclass. Property imposed divides society into unequal classes.

The industrial revolution sharpened that knife edge of division and upset old balances. The thought leaders of the Industrial Age theorized about new social orders that could better align distribution of property with labor. As the catastrophic wars of the twentieth century unfolded and the anarchist movements faded, these ideas crystallized into two main competitors: state-regulated communism and state-regulated capitalism. Communism abolished all private ownership of the "means of production" for ownership by the state. Capitalism permitted private ownership but married itself to socialism. Socialist-managed capitalism used state power to redistribute wealth or address failures of private property and markets, real or imagined. These approaches diverged over theories of property but converged in their calls for an authoritarian state to manage economic activity including property rights. Theories of civil society based on the self-sovereignty of the individual could not compete with theories based on powerful states, for raising armies and making war. Political and philosophical leaders rejected classical liberal or laissez-faire ideas of governance, along with newer libertarian or anarchist ideas. Many people came to regard most economic freedoms as antiquated and inapplicable in the industrialized and militarized 20th-century world.

By the time "post-industrial" entered common parlance and the twenty-first century began, state-regulated communism had failed as a viable system of governance. Although it has emerged triumphant from its competition with communism, state-regulated capitalism is now on the verge of great instability, and perhaps failure. Sovereign debt soars well beyond all historical precedent or hope of repayment. Wealth becomes ever more concentrated. The middle class transforms into a debtor class dependent on government handouts, and clamors for less independence and more government control. Central bank manipulation grows to extremes as strange as negative interest rates and coins worth less than the dross they contain. Governments fall under the control of international corporations that dominate their mass media, elections, courts and bureaucracies. Work opportunities and social mobility stagnate. The masses feel insecure in their futures, as their social support networks fail or evolve into predatory monopolies. For all its problems, few accept the possibility of any real alternative to state-regulated capitalism. Even many on the fringe are peddling old ideas, tried and rejected by earlier generations. All are divided by notions of property. Factions on the "left" distrust private property. Factions on the "right" distrust everything but their own definitions of private property. Conflicts over property threaten to divide the future as they have divided the past. Disagreement over the definition and proper use of property impedes social progress and causes violent conflict including war.

Social promising teaches a middle way: all claims of property are subject to principled self-sovereignty. This middle way might act as oil on the troubled waters of social discourse, unifying the left and the right. Once adopted, voluntary property will fill the right-left divide, or if you prefer, will dissolve the divide entirely. However, voluntary property as presented here is new, and takes getting used to. Academics are unaware or scornful of it. Members of voluntary society must put voluntary property into practice before academics will consider it possible. If you have read this far, you may be a pioneer who will experiment with this new way of allocating natural resources and products of human labor. Progress is up to you.

Voluntary property is coherent, meaning anybody can evaluate claims under voluntary property according to a rational process. Voluntary property has a two-part, if-then structure just like every other type of claim under social promises or law. The first part of property is its basis, meaning its metes and bounds, and its conditions for ownership. The second part of property is its rent or use value. The property claim prevailing between conflicting social promises imposes the least burden on the property's trespasser. Title between any two parties belongs to the one who first satisfied the most stringent of the parties' social promises about respect for property. Using these basic principles, voluntary property produces predictable results subject only to disagreements about the facts or the meanings of words, just as with any other rule.

Voluntary property is logical, but can it produce just results? Will it provide outcomes more just than those provided by property rights imposed on the unwilling? Only time will reveal if human society can implement voluntary property on a large scale. But voluntary property is no less logical than property rights based on labor theory or on territorial sovereignty rooted in military might. Justification for voluntary property rights is rooted in equal self sovereignty and a fair balancing of competing interests. Each member fulfils their own social promises to respect the property rights of others, and each defines the property they will respect. Cooperation and mutual respect for self-sovereignty protect and develop those natural resources and products of human effort that people value most, once people understand.

To develop your understanding of voluntary property, you must embark on a mental journey. You must re-imagine the ancient human institution of property from its foundations on up. This book aims to illuminate your journey, which you must walk with an open and inquisitive mind to progress. Along the way, detailed examples will clarify the abstract principles of voluntary property law in concrete terms and show both its rationality and its usefulness.

Bridging the Property Divide

Property divides owners from non-owners. Voluntary societies unite owners with the poor through shared veneration of personal sovereignty, the path of adapting to diverse beliefs about property without suppressing minority opinions. Promise communities free their members from complying with rejected or unknown property systems of others. Members are also free to join and comply with any property systems they want to use. But there will always be conflicts over natural resources between the poor and owners, and between competing claims of owners. In this essay, we'll consider how respect for personal sovereignty under the Three Promises can solve conflicts about what can be property. Willy the

Wanderer, Veronica the Vandal (she's not a bad person), and the shipwrecked crew of the Jolly Tucker will be our examples.

Before we reach those examples, consider our context. There are three basic states of voluntary society: zero, 100%, and everything between. A society can deny individual sovereignty in every possible respect, can value it above all else, or exhibit a mixture of attitudes about righteous limits of self-sovereignty. Perfection is impossible, so reality is always an in-between state, a mixed bag, often biased towards one pole or its opposite. We'll start by assuming our adventures in diverse coexisting property rights happen in an imaginary society that is 99.999% voluntary, where everyone embraces the Three Promises. An overwhelming majority defend the integrity of their decentralized system for justice and order, and penalize behavior that undermines it. Equal non-hypocritical self-rule is supreme, and all social obligations (including obligations to respect the property of others) arise only by social promising. However workable our assumed endpoint is, making the assumption helps us explore logical conclusions of voluntary property systems. The cultural context is alien to modern readers, who will need to suspend their disbelief to accept the possibility that property can be voluntary. After understanding how property works in a society where everybody governs themselves by the Three Promises, we'll dial back the assumptions and peek at voluntary property where coexisting with imposed property laws.

Societies skeptical of self-rule will impose uniform property systems on everyone. Such societies have predominated since history began; if you've grown up in one, you may find voluntary property alarming or impractical. Take comfort in knowing familiar property systems will be around for as long as people want them. Or maybe you can't wait to see the present property systems replaced by a self-sovereign system. Then this chapter will help you understand the implications of voluntary property and guide you on your journey there.

There will always be people who don't own property. In our hypothetical voluntary society, different definitions of property will be unlimited in number. Many will choose not to own property of all known types. Most will avoid making social promises respecting the types of property they consider overreaching, or types of property they don't intend to ever own. You might think a society of owners and non-owners could not exist without class systems, oppression, or constant conflict. But in voluntary society, personal freedom to disclaim property rights diffuses social tension and encourages cooperation. Owners and non-owners have reasons to avoid abusing rights respected by others, whether those rights arise from respect for property, or from respect for personal sovereignty. Under the Three Promises, personal sovereignty always comes first.

Lack of ownership leads to failure of reciprocity between owners and non-owners. Recall the "Impossible Reciprocity Problem" that comes up in voluntary justice, discussed earlier. When a person cannot ever be in the same circumstances as others, that person need not obligate themselves for those circumstances. They may be tempted to place burdens on others for situations they are immune from, or to promise only trivial penalties for wrongs they cannot suffer. Despite the temptation, everyone has an incentive to be reasonable and avoid offending others. Nobody enjoys special privileges got by political fiat. A person can make no social promise without carrying burdens that reciprocate those he would place on others. The Third Promise ensures it. If a social promisor attempts to place unreciprocated burdens on others, the source of hypocrisy will be clear. Those who would place burdens on others without willing to carry the same burdens themselves will fail, while revealing a character that is obtuse or unfair.

The Impossible Reciprocity Problem often comes up with social promises regarding property rights, because not everybody wants to own the same types of property. Those who intend to never own or use property of a type will have no reason to make social promises respecting that type of property. Although most will own personal property, some may own no real property (e.g., land), or no "intellectual property."

Consider, for example, the case of copyright. Producers of creative content will enforce their copyright claims, if copying deprives them of income or reputation. But consumers of creative content might want no penalties for copying or using the creations of others, under any circumstances! Under the principle of reciprocity, there is no way for a content creator to enforce a copyright claim against someone who refuses to make a social promise respecting copyright. But a ledger of published social promises offers content creators a certain refuge. Copyright holders can require their customers to identify their social promises touching on copyright before providing access to copies of creative content. The copyright holders can deny access to their protected copies for those who refuse to reveal a social promise the holders find acceptable.

The promise ledger acts like a license made under contract, except everybody sets their own conditions, so the ledger frees as much as it binds. People can lie about their social promises or make social promises they have no intention of keeping but do so at great peril to their own precious reputations. Owners with reasonable defenses for their property claims (e.g., digital protection means) are better off under a self-sovereign system than under an imposed property system. Imposed property laws cloak people who intend to break the law. Imposing one law cloaks disagreement, but does not eliminate it, depriving everybody of the right to openly follow their own moral beliefs about property. The diktats also deprive everybody of any good reason to ask others to reveal those beliefs as a precondition to transactions, because dissent on the microeconomic scale is irrelevant when all must follow the same law.

What about people who reject all real property claims, or even personal property claims? The publication requirement provides a check against insincere making of promises respecting property. The example of Willy the Wanderer illustrates how the interests of property owners and non-owners balances in a self-sovereign, social promise system. Suppose Willy the Wanderer makes social promises that disclaim all rights under real and personal property. Willy does not recognize theft as a possibility and can be dispossessed without complaint. No one can charge Willy with trespass or theft, but neither can Willy enjoy social protection for any of his belongings; he cannot expect others to respect his belongings.

With no personal property rights, Willy can only possess things nobody else wants. If you do not want Willy sleeping in your house, lock the door — he cannot get the tools to break and enter. If you find him sleeping in your unlocked garage, you cannot complain that he has broken any social promise. But you can act. You can lure him out with the promise of a hot meal, and then secure the garage, if you please. You can remove him without breaking your own social promises, and he cannot complain about it. Recognizing no right to possess territory, Willy has no justification for defending his possession of the garage. You can defend yourself against unlikely violent resistance to eviction by Willy without violating your honor if you have promised to recognize a right of self-defense. Willy will not resist because he knows how social promises work.

Whether or not resisted, land owners can evict trespassers without risk, so long as they do so without violating the weaker of their own social promises or that of trespasser. Wanderers like Willy recognize no real property right, and with that, no right of occupancy. With no right of occupancy, they cannot complain about safe relocation to a similar place. They cannot object to a removal from one place to another accomplished without breaking of the weakest applicable social promise. Usually the weakest promise will penalize tortious conduct such as fraud, assault, or battery causing tangible harm; harmful acts that all recognize as wrong and wish to avoid being victims of. Those like Willy who want social recognition for a right to stay put must publish a social promise granting them that right. But making such promises validates others' claims to real property.

Suppose Willy is clever and makes a social promise to pay damages for touching or moving another even if no harm results. Under TROTWET, such a social promise would have effect only when those who remove him have promised an equivalent obligation. But landowners would make no similar promise, because they have no need for it. Landowners can rely on their property rights, instead. Willy will have no remedy for gentle evictions from landowners' property, while making people of good conscience less likely to give him friendly touches!

Is this balance of rights and obligations so bad? Does it not leave everyone an option to exist in undefended spaces, with their personal dignity and social status as principled wanderers intact? Is it not how the humane parts of the world work, anyway? Few people today would follow Willy the Wanderer in making no promise to respect real or personal property, but any who did would be free to wander at the risk only of their personal property. Most sensible wanderers would respect personal property rights, to protect their own moveable shelters, food stores, money, clothing and tools, and to avoid unnecessary controversy. They would need to respect personal property to secure for themselves survival, and to live at peace with their neighbors. Wanderers can promise to not damage or steal personal property, and to pay for damage they might cause. Those like Willy would not make promises respecting real property because they place a higher value on freedom of movement than the right to stay put somewhere. This value scale is not uncommon even today. Where the Three Promises govern, vagrants can wander within the bounds of their own social promises while remaining honorable members of society. Free of claims of trespass, Willy the Wanderer can prosper and contribute to the welfare of others without burdening himself with real property.

Wanderers only seek freedom to travel and encamp, but what about principled vandals? What about those who would destroy the labor of others, for good reasons or bad? We see principled vandals at work in the present day, in saboteurs who wreck the tools of those they oppose and hackers who break cryptographic protections in pursuit of some social purpose. Suppose, for example, Veronica the Vandal believes that accumulating any excess personal property is sinful, an affront to Mother Earth and future generations. Her mission in life is to discourage others from accruing what she regards as excess personal property. The only personal property she respects is that needed for immediate survival: the clothes on her back, a covering and simple shelter of natural materials to avoid perishing from extremes of climate, the food on her plate, and tools or medicines she can carry on her person. She would return human society to a lifestyle of subsistence hunter-gathering, as nature intended. To hasten this goal, she vandalizes what personal property she can, things like fences, homes, factories and industrial farms, while always being careful to do no physical harm to any person.

Do the Three Promises allow idealistic vandals like Veronica to destroy hard-earned property without recourse? Only in theory. A failure to promise recompense for the willful destruction of property does not come without consequences for Veronica. Given those consequences, both Veronica and the owners of the property she would destroy are better off under a Three

Promise system than under an imposed property system that treats Veronica as a criminal and violates her sense of justice.

Imposed property systems criminalize and make martyrs of their opposition, suppressing dissent and building social tensions. The 20th-Century wars between communists and capitalists are among the abundant evidence of these tensions. Often, opponents of unjust property systems do their work in secret and hide behind the cloak of the law. Motivated resistors are undeterred by the laws of their oppressors, and those same laws deprive both sides of common ground for mediating disputes.

Under a Three Promise system, there is always some common ground. Veronica the Vandal values human life and equal sovereignty, or she would not be a member of voluntary society. The same is true of the owners whose property she destroys. Since she respects personal property of some types, and values human life, she puts her honor and reputation at stake with every act of destruction. The opinions of neutrals will weigh on her actions. If she goes too far, she can suffer the grave penalty of shunning because she performs her actions in plain view. Since her aim is political, she cannot risk the disfavor of people holding moderate positions. Others will urge her to support the property rights of allies who would preserve parts of the Earth for the human uses she prefers. All these social factors and more will constrain her vandalism to unpopular targets. Even more important, her freedom to live by her own social promises will bring her into dialog with her adversaries, in marginal cases. In a social promise community with a healthy market for conflict resolution service, such dialog will bring about settlement of differences without wasteful destruction, and restoration of peace.

To illustrate, suppose Veronica opposes slash-and-burn agriculture. She organizes Amazonian tribes against the practice, teaching them how to sabotage big farm equipment and to make social promises like her own. Veronica and her tribes recognize "hand tools or powered implements of less than 2500 Watts peak power" as personal property, but no other equipment qualifies in their view. They view large equipment as a community resource or as targets fit for destruction. Veronica and her allied Amazonians hold sway in the lands close to the rain forest. Their depravations give pause to farmers destroying the forest, by raising the cost of industrial farming close to Amazonian territory. But no one can declare war or bring successful suit against Veronica and the Amazonians, so long as they operate within their social promises. Because of her activities, only boutique farmers dare cultivate territory close to the rainforest, using hand tools and small-scale equipment. Opinions about Veronica are mixed in the buffer zone. Farmers as a class are skeptical of destruction of property, but most recognize that Veronica's vigilance makes their homestead farms feasible, protecting them from being taken over by the large-scale agriculturists located closer to the urban areas.

The further one travels from the rainforest, the more the natives shun vandal promisors like Veronica. It is harder for Veronica and her allies to operate without blowback. Fuzzy zones mark transitions between jungle and factory forces and help preserve a balance. The balance does not come by imposing a conqueror's will on native peoples, but by unforced expression of social preferences of the people on the land. Consider a micro view: one day, Veronica leaves the jungle and travels to the nearest city. Not far from the city, she spots an expensive harvesting combine and disables it, causing the combine's owner substantial losses. The farmer apprehends her, and she consents to voluntary due process. She rests on her social promises before the neutral, who finds she is neither hypocritical nor honor bound to pay for the damage she caused. But the destruction so far from the rain forest creates outrage in the modernized agricultural zone. No one will sell her food or supplies. Anonymous residents of the area pay the local ruffians to harass her, taking all her baggage and money. In doing so, these ruffians act with honor. The ruffians have made sincere social promises even weaker than hers; they earn their living as the local protection force against Veronica and her kind. She can make no claim against them. Outnumbered, reviled, and without protection of her social promises, she returns to the safety of the jungle. The balance of customary property rights arises from the people and preserves peace.

If Veronica's world seems too chaotic for your tastes, is it worse than establishing uniformity by conquest, slaughter and genocide? Suppose the Europeans, upon discovering the New World, respected the aborigines as equals. Suppose both aborigines and immigrants considered it unethical to kill or endanger members of the other group to impose their social preferences on others. But the property systems of the two groups were in conflict. Most aborigines lived by traditional hunting, gathering, supplemented by small-scale bio-diverse gardening. Most rural immigrants kept herds in fenced pastures and planted monoculture crops in fenced fields. These competing uses relied on competing property systems. At first, both sides destroyed property wherever the two systems came into conflict. Over time, by submitting marginal cases to due process before neutral jurists, the people developed customs for coexisting without destroying what others lived to build and protect. So long as all sides valued and respected the values of those holding different beliefs, there was a way to work out differences with minimal offense to others. Had the aborigines and immigrants followed this process in the New World, the Americas would enjoy a much more diverse fabric of peoples, cultures and uses of the land than exists today, with less tragic and cruel loss of life and homes along the way. Voluntary property happens when no group seeks to dominate and force its views about property on others. The right to exclude becomes a social promise to respect exclusionary claims each member desires the social power to make. The power of that desire can expand only to the extent others desire the same powers because all social power derives from mutual respect. As is true today, the most powerful possible property claim is one that all others respect.

Our last thought experiment borrows from 1960's American television. Two tourists, Nancy Neutral and Danny Diligent, charter the Jolly Tucker for a three-hour cruise from Captain Randy Radical. Captain Randy forgets to check the weather forecast, the Jolly Tucker runs into a terrific storm, and breaks apart on a reef near an uncharted island. The island has all the basics for survival of dozens of people: abundant coconut palms, fresh water, and a lagoon full of seafood. Danny reaches the island first. A diligent capitalist, he claims ownership of the island by first discovery. He bolsters his claim by "mixing his labor with the land," constructing a shack and planting a small coconut grove. Nancy and Randy swim ashore a few days later because the tide carried them far out to sea with debris from the wreck. Danny demands they each pay rent or leave the island and sets the rent at ten hours labor per week. Nancy like Danny is a capitalist and agrees to pay the rent demanded. Randy is an anarcho-mutualist who does not recognize first discovery as a valid basis for ownership, nor any claim to unused land. Randy goes to live on the other side of the island without agreeing to pay Danny rent. Nancy lives in Randy's camp, but returns to Danny once a week to fulfill her rent obligation.

Suppose the three castaways had never heard of social promising or the Three Promises. Danny is outraged by Randy's refusal to pay rent, which Danny believes is more than reasonable and justified by the only correct viewpoint about property: his own. Randy thinks Danny's claim to the island is ludicrous. Nancy just wants to get off the island safely. Danny has a lot of time to consider his claim to the island, and soon realizes that the island is his kingdom, with Randy and Nancy his subjects. This is too much even for Nancy, but she plays along so long as Danny does not ask more from her than ten hours labor per week. Randy thinks Danny has gone insane. Danny is not insane, however; he is a rational capitalist who realizes Randy's attitude is a threat to his sovereignty over the island. One day when Randy is out fishing he destroys his camp. In retaliation, Randy destroys Danny's camp. Clash of unbendable property laws leads to violent conflict. The conflict results in "national" borders and estrangement of the castaways from one another, or worse, war and murder. Just as every real property claim will conclude when elevated over personal sovereignty.

Now suppose that the three castaways thought of property as bendable by personal sovereignty. The three know about voluntary property and follow the Three Promises. Danny can make his property claim, and Nancy as a fellow capitalist can pay him rent or a purchase price to preserve her honor, but Danny has no basis for demanding rent from Randy. If Danny presses his claim for rent, Nancy and Randy will remind him he has no right, because Randy does not recognize claims to unused natural resources. Danny's enforceable claims against Nancy cannot exceed what Nancy respects (she might want to rethink her capitalist bent), and his claims against Randy cannot exceed what Randy respects. Danny cannot be king of the island, and the three castaways can coexist without borders. Voluntary property happens when you value self-sovereignty more than ownership of things.

If humanity can ever obtain self-sovereign society, it must first pass through a transition in which some govern their actions by honor, and others by the diktats of a coercive authority. Civilization can be always in a transition state, with the plague of violent authority spreading where self-rule and mutual trust break down. A social promise society can exist as a self-organizing, borderless club within the world of conventional national and international laws. Imagine that! Club members use voluntary property among themselves, and state-mandated property systems with outsiders. Club members invent and establish registries of real, personal, and intangible property, to any degree they find useful.

Crypto-currencies and similar blockchain registries provide present-day examples of such registries, with coders writing the property rules in computer code. Code stores like GitHub are registries of open-source code, with rules written or unwritten for who owns the root code that any can branch out from. These voluntary registries are already competing with governmental and corporate systems run by fiat.

Competition of voluntary and compulsory property registries will intensify. Three Promise clubs will expand on these notions of private registries and self-organizing networks, by registering the conscience of each self-sovereign as if a crypto-currency, its value to be revealed and transferred to trusted persons as each self-sovereign decides. The ultimate property of every promisor will be an undetachable reputation. If people value their reputations in voluntary society, that ultimate property will inform and illuminate all other forms.

Two Parts of Property, and Their Dance

Every claim against another contains two parts: first, the elements that give rise to the claim itself, without which it fails. Call that its "basis" or "condition." That's the first part. The second part is the recompense the wrongdoer must pay if the claimant proves the claim, its "damages." If 'A' then 'B.' Condition followed by consequence. The species of claims called property shares this two-part structure with general claims. Property's first part supplies its legitimacy. For example, owners may justify their ownership as being fruit of some labor or discovery, or as transferred from a prior owner. Property's second part defines its price for purchase, rent, or penalty for trespass.

We can analyze a two-part claim as the sum of its parts, or as two parts. As the sum of its parts, we test the whole effect of each claim to determine which of two claims is weaker. We consider the claim requiring the least damages to be weaker, and therefore applicable. The stronger claim has no effect. When analyzing the parts as separate agents, we use a different approach. First, we break each claim into its two constituent parts. We put the four broken parts in a basket, and from the basket pick the weakest basis, and the weakest damages. Then, we hold that combination to be the weakest promise, whether the parts come from the same promise or from two promises. Either way — in whole or in part — we apply the weakest law.

So which method of analysis should we apply in real life? Perhaps since people only make promises in unbroken form, we should only apply them as unbroken wholes. One could counter that the two parts making a "whole" is arbitrary, so we should consider each part on its own. We can argue this debate or end it with a bang. The "bang" is this: whatever arguments made are a waste of breath, because in real disputes it is never necessary to argue the point. Social promises could say things like "Both parts apply together, or not at all." But many social promises will not be so detailed. Sometimes the social promise will not express how its parts apply, and disputants may disagree about how to apply it. How can we say it doesn't matter?

For that, first consider the nature of "if" in social promises that are *not* about property. Given two different conditions 'A$_1$' and 'A$_2$' applied to determine whether the conduct of a defendant creates liability: either (1) both (or neither) conditions apply, so which condition applies does not matter to whether liability exists; or (2) only one condition applies, so which applies matters. If both apply, then the promise with the weaker consequence applies. When the facts satisfy the conditions of both social promises, the only way to distinguish the social promises is by their consequences. If only one conditions applies (e.g., A_1 only), we shouldn't separate it from its consequence (e.g., from B_1), because no one ever intended the other consequence (B_2) to apply under the conditions of A_1. In fact, the holder of rule (2) is a non-promisor under the circumstances specified by the other rule (1). No case exists for a neutral to try. Triable cases can only exist when facts satisfy the conditions of all the parties' social promises. Both the claimant and the defendant must recognize that liability for the accused conduct exists. When the claim is wrongful harm, the weakest consequences always applies. The facts satisfy the conditions of all promises or there is no case. Not so, for claims based on property.

Claims of property right are distinct from claims of wrongful harm done to a victim. With harm to an injured party, the claimant, the injured parties or their legal representatives and successors own the claim. With property, unrelated people can claim ownership of the same thing for different reasons. For example, one might claim land as an ancestral inheritance, and another claim the same land based on homesteading. For these conflicts, we must hold either that only one has a valid claim to the property, that both own it, or that neither owns it. It is possible to encounter property disputes in which $A_1 \neq A_2$. It is not only possible, it is inevitable. We will need fair and non-arbitrary ways of resolving these disputes. Unlike with claims based on wrongful conduct, with property we cannot say "no one ever intended the other consequence (B_2) to apply under the conditions of A_1." Conflicting conditions of property must apply to the same subject (i.e., the property itself) or else the conditions are not in conflict, and both parties intended the consequences to relate to the same subject.

Property is a distinct type of claim, but why should social promisors regard the property's basis and its exclusionary consequences as separable? Consider the consequences of treating the basis and the consequence of any person's promise only as a unified whole. Suppose Alexandra (1) claims ownership of land by inheritance from an original homesteader, and Bill (2) claims ownership of the same land by adverse possession. Alexandra brings a claim for eviction and extinguishment of Bill's claim, and Bill counterclaims for title and extinguishment of Alexandra's claim. For simplifying the hypothetical, assume that Alexandra and Bill both recognize that the land has been vacant and unused prior to Bill's adverse possession, and that Alexandra inherited from an original homesteader. Resolution of the dispute comes down to how the conditional parts (A_1) of Alexandra's property law and (A_2) Bill's property law treat the facts of Bill's adverse possession of the land.

In this, assume that $A_1 \neq A_2$, because the property promises differ on requirements for perfecting a claim of adverse possession. Bill has satisfied his own rule for perfecting adverse possession, but not Alexandra's. Both require continuous homesteading for three years to establish a claim. Once a homesteader does so, Alexandra will not recognize a subsequent adverse possessor until completing five continuous years of open and adverse possession; Bill recognizes the adverse possessor after three years. He has been homesteading openly for four years. Assume also that Alexandra and Bill have made social promises with different consequential parts ($B_1 \neq B_2$): Alexandra's consequence (B_1) provides that the owner has the power to evict, while Bill's consequence (B_2) provides that the owner must provide squatters on vacant property with an option to stay if paying a fair market rent.

Alexandra's conditional part (A_1) differs from Bill's (A_2), although Bill and Alexandra agree on original conditions of ownership. Her consequential part (B_1) is stronger than his (B_2), because Bill grants no power to evict anyone from land vacated by its owner. Whether Alexandra's "whole" property law (A_1+B_1) is weaker or stronger than Bill's "whole" property law (A_2+B_2) is indeterminate. It is impossible for a neutral to determine which law is weaker. In the abstract, discernment between the relative burdens imposed by conflicting property promises is impossible, because of the different conditions and different consequences applying to the same subject property. The determinate path requires that the neutral consider the separate effect of different parts of property promises. The separate promises matter whenever ownership of the same underlying asset is at issue between promisors who set different conditions ($A_1 \neq A_2$) and consequences ($B_1 \neq B_2$).

Regarding the parts as separate promises, the neutral would recognize that the defendant's preferences control which condition and which consequence apply. If Alexandra claims against Bill, Bill will prefer his own conditions of ownership and so Alexandra cannot prove she has ownership superior to Bill. If Bill claims against Alexandra for title before possessing for five years, Alexandra will prefer her own conditions of ownership and Bill cannot prove he is owner.[11] Either way, when Bill's adverse possession has lasted at least three years but less than five years, neither Bill nor Alexandra will have ownership superior to the other. Even if Alexandra can prove she is owner (e.g., if she and Bill promised identical conditions of ownership), Bill can stay on the land rent free as a tenant for payment of a fair rental value to Alexandra, because his consequential promise is weaker.

This view of property is not so strange, once we view property rights as based on an exchange of social promises. With social promises, it is only natural to express our conditions for respecting the property of others as one promise, and our promise to pay damages as another. For example, we might promise to

---

[11] See Chapter 4, under "Determining the Lesser Penalty."

respect all real property purchased for value in a voluntary transaction from a legitimate owner and set other conditions as exceptions for special circumstances. These conditions are independent of our promise to pay damages for violating the property rights of others. We cannot prevent members from making social promises tying conditions for recognizing a property right to a promise to pay damages. But we will seldom have cause to link special conditions with special consequences for property. The simpler approach is to count all property of the same type worthy of the same measure of damages, whatever we believe is right. The astute promisor will recognize that making separate promises increases the chances that what they have promised will be the prevailing rule. Prudent members will separate their conditional property promises from their promises to pay damages.

We can boil this essay down to a simple rule. For conflicting property claims, test the separate effects of the different parts of the property claim: the condition and the consequence. Let the weakest condition and the weakest consequence prevail, even if promised by different parties. This evaluation in parts avoids indeterminate outcomes and favors reasonable use of the underlying asset. No other approach is fairer or more useful.

Competing Property Claims

In the preceding essay we considered conflicts between those who recognize property, and those who do not. Here we will consider competing property claims, when two or more members of voluntary society claim ownership over the same thing. Before diving in, remember that your property in voluntary society exists only because of others' promises, their commitments to respect things you would claim dominion over. Just as the property rights of others depends on your commitments to respect their property based on your promises.

We introduced scenarios earlier about clashes in property promises,[12] when considering affirmative defenses. Another example illustrates how voluntary property balances claims to uncultivated lands and encourages use of idle assets for human sustenance. Suppose one person (Lysander) promises to respect claims of adverse possession so long as the squatter's use is open and unchallenged for three years. Another person (Murray) promises to respect claims based on as little as one year of unchallenged use. Murray squats unchallenged on Lysander's land for 2 years, at which time Lysander brings a claim to evict Murray. Suppose that Murray counterclaims to take Lysander's title. Applying the Third Promise (TROTWET) to Lysander's claim, Lysander wins if the neutral treats Murray's adverse possession as an affirmative defense to Lysander's trespass claim. Lysander holds the weaker shield, requiring three years of use instead of only one. Murray must use Lysander's more stringent standard of affirmative defense to Lysander's claim. But under Lysander's rule, Murray's adverse possession is not long enough to grant him ownership of the land.

If Murray brings a claim against Lysander for ownership based on his social promise to respect three years of adverse possession, Murray loses because he has only possessed for two. Lysander gets the benefit of his rule on adverse possession when defending. Although adverse possession can be positive law conveying a right to bring claims for title, the "weaker tool" is the rule that calls for a greater burden to prove ownership. Lysander's rule is the weaker tool, because it results in lesser damages to the defendant, and a greater burden on the claimant to show ownership. But when a social promise about adverse possession reads only as

---

[12] Chapter 4 at "With Negative Promises, Reverse The Sign," *supra.*

a defense (e.g., "I will not evict or claim rent from adverse possessors of greater than three years") then nobody can claim for title on it, period.

Adverse possession illustrates an interesting characteristic: whether written as a positive law or an affirmative defense, the rule imposing the greatest burden to establish ownership is in both cases the weaker tool. From this we can derive an axiom: property claims based on more stringent antecedent conditions will prevail against comparable claims based on less stringent conditions, whether analyzed as positive promises or affirmative defenses. Lysander can evict Murray even if Murray relies on an affirmative defense of adverse possession (assuming Murray's promises respect owners' right to evict and the basis for Lysander's original property claim), and Murray cannot win title to Lysander's property, under the original hypothetical.

The hypothetical does not exhaust all possibilities. Murray can assert rights against more senior holders of property claims if he makes suitable social promises. For example, if Murray does not wish to play Lysander's "game" of rightful occupancy by adverse possession, Murray can make a different social promise. He can promise to respect property justified by more stringent conditions than Lysander's law. For example, suppose Murray promises to relinquish title over plots of one acre fallow for at least five years to the first homesteader who maintains open use for five years. Lysander claims hundreds of acres of farmland, then allows it to go fallow and unused for over five years. Murray fences off a few acres within Lysander's claim and cultivates a bona-fide homestead farm, basing his right to do so on the positive right of property recognized by his own promise. After five years Murray's homestead remains. Lysander then claims against Murray for eviction because Lysander holds title under a social promise that requires no homesteading use. Lysander's claim fails, because Murray's holds the weaker social promise, the one with more stringent conditions. Murray holds the weaker tool when Murray is the defendant, and Lysander has no legitimate claim to the land Murray has improved.

Instead of defending, suppose that Murray claims against Lysander for title after homesteading for five years. Murray's promise supports his right to stay on the land as an owner-in-possession, for being the weaker rule. Lysander cannot evict Murray, but neither can Murray extinguish Lysander's title. Lysander has made no comparable social promise to relinquish title. Note this difference from the first scenario: in the second scenario, Murray makes a social promise allowing annulment of his own property claim, were he to fail to maintain his own homestead for five years. It cannot be an affirmative defense, because as hypothesized it grants the right to bring a claim for title. Once proving his right to homestead, Murray retains his inferior title for so long as the five acres he has fenced off do not go unused for over five continuous years. Consistent with the general axiom, Murray's positive law in the second case has a more stringent condition: a need to homestead the claimed area. His right to homestead coexists with but cannot extinguish Lysander's claim to the fallow land.

Lysander is not helpless against homesteaders like Murray. If Lysander wishes to prevent establishment of inferior claims and discourage homesteading on his wild and fallow lands, he must patrol his land and defend its borders. He may check the social promises made by anyone passing into or discovered on his wild lands and eject those with homesteading promises like Murray's. Many people will step up to help Lysander defend his wild lands, if they regard his property claim worthy of defense (e.g., as protecting a nature preserve). If Lysander is incapable of this minimal level of defense, his failure to defend is evidence that his property lacks social value, and its eventual demise to homesteaders entails no net loss of human rights.

Differences in substantive real property promises can cause stalemates wherein one party cannot evict and the other cannot gain unfettered title. Such stalemates in property claims are a feature of social promising, not a bug. "Stalemate" is not the most descriptive term. A culture of toleration for inferior claims describes the balance better. Inferior claims are those resting on social promises to respect property claims made with less stringent conditions than competing claims. Inferior claims can coexist with superior claims, without one extinguishing the other. Coexisting claims are neither impossible nor unfamiliar, even in the present day. For example, the same plot of land may be subject to different layered titles, such as fee simple title, tenancy, mineral rights, and easements. These different rights can be separable for ownership or transfer. Likewise, present day regimes allow division of the same intangible copyright, trademark, or patent into different licenses and ownership claims, and inferior rights such as "fair use." Layered claims under the Third Promise are no less possible, and capable of adjudication by competent neutrals.

Although the toleration of inferior claims might sometimes cause problems, it supplies a balance between inappropriate property claims by a few and natural property rights expectations of the masses. Conflicts such as Lysander and Murray experienced do not happen in a vacuum. Such conflicts occur in a social context with different numbers of people making social promises on different wavelengths of the property rights spectrum. The reasonableness of each member's social promises about property will be interpreted within the prevailing culture. Although allowing for variation and ways of relieving tension between conflicting promises, a dominant property culture will leave strange or offensive promises unenforceable in most cases. To illustrate, suppose Lysander promises to respect land titles justified by gazing at the claimed land. By making such a promise, registers his status as a fool. He has made a promise that the Rule of The Weakest Tool renders unenforceable in almost every conceivable instance. Peers will expect property rights to be earned.

These examples illustrate a foreseeable side effect of the Three Promises: leveling of property claims. Once adopted, the Three Promises will push property rights towards the least that most members believe acceptable. That least will lie near the greatest that members can hope to own. It will become impossible under the Three Promises for durable classes divided between property owners and non-owners to arise. Whenever great inequities arise, those who lack any realistic hope of gaining a specific class of property will adapt. The dispossessed will adapt by making promises that do not recognize the remote property claims of the elite, or that supersede existing claims by setting more stringent conditions for ownership. Elitist property claims will be unenforceable; the fewer the people who respect a rule for property, the less value the claims will have. Advantages of voluntary property will include encouraging socially valued use of idle resources and providing grassroots relief from concentration of unearned property in the hands of a few. Members will enjoy these advantages if the property they use and enjoy is protected by the social promises of fellow members.

On Selecting the Weaker Property Claim

When disputants have made identical social promises respecting the same subject property, determining the rightful owner depends only on the proofs of facts that the parties advance. But when they have promised different conditions for ownership (i.e., if $A1 \neq A2$) or different consequences for trespass (i.e., if $B1 \neq B2$), the neutral path follows the weaker condition, and the weaker consequence. To know the weaker consequence is easy: it's the least burdensome, which is always the same as the consequence preferred by the losing party. Knowing the weaker condition is trickier because the conditions determine the winner and loser. We can't rely on the winner or loser to choose the weaker condition because we don't yet know who that will be. We need an independent measure to determine which condition is weaker. For comparing conditions of ownership, we can look to "stringency" of the conditions for ownership, to determine which of conflicting property promises is the "weaker tool." Per the Third Promise, the underlying ethic avoids laying a higher burden of ownership than any party has promised to bear.

Stringency of conditions is like validity of title to property. Validity of title is a familiar concept and depends on whether the claimant has satisfied the conditions for claiming ownership. Questions of rightful title are no less applicable in social promising where the promisors participate in determining the conditions. Stringency of conditions arises when two disagree over who is the rightful owner. In those cases, the neutral must decide which set of conditions to the property claim should apply. In a stable society, controversies involving conflicting conditions for ownership will be rare. Such disputes are more likely during times of revolution when views regarding property are undergoing rapid change. Even when disputes involving stringency are seldom heard of, conscientious members will want to know of the possibilities and hazards of setting their own conditions for claiming ownership. As members progress in understanding and use of social promising, their social promises will evolve and become more sophisticated. Their social promises will come to reflect a more well-considered view of property rights, in which conditions for ownership play a fundamental role. Stringency is fundamental.

Stringency fulfills the Third Promise to lay no burden on another you are not willing to do for others. Social promises create obligations on others only by promising those others as much as the promisor would receive. Each member can expect no more than they promise to others. The least burdensome of the promises must apply, but a question remains. Which condition of ownership is least burdensome, the condition that makes ownership easier, or harder? On whom does the burden fall? When two quarrel over ownership and one loses, the loser suffers the burden of the social promising. The burden is least on the non-owner when the burden is heaviest on the one who claims ownership. The most stringent condition applies. Suppose we apply the least stringent condition instead. Then everyone in the contest will satisfy the conditions of ownership, and the only issue will be who satisfied first. That way of judging will encourage a race to promise respect for frivolous conditions of ownership and embroil owners in litigation over who satisfied a frivolity first. Applying the most stringent conditions of ownership makes better social policy. It ensures that people work for what they would own and discourages frivolous property claims.

Stringency measures the personal difficulty of gaining first ownership of an asset. Its measure is not dependent on whether the asset is unowned, or subject to property claims by others; we measure its magnitude in the same way for original claims and for claims made by adverse possession. With any social promise to respect ownership, ask what a person must do and for how long to establish a valid claim. Look at the intensity of labor, capital and risk involved. Exclude consideration of transfer costs (e.g., selling prices) for the property in stringency comparisons, to avoid undermining the validity of gifts or inheritances. Examine whether prior transfers are valid, the conditions for the original claim of ownership, and conditions for adverse possession that might extinguish an original claim. Do not let stringency depend on a subjective emotional state of the owner. To be useful as tool of justice, stringency must be objective. We must be able to determine an objective difficulty of establishing original title to property in any chain of ownership.

You might regard stringency on a linear scale extending from zero towards infinity. At the zero end of the scale is the claim of a person over her own body. The body precedes formation of the self-sovereign promisor; once the promisor emerges from the organized system of matter making up the body, the person need take no social action to make a claim of ownership over that system of matter. They need but live. Ownership of the body by the person is automatic, because in a natural sense the body "owns" the person living through it, who depends on the body for existence. The stringency of the condition for self-ownership is zero and likewise the right to self-ownership is infinitely strong. No other person depends to a greater degree on another's body, and hence no person can have a superior claim over another's body. At the infinite end of the stringency spectrum are impossible tasks, such as landing on a planet moving away faster than it is possible to travel toward it. Between zero and infinite stringency lies alienable property, what people can trade.

Stringency is objective, but not strictly quantitative. It may have quantitative aspects, such as time, space, mass, continuity or quantity of information. Stringency increases with these quantities of action. The smaller the volume of space, mass, or quantity of information over which the claim extends per "unit of action," the more stringent the condition. Relationships between the action and beneficial uses of the asset can also be important. The more a task relates to a beneficial use of the property, the more weight the task deserves. To be clear, a task is intentional if directed at an objective. All intentional action is personal (fictions can't form intents), so only persons can perform tasks. Action emanates from the body and has effects beyond the body of the actor. Objective actions and their effects are observable by others. Although thought may be action, it is not absent outward expression observable by others. Parties should not expect their thoughts and intents to have weight in establishing a property claim unless expressed by word or deed.

Neutrals can evaluate stringency based on these and other objective factors and use stringency to determine the "weaker tool" between competing claims to the same property. They can determine original ownership based on the facts and on the social promises of the parties making competing claims. The social promises determine the rule to be applied. The neutral determines the rightful obligations for original ownership separate from the remedies attached to violations of the property right. Stringency is not relevant to the remedy for violating a property right. Determining the least burdensome remedy is easy: just let the loser decide which of the promised remedies they prefer.

Some examples will help to illustrate stringency analysis in operation. Consider, for example, conditions for a claim over vacant land. Alice promises to respect the land claim of any person who performs 100 sit-ups within an hour on a piece of vacant land within a 100-meter radius of the spot where the sit-ups were performed. Bill promises to respect the land claim of any person who walks around a perimeter of the same plot of vacant land at least once per day, for thirty continuous days. As far as Bill is concerned that person owns all the vacant land within the perimeter. Cindy promises to respect the claim of anyone who builds a house on vacant land and sleeps in the house for every night for a year as owner of the house, the land it sits on, and any land adjoining the house that the owner cultivates using hand-held, manual tools operated for at least a year. Doug's promise is the same as Cindy's, except that it requires performing the actions after building the house for three consecutive years. Edward's promise is the same as Doug's but allows the owner to cultivate using powered equipment. Frank promises to respect any claim to vacant land that the owner has enclosed by a barbed-wire fence of at least three continuous strands on poles four feet high. Georges' promise is the same as

Frank's but specifies a stone wall at least one foot wide and three feet high.

If any two of Alice, Bill, Cindy, Doug, Edward, Frank or George disagree about ownership of the same parcel of land, how should a neutral determine which conditions to apply? For simplicity of example, we'll assume that the conditions apply only with vacant land, and no pre-existing ownership claims by any social promising member exist. Also assume that all the parties' social promises agree about documentary conditions such as registering the property claim in a public registry, and there are no disputes over proper notice of the property claim. Assume all other conditions are equal.

Supposing all seven property promises were at play, a neutral might rank them as follows, from most stringent (weakest tool) to least stringent:

1. Doug requires hand labor for cultivation and harvest over the entire land surface claimed, plus building and living in a shelter on the land. This labor is related to the utility of the land for sustenance and shelter, involving work performed on the land itself. Moreover, Doug's law requires the labor to continue for the longest amount of time (three years) before he will recognize a claim of ownership.

2, 3. Cindy or Edward: Does Cindy's requirement of manual cultivation by hand tools outweigh Edward's longer time requirement? Which is easier per unit area, farming for one year using hand tools and manual labor only, or farming for three years using modern farm equipment? To answer this question, a neutral might consider evidence on personal labor required to cultivate and grow a crop per unit of land, by hand versus by modern machinery. If modern machinery reduced the labor needed by over 2/3, the neutral might decide that Cindy's law contained more stringent conditions, because it required more labor in one year than

Edward's law did in three. Other factors might include the extra two years of residency required by Edward's law, plus the greater capital cost of machinery as compared to hand tools. How a neutral would consider such other factors in a stringency balance is uncertain. The outcome would depend on the circumstances and quality of the parties' respective advocacy, and the neutral's biases. Attempts to predict a certain outcome in theory are futile. The futility of theory does not mean the law is broken. Close cases are always unpredictable, even when only one rule applies. Neutrals would urge compromises when conditions are too similar to be distinguished easily.

It might seem unfair to consider the capital cost of tools as related to ownership of land. Although the cost of tools is related to ownership of the tools themselves, it is at least one step removed from ownership of land. Therefore, a neutral might assign a lower weight to using expensive tools as a rule.

4. George: Building a stone wall around vacant land has little to do with the utility of vacant land, but at least it involves erecting a structure on a significant part.

5. Frank: It is easier to build a barbed-wire fence than a stone wall.

6. Bill: It is easier to walk around a plot of land for thirty days than to build a barbed-wire fence around it.

7. Alice: 100 sit-ups are trivial and have no nexus to the surrounding 100 meters of land.

If the property claims of these seven overlap, the most stringent condition applicable to the area in dispute would apply to determine the first rightful owner. Even if making a claim, Doug is not necessarily the rightful owner. Instead, the first person to fulfill the conditions specified by Doug's law would be the rightful owner. What happens next would depend on the claimant. For example, if Doug is bringing a claim against Bill to prevent him from walking through his land, whether Doug gets the remedy he seeks will also depend on the exclusionary privileges of the different promises. If, for example, Bill's law does not recognize a right to exclude others from walking across open farms or fields, Doug can get no remedy under social promises to prevent him from doing so. Neither could Bill prevent Doug from walking across Bill's farm lands.

What if a claimant relies on the actions of robots under his control, or paid agents? Neutrals who understand the root of social promising in personal sovereignty would limit stringency assessments to personal actions of the owner. Actions of a paid agent would accrue to the benefit of the agent. If the agent establishes a property claim, the agent can convey the associated property right to his employer. Since stringency requires personal action, a person who hires employees risks destroying the validity of his property claim, and the more employees hired to establish a claim over the same natural resource, the more uncertain the outcome would be. If a person cannot perform the labor to establish a property claim, the person is best served by hiring a single reliable agent to establish the claim under a contractual obligation to convey the property to his employer once earned.

If the claimant's social promise allows for extending the reach of his action using machinery (robotic or otherwise), he risks diluting the stringency of his conditions just like Edward. Application of stringency under TROTWET preserves the natural law basis of property in social promise societies, by favoring personal action directed towards extracting the utility of the natural resource over which competing claims arise. Seniority is not a controlling factor in stringency analysis, enabling latecomers to supersede earlier claims when left alone to labor on undefended property. Stringency might sometimes provide results analogous to state laws providing for adverse possession. Claims over unused and undefended resources will always be less stringent than claims over resources in active use and patrolled, unless competitors agree otherwise. For example, a guild of scavengers or prospectors can set rules for staking claims despite any stringency analysis. Those rules will apply to members of the guild only. Guild members will therefore have a motive to exclude outsiders from their hunting grounds.

Stringency can apply to real property or other natural resource claims. It might arise in other contexts. For example, when assessing competing claims to intellectual property, conception, originality, inventiveness, creation, publication, production, use, sale, and other acts relate to stringency of competing claims to an intangible asset. Those who disfavor intellectual property might put their preferences into effect, by adopting promises with high stringencies and no or low penalties. Regarding personal property, stringency might become a factor in disputes between different people involved in manufacturing the same product. To assess the relative degrees of ownership of a finished product, the most stringent standard for establishing ownership among the parties in dispute would apply. Stringency should be most useful in relation to claims over real property and other natural resources, over which competing original claims over the same property are more likely to occur. Competing original claims are less likely over personal or intangible properties, which owe their existences to corresponding acts of labor. The acts that create personal or intangible properties will always provide the most stringent basis for related property claims, with disagreements arising out of factual questions such as who performed the creative acts or received ownership of the creations by contract.

Natural resources exist independent of any acts performed by persons. A natural law basis applies for assessing competing claims based on conflicting promises over such resources. Stringency analysis provides a basis for choosing the law that governs original claims over natural resources, in a manner analogous to TROTWET in positive law claims and affirmative defenses. Stringency expresses the same principle of conflict resolution – the law of the weaker tool – in context of conflicting promises for earning ownership over preexisting resources. Stringency resembles a natural law basis for property, which roots all property rights in self-ownership of the body and the products of one's own bodily labor.

Stringency, however, is not itself property law, and does not define what property is. Instead, stringency testing is a conflict of law principle between competing property claims over the same subject, for that subset of cases wherein those making the competing claims hold to different social promises setting conditions for respecting property. Being a principle for resolving conflicts of law, it cannot impose uniform conditions for property claims on all members of society. Instead, it operates on the same ethical principles as natural property law to check assertion of more expansive property claims against less expansive claims legitimized by more stringent requirements for labor as a condition of ownership. Freedom to define conditions for ownership allows for unlimited variety in private property within social promise societies. Comparison of stringency governs competition between competing property promises within voluntary societies according to ancient natural law principles.

Forking the Chain of Title

Developers of open-source software have introduced the term "fork" to describe creation of new open-source software versions not controlled by the original developer. For example, many crypto-currencies depend on forks of the highly successful and open source Bitcoin software. Control of a software fork can be analogized to ownership. The open-source community deserves recognition for demonstrating that forks in control over assets can be useful and non-damaging to original owners. In the world of traditional property, no forks are allowed. Chains of title may not branch. Most property cannot be replicated like software and cannot have more than one entity holding title at a time, even if subject to multiple liens or other subordinate rights.

In the revolutionary world of social promises, forks in chains of title are possible. Each new branch of the chain is based on more stringent conditions for ownership than the branch it sprouts from. The new, more stringent branch pertains only to those who accept its conditions for ownership, including those who accept less stringent conditions. New branches cannot form where it is impossible to satisfy conditions more stringent than the owner has satisfied. For example, an owner holding title under the conditions of homesteading and active cultivation for three continuous years will be secure. Nobody else can satisfy more stringent conditions for ownership if the owner defends his ongoing possession and use of the land, we suppose. If the owner abandons the homestead, he may lose title to another who first satisfies the owner's conditions for ownership, or conditions of equivalent stringency. But usually a person unable to continue use of a homestead will transfer title to a capable homesteader before an intervenor can fulfill the homesteading conditions. In either case, the chain of title does not fork. The same conditions for ownership apply, and only one can satisfy those conditions first.

Forks in chains of title over natural resources will arise beyond frontiers in areas free of prior claims based on actual use. For example, suppose Edith the Explorer travels through the asteroid belt, cataloging the objects to be found there. She claims ownership over every asteroid she extracts at least one gram of material from, carefully documenting each discovery and samples. Her claims are respected by other space explorers, who make social promises around asteroid sampling like Edith's. Edith registers her claims in an Explorer's registry. Manuel the Miner does not respect claims based on sampling and therefore gets no access to the

Explorers' registry. Manny operates a mining vessel that processes iron, carbon and other materials from asteroids into steel and other iron alloys. Manny promises to respect asteroid claims of other miners based on first active mining. Other miners respect similar conditions and keep their own registry of ownership based on mining. Some asteroids appear in both property registries. The chain of title for those asteroids is forked. They appear in a less stringent Explorer's registry, and in a more stringent Miner's registry. Protective of their discoveries, the Explorers keep their registry private. Only those who are honor bound by their promises not to deprive any explorer of the benefit of her discovery can access the registry.

Suppose Edith discovers that Manny is mining one of her asteroids. She brings a claim against him for trespass and they submit the dispute to a neutral. Considering the social promises of Edith and Manny, the neutral holds that Manny owns the asteroid because he was first to satisfy the more stringent Miner's conditions for ownership. Therefore, Manny is not liable for trespass. Suppose Edward the Explorer reads about the neutral's decision in *The Asteroid Home News*. Ed sells the location of the asteroid to one of Manny's mining competitors, Monica. Discovering the sale, Edith brings a claim against Edward. She wins, because Ed is an Explorer and respects her conditions for ownership. Meanwhile, Monica lands on the other side of the asteroid and sets up a competitive mining operation. Edith cannot win against Monica for the same reason she could not win against Manny. Depending on the facts and on the details of the conditions for ownership promised by Monica and Manny, he might have a valid claim against Monica. Let us suppose that Monica has done her due diligence before landing, and Manny has no good claim against her. Monica and Manny each own separate claims to different parts of the asteroid, instead. Unsatisfied with her win against Edward, Edith hires a mining ship and lands on the asteroid. If Edith can satisfy the conditions of ownership observed by Manny and Monica, she can own part of the asteroid alongside them. If she cannot, she will be liable for trespass to one or both them.

Humans might never have asteroid claims, who can say? But the same principles apply on Earth and allow for different levels of ownership of the same asset. Balancing interests results with minimal litigation and no one in charge. We will explore further examples of forks in property titles later in this book, especially in the chapter titled *Preserving the Public Good.*

First Ownership and Abandonment

Forking multiple layers of title is one approach to living with differences in conditions for establishing ownership. It allows different communities to exchange and develop different economic value from the same resource. The asteroid example showed how both explorers and miners can use different activity to establish different ownership claims. Forking of titles (which might also be called toleration of inferior titles) can work well when there is a reason for communities interested in a type of asset to cooperate, as between mineral surveyors and miners.

Not every group of competing owners will be collegial. Some uses of assets are not compatible. For example, preservation often conflicts with development or extraction of resources. Sometimes property needs a quiet title to be useable for the owner's purpose. For example, personal homes are closely tied to the individual personas of their owners. People demand a sense of security in their right of ownership of their homes. Ownership of farms and factories rests on similar assumptions; lack of security discourages investment. Once ownership is established, people expect the ownership will endure until the owner dies, sells the property, or abandons the property. The first owner determines all later owners.

In traditional property systems for land, first ownership in any title chain usually involves conquest and award by a sovereign, such as a king or nation-state. Original titles rest on conquests, however ancient or recent. Libertarians and anarchists have postulated theoretical "natural" bases for first ownership but have failed to obtain universal acceptance of any one rule for determining the first owner. We cannot expect universal agreement on conditions for first ownership within voluntary society. How then can owners enjoy quiet title?

The answer is always by making social promises with adequate stringency for conditions of ownership and abandonment. Suppose Sam the Surveyor promises to respect land titles by original survey. Sam holds the first person to survey a piece of land to be the original owner. Sam's promises recognize no process for abandonment or adverse possession; the original owner or her heirs owns until sale or gift to another. Harriet the Homesteader is a classical liberal who recognizes the first homesteader as first owner. Harriet recognizes sales, gifts and inheritances, and recognizes abandonment. Harriet promises that after ten continuous years of nonuse or three continuous years of adverse possession she considers property claims to be abandoned. Sam surveys large areas too large for him to police, and Harriet sets up her homestead on Sam's land unnoticed for three or more years. We have considered a similar example, and already understand how it works out under social promising.[13] But there is more.

While perusing the Free Aborigines Online Library, Aaron the Aborigine discovers solid evidence that his direct ancestors surveyed and lived on Sam's land including Harriet's homestead

---

[13] Neither can claim the other's title, because each is entitled to their preferred condition of ownership when defending against a claim by the other.

more than a century before Sam surveyed the land. Aaron can also prove he is the sole surviving heir of his tribe. Aaron's social promises are the same as Sam's. Aaron claims title to Sam's lands, and wins under Sam's law. Aaron cannot win against Harriet because of the intervening abandonment, even though his ancestors homesteaded the same land. Sam's non-recognition of abandonment or adverse possession made his claim vulnerable to prior claimants like Aaron. Harriet's recognition of abandonment or adverse possession make her secure in her claim for so long as she homesteads the land. The example illustrates why many will make social promises that respect abandonment and adverse possession: doing so shields them from claims based in antiquity.

Where ultimate ownership is based on conquest, on the military and police power of some collective, individual owners never possess secure title. Every property can be seized for failure to pay taxes, by eminent domain, or by abandonment. Voluntary property can remove the first two avenues for attacking title, leaving only abandonment or its close relative adverse possession capable of breaking title chains. People will continue to recognize abandonment and adverse possession as a shield against claims by long-absent people. No property claim should be invulnerable in any fair system of law, but property titles will be more secure under social promising than under systems based on conquest.

Conquest and Evolution

Police force backs most of what people consider "property." And the sovereign state backs what most consider "police force." The ruling regime decides what can be property, and how its subjects must resolve conflicts over ownership. The government defends its right to rule and claims sovereignty over conquered territory.

We might forget the property we own would not exist were it not for the conquest of territory by our rulers or their predecessors.

The justification for original property claims by conquest is far back in history, and we examine only recorded title chains of more recent owners. Title searches examine the property's chain of title only so far back as some incontestable ancestral title. Political activists sometimes challenge legitimacy of original property titles, but no judge of the ruling regime has authority to declare these original titles illegitimate. Only political revolution be it violent or peaceful can overturn original titles. The ultimate authority for the property we know under state law is power. The root of every property claim is the ability of a sovereign entity to defend that claim, with violence when needed. This old notion of "might makes right" only pertains to sovereigns at war. It's not helpful for deciding conflicts between equal sovereign individuals bound by the Three Promises to an ethical order.

In voluntary society, we cannot use conquest as a justification for ownership. Conquest requires much work, but such labor counts for nothing in tallying up rights of ownership. War is the violent alternative to due process. It cannot provide a basis for justifying claims between equal sovereigns who reject violent conflict as a legitimate means of dispute resolution. Individual sovereigns can in theory agree to settle disputes over property using a physical contest, but sovereign nations are collective entities without meaning in disputes between sovereign individuals. Whatever my citizenship, I cannot demand that others recognize the acts of any nation or other collective fiction as bearing on individual rights, without relinquishing my self-sovereignty. Without self-sovereignty, the Three Promises are dead.

War is sovereign struggle for dominion, pursuit of which without regard for the rights of others is immoral and often leads to hideous consequences. Even if we overlook the immorality of war, effectiveness of any military conquest is unrelated to the labor spent at war. For example, a clever tactician or one possessing superior weaponry might gain control over a resource while laboring less than a competitor. A single soldier possessing a working machine gun might wipe out an entire troop of aborigines who had never encountered such a weapon before and possess their lands. Foreign invaders can carry diseases that decimate native populations with no labor, but that tragedy does not amount to abandonment of native property rights. The labor of war can provide no justification for a property claim.

People alone can wield political power, and by their human natures exercise power for their own self-interest and for detriment of their adversaries. Rulers may exercise their powers subject to universal moral considerations, returning us to seeking justification based on moral virtue. The power to act cannot justify the act. This premise underlies every system of justice and right rule of law that acknowledges individual rights and does not set up the ruler with power over morality itself. Rule of law means that power cannot be self-justifying. In most parts of the world, *possession* of property is a concept distinct from ownership. We need no law to decide who possesses property; possession is a question of fact. Law determines who holds the *right* of ownership, which can include possession. Possession is separable from ownership, as when another rents or borrows property from its owner, or in cases of theft. Owners must follow established rules to earn honorable status as owners.

Social promising is no less a rule-based system. In it individuals define their own morality but not that of others, and all bow to the Three Promises. Voluntary property arises in that context, as do conflicts between rules for establishing original property claims. We have introduced stringency as a tool for determining the rightful rule governing ownership of property consistent with the Third Promise, when social promises conflict. We have assumed that wars of conquest cannot provide a moral basis for a claim of ownership, but a related issue remains.

When comparing the stringency of competing property claims under social promising, should we consider labor spent in defense of the property at issue? In the prior section, we proposed that respect for labor spent to establish a property right should depend on a meaningful relationship ("nexus") between the labor and the property's beneficial uses (its "utility"). Otherwise, we would have to credit labor for unrelated purposes, leading to absurd and unfair results. For example, Paul might work hard to keep his hair colored a precise shade of pink. He should not expect others to respect that labor in a claim of ownership over a piece of land absent a nexus. Nexus seems unlikely in Paul's case, but suppose he mines the substance he needs to color his hair from the land? The "nexus" requirement is familiar in legal reasoning whenever necessary to characterize the significance or value of some act. Nexus works for our purpose here.

What is the nexus between defense and utility of property? Defense is not necessarily related to beneficial use of property. For example, excluding others is part of the utility of a fence, armed guard, or other barrier, but is not part of the utility of the property itself. If you doubt this, consider that property protected by a perfect barrier has no utility, because no one can access it. At the opposite extreme whatever is indefensible cannot be property. Between these two extremes, policing a property to control access and manner of use can relate to beneficial use. There can be a nexus. Efforts in defense of property can justify a claim of ownership, when a nexus between defense and utility exists. We must exclude the relative powers of competing claimants from determining who is the rightful owner, to avoid turning social order into a justification for exercising power over others. We should look instead to the claimants' social promises, the nature, purpose and extent of their respective labors, and the utility of the property.

Under social promising, individual sovereigns take responsibility for their own defensive measures, and more than one can defend the same property. Within social promise communities, members can police uses of a property without having dominion. For example, suppose Boomer the Beachcomber lives in a driftwood shack by Sandy Cove, a delightful bit of beach on a semi-tropical shore. He does not exclude others from visiting or using Sandy Cove for purposes that do not conflict with his. He picks up litter, disposes of refuse washed up on the beach, enforces civil behavior by regulating visitors who threaten other' quiet enjoyment of the cove, and acts as a lifeguard. His policing efforts make the cove a nicer place for him to live, and benefit most visitors, too.

Recognizing the popularity of Sandy Cove, Fiorina the Fencer encloses the property with a fence and charges admission for entry. Suppose Fiorina lives by her promise to respect property first fenced by others. Boomer lives by his promise to respect caretaker's territories if maintained open for public use. Boomer's promises permit him to dismantle fences erected by others in defense of his property, so Fiorina cannot complete her fence without forcing Boomer to desist from his deconstruction efforts. Suppose she completes the fence while Boomer is on vacation. Boomer returns home and discovers her fence, and so a clash of social promises arises. To make the hypothetical interesting, suppose the investigating neutral finds that Fiorina's fence-building promise requires more work than Boomer has done in all his time as caretaker of Sandy Cove, and that Boomer had abandoned his caretaker claim by long absence. Fiorina will be the owner if the neutral compares stringency of promises without considering the nexus between the labor and the property. Suppose Fiorina's only purpose for fencing was to charge other users rent for using the cove. A neutral might hold that the nexus between the labor to build the fence and the utility of the land was too weak to support her claim, and that Boomer's promise was the more stringent of the two because of its greater nexus to the utility of Sandy Cove as a public park.

Fiorina's purpose in fencing the land is a factor. Suppose she built her fence to protect an endangered species of ninja turtles who can breed only in Sandy Cove when the cove is empty of people. The neutral might reach the opposite conclusion if the cove's utility as a preserve outweighs its utility as a public park.[14] Nexus between a defensive measure and a property depends on the purpose of the defense.

As the example of the Sandy Cove suggests, property systems based in social promising provide flexibility in how members make ownership claims over natural resources and can allow owners and different uses to coexist. In the previous section, we considered the concept of forks in titles, of coexisting ownership in different registries. Perhaps the claims of Boomer and Fiorina will end up in different registries. Whatever the outcome, the property of tolerating co-existing ownership claims creates a path to reform for property titles of questionable merit, such as those awarded by states.

The plain illegitimacy of property title chains administered by states is an obstacle to formation of just property systems and has caused violent revolutions. Established chains of title remain until overthrown by political fiat based in the pure exercise of power, by occurrence of catastrophic, complete destruction of the title system, or by voluntary agreement of the title holders. The pure exercise of power is illegitimate for those who esteem voluntary action, leaving apocalypse or voluntary agreement as the remaining possibilities. Voluntary property systems here provide another

---

[14] Under the Third Promise, Fiorina cannot evict Bill even if the neutral opines that she is the owner of Sandy Cove, as we explain elsewhere.

advantage: a peaceful path to a system of just property rights, with no intervening apocalypse or miraculous sudden political transformation. Apocalypse is as undesirable for voluntary society as for states, and faith in miracles is no plan for action. Healthy voluntary societies will ally with states to prevent calamitous disruptions in social order. Instead, voluntary property enables a gradual and voluntary substitution of just property systems for old property systems that originated from exercising power.

How does voluntary property do this substitution? By enabling gradual development of a flexible, multi-layered system of property, coexisting but separate from the system of property maintained by states. This independent system of property can not affect old systems of property, without itself being legitimized by the state. Voluntary property systems cannot notice state-determined property laws, because voluntary conflict resolution systems must rest on social promises made by individual sovereigns. As voluntary property systems succeed, they will grow in social power and influence. Once most people living under a state are members of voluntary society, and voluntary property systems have stood the test of time and earned the people's trust, the old systems of titled property will fall out of use, being unneeded and no longer wanted.

The most effective way to vote is with your feet. We accomplish true reform by walking away from gross imperfection towards a more perfect and sustainable order. Walking away is pointless without a better destination. Voluntary property will enable people to invent better alternatives to old systems of property, being separate, coexistent, and non-threatening. "Galt's Gulch" as a refuge for individual sovereigns needs no geographic boundaries. Room in our hearts and minds for voluntary property will suffice.

Voluntary Intellectual Property

Whether and to what extent intellectual property (perhaps better called *intangible* property) can be a legitimate form of property is controversial among capitalists, anarchists, socialists, and many others. Although cutting in a different direction, this controversy resembles the old right-left divide that has been the source of so much strife and misery in recent centuries. The controversy will never go away, until the tensions that create it pass out of existence.

Voluntary property avoids the controversy of intellectual property altogether, neither banning nor requiring it. More generally, social promising can heal divides over morality, enabling self-organizing society to grow in power and influence despite such divisions. The Three Promise system enables a universal self-organizing society precisely *because* it accommodates deep divisions in moral outlook via its foundation in self-sovereignty. Anything can be voluntary property, but property rights can only be enforced against those who accept those rights as legitimate. Voluntary property will include forms of intellectual property, because some of the general population will either recognize certain intangible rights expressly or recognize other rights that produce results like those resulting from intellectual property.

Most national governments recognize four basic classes of intellectual property: trade secret, copyright, trademark, and patent. Voluntary property rights are possible in each class of property, and worth considering. Useful by itself, intellectual property in voluntary forms also provides a basis for comparing with forms imposed by states. Better solutions exist than those imposed by political fiat.

Unlike more tangible property rights, the value of intangible rights based in information (e.g., patent rights) can be decimated by a single infringer. For example, the value of a trade secret can be destroyed by a single leak. Likewise, if any are free and willing to aggressively ignore claims of trademark, patent or copyright by selling competing products that make use of someone else's intangible property rights, the value of such rights are decimated, even if most would observe those rights. It is fair to ask whether voluntary intangible property can have any substantial value, in practice. This question of value is considered in the final portion of this section on voluntary intellectual property.

Privacy and Trade Secret

Privacy can include two duties: a duty to preserve an existing level of secrecy about information, and a duty to refrain from publication of information. Breach of the second duty — the duty to refrain from publication of private information — is a tort that blends in with breaches of similar duties, such as the duty to refrain from defamation. Claims based on the duty to preserve an existing level of secrecy include trade secrets, meaning secrets with economic value. The duty to preserve secrecy might arise in various ways: by contract, by fiduciary relation, or by existence of an intangible property interest or duty of care. Claims based in contract or fiduciary obligation do not rest in property. Property is a right to exclude. A property interest in trade secret means one who discloses or uses a trade secret without the consent of its owner is committing a trespass on the owner's property. What qualifies information as trade secret can vary. Its status as a protectable secret depends on maintenance of confidence by its owner. The owner of the secret information cannot disclose it except to those under a fiduciary or contractual obligation of secrecy, or it loses its secret character. A connection exists between trade secret property rights and contracts or fiducial relations. Trade secret as property extends beyond those relationships, penalizing the information thief or spy.

156

Using social promises, people may reject any intangible property interest in trade secret, expressly or implicitly. People can define trade secrets in different ways and adopt different penalties for trespass on trade secret property. For example, Isaiah may promise, "I will not publish or use trade secret information without consent of its owner, and if I break this promise, will pay the owner fair value for the damages my publication or use has caused, if any." Peter may promise nothing. Suppose Peter operates a hedgehog delivery service, and his most valuable business asset is his client list. Isaiah may steal and use Peter's list with impunity, assuming Isaiah has not agreed to a duty of secrecy for some non-property reason. If Isaiah is the one with the hedgehog delivery business, Peter is free to steal and use Isaiah's list without risk of facing a claim by Isaiah under social promises. Peter's silence means that no intangible property right in trade secret exists between Isaiah and Peter. Weaker tool analysis leads to that result.

Consider a different hypothetical, involving Irma and Paul. Irma has adopted the same social promise as Isaiah and is in the even more ambitious business of running a hedgehog stud service. Irma has a trade secret method for increasing hedgehog virility ten times more than normal. By using this method with clever marketing and astute management, she is eliminating her competitors. Paul has adopted a different promise: "I will not publish or use trade secret information without consent of its owner, and if I break this promise, will pay the owner fair value for the labor spent creating the trade secret information, if any." Out of desperation, Paul steals Irma's method, to save his failing hedgehog stud service. Irma brings a claim against Paul, proving two things: first, that Paul has stolen and used her trade secret method, and second, that she developed the method out of an intensive research effort that cost her 1000 Bitcoins. But she proves no actual damages from Paul's use. Paul owes her nothing, because under the principle of the weaker tool, she cannot ask for more than she has promised (fair value of damages) and has proved no damages from Paul's use. If she proves damages, Paul will owe her damages so long as not exceeding 1000 Bitcoins — the limit of her own rule. If she proves damages but admits that the hedgehog virility method came to her in a dream with no labor expended, Paul owes her nothing no matter how much damage she proves. Paul's rule (fair value of creational labor) is weaker under those circumstances. Once again, the weaker rule applies.

So far, we have analyzed the strength of intangible property claims based on their consequences. Like any other form of property, we can also analyze intangible property based on stringency of its antecedent conditions. For example, one may declare that the only owner of a trade secret is the person or people who have created it, or their successors and heirs. Another may say possession of a trade secret is enough for ownership, so long as not gained by force or fraud. The first condition being more stringent, it applies if those two conditions come into conflict.

These examples show that privacy as property fits within the framework of voluntary property.

Copyright

Copyright penalizes the use of creative expression claimed as property. It differs from trade secret by springing into being with publication, requiring creative expression, and excluding ideas. Copyright applies only to creative personal expressions and is mortal like its authors even for immortal expressions. The originator of copyright is the person: the individual artist, author, or creator of content. To create a work that by wide esteem outlives its copyright is a high honor. And it is no dishonor to live by one's copyrights in creative expressions. To do so is proof that the expressions have value.

All is not sunshine and daffodils; muck underlies. A fuzzy gray zone lies between the public domain and private property. Ideas and basic building blocks for expression (e.g., words and phrases) are in the public domain. We can own only what owes its existence to our creative labor, expressed in a tangible medium. Taken too far, claims over creative expressions violate more fundamental principles, such as free speech and free thought. To curb these abuses, states have evolved legal doctrines such as "fair use," the "idea-expression dichotomy," and "minimal authorship." Fair use protects free speech uses that do not deprive creators of the economic value of their creations. Commercial use is not fair use. No one can copyright ideas, and minimal authorship means trivial creations are also ineligible. Copyrights are never perpetual, expiring after a definite time. Details of these limitations vary by state, which variances are not germane to the purpose of this writing. Much controversy exists over details of state law about copyrights as over any law imposed by political fiat against the will of minorities or hapless majorities. Politicians argue about policy justifications for copyright laws while representing powerful constituents with conflicting interests. We won't get entangled in such details here.

Instead, we'll consider copyright as voluntary property in a three-promise scheme. How does copyright fit into the scheme of voluntary property? This essay began by observing differences between trade secrets and copyrights. We should notice the similarities, too. Like trade secret, copyright is an intangible right in certain information. We can analyze conflicts between social promises respecting copyright like we did for trade secret. As between any two social promises, the most stringent condition determines whether the copyright exists. Authorship is a universal condition for copyrights. Differences will arise in the exceptions, such as fair use for example. If the copyright exists, the lightest penalty promised applies. Earlier in this book, we considered conflicts between people who make social promises respecting copyright and those who do not. We concluded that both sets of people are better off with the freedom to make their own promises than when coerced to accept a single copyright law. Here, we will consider examples of more nuanced conflicts between promisors respecting copyright. Before we get to those examples, we will consider social policy aspects of traditional copyright law and voluntary copyright law.

The U.S. Constitution of 1783 allows Congress "To promote the Progress of Science and useful Arts, by securing for limited Times to Authors and Inventors the exclusive Right to their respective Writings and Discoveries." How does a public policy justification such as "promotion of progress in the arts and sciences" justify intangible rights in social promise society? Justifications and motivations are as multifaceted as the people making up the community. The legislature is the entire body of members, each of whom determines their own social promises. Concern over public policy or fairness, such as desire to reward skillful artisans for their labors will motivate civic-minded members. Self-interested objectives, for example gaining access to restricted content, or gaining a higher quality of access, will motivate. Moral principles may also motivate those who abstain from recognizing copyrights. Some believe it wrong to make any claim of ownership over free expression. All will be free to live by their individual beliefs. Without central authority to force any scheme of copyright, debate about justifications for forcing schemes on an unwilling public disappears.

Individual creators will find pragmatic motivations for promising to respect stateless copyright when they join social promise society. Their audience need not also be members of voluntary society although if many are their promises will supply additional motivation. Membership in voluntary society will motivate adoption of copyright by creators of content. Only by respecting copyrights of others can the creators receive reciprocal respect for their own copyrights. One cannot ask for recognition of one's own intangible property in voluntary society, without recognizing the same intangible property of others. Making reasonable copyright promises will create social pressure for others to make the same or similar promises and reveal those who refuse to do so. Those claiming copyrights to digital content can prevent those who acknowledge no respect for copyrights from accessing the content, using cryptographic keys or other access control mechanisms. Content providers may withhold content and content keys from any who do not make acceptable promises about copyrights. Those who care little about receiving access to protected content can avoid unwanted obligations by making less expansive promises regarding intangible property rights, or by forbearing from any such promises altogether.

Social promises regarding property will differ. Let's consider examples. Cassie is a true believer in copyrights while Sam is skeptical. Both hold that creators should receive fair compensation for their labors but differ about what is fair. Cassie promises to not copy or derive new creative works based on the creations of others, without permission. Sam promises to not make or sell copies of the creative expressions of others without permission, but nothing more. Sam writes an epic fantasy, "The Quest Against Bruhaha," about a magical dwarven elf who leads an army of unicorns and fairies against the evil Lord Bruhaha to save the Kingdom of Avalai from the powers of darkness. Cassie enjoys the story and discovers Sam's social promise regarding copyright written on the cover page. She writes a variation on the story, using the same characters and settings. But she writes a new storyline in which the evil Lord Bruhaha ends up the hero and calls her story "The Redemption of Bruhaha." Cassie's story also becomes popular. Sam complains to Cassie about breaking her own promise not to derive new creative works based on the creations of others without permission. Cassie need not apologize. She need only remind Sam that if he wanted her to keep her promise, he should have made the same promise himself!

The result would be the same had Cassie written Quest first and Sam had borrowed from it to write Redemption. Then Cassie would have no complaint against Sam, either. This is the more likely scenario, in which everybody conducts themselves according to their own promises.

Enter Cindy, a copyright true believer who made the same social promises as Cassie except for promising to pay a lower penalty for violating her promises. Had Cindy written Quest, then only Sam would be free to derive Redemption from Quest without Cindy's permission.

If Sam wrote Quest and wants to stop Cassie, he might assign his rights in Quest to Cindy or better yet to someone who has made the same or more stringent social promises as Cassie. Cassie could not publish Quest without permission from Cindy, due to their matching reciprocal promises. Suppose Cassie publishes Redemption anyway, and Cindy brings a complaint. Cassie is liable for the lesser of penalties promised by her and Cindy, which is Cindy's. Suppose Sam assigned to Kafka, who has made the same promise as Cassie and Cindy except for promising a penalty of lifetime involuntary servitude for willful copyright infringement. Then Cassie will be liable to Kafka for whatever lesser penalty Cassie has promised. These results flow from an assumption that the underlying copyrights in Sam's work are separate from what Sam has promised regarding copyright. That assumption deserves examination.

Sam seems to enjoy an advantage by promising less than Cassie. He is immune from claims for borrowing story elements from others while preserving hope of economic benefit from those who borrow from his creative works. He can pursue that hope by assigning his rights to another, for example Cindy. But he cannot assign his rights without risk. He will pay a price for the assignment because Cindy will not get involved for free. Beyond that, many promisors may regard assignments like Sam's as having no effect beyond what the original holder of the right possessed. So if Sam has no right to complain about those who borrow from him, neither does anyone he might assign his rights to. Sam cannot enlarge his property right by assigning it to another. This idea might take hold among neutrals who hear complaints about copyrights, or other property. In addition, promisors can make the precept a part of their social promises regarding copyright, by limiting recognition of assigned copyrights to rights recognized by the work's original authors. If such limitations become popular, producers and distributors who make their living by receiving copyright assignments will encourage creators to make standard social promises regarding copyright. Most creators who rely on others to make a living from their works will make whatever social promises leaders in their chosen industry find acceptable. If they refuse to make standard promises, they will diminish or destroy the economic value of their own works. Without a monopolistic legislature to corrupt, the free choices of producers, consumers, and creators will regulate industry leaders. Acceptable promises will balance competing interests of these different groups.

Free riding is an everlasting temptation for consumers, but when depriving creators of a reasonable fee comes at the risk of personal dishonor, the stakes are high. Honorable members of voluntary society who have promised to respect copyrights will protect their own reputations by paying their obligations when due. Principled and no less honorable deniers of copyrights will not ask fellow members to risk their reputations by breaking their agreements. Creators will protect valuable digital data by strong encryption, difficult to break even for determined thieves. Creators will also distribute copies under license, requiring recipients to avoid unauthorized copying and to prevent access by members who do not recognize copyrights. Copyright holders will trace the source of unauthorized copies, using digital and analog watermarks. Most consumers will not want to risk their reputations and access to high-quality protected content by copying. Piracy of digital content will exist only at the margins as it does today. But those margins may shrink, as personal reputation becomes more important and tracking tools become more capable. We can expect digital content protection to only improve, leaving non-digital uses such as creating derivative works with less protection. Under voluntary copyright, we can expect to see artists using the concepts and storylines of others to provide alternative offerings. Consumers will have more choices than ever, without depriving creators of a fair ability to earn a living from their creations.

Voluntary copyright is vast enough to make up its own field of social promising. It will be important wherever a demand for creative content exists that the labor of skilled artisans fills. Before society can evolve to exclusive use of voluntary copyright, it might need to pass through a transitional period using copyright rules based in both state and voluntary paradigms. For example, creators might hold both types of copyright, enforcing only social promises against members of voluntary society, and only state-based copyright against non-promisors and legal fictions like corporations. Due to its greater adaptability and more competitive service industry, voluntary copyright may become the favored vehicle for allocation of income from created content. Many will perceive it fairer to creators and consumers, and more efficient all around. If it cannot do these things, it will not exist. Voluntary copyright cannot displace copyright based in state law unless by providing superior results.

Today, governments offer well-developed registration services for copyright. Voluntary society can make use of these existing registries when expedient. In addition, social promisors may wish to introduce and use competitive voluntary registries for copyright or other property interests. For example, universal worldwide registries using of blockchain or similar decentralized data storage and retrieval technology may provide advantages such as greater security, flexibility, convenience, or economy. A single public registry might hold property information from around the world. Alternative registries might augment instead of replacing governmental registries. For example, a voluntary registry might include information about social promises or title history irrelevant to non-voluntary systems of governance, while also cross-referencing voluntary records to registries maintained in the name of mandatory law.

Copyright scofflaws proliferate even today but have not destroyed the value of the state-law copyrights which remain the basis for large and growing industries. Neither would copyright scofflaws be able to destroy the value of voluntary copyrights. Opportunistic disregard for copyright would be less in a social promise system than in a state system, and not only for psychological reasons. Scofflaws scorn state-mandated copyrights as made for corporate special interests by corrupt legislatures, providing a moral excuse for ignoring state law. Voluntary copyright provides no such moral cover. Each person who would do commerce involving created works of expression must take a visible position on the moral legitimacy of copyright in the natural law sense as a product of labor. And each member of voluntary society may craft their own law of copyright as right in their own eyes. There will be no excuse for not following an unjust law, or for hiding one's own moral views. Voluntary compliance is likely to be high, because reputational harm for hypocrisy — e.g., the unwillingness to keep one's own promises — will be severe.

We can only speculate about the exact forms that social promises about copyright might take. But we can be optimistic about social promisors working out fair, efficient, and close-to-total-consensus views on copyright wherever communities desiring to reward content creators exist. Social promisors will in fair measure allocate rewards from the labor of creating, producing and distributing creative content to those who do the work and bear the risks.

Trademark and Similar Rights

Trademarks protect informed markets. As property, trademark is a right to exclude others from using a mark to identify goods or services in commerce. A mark can be a name or phrase; it can also be a graphical design, static or animated. Sometimes, a mark can be a feature of a product that consumers use to indicate origin such as a distinctive color, shape, sound or scent. Trademark rights are not independent of actual use in commerce. Only actual or imminent use of a mark as a source indicator for some item of commerce confers the privilege of excluding others from use of the same or confusingly similar mark. The rights exist only for so long as the owner of the source mark is making use of the protected mark or preparations for its use. Those who stop using their trademark abandon it to others.

Every voluntary trademark exists only by the social promises of others. It emerges from the promises of others to avoid using trade names likely to mislead or confuse consumers. Stated that way, the social promises supply their own justification: enabling consumers to know the source of items in commerce by respecting accurate information about sources. Misleading consumers about a source of goods can be fraudulent, but trademark rights extend further than preventing fraud. Trademarks prevent others from using a distinctive source indicator (mark) that is like a protected mark, even when there is no intent to defraud.

A voluntary trademark right resembles but is distinct from a right of personal identity. To assume the identity of another person is fraudulent, justifiable only in rare circumstances such as necessary self-defense. Social promise societies depend on the universal use of accurate personal identities, without which there can be no reliable personal reputations. Without reliable reputation information, voluntary society cannot unlock the power of credit based in mutual trust. Every transaction becomes a dangerous back-alley exchange, destroying the benefit of belonging to voluntary society.

It's easy to recognize that identity theft is wrong and destructive. Good people will promise not to do it except in necessary self-defense. Or they will make a broader promise to not defraud. Use of another's identity to deceive a victim is fraudulent. However, victims include those whose identities are stolen, and not only those who the thief intends to deceive. Identity theft does not always involve deceiving anyone with intent to harm. Data thieves often steal identifying information without deceiving those to whom the identities belong, for example by hacking into records held by a third party. Those neglecting to make a reasonable promise respecting personal identity and the privacy of personal identifiers will tag themselves as being dangerous to deal with.

Although personal identities are unique, personal names seldom are. Different people may use the same name. Personal names do not establish identity and cannot be property under present-day copyright law unless used for commercial purposes, e.g., "Jonny Stryder's Famous Shaving Cream." But in the universe of social promising, members can make any claim the social promises support. Social promisors may respect personal names as property rights but can only enforce such rights against those making similar promises. Since most personal names are not unique, few would promise to avoid using a name that someone else is using first — at least for now. Attitudes about personal names may change with time.

Consider cybersquatting or domain squatting in which squatters hold domain names without use. Speculators are free to "squat" on as many domain names as they care to, subject to paying a small annual fee. However, regulators have made domain names subject to trademark rights, in that holders of trademarks rights can compel holders of domain names that infringe a trademark to relinquish their domain names without compensation. In a voluntary society, people who do not recognize trademark rights would be free to cybersquat and exact tolls on trademark holders. Such squatters can enjoy no trademark rights themselves. Whether that balance is fair is a matter of opinion. Voluntary trademark holders can avoid the problem by securing the domains they want before committing to any trademark.

Conflicts in social promises respecting trademark are possible, and we can reconcile such conflicts using weaker tool theory. Social promises can set different conditions for creation of a property interest in a trademark. For example, Frank recognizes the first person to use a mark for commerce as the owner of the mark. Leibniz recognizes as owner the one who makes the most use of the mark, determined by integrating the economic value of the use over the preceding three years. Both promise to cease using any marks owned by others. Suppose Frank uses the mark "CALCULINDO" for his mobile crypto-wallet tracking software in 2019. Leibniz uses CALCULINDO for the first time in 2020 for financial planning and expense-tracking software. Demand for Leibniz's product exceeds demand for Frank's product right away. By the end of 2023, Leibniz can show three years of sales much greater than Frank's. Frank used first and later, Leibniz used most. Who owns the mark, then?

To attack Frank's ownership claim, Leibniz might argue that maximum sales over a period of years is a more stringent condition than first use. The most stringent condition of ownership applies, so Leibniz will argue that because his sales are higher over three years, he should own the trademark right. He will lose the argument. Frank was the first to complete a three-year period of sales, making Frank first owner even under Leibniz's conditions. Otherwise, no title would be secure; ownership could change daily depending on who's running average sales were higher for the day. So far as Leibniz is concerned, Frank owns the mark. Leibniz must cease using CALCULINDO or suffer grave risk to his reputation.

What if Frank promises to cease use without promising to pay damages for trademark infringement while Leibniz promises to pay a reasonable fee without promising to cease use? Frank cannot prevent Leibniz from using CALCULINDO no matter how soon Frank acts. The most Frank can receive is a reasonable fee for Leibniz's use. But even if Leibniz can prove ownership of the mark superior to Frank, he will have no right to demand damages for trademark infringement from Frank, who has promised only to cease use.

Suppose Cindy uses CALCULINDO in 2024 for mobile payment software. She promises to recognize the first person to sell 100 Bitcoins worth of a marked item as the owner of the mark. She reaches that threshold in 2025 when Frank's total sales have reached a cumulative value of only ten Bitcoins. Can Cindy win ownership as of 2025? We can argue either side of the stringency question, regarding which condition of ownership is more stringent. But even if reaching a sales target is a more stringent condition than first use, Cindy satisfied her condition too late. Frank satisfied his condition of ownership in 2019 when he became the first member of voluntary society to use CALCULINDO in commerce. Frank already owns the mark, so Cindy must show that Frank abandoned the mark before she can claim ownership. We can draw an analogy to adverse possession in tangible property, while recognizing that "possession" with trademarks can mean nothing other than use in commerce without being something else (e.g., a copyright). Even if Cindy was using CALCULINDO openly and Frank ignored her use, Frank has not abandoned the mark if he is still using it in commerce. Cindy will win only if both she and Frank began using CALCULINDO on the same day. For trademark rights, first and continuing use in commerce are the natural conditions for ownership.

The concept of "natural conditions for ownership" needs explaining. Don't promisors determine which condition they will accept before recognizing another as owner? How can one person's preferences be more "natural" than another's? Trademarks are a reputational form of property because their value does not derive from scarcity but from commercial reputation and goodwill earned by participating in the market. An infinite supply of possible trademarks exists, waiting for discovery by anyone with a little imagination. Because the supply is infinite, we provide a benefit without social harm by granting an exclusive right to the first commercial user of a mark for so long as their use continues. We foster development of useful social assets: reputation and goodwill. Nor is there any social benefit from granting trademark rights to anyone not using their mark in commerce.

Likewise, the sole justification for social promising rests in providing a social benefit: liberty and justice for all. When we make social promises recognizing rights subject to conditions providing a social benefit without harm, we fulfil the purpose of social promising. Our conditions are "natural" in the sense of following the purpose of our social promising. Our application of the Third Promise using stringency of condition reaches the same result as consideration of our natural purpose. The agreement in results is evidence that our analytical framework is sound.

Trademark registries inform others that a trademark exists, and how it is being used. State-run registries already exist for this purpose. Operators of these registries screen trademark applications to ensure that the trademarks they register are distinctive and not in conflicting use by others. A register of voluntary marks might accomplish the same functions as state-run registries at a more efficient cost but would not confer any right enforced by the police power of the state. Therefore, voluntary trademark holders have a reason to prefer state-run registries for so long as the costs and requirements for state registrability are reasonable. Members of voluntary society can treat state-registered intellectual property rights as voluntary for other members and according to state law for non-promisors. They can augment state registration with information pertinent to social promises kept in open-source voluntary registries.

If voluntary society becomes prevalent, well-established state-run registries might evolve into self-funded agencies registering voluntary intellectual property rights that work in social promise frameworks. The U.S. Patent and Trademark Office is already self-funded, earning more in user fees than it costs to operate. The patents and trademarks it examines and registers are not voluntary, but we can make them so with political power in the state system. To finish the revolution, we need only use patents, trademarks and other state-registered property rights under the Three Promises when dealing with our fellow voluntarists. Nothing stands in our way but ourselves.

Patent

Patents are certificates of limited monopoly granted by a state as an incentive for inventors. For example, in the United States inventions that are new, not obvious, and not abstract ideas are eligible for patenting. With the certificate comes a right to exclude others from making, selling or using the invention without license from the patent holder, for a limited term. Patents are younger than other monopolies, being first granted by the U.S. Congress in 1790. States justify their grants of monopoly as incentives for investment in new technology, benefiting the public. Maybe patents can help new technology grow. The introduction of patent law coincided with the industrial revolution in the West, along with other social changes. Post-Enlightenment advances in science, the American revolution, and the growth of international trade and free enterprise all played a role. Patents were a part of the mix.

We can debate whether states realize their public policy justifications for patents. Patent law has had negative impacts, contributing to corporatization of economic power, less diverse markets and skewed investments. In certain areas (e.g., health), patents have contributed to diversion of research and investment away from older technologies ineligible for patent, when the older technology would provide superior results for consumers.

Patents benefit the state. Before patents, private guilds formed to protect trade secret knowledge. Patents weaken trade secrets. Instead of private guilds, patents engender a government-dependent class of inventors, bureaucrats, lawyers and entrepreneurs, while increasing government revenue. Little wonder states around the world have been willing to adopt patent laws since the U.S. Congress led the way in 1790.

Patents differ from other forms of intangible property. Patents don't exist unless the state permits them. Other forms of intangible property rights arose by interaction between members of civil society. The original civil law nature of trade secret, copyright and trademark has persisted despite political action to co-opt more traditional forms of intangible property. Politicians want to transform all property rights into state licenses; doing so increases the politician's powers.

Patents are distinct from other intangible property in another respect: how far the exclusionary right extends is often unclear. Judges determine the exclusionary right based on the patent claims that the patent holders write. Uncertainty of scope and the role of patent owners create justification for examination of proposed patent claims by the state. The state must approve claims before allowing patent holders to enforce their patents. State patent agencies and legislatures create rules defining what inventors may patent. These rules limit claims to what the inventor invents, meaning technology that is new and non-obvious (or inventive) because of what the public knows when the inventor first applies for a patent.

In voluntary society, no state exists to grant patent rights. Is there any reason to suppose that voluntary society would make use of similar property rights? How might such rights operate? Like every other property right, patents rights can exist in voluntary society only by the social promises of others. A voluntary patent is a social promise to reward first inventors for the value of their inventions. Claims for the promised rewards are only valid against those making this promise. Members might resolve conflicts between patent promises having different conditions and consequences using the two-fold analysis based on the least burdensome (weakest) property right, as this book explains. Claimants could not bring patent-like complaints unless the social promise of both the claimant and defendant allowed it. Damages for infringement of a patent right would depend on the least burdensome rule of the parties.

As with copyrights and trademarks, inventors may register their inventions with a registrar, which may or may not be a state agency. If the inventor registers the invention in a stateless registry, its validity can be tested by a neutral after the registration is asserted. "Validity" in a social promise system entails determining whether the invention complies with the conditions for the patent right spelled out by the inventor's promises and the promises of any the inventor would enforce against.

Just as voluntary copyright enables creators to realize value in voluntary society, so voluntary patents will enable inventors to realize value for their inventions from other voluntary society members, without resorting to the state. Most members of voluntary society will have no personal interest in protecting patent rights. Invention is a niche activity that few people engage in. But there are reasons non-inventor members might want to recognize voluntary patent rights. Inventors can identify those who refuse to recognize patent rights and encourage them to become patent promisors. For example, inventors may refuse to sell their inventions or scarce technological wares to non-promisors and enter secrecy pacts with those who buy their inventions. Inventors may shun or boycott non-promisors and focus on inventing things they can maintain as trade secrets. Those who invent may organize guilds to magnify the effect of their protective measures. But inventors cannot bring claims against non-promisors who are fellow members of voluntary society. Therefore, members who don't need favors from inventors or their guilds and supporters might find it convenient to promise no rewards, or only trivial rewards, to first inventors.

Self-sovereigns seeking patents might make use of government-run patent agencies and registries for record-keeping, for so long as such things exist. Holders of voluntary patents could specify their own consequences for claims of infringement and avoid state-based due process for voluntary due process. Other modifications of state laws by voluntary patent adopters may include, for example, declaration of a shorter or longer patent term than granted by the state, different methods for computing damages, and different standards for patentability. Members may promise different standards for obtaining patents (in our parlance, "conditions for ownership") than state agencies, but doing so would eliminate using state agencies to keep track of things. Voluntary standards could be more restrictive, or less restrictive, than present standards under state law. If a member of voluntary society adopts different standards for patentability than adopted by the state, a neutral must apply those standards without guidance from any state agency. Experts in patent standards can exist outside of the state, but such is not near at hand. It would be more convenient to use the existing resources of state agencies for patent granting and registration for so long as social promise communities are in the minority.

Many state-run patent agencies are funded by user fees; for example, the U.S. Patent and Trademark Office has long derived more revenue from user fees than it spends on its own operations. Self-supporting state agencies might transform themselves into voluntary agencies, by gradually accepting the principles of social promising among the population they serve. Members of voluntary society will abstain from suing one another in state courts, bringing their claims instead based on social promises in stateless forums. So long as the existing patent agencies apply a legal standard (or legal standards) that is (or are) used in social promising, the agencies will continue to exist on the user fees of patent applicants. However, to the extent voluntary standards for patentability diverge from the prevailing state standard, competing stateless agencies or agencies belonging to other states can enter the market to compete with the established state agency in certifying patent applications under voluntary patent standards.

Instead of registering a patent with a centralized registry, any member of voluntary society can publish their invention and any related patent claim using the voluntary society's system for publication of social promises, claims, and reputation feedback. In a system in which law emerges from the social promises of self-sovereigns, examination of patent claims by some certifying agency

175

will become less valuable. Whether patent-certifying agencies can survive the demise of coercive patent systems will depend on the extent to which voluntary standards for patent rights exist, and the number of different standards in use. For example, if 1 billion people worldwide promise to respect voluntary patents that meet a certain standard, or only a few different standards, the economic ecosystem should support several efficient patent-certifying agencies. If there are too few users of voluntary patent law, or too many standards in use, there may be no functional certifying agencies. These and other outcomes are possible.

Whatever forms voluntary patent rights might take or whether such rights will exist are as unpredictable as the future desires of free people. Voluntary patent rights can and will exist if enough free people make social promises respecting first inventor rights.

Other Intangible Property

The examples of trade secret, patent, copyright and trademark do not exhaust the possibilities for intangible property rights in any conflict resolution system, voluntary or otherwise. For example, intangible property rights that are neither patent-like nor copyright-like have arisen in open-source software. Founders of open-source programming projects enjoy by community norms of behavior the right to maintain control over their own open-source projects.[15] They can earn social credit and recognition for their contributions to code.[16] These norms arose organically from community consensus in a certain context and are analogous to "moral rights" recognized by some states. In voluntary societies, intangible property rights will be highly adaptable to environmental

---

[15] Coding Freedom, Gabriella Coleman 2013, p. 123 (re. Debian).
[16] Id. at 117.

conditions and take many new and interesting forms that cannot be anticipated. These rights will practically exist only if their fairness is widely recognized.

On Value

The body of trustworthy promises we enjoy by becoming promisors ourselves has value, to be sure. The overhanging value of obligations based on individual honor is the greatest intangible asset possible. Using infinite complexity of language and powered by trust, promise networks can do almost anything. Unlike laws imposed by politicians elected by magical popularity rituals, the network of promises does not pretend to be homogenous. Like-minded people will join you in recognizing the rights you respect. Others won't. So it works under empire, too, except for greater license to despise rules imposed by the whim or avarice of politicians. When those who respect your intangible property act out of their sense of personal honor, you enjoy honorable value. Those who will not respect such property offer such as they produce for public use. You are better off on both sides. And you can tell the sides apart by their social promises.

Too idealistic? Of what value is a copyright if copyright non-promisors may steal? That's a fair question when people despise copyrights. Plenty get their software, games, videos and other digital stuff from torrents, despite laws forbidding such copying and sharing. The pressure of digital copying has transformed the market for content, but not destroyed it. Consumers still reward producers for producing popular content. Content producers use many tools and methods to reduce unauthorized copying and make it less profitable. Their efforts are not without effect; it is possible to defend electronic content from lazy freeriding. But if many people respect copyright out of their personal sense of honor, they show themselves as desirable consumers. Producers can market to them as a class. Promisors have more influence with producers than non-promisors do. Consumers and producers are both off knowing their mutual supporters. None need stain their honor by extracting value from the unwilling under coercion, i.e., by committing theft.

We can treat property in accord with rational economics. By that economics the value of any right will depend on its base, on the collective resources and wills of the self-sovereigns who respect that right. Property of a despised kind will always be of lesser value than property of a respected kind. Such is the nature of property. Nor will people despise property without reason. If people think it wrong to claim something as property, we cannot deny their self-sovereign right to live by their own beliefs.

Free-riding is the perennial problem. There will always be non-promisors wanting to take the labor of others without compensation, including using valuable information created by others. Consider copyright, for example. Statist legal systems cannot end disregard for copyright laws, despite strict laws and vigorous enforcement efforts. Copyright still has value, or no industries could grow up around it. Copyright will continue to have value under voluntary systems, for several reasons. First, the personal honor of those who profess respect for voluntary intellectual property is the best defense for creators. The risk of an identity as a thief and hypocrite will not be worth the benefits of breaking their own promises. Digital protection techniques will discourage most consumers from bothering with unauthorized copies, even consumers who do not recognize intangible property as valid. Competition and low distribution costs will keep prices affordable, making "piracy" of copyrighted material unappealing for most people. It will be more convenient to pay a small fee to get access to high-quality protected content from its creators. Moral arguments made by copyright holders or fear of legal action might persuade a few, but convenience rules the day for most. Pragmatic compliance works even better for voluntary rights, in which members know each other's promises at the point of transaction.

In addition, no one loses rights under state laws just by making social promises respecting intangible property. Instead, one exchanges a state-mandated property right for rights promised by others, to the extent not greater than what one has promised others. Promisors lose state-mandated rights only so far as the state rights exceed those promised by others and by themselves. They lose no state rights against non-promisors. Total silence on the question of voluntary property may cause a society member to be a non-promisor, and vulnerable to claims under state law.

Members can avoid or recapture claims based on state law from voluntary society members by their own promises. For example, by (1) adopting the promise of "I will recognize no voluntary intangible property right and waive my intangible property rights granted under the law of any state." Another (2) might make the same promise, except for recognizing voluntary intangible property right 'X'. A third (3) might promise: "I will recognize no voluntary intangible property right, but reserve my intangible property rights granted under the law of any state against any who do not excuse me from claims based on those rights." A fourth (4) might make the same promise as the third, except for recognizing voluntary intangible property right 'X'. Four combinations of law and ten (4+3+2+1) unique conflicts of law are possible between members of voluntary society. The different possibilities are summarized by the table below, in which 'V' stands for "Voluntary" and 'IPR' stands for "Intangible Property Right."

Parties in Dispute	Party 'A'	Party 'B'	Result
1-1	No VIPR State IPR Waived	No VIPR State IPR Waived	No IPR of any kind is enforceable
1-2	No VIPR State IPR Waived	VIPR 'X' State IPR Waived	No IPR of any kind is enforceable
1-3	No VIPR State IPR Waived	No VIPR State IPR Reserved	No IPR of any kind is enforceable
1-4	No VIPR State IPR Waived	VIPR 'X' State IPR Reserved	No IPR of any kind is enforceable
2-2	VIPR 'X' State IPR Waived	VIPR 'X' State IPR Waived	'X' only is enforceable
2-3	VIPR 'X' State IPR Waived	No VIPR State IPR Reserved	No IPR of any kind is enforceable
2-4	VIPR 'X'	VIPR 'X'	'X' only is enforceable

Parties in Dispute	Party 'A'	Party 'B'	Result
	State IPR Waived	State IPR Reserved	
3-3	No VIPR State IPR Reserved	No VIPR State IPR Reserved	State IPR only is enforceable
3-4	No VIPR State IPR Reserved	VIPR 'X' State IPR Reserved	State IPR only is enforceable
4-4	VIPR 'X' State IPR Reserved	VIPR 'X' State IPR Reserved	Either 'X' or state IPR is enforceable

Reservation of state IPR (or any other state-granted right) while adopting voluntary rights does not entail contradiction and enables coexistence. This is as true for other forms of property as for intangible property. Nor is reservation of state rights odious, so long as limited to those who have likewise reserved state rights, as must be so in Three Promise systems. By adopting a voluntary intangible property right 'X' while reserving state rights, a person can gain the right to enforce 'X' while losing enforcement of rights only against those natural persons who do not promise to disclaim 'X'.

Any member of voluntary society is always free to pursue state law claims against non-promisors. If the member waived state rights by their social promises, non-promisors cannot enforce waivers made by promisors. So those who prefer enforcing rights under voluntary process have no reason to reserve state rights by their social promises. Reserving state rights exposes the voluntary society member to state-based claims by other members of voluntary society, undermining the purpose of voluntary society. Members who adopt voluntary IPR are likely to waive state IPR against other members of voluntary society. They will keep their voluntary rights against those who have adopted compatible rights, and their state rights against non-promisors.

Concern for reputation must be present, or useful voluntary society does not exist. With concern for reputation, those who have promised to respect any form of property, intangible or not, will feel social pressure to fulfill their own promises. Compliance with voluntary intangible property rights is likely to be high, and this will shrink the market for infringing products. Members of voluntary society will not purchase products they suspect of infringing on intangible property rights of others. The market will segment into a set of consumers and sellers who respect no intangible property rights, and one or more sets of consumers and sellers who recognize similar forms of intellectual property rights. These different segments will coexist without cross claims, creating diverse opportunities for different economic players.

The lack of compulsory property rights does not mean there is lack of enforcement power in voluntary society. Sometimes members will avoid expressing disrespect for property rights even if they do not recognize the property right at issue. For example, consider a technology guild that enforces trade secrets among its members. The members of the guild also promise to respect guild-approved patent rights held by guild members. Let's assume that the guild avoids violating state laws, such as antitrust, and develops valuable trade secret technology and patent rights. Members of the guild bind one another by elements of contract, fiduciary duty, and property. Guild members will seldom risk their good standing by violating the rights they have promised to respect. Outsiders will not ignore the guild's claims to intangible property, if it has market power and valuable trade secrets. No society member will want to anger a powerful guild. A proper guild will not aggress in retaliation but will refuse to do business with those who do not respect its claims to intangible rights. If the guild is large and well-coordinated, controls access to essential technology, or is popular, open opposition to its reasonable claims will come with disadvantages, expense, and reputational harm. Guild power will reduce but not end trespass on the guild's intangible property rights. Intangible property "rogues" may exist and work as they wish but will find that status as rogues will limit their economic opportunities for dealing with guilds. Imagine for example a wireless telecommunications guild that will not sell its products to consumers unless they make social promises respecting certain property rights. Guilds are cartels, and not invulnerable to market pressure from competitors. Hence, the survival of the guild depends on creating value by pooling the trade secrets and inventions it would claim rights to.

Because of the boundless, innovative ways members of social promise communities can create and enforce voluntary intangible property, intangible property will be more valuable than is possible when compliance depends on state compulsion. Voluntary intangible property may be narrower in some respects, and broader in others, than what we experience under state systems. It is impossible to predict the exact forms that will exist. By creating alternative rights and more effective enforcement mechanisms, intangible rights based in social promises will exert pressure on compulsory forms of property. We hope this pressure will cause state-imposed rules to evolve into more acceptable forms until no one's view of property is imposed on any natural person.

Recounting Advantages of Voluntary Property.

Voluntary property is superior to other property systems. Its advantages include accommodating diverse moral worldviews, preventing accumulation and use of property as a tool for domination of others, better aligning property rights with socially beneficial uses of natural resources, encouraging diverse uses of natural resources and diverse lifestyles to coexist in harmony, and providing a gradual evolutionary path away from traditional property systems based in power to a more just and beneficial system. Meanwhile, voluntary property can provide all the benefits of traditional property, including encouraging and rewarding productive labor and investment, and facilitating allocation of resources to their highest and best uses.

Evolution towards voluntary intangible property will be gradual. But after enough social evolution has occurred, the voluntary approach will produce results fairer to the actual producers and less advantageous to market intermediaries who do not add value in proportion to their added cost. Entrenched owners cannot use their property claims to oppress the poor. Instead, they must demonstrate the benefits of their property systems to a community of self sovereigns.

Perhaps you are not convinced that voluntary property is better than property defined by the decree of some ruler, ultimately backed by a coercive police force controlled by political fiat. In the remainder of this Guidebook, you will encounter voluntary property considered in various conflicts over the use and control of resources. Keep an open mind and read on!

Chapter 6: Due Process & Enforcement

First Look

Equal sovereigns can settle their differences however they please. By promising in advance to follow specific process for peaceful resolution of disputes and by keeping their promises, sovereigns signal their comity for others. They become safe neighbors for one another, entering community under rule of law. We know from experience that people can cooperate by agreement and mutual trust, without threats of violence or fraud. So due process rules can emerge from exchanging social promises as can other mutual understandings. In social promising, process is "due" when accepted without coercion or fraud by every party that takes part in it. Social promises are tools for reaching mutual acceptance of rules for social behavior.

Big questions for due process among individual sovereigns are what social promises are best for each person (as always), how to resolve clashes between different promises, and what happens when disputants refuse to agree on a process and forum for hearing their dispute. We'll make a few assumptions: no state exists to shift the cost onto taxpayers and maintaining a reputation as someone who will settle grievances using a reasonable process is important. For a first look, suppose your promises to divide up the costs of minimum viable process in a specific way and to accept the verdict of any neutral you have agreed to are all you need to preserve your good reputation. You'll negotiate what "minimum viable process" means on a case-by-case basis. You can be more specific if you please, and people will judge you by the promises you've made.

No one can imagine the myriad solutions to process problems that billions of free sovereigns will invent. It is even harder to guess what schemes to subvert fair outcomes depraved people will try. It's still fun to discuss possibilities, and vital to spot basic problems and their potential solutions.

Kernel

In traditional legal systems, due process separates the rule of law from the arbitrary exercise of power. A government monopolizes enforcement power and promotes the conceit that fair process is a precondition to all its coercive acts of justice. Take away the monopoly, and process loses its bureaucratic purpose: legitimizing a collective sovereign. Process becomes a tool for persuading our fellow individual sovereigns that our actions are just. Our promises to respect due process assures others we are fair and peaceful people. Lacking any central authority, definition of due process in social promising emerges out of the power and responsibility of each person to publish their chosen social promises. No single standard applies to due process, instead, different ideas interact and are mediated by the Third Promise. When parties do not agree on a process for dispute resolution, their Third Promises compels use of the least burdensome of the processes they have promised to follow. In this chapter, we explore what picking the least burdensome process might entail in different circumstances, what promises touching on due process are likely workable, and what happens when conflicting parties refuse to cooperate.

Claims in social promise community are not "legal actions" in the sense of invoking external authority. Claims are events recorded in a registry. They don't involve what governments call "law" at all! Still, the claim and its consequences touch on the honorable rights and obligations of community members. The claims are legal in a philosophical sense. Claims justify judgments on the morality of others, without imposing an alien moral standard.

We judge our neighbors by their social promises and their responses to claims based thereon.

Absent meddling by governments, due process is easy. To the extent due process provided by government courts fails to meet demand, many private organizations offer private process for those litigants able to afford alternatives. Market-based arbitration services can create their own rules for due process, directed at resolving disputes using a settlement process agreeable to their clients. One challenge with private arbitration is compensating for unequal economic power in the market for arbitration services. Large players can impose private arbitration by contract on individuals having little economic power, creating advantages for corporate entities. Social promising does not banish contracts. It can cultivate innovation and fairness in dispute resolution by empowering each person to point out their own acceptable processes using a Three Promise framework.

When dealing with a corporation, individuals need ask only whether it abides by the Three Promises. Individuals need not ponder the relative merits of private arbitration or government courts, both expensive forums in which large corporations enjoy the advantage of size and expertise. Suppose a corporation does not respect social promising. Its customers can discover its contempt for self-sovereign process, and deal with another. Members will find another provider willing to respect process according to social promises, and to demand no more of others than they will do themselves (the Third Promise).

Disputants in social promise society may select a resolution service or set of private rules before a dispute arises, for example as part of a contract. When no contract requires a specific process, litigants may submit to any settlement process they want, using such resources for settlement as they can find. Any person or group of persons capable and willing to lead a defined settlement process for resolving disputes using social promises can do so. And they may do so for some fee, or *pro bono*, as they wish. We call these people "neutrals." We would like them to work without state interference in their function as trustworthy independent fact-finders and mediators. But to the extent they commit fraud or other harmful acts under state law, they are not immune from prosecution.

States restricting the practice of law to licensed individuals may create risks for neutrals hearing disputes based on social promises. Neutrals can get law licenses if they please, but the state cannot ban others from acting as neutrals without subverting the market for neutral services. Competition without restriction on supply of neutrals is vital for healthy social promise ecosystems. Requiring law licenses restricts supply, and poisons it with motivations to support the power of the state. Are social promise neutrals "practicing law," in the sense of doing an activity the state forbids except to its licensees? It depends on the settlement process being applied, and on who is determining what "practicing law" means. A state actor might regard any positive involvement in settlement process as the practice of law if the settlement affects rights of the participants under state law.

There is the escape hatch. Social promises are not state law, and those who assist with settlement under social promises are not practicing law. So what if settlement under social promises can obviate the need to use state law for dispute resolution? States encourage private dispute resolution as a matter of social policy. To avoid risk, neutrals unlicensed by the state should generate no contracts or other instruments that create or destroy state law rights or obligations. If the parties want contracts and instruments under state law after settlement, they have alternatives. They can hire a state-licensed lawyer to carry out their settlement terms by the state's legal instruments. Or they can create their contracts and instruments themselves without using a lawyer. Unlicensed neutrals should refer their clients to licensed lawyers or self-help resources for acts of legal significance under state law. All participants should cooperate to deprive states of grounds for interfering in voluntary process. They can do so by exercising their freedom to avoid entanglement with state-regulated activities. They can avoid using state-granted police powers and rely instead on the value of trustworthy reputations in voluntary society to preserve the peace.

There is at least one type of process that cannot touch on a person's rights under state law: a game without wagers. The state might claim to license operators of gambling establishments. It will dare not require licenses for playing board games, video games, or hopscotch, lest its greed and folly become too plain. If participants of such games earn non-transferable reputation points only, state regulators will find it hard or impossible to regulate honor games as money transfer activity as they have with crypto-currencies. The first systematic application of social promising may arise in an online multiplayer game, if it hasn't already.

Many resources already exist for private dispute resolution. Most such resources apply state laws, but self-sovereign process rules will work just as well. Private judges are as happy to decide the case under a Three Promise framework as under state law. State courts might discriminate between outcomes under the Three Promises and outcomes under state law, or may regulate private judges, but these aspects concern coexistence with state law: a subject for a different section of this chapter. This Guidebook refers to settlement agents operating under self-sovereign, social promise frameworks as "neutrals," and state-regulated private judges as "arbitrators." These labels are arbitrary – pardon the pun – but useful to make distinctions when necessary. Nothing prevents a neutral from also being an arbitrator, or an arbitrator from also being a neutral. In a thriving social promise ecosystem, many neutrals will not be arbitrators; others will be.

Members will judge neutrals based on the rules of due process. They will determine those rules by agreement or by selecting the least burdensome process from those promised. Whatever the due process rules, in modern legal systems outcomes of judicial proceedings often disappoint parties to a dispute, causing them to seek appeal. Whether a rehearing, appeal, or some other review process is available will vary in different circumstances. There are different ways to ensure quality of the neutral services, and appeal may not be the most optimal or cost-efficient mechanism. A free market in neutral services and process rules should offer many alternatives for ensuring the accuracy and quality of neutral opinions. That market should also enable swift enforcement of just neutral opinions without unnecessary delay.

"Enforcement" in social promising includes compelling compliance with promised obligations and penalizing noncompliance. The main tool for enforcement is reputation. Neutral opinions and process details become part of the social promise records of all the involved parties. Members may encrypt their settlement records but will experience pressure to unlock their due process histories for anyone with a reason to know. Every interested member may act on another member's process history, without violating the rights of that member. Members of the community of equal self-sovereigns will feel pressure to fulfill their own social promises, subject to due process for establishing fault and determining the remedy if any.

Some members will refuse to follow neutral opinions, judging the cost of compliance greater than the benefit of preserving their reputations. Those owed unpaid obligations are not without recourse. Winning claimants can hire freelance enforcers, just as they can today. Self-sovereign enforcement occurs without central authority over enforcers. Those who work to enforce neutral opinions will experience vigorous regulation from market participants and will enjoy no special privileges to protect from claims of malpractice or abuse. So only respectable neutral opinions will attract competent people willing to take on enforcement risks. We will consider further aspects of enforcing social promises in the Basket of Nuts.

Basket of Nuts

The Neutral

In social promise communities, neutrals serve as intermediaries. They might offer opinions on disputes, make findings regarding lost or abandoned property, act as escrow agents for exchange of property or information, or do any other task that requires a trusted intermediary. Although the Guidebook focuses on their role in conflict resolution, don't forget that they can do other jobs. Neutrals are the lubricant that makes social promise community work.

When helping to resolve conflicts, neutrals base their opinions on the published social promises of the parties and facts of the dispute at hand. When acting within social promise community, neutrals do not opine or advise about state laws or regulations. Some neutrals may wear more than one hat, for example, a "neutral" hat and a "state-licensed " hat. Wearing the neutral hat, they can take on different tasks depending on the social promises and instructions from the parties. Some neutrals may operate like common-law judges, overseeing procedure and letting the competing parties or their advocates develop the evidence and reasoning. Others may work more like civil-law investigative judges. Still others may operate more as mediators, peacemakers or counsellors. Some may resemble or act as members of a jury. Neutrals can work as individuals, or as a team. There are no constraints beyond the choices of the participants in dispute resolution processes, economic factors in the marketplace for settlement services, and basic elements of due process. Alternative ways of resolving disputes can coexist in the environment of freedom from monopolistic authority that social promising provides.

Whatever task they are performing, neutrals operate under expectations of the community that the neutrals serve. A state or other authority has no rightful power to determine who may act as a neutral, or what due process using social promises must comprise. The responsibility to select and empower neutrals rests with the disputants alone.

When the defendant and claimant agree on the choice of neutral and do not contest the process used by the neutral to arrive at an opinion, due process is easy. The parties' agreement controls the process used. Not every case will be easy. Problems can arise when disputants do not agree on choice of a neutral or due process, which we will consider below. Other problems arise when a party alleges that the neutral is biased, does not follow the agreed process or arrives at an erroneous result. We consider the latter problems in the essay titled Ensuring Quality. We consider more advanced topics in due process, for example, justice for the poor and deciding unopposed claims, in Chapter Ten.

Self-sovereigns take the first steps towards fair process by agreeing on a neutral to hear their dispute. They can assure fellow sovereigns by making social promises revealing their minimum acceptable standards for neutrals and processes. Community members will not choose unreasonable conditions for selection of a neutral because their conditions only apply to themselves. Social pressure adds a further disincentive: members will not want to mark themselves as being difficult to deal with. For example, suppose Sue has litigious tendencies. She promises to accept any unbiased neutral who has opined in at least 50 prior cases and favored the claimant at least 60% of the time. Jordan hates litigation and promises to accept any neutral of similar experience who has favored the defendant at least 60% of the time. No neutral can satisfy the conditions of both Jordan and Sue. If Sue brings a claim against Jordan, which social promise is weaker and therefore applicable? Jordan's promise is always weaker for the claimant and stronger for the defendant. Sue's is the opposite, always weaker for the defendant and stronger for the claimant.

The social promises of Sue and Jordan are alike in their cost but differ in their relative burdens. Sue's promise always favors the claimant, and Jordan's the defendant. If we consider only the burden on the defendant, we might encourage people like Jordan to set extreme conditions in their social promises. Jordan might reserve the right to refuse any neutral with less than a 99% acquittal rate, for example, granting himself veto power over almost any neutral a claimant might choose. But if Jordan sets a 99% rule, he marks himself as a target for aggression. He cannot bring claims against his aggressors without being stuck under the No-Hypocrisy Principle with his own 99% rule. We should not allow those who promise to accept only defendant-friendly neutrals to enjoy more claimant-friendly promises of their chosen defendants. Likewise, defendants who have promised to accept only claimant-friendly neutrals should not get the benefit of more defendant-friendly promises made by their accusers.

When potential hypocrites are on both sides of neutral selection controversies, such as when Jordan brings a claim against Sue, it is impossible to check the hypocrisy of one without tolerating the hypocrisy of the other. If we hold Jordan to his rule, Sue enjoys a defensive advantage greater than she has promised to others. But if we allow Jordan to enjoy Sue's neutral selection promises, we reward Jordan's hypocrisy. Since we cannot apply the No-Hypocrisy Principle without also negating it when choosing neutrals, we need a different approach.

By the Third Promise, none can demand that another carry a burden greater than they have promised to carry themselves. A promise to refuse neutrals that do not meet the promisor's conditions is a burden placed on the other party. If the other party has not set conditions similar enough to find at least one neutral satisfying both sets of conditions, then by the Third Promise neither party's promise creates obligations for the other. Neither set of conditions applies. The parties must agree on a neutral despite their promised conditions, or they cannot resolve their dispute as cooperating self-sovereigns. If one proposes reasonable options that the other rejects without good reason, each bears the credit or blame of their decisions.

Whether one or both parties come to the neutral's table, the neutral serves her client and the community by opining the facts and the rights and obligations of the parties. By providing her opinion, she exposes credit and blame where due. She enables each member of the community make their own judgment of her comity as a neutral. She builds the network by adding to community assets. She does not decide the fate of others, and rules over only herself.

Selection of the neutral is a responsibility and privilege shared by both claimants and defendants. Promises like Sue's and Jordan's to accept only biased neutrals break the system, as promises to aggress for arbitrary reasons (e.g., ethnicity) do. Incoherent self-contradictory promises, such as promises to accept biased neutrals, will only earn dishonor for their makers.

Promised conditions for neutral selection can fail to result in anyone acceptable to both parties, without calling for explicit bias. For example, Jennifer might promise to accept only neutrals living in Japan, while David might promise to accept only neutrals living in Denmark. The social promises of Jennifer and David cannot guide them to a neutral that fulfils both of their conditions, despite lack of explicit bias. Jennifer and David end up in the same position as Jordan and Sue. They must bend their conditions and find a way, or they will unable to resolve their dispute by neutral consideration of the facts based on their self-sovereign social promises. They and they alone must bear responsibility to agree on a neutral.

Promising to refuse neutrals that don't meet your conditions is pointless. But there are reasons to promise to accept neutrals that meet your conditions. Although you cannot impose your conditions on others, you can use the conditions to reassure others of your fairness in resolving disputes. Reassurance may encourage others to form trust relationships with you. At root, willingness to submit disagreements to a neutral operating a fair process for dispute resolution is a virtue upon which social trust depends.

Whether guilty or innocent, defendants always have a motive to refuse due process. Without a neutral opinion, the public has little basis for assuming they owe restitution. By refusing to submit to a neutral process, guilty defendants can hope to escape liability. Innocent defendants can hope to escape the costs of raising a defense or the consequences of a neutral's mistake. Nobody loves due process except for those who make their living by it. But submitting to due process is better than the alternative: life without social order.

Well-designed social promise communities will motivate members to agree on due process under a neutral. The burdens of using due process should be less than what we experience when government claims a monopoly over judicial process. Those who make social promises and then refuse to submit claims based on their promises to fair process will sully their own reputations. Notice of claims made and left unresolved will accumulate in social promise registries. Community members will regard those who make or receive many unresolved claims with fatal distrust, foreclosing all but the most minimal social opportunities. Successful self-sovereigns will make and receive all formal complaints with care and diligence. Maintaining social trust will be one of their highest priorities.

It may sometimes happen that no neutral or forum acceptable to both parties is available to hear a case, with no malice or unreasonableness involved. In such cases, the claimant may publish the claim and wait for the market to provide a suitable neutral and venue. Neutral service providers can monitor published claims and react to satisfy market demands.

When disputants control their selection of neutrals, they foster a free market for neutral services and maximize the chances that due process will be unbiased and competent. They deny grants of judicial authority to any person or collective. When participants regulate the market by their free choices, any who would work as a neutral must earn a reputation for neutrality and competence. Openness of the market to all providers, lack of entrenched market positions, and transparency provided by sharing of reputational information among promise enforcers and litigants provides optimal regulation.

None can own the market for neutral services. Neutrals unable to produce cost-effective and durable settlements must improve, or face replacement by those more competent. Openness to unfettered competition in the market for due process services provides a reasonable basis for assuming, in the general theoretical case, that a sufficient supply of unbiased and competent neutrals will be available. No authority prevents willing participants from servicing demand, and so prices adjust until supply meets demand.

The free market in neutral services eliminates mandatory jurisdiction. Contempt of court is no longer punishable by prison but only by creating a durable record of the offender's misconduct, if any. Neutrals cannot enforce penalties for failure to submit to process by police power. The power of neutrals, like everyone else, rests in their reputations. Each holds a carrot and a stick. The carrot is reputation, applied to restore the reputations of the disputants by facilitating honorable resolution of their grievances and making a record of their virtuous conduct. The stick is also reputation, applied to convince the community of the social offenses of those who would live by self-sovereign justice but fail to take responsibility for keeping their own promises. When refusing to agree to a proffered neutral, a party should state a cogent reason why the neutral is unsuitable and propose an alternative. Self-inflicted damage to reputation will be the cost of unjustified refusals.

Respected neutrals are rare in humanity, outside of families or small tribes. Can they exist without compulsion in large societies of strangers? Perhaps every neutral serves political interests. Perhaps the neutral's opponents will always object to her opinions. If so, no neutral can earn universal respect. Conflicting moral views will always exist and will play out in violent conflict. For those intolerant of differing moral views, police power to enforce controversial judgments made under one uniform law is the only power they believe capable of avoiding violent social conflict. To avoid destructive wars, police power must be a monopoly, allied with legislative and judicial monopolies. If you believe this you may as well shut this book, abandon your hope and go back to coping with Orwell's eternal boot.

If you doubt the universe could be such a dismal place for humanity, read on. We can hope for better outcomes. People can learn to accept moral differences without violent conflict. They can learn to use social promises to understand how others operate, and avoid relationships that will lead to anger, distrust, hatred and violence. Even if some never learn to tolerate moral differences, that will not prevent others from joining in supportive, tolerant networks. Neutrals will work within those networks, promoting the underlying ethic of personal sovereignty: morality by self-rule.

Suppose there exists a class of people who oppose personal sovereignty. Members of this opposition class will not obey the rulings of neutrals on social promises, but neither will any expect them to. Likewise, opponents of self-sovereignty have no social standing to bring anyone to account for their social promises. Social promises create no obligations for or to those who promise nothing. The Three Promises separate the wheat of society members from the chaff of non-promisors. Honorable sovereigns will accept any unbiased neutral competent to opine on the case. Society members will obey respected neutrals or earn status as non-promisors and hypocrites.

The more a neutral's opinions are respected, the greater the reasons to hire him. The best neutrals will usually be more expensive. But even a child can point out the emperor has no clothes and be believed over exalted liars. Where the people are free and unafraid, truth rules the day more than power and allies itself with compassion and healing. No matter who you are, the next great neutral might live in your neighborhood, or might even be you.

Voluntary Due Process

Due process between self-sovereigns has a different meaning than due process by states. Unlike subjects of territorial monopolies, self-sovereigns need not protect litigants from the overwhelming monopoly power of the state. Debating the proper standard of due process for government to apply as if violent monopolies were acceptable is counter-productive. We should instead learn to resolve conflicting preferences for procedural due process among ourselves, and to give weight to opinions according to the probity of the processes used to reach them. To grasp voluntary due process, we must turn conventional notions of due process inside-out, from the viewpoint of the individual sovereign.

We cannot prove that voluntary justice is achievable by assuming participants who practice it will be just. Selfishness will always tempt away from righteousness and people will hold conflicting concepts of what justice is. Under those inevitable conditions, it is up to the community to involve itself in defining and evolving due process as part of each person's ordinary diligence in their social affairs. We will achieve more just processes by weighing each opinion about any member's claim or defense based on the process used to derive the opinion. If the process is unfair or injudicious, we should regard any related opinions with suspicion.

Let's start by considering traditional views on due process. U.S. Federal Judge Henry Friendly once provided a list of procedural due process elements: an unbiased tribunal; a notice of proposed action and grounds asserted for it; an opportunity to present reasons the proposed action should not be taken; the right to present evidence, including the right to call witnesses, to know opposing evidence, and to cross-examine opposing witnesses; the right to a decision based exclusively on the evidence presented; an opportunity to be represented by counsel; a record of the evidence, and written findings of fact and reasons for the decision, prepared by the tribunal; a right of appeal; and at least for criminal trials, a right of public attendance.[17]

Those who place trust in state sovereignty assume that a state monopoly can provide the first item in the list: neutrality, through democratic process or other basis for authority. Statists busy themselves with identifying and debating the factors that procedural due process entails while downplaying the problem of using state monopolies to administer justice. We can conceive of other items to add to due process elements and debate their optimal forms. We might add elements such as a right to a jury trial (helpful for decentralizing judicial power), a statement of law, a convenient forum, and a source of law independent of the tribunal to our list of

---

[17] Henry J. Friendly, "Some Kind of Hearing," 123 U. Pa. L Rev. 1267, 1310-11 (1975).

desirables. However long or detailed our list becomes, in actual practice each item can be tainted beyond repair by bias in the tribunal. If the tribunal is biased, all other factors become as props in a due process theater for disguising injustice.

But if the tribunal is unbiased, wise, and seeking justice, we can trust it to adopt whatever due process tools are fair and appropriate for the case at hand. In the hands of a competent and unbiased neutral, lists of due process factors describe a flexible toolset for quality control. The best tools in the toolset may vary from case to case, depending on the preferences of the parties. Neutrals need impose no requirements on due process beyond the framework of the Three Promises. That framework creates consensus around a set of basic requirements for voluntary due process: first, that the parties' expressed their social promises to each other (e.g., by publishing in a public registry) before the dispute arose; second, no one can demand performance of an obligation greater than another has promised, or greater than they have promised to others. These principles are subject to a condition: when the parties cannot resolve their dispute without help, just resolution requires an unbiased neutral competent to apply their social promises and determine what the evidence shows. Just process unfolds from the skill of the neutral and the social promises of the parties.

Each social promise about due process informs others what the promisor will accept as just if exercised against her. Being sovereign over herself alone, she cannot dictate to others what process they must follow when prosecuting a claim against her, or what process they must accept when she is the claimant. It is up to the claimant to use a process acceptable to the defendant.

Suppose you are a claimant. How do you proceed? Follow the Third Promise and be no hypocrite. Use the process the defendant has promised or agreed to accept. If the defendant has not promised to accept a certain process, then you must agree with her regarding the process you will use. In negotiating, you will feel pressure to follow your own promise if more rigorous for you. When you can agree with the defendant regarding the choice of neutral, the neutral can assist you and the other side to agree on a process. If you cannot agree with your opponent on a process, your dispute will fester without honorable resolution, impacting your reputation.

Sometimes defendants or claimants prefer festering to honorable resolution. When they make this terrible choice, it is not without reason. One of them fears that the results of honorable resolution will be worse than indefinite festering of a claim. To make that equation balance, either the claim is insignificant, or the stakes are high. If the claim is insignificant due process serves no one's interests, or if both parties prefer to avoid process, then the claimant will not raise the claim. If the stakes are high, the party that desires honorable process will push the costs of festering higher and of settling lower, to tip the balance towards resolution. Often that party will be the claimant desiring restitution. If the defendant will not agree to take part in reasonable process, the community will have good reason to conclude that the defendant fears fair judgment. Sometimes the claim will be spurious, and it will be the defendant who desires process to clear the cloud on her reputation. When the claimant refuses reasonable process, all can conclude that the claim is false. When refusals of process persist in a durable register, the consequences for the refuser's reputation and the claim itself will not fade. Due process will happen when reputation matters.

Who pays for process costs? Justice involves restitution although not always in monetary form. By the principle of restitution, the loser should pay the process costs. Winning claimants cannot have their losses restored in full unless someone else pays their costs. Winning defendants should not have to pay the cost of the claimants' error. Restitution is important but is not the only consideration.

At root, responsibility for process costs is a matter for agreement between claimants and defendants like any other aspect of due process. Parties may split costs as a hedging strategy, or to ensure that the neutral has no incentive to decide against the party best able to pay. Claimants may sometimes be willing to pay for process to entice the defendant into accepting process. Wealthy defendants might pay for process when faced with claims from poor claimants, to show magnanimity or to provide for adequate process when the opponent is poor. The wealthy have more to lose from festering claims or inadequate process. There are plenty of reasons to deviate from "loser pays." Self-sovereigns may choose and promise alternatives for funding process costs as in all other social matters.

Options for promising to follow due process include heavy obligations, light obligations or no obligations. Recall you can obligate only yourself. You may need to honor your heavy promises when bringing or defending against claims. A heavy promise strategy entails a risk of high settlement process costs. Others will read your heavy process promises as a signal you prefer to avoid formal settlement process and may engage with you in riskier ways. You never know whether riskier engagement will be to your benefit or detriment. Either outcome is possible. Promising light obligations informs others of your preference for formal settlement processes. Those who bring claims against you know the process will not be expensive if their process obligations do not exceed yours. Making no due process promises preserves your flexibility and hides your preferences from others. Silence on due process may become a popular choice. Neutrals will become experts on due process and offer menus of process options suitable for different cases. Whatever the parties' due process promises, once the market for neutral services becomes established the parties will often agree on a neutral and a process as a package deal.

What makes process obligations "heavier" or "lighter"? In a word, cost. Three neutrals are about three times more expensive than one. Proof beyond a reasonable doubt is more protective than preponderance of the evidence, and more expensive to prove. Liberal rights to pre-trial discovery can drive up everyone's costs. The basic approach of adding up and comparing the total economic costs of different due process rules has an appealing simplicity that may encourage its use to compare process rules. But which process will cost more may sometimes be unclear. Suppose Jillian promises to accept nothing less than three neutrals, all of whom must be unpaid volunteers. Henry promises to accept only one neutral and is silent regarding payment. A neutral might reason that one neutral is less burdensome because Henry promises nothing regarding payment. Supposing the second rule requires a minimum payment to the neutral, the answer is less clear.

Whatever the finer points, the path to voluntary due process boils down to enabling negotiations over process between sovereigns with a motivation to agree and equal self-sovereign power. If a community of self-sovereigns fails to produce these earnest and fair negotiations between its members, it cannot achieve just society.

Due Process and The Blockchain

Blockchain is a form of secure distributed public ledger. Truth about blockchain as a tool for due process is true of other public ledger forms. Construction of blockchain registers is controlled by a software application, which programmers encode to operate as desired. The controlling application is open source and licensed under a general public license, so no single entity can control information content in the register. Operation of the blockchain application for social promise community will include at least two ledgers.

One ledger will contain social promises and other statements signed by a single user. You might call it a Promise Ledger or Single-Party Ledger. The Promise Ledger for each user contains information under the control of a single user, in some ways like a social media page on which only one user may post. The application for writing and accessing the Promise Ledger may include features encouraging users to economize and submit high-quality information relevant to the ledger's social purpose. The Promise Ledger may avoid recording crypto-currency transactions, to avoid state regulation.

Another ledger will contain entries reflecting on content in the Promise Ledger, signed by multiple users (e.g., two or more). You might call it a Reputation Ledger or Multi-Party Ledger. Two or more users of the Promise Ledger must sign every entry in the Reputation Ledger, or the application controlling the Reputation Ledger will not add the entry. Disputants and neutrals will use the Reputation Ledger to make records of voluntary due process. Some records will be signed by three or more parties: at least two disputants and one neutral. Other records will be signed by only two people, which could be two parties and no neutral, or a claimant and a neutral.

When the parties cooperate and reach a resolution together, all may sign a record in the Reputation Ledger memorializing their agreement and satisfaction of obligations. This multi-party record can offer powerful evidence of cooperation and agreeableness and is useful to discourage any disputant from reneging. Where the parties have agreed to use a neutral, it's still up to them to decide whether to put the neutral opinion in the Reputation Ledger. In some cases, the disputants will record no more a note of agreement and satisfaction in the Reputation Ledger without a record indicating a dispute. Few will want a reputation as a frequent defendant or claimant.

The possibility of settling a dispute without creating a record creates an incentive for parties to agree on due process. When the defendant refuses to cooperate, the claimant can hire a neutral to evaluate the claim and create a record in the Reputation Ledger. A record signed by a claimant and a neutral will have the weight of its signers behind it. Except in cases with no defendant,[18] this weight will fall on the self sovereign who shows contempt for due process. Defendants who refuse due process without good reason will pay a heavy cost in reputation, if the claimant hires a respected neutral to opine against them. Records in the ledgers are permanent. Besides settling on the claimant's terms, the defendant's only recourse for mitigating a ledger record is to hire their own neutral to write an opposing opinion. Parties can conduct litigation in the Reputation Ledger by recording volleys of neutral opinions. Such volleys will be expensive and harmful to the reputations of both parties. It is better for both to agree on a process and neutral who might enable a quiet settlement.

Details of the Promise Ledger and Reputation Ledger are beyond the scope of this edition.[19] Well-constructed ledgers will create incentives for promise community members to engage in due process, using mechanisms as explained above.

Ensuring Quality

Voluntary due process occurs by agreement but is not infallible. One or both parties may believe the neutral made a

---

[18] See "Unopposed Claims" in Chapter 10.
[19] See "Infrastructure Design" in Chapter 12 for further discussion of blockchain and other ledgers.

mistake or is biased. Aggrieved parties can register their arguments and evidence that an error has occurred, putting others on notice of a controversy. They can rehear the case or portions of it and agree on a different neutral. Rehearings should be unnecessary in most cases. Still, when the stakes outweigh the costs of further process, the losing party will want a do-over. For greater social benefit, delays in enforcement and overturning of neutral opinions shouldn't happen except to avoid irreparable injustice. The injustice should outweigh the costs of process to correct the error. Where the risk of error and irreparable injustice is low, challenges to neutral opinions delay and increase cost for no good reason. Better approaches avoid error, inefficiency and delay. Free choice by the parties of their original neutral is the best tool for achieving efficient and accurate justice. We'll examine reasons below.

Quality by Choice

Successful neutrals provide opinions followed by the people who matter. "The people who matter" vary depending on the claim and the parties. In cases exposing deliberate malfeasance, everybody matters because the punishment is the general stain on reputation. In civil disagreements, those who matter have power to carry out the neutral's remedies, to penalize misconduct, or to shun. With self-sovereigns, each neutral's authority derives from her power to persuade. When neutrals can compel none, persuasion becomes a greater and more judicious authority than any power imposed by the barrel of a gun. Voluntary justice grows powerful by enabling choice between independent neutrals.

This hope can be hard to believe. We are all too familiar with the alliances between territorial monopolies of police power and monopolies of judicial power known as "government." Government-appointed enforcers obey no judicial edicts except those of government-appointed judges. The ubiquity of government by states beckons us to believe that alliances between courts and enforcers are inevitable. Competition in exercising power breeds quests to seize monopoly power and reap unearned privileges. Are polycentric conflict resolution systems doomed to devolve into judicial monopolies, in which only one law capable of rendering enforceable judgments exists? Not if people insist on self sovereignty. In a self-sovereign society, forces preventing monopolization arise from innumerable inter-sovereign relationships. All self-sovereigns hold the three civil powers: legislative, judicial, and enforcement in equal measure, correlating to the power and freedom to live by one's own social promises, the duty to hold yourself and others to the same neutral standard, and the power to act honorably in exigent circumstances. These powers have no honorable force unless subject to the scrutiny of all affected by them.

Consider the benefits of possessing voluntary "judicial" power when acting as a neutral. When powerful enforcers will enforce your opinion, you gain an economic benefit. You can better attract clients, who will bid for access to your neutral services and respected opinions. Claimants can avoid the cost of persuading enforcers by hiring you. Defendants can likewise avoid the cost of error. The higher the stakes, the more you are worth. Great wealth in dispute will hire expensive but competent professional neutrals. Volunteers and interns will hear minor disagreements. Most cases will fall somewhere between the extremes. The virtual neighborhood will supply a neutral of desired quality for every pair who seek to resolve their dispute with self-sovereign honor. Using modern technology, self-sovereigns can extend the virtual neighborhood to the world.

Neutral service providers hold no coercive advantages over their competitors. They can force nobody to hire them. Their only advantage is a better reputation, which all must earn on their own. The earn their good reputations by performing high quality services (e.g., prompt, courteous, and accurate) and by issuing high quality opinions without cause for malpractice or negligent enforcement claims. A neutral may seek certification or higher rankings from various consumer rating or certifying organizations. The certifying agencies must grow and protect their own reputations by not certifying or ranking without good reason.

A neutral forum with a reputation for poor quality opinions will have a hard time earning respect. Enforcers will fear liability arising from negligent enforcement of defective opinions. Diligent enforcers will examine opinions of a neutral who lacks a proven reputation before enforcing. The extra examination will raise process costs and sometimes make the opinion unenforceable.

Under their own social promises, neutrals can be liable for issuing incompetent or biased opinions. Law enforcers can be liable for enforcing opinions they knew or should have known were of poor quality. Prudent enforcers will refuse to enforce inferior opinions. Parties may wish to self-enforce shoddy opinions issued by sham neutrals under their own influence. But absent fraud, their opponents won't agree to use a biased neutral. Unless both parties agree on the neutral, due process and justification for enforcement do not exist. If one party is tricked into agreeing to a biased neutral, the other risks liability for enforcement of a corrupt opinion and for subverting due process.

Free choice will make sure that neutral opinions have the best possible quality for the cost incurred. The society of sovereigns need only keep the right to perform neutral services open to all fellow sovereigns and compel none to submit to any neutral.

Authority and Hierarchy

The practical effect of an opinion depends on its author's reputation. Successful neutrals will be famous for their persuasive powers. Opinions of neutrals having unknown or poor reputations will have little weight. Justice between self-sovereigns is both democratic and individualistic. It is democratic because the weight of any neutral opinion or partisan argument about it depends on popular assessment. It is individualistic because every self-sovereign may ignore the reputational stain of neutral opinions as they please. No court of neutrals has ultimate authority or power to compel, except by persuasive opinions. No law requires enforcement agencies to enforce defective opinions or excuses them from doing so. Contrast this to any justice system imposed by the state. A monopoly court's reputation for persuasiveness doesn't matter in enforceability of judgments. Its reputation for holding monopoly power is all that matters.

In common law systems recognizing binding judicial precedent, appeals are the primary mechanism for reversals of judgments. Litigants appeal to higher authorities in a judicial hierarchy. Hierarchical appeals courts exist to benefit the judicial system, and not to benefit litigants. Appeal functions to maintain consistency between rulings of lower courts and to keep lower courts in check. The threat of being overruled on appeal prevents renegade courts from ruling contrary to the will of the highest court. Correcting injustice and satisfying litigants are secondary purposes from the court system's perspective. With their monopoly on judicial services, statist courts have less reason to care about whether the parties perceive the system as just and effective. Instead, the politically appointed court must concern itself with avoiding offense to those holding power over it. If displeased, powerful players might threaten funding for the court, instigate impeachment proceedings against judges, fund the political campaigns of competing judges, or take other political action.

The motivation and operation of appeal is different in social promising. Judicial precedent and hierarchies of judicial power do not exist. The only worthwhile appeal is to a neutral of equal or greater reputation. Appeal to a higher court to maintain consistency between neutrals or resolve ambiguities in law is unnecessary.

Social promising fills the gap left by losing judicial precedent, by empowering all to define their own social promises. If ambiguities with real consequences persist in social promises, it will be because the people prefer the ambiguity to greater clarity. If people want more specificity, they may make more specific promises. Each person can change their own vague or imprecise social promises as neutrals and commentators point out problems with older practices. Upgrades to social promises may resemble software upgrades in today's world, but with less pressure on users to upgrade and no single programmer in charge. Each member "owns" their own social promises in the public domain.

Lack of binding judicial precedent doesn't mean there can't be influence, and reputation, and persuasive precedents. Influence without compulsion will thrive and illuminate fair conflict resolution in voluntary society. The only authority will be what is most reasonable, durable, and true, in the neutrals' treatments of social obligations the disputants have promised, and the facts of the conflicts as revealed through due process.

Enforcement Liability

Those facing enforcement action can defend by proving the underlying opinion is defective to anyone who would enforce it. Defendants can petition enforcers to stay their enforcement actions until a worthy neutral can confirm its merits. They might file a malpractice claim against the neutral who rendered the opinion. A malpractice claim puts would-be enforcers on notice of a dispute over the opinion. Reputable enforcers will wait to see how the challenge plays out before risking malpractice liability for negligent enforcement of a defective opinion. Even when the claimant is enforcing an opinion herself, she will feel the same pressure as a hired gun. Placing the enforcer on notice of a disputed opinion will create settlement pressure like that created by appeal. The ability to attack opinions will also create pressure for higher-quality opinions in the first place, because parties to bona fide disputes share an interest in finality. Those seeking to delay or subvert justice might seek opinions of poor quality. Liability for enforcing unjust opinions is an effective check against fraud or incompetence by neutrals, and one lacking under statist systems.

Can neutrals place themselves beyond reach of malpractice claims, by crafting limited social promises? Yes, but who would hire them? Without agreement of the parties to the selected neutral no just process exists. Enforcers are in a different position. One party hires the enforcer, who owes loyalty to their employer. Some enforcers may adopt a reckless style and make themselves judgment proof. They might protect themselves by living without property others can seize while wearing complaints about overzealous enforcement like a badge of honor. Their victims can brings claims against them, but the enforcers have little or nothing to lose.

A more extreme style of enforcer makes no social promises at all, living beyond the reach of voluntary due process. Non-promisor enforcers care nothing about neutral opinions, working only for compensation and plunder. These enforcers are of the worse kind. Hiring them will damage their employers' reputations.

A victim of reckless or non-promisor enforcers might lodge a complaint against the one who hired the evildoers. A complaint over hiring agents won't stick unless the employer made a social promise to be responsible for her agents. Respectable self-sovereigns will take this responsibility. To do otherwise would be to advertise themselves as miscreants. Vengeful victims will punish miscreants by the same evil instruments the miscreants fail to disavow. The instrument here is action through evil agents for which the actors escape responsibility. Members might prevent other abuses of process using similar deterrents.

If those accused won't agree to due process and won't take responsibility for proven abuses, their accusers can exploit those abuses in revenge. This statement is unbelievable enough to deserve an example: Lorna and Alexa are close friends and novice criminals. Lorna is a dealer in antiquities and Alexa is a respected neutral. Lorna sells a fake Dong Son drum to Reuben and colludes with Alexa to hide the fraud. She convinces Rueben that the supposedly 2700-year-old drum is the oldest and most significant example of its kind, when it is a fake made in a smoggy part of China about five years prior. Reuben pays a ton of money for the drum — five whole Bitcoins — so when Reuben discovers the lie, he is pissed. He brings a claim against Lorna. The two agree on Alexa as neutral while keeping Reuben ignorant of Alexa's relationship and collusion with Lorna to defraud him. Alexa hears the case and issues her respectable opinion: Reuben has not proven key facts to convict Lorna. This opinion is hogwash, but Alexa conceals her opinion's rottenness well. So the two cheat Reuben of his Bitcoins.

A while later Reuben sees Lorna and Alexa indoor parachuting together in a tornado of high-denomination bank notes and puts 2 and 2 together. He hires Jeremy, a private investigator with connections in the Mossad. Jeremy uncovers the fraud. When Reuben prepares to bring a claim over it, he discovers that Lorna and Alexa renounced all their social promises before they plotted to defraud anyone. Reuben is the victim of his own lack of due care. Will Reuben get his revenge by staging an elaborate plot with Jeremy to reverse the fraudulent justice he had suffered? Not on these facts! If Reuben wants his Bitcoins back, he'll go after them any way he can. If he can borrow espionage tools and muscle from Jeremy, he'll use them. Lorna and Alexa are non-promisors! No reason to hold back. He might go after them with torches and pitchforks. Since they married each other and went to work for the

California Highway Patrol, maybe he'll sue them in state court instead.

Few will suffer unbridled aggression, so few become non-promisors. Most will make at least basic promises like no fraud. That simple promise would have been enough for a claim against Lorna and Alexa. That is how most abuse of process claims will end, in front of a neutral, with restitution paid and much regretted loss of reputation. Avenging abuse of process by abuse-in-kind has a pleasing symmetry to it but is almost as impractical as all those extra dimensions of string theory.

Malpractice

Dissatisfied parties are not without options for redress of error by a chosen neutral. One option is to bring a claim against the neutral for malpractice. Most professional neutrals will respond to market pressure and make social promises permitting such claims. Requirements for proving malpractice might vary, but with free and open competition between settlement service providers, requirements cannot be onerous. Reasonable promises might require the claimant to prove a failure of the neutral to follow a professional standard of care, and consequential damages. The market would determine such requirements as with all other rules in social promise community.

Will malpractice liability become severe enough to choke off the market for settlement services? Today, litigation creates winners and losers. At its conclusion, most times at least one party feels dissatisfied. Sometimes all the parties are unhappy, angry at the lawyers and judges involved, and ready to lash out. If neutrals do not have immunity from malpractice, what prevents ordinary dissatisfaction from generating malpractice claims in almost every case? This question is empirical. Actual outcomes will vary based on many factors, for example, the culture in which neutral settlement occurs. Parties using social promises will have more satisfactory experiences than under state laws, for reasons outlined below. Malpractice claims will be the exception, not the rule.

First, by the Third Promise no self-sovereign can enforce any obligation they themselves have not promised to others. Defendants of valid claims will have promised the obligation or a greater obligation; nobody is coerced to make undesirable promises. Neither the defendant nor the claimant will believe the obligation in dispute is unfair. They will have no reason to feel aggrieved about being asked to keep their own promises.

Second, neutrals are not immune from malpractice liability. Immunity is an affirmative defense, limited or unavailable under the Third Promise. Competition with other neutrals would lessen restrictions on malpractice liability made by limiting positive promises. Also, parties can make their social promises around fair process subject to a condition that the neutral accept malpractice liability. Whatever the parties' social promises, successful neutrals will take responsibility for the quality of their services or lose business. They will take pains to satisfy all parties as much as possible. If it became necessary to rule against a party in the interests of justice, the neutral will be more likely to explain to the injured party why the ruling was necessary and gain at least grudging acceptance.

Third, neutrals will be more active in promoting settlements than when they are immune from malpractice. Malpractice liability is less likely to arise, and clients are happier, when the neutral can get both sides to agree on a compromise.

Fourth, if malpractice became a large systematic problem for all neutrals, neutrals as a group will adjust their social promises. They would make social promises with more restricted obligations around malpractice issues. The market would adjust to provide neutrals with less exposure to malpractice claims.

Fifth, neutrals will form associations for promoting standards and reducing malpractice risks they face as a group.

Sixth, competition for customers will increase the quality of services, as in every free market. When neutrals satisfy their customers, their customers will not bring claims against them.

Seventh, suing a neutral for malpractice costs time and money, and might fail. Therefore, dissatisfied parties will avoid making malpractice claims where the risk of loss exceeds the amount at stake.

Malpractice will rarely arise in a free market of self-sovereign neutrals. Instead, risk of potential malpractice claims will motivate professional neutrals to mitigate that risk by increasing customer satisfaction.

Responsibility for Cost

Could a losing litigant forestall enforcement by challenging every opinion against him? In theory, if the promises of parties allow. But customs such as "loser pays" and reputation scoring make unreasonable intransigence self-defeating. Each later loss diminishes the chances of eventual success while increasing costs. Neutrals with good reputations become reluctant to accept cases decided by another of good reputation. Finality of neutrals' opinions will affect their reputations. After one or two prior opinions exist, every later neutral has a reason to believe their opinion will not be final, too. Opinions by neutrals of solid reputation will usually stand. Later opinions by lesser neutrals will seldom if ever outweigh those of more reputable neutrals.

If risk of endless litigation becomes high despite the countervailing factors noted above, members can adjust their social promises around due process to reduce the risk. For example, a member might promise to submit to due process for no more than a certain number (e.g., 1, 2 or 3) of sequential opinions. When either party has made such a promise, to preserve honor neither party need cooperate with a neutral hearing after reaching the specified number of opinions.

Where new evidence of innocence renders an opinion invalid, malpractice will seldom give right relief. Instead, the relief lies in a retrial of the original claim, given the new evidence. Any who asserted an opinion made unjust by new evidence will be liable for the harm caused. Most people will promise to not enforce false claims out of self-interest and social pressure. A promise to not defraud others is enough to create liability for one asserting a false claim. Where the veracity of exculpatory evidence is in doubt, the claimant and defendant can agree on a rehearing.

A losing defendant seeking to weasel out of an opinion might instead consider finding a sleazy, judgment-proof neutral to hold the original neutral guilty of malpractice. A difficulty with this approach is the short supply of neutrals who are both sleazy and judgment-proof enough to provide an unjust opinion, while being credible enough to have weight. In most cases, the sleazy malpractice opinion would have little weight. Being given little credit by anyone, it would not prevent the original opinion from being enforced against the losing defendant.

Voluntary Right of Appeal

Only appeal has the power to correct errors in opinions that the opinion's author refuses to acknowledge. What higher power can correct such errors? Among self-sovereigns, without new evidence only one with a reputation greater than the opinion's authors can outweigh the original opinion. The best neutrals will work on appeals, which should cost more than first opinions per unit of labor involved.

To reduce risk of malpractice liability, groups of neutrals may offer appeal and other quality control measures as part of their services. Those hiring such groups might agree that any opinion of a chosen neutral is not final until the parties waive or complete all appeals. Parties might bring their business to service providers offering appeal to reduce the risk of poor quality, unenforceable opinions. Besides appeals to a higher power, quality control measures may include, for example, services such as random audits of juror performance, quality ratings, customer service ratings, use of expert systems and other artificial intelligence, and other measures. Competing service providers will develop innovative and cost-effective ways to resolve disputes over the quality of their opinions, if only to enhance their own reputations as neutral, fair and competent neutrals.

Might claimants choose forums offering no appeal or other quality control? They might, to reduce expenses. Parties will select more reputable, comprehensive neutral services for important cases, and cheaper, less comprehensive services for less important cases. Statist systems offer similar options to the claimant, in different general and limited (e.g., small claims) courts. Often, limited courts have corresponding limited or no right of appeal, even in statist systems.

Instead of agreeing to a process that includes appeal, people may make social promises to submit to appeal after a first opinion. Such promises will only apply when both parties have made them. None cannot hold another to an obligation without promising the same obligation themselves. Members who value appeal can give their business to like-minded people. They will agree with strangers by publishing their social promises. Whether self-sovereign society will make much use of appeal is an empirical question.

A market free to its deepest bones will dispute opinions of fitting quality. Using the tools of self-sovereignty, social promises, competition, free choice, reputation, responsibility for costs, and malpractice liability together (all are necessary), quality will be suitable in almost every case. Free people will sometimes participate in activities like rehearings, stays of enforcement, and malpractice claims in pursuit of greater justice. Quality depends on keeping markets for dispute resolution free of influence from any collective with the power to make laws or to shield members, neutrals and enforcers from consequences of their evil or incompetent conduct.

Enforcement

Reputation the Foundation

"Enforcement" can have different meanings. In social promise community, enforcement includes revealing wrongs proved by due process, and empowering all to act on their knowledge as they believe honorable. Some prefer quiet avoidance, others vocal shaming of wrongdoers; a few recognize condemnation as an opportunity for win-win redemptions. Enforcement can include other things. If social conditions allow, enforcement might include more assertive remedies, like repossessing stolen property, attaching a lien, taking an eye for an eye, or a tooth for a tooth. All enforcement involves an attack on a person or deprivation of property justified by prior due process. These attacks diminish the convicted, by diminishing their reputation, their health or freedom, or their property against their will. Enforcement involves such attacks but is subject to limits. The just attacker refrains from acting beyond what prior due process confirms. Limiting themselves by due process, attackers become enforcers.

Enforcement has two measures: its effectiveness and its justice. These two measures intertwine. Enforcement is effective when it accomplishes its purpose. If the purpose is unjust, so is the enforcement. Unjust effects will likewise taint a just purpose. What purposes are just? Between equals, only one penalty is just: payment of restitution. Deterrence in the sense of executing a penalty harsher than restitution to set an example for others is brutalizing a victim to make others afraid. It is terrorism.

We might justify punishment as needed for breaking evil wills. Breaking wills violates self-sovereignty, which entitles all to their wills be they good or evil, and lays responsibility for consequences of evil on the wrong doer. Those who make no supportive obligations to others will lack rights afforded by obligations of others. They become prone to punishments that violate no party's social promises. But even if we agree restitution is the only remedy consistent with self-sovereignty, difficult issues remain. What is the right remedy for murder and other losses without price? What enhanced punishments should we apply to malicious harms? The issues are more than these.

Those in voluntary society are lucky. They need not debate one another about something that cannot exist: a perfect measure of justice for every harm. All they must do is pronounce the measures each will accept as just penalties, should they harm others. The effect of their individual promises must not rest on any agency with a monopoly on enforcement powers. It must rest instead on the individual honor of each sovereign, exercised by the keeping of their promises. Their police are self-organizing autonomous sovereigns, restrained from forming monopolies by their own promises, without which no one will hire them. No monopoly grants them immunity for unjust acts. Each will be liable for their individual actions and judged by their individual promises. They will avoid doing things that others can bring claims against them for. They cannot be non-promisors without earning a non-promisor's reputation, and with that comes distrust and risk of unbridled aggression.

A community of free enforcers will develop effective techniques with minimal risk of blowback. Communities of voluntarists will start with enforcement by reputation only, to avoid provoking the powers-that-be. Voluntary enforcement power is not a switch that society can flip at will. It is an emergent phenomenon that develops as voluntary community increases in size and social power. Enforcement without monopoly and coercion needs a valued community of persons to be effective. Unless members value their community and their reputations within it, voluntary enforcement is meaningless. When self-sovereigns fail to create a community offering neutral due process in which all fear loss of reputation for breaking their social promises, they lose their sovereignty. They submit to rule by collective police forces vying for monopoly power.

Value is a flexible proposition, resting on intangible scales in the minds of self-sovereigns. People value community for many reasons. At root, communities build value by supporting their members. Build they must, to enlarge the domain where self-sovereign order holds sway. Where community satisfies the value scales of its members, promise-breaking has consequences. Promise-breaking is hypocrisy: promising one thing and doing another. Earning a reputation as a hypocrite creates limits on future possibilities. Known hypocrites lose the privilege of trust from other community members. Deprivation of reputation will sting if members value their honorable status in the community.

Without effective enforcement, voluntary order has no power. Valued community is a precondition to operation of social promising, just as opposing teams, a ball, and a playing field are preconditions for football. Players need a reason to play. Once they will play, they need other supports to play their game. For Three-Promise reputation games, these supports include an educated public able to make durable and convenient records of their social promises, as in the social promise registries. Other necessary supports include reliable personal identities, verifiable feedback, neutral due process for settling disputes, and a possibility of enforcement. Depending on the nuanced character of the game we want, we can add other supports, and reconfigure a bit. The basics will remain. Reputation must matter, and contempt of voluntary due process must have consequences. For example, neutrals might make a permanent record of contempt in a record associated with each offender. Those who show contempt for fair process cannot remove the stain without satisfying the underlying neutral opinion or proving its error.

Don't confuse popularity with reputation. We are familiar with rating systems for service providers, sellers and buyers in online bazaars, and comments on social media. Such ratings have their uses but are measures of popularity and whim. If we can't confirm popularity scores by neutral due process, the scores measure something other than trustworthiness. To the extent a system measures people for conduct that does not violate their own social promises, it measures nothing pertinent to self-rule. Even the term "reputation" fails to convey a sense of a record of moral conduct, testable by neutral due process, by the measure of each's social promises. That record differs from anything you have seen before. We call it "reputation" for lack of a better word. "Testable self-determined moral profile" is more descriptive, but unwieldy. We'll stick with "reputation" in this Guidebook, understood as a self-determined moral profile subject to proof through neutral due process in a community of social promisors.

Enforcement unsupported by a valid opinion of an unbiased neutral makes the enforcer liable to a victim. She puts herself at risk of a claim for damages and loss of reputation. But enforcing while complying with a respected neutral opinion enhances her reputation and protects her from liability. If the enforcer obeys the neutral opinion, liability belongs first to the neutral. If the enforcer and the neutral collude to do evil, then liability belongs to both. Enforcers looking to avoid unnecessary risks will not enforce the opinions of untrusted neutrals. They will be careful to avoid force beyond the extent permissible by the social promises. For example, if the social promises of the parties involved permit no death penalty, the enforcer may not kill nor would any valid opinion allow an execution.

Suppose a member hires a non-promisor to enforce a valid neutral opinion. Is the member liable? Only if the non-promisor acts outside the opinion. The non-promisor is the least protected person in this scenario. Social promises protect all the others. Suppose Oscar the non-promisor works for the municipal police force. He's not into the social promise thing, but some of his buddies moonlight as bounty hunters for self-sovereigns. It's not dangerous work. Attracted by the pay, he answers an ad by Mona to recover stolen property from Roger, a rogue bounty hunter. Roger like most bounty hunters is a social promisor who lives by the "Bounty Hunters' Oath." The Oath makes an offense against one into cause for revenge by all, within limits afforded by the offender's social promises.

A respected neutral has convicted Roger of failing to share proceeds with Mona. The neutral opinion forbids violence, but being untrained and ignorant, Oscar confronts Roger and breaks his nose. Lacking any social promises, Oscar has no protection within voluntary society against revenge by Roger's fellow bounty hunters. Oscar had better hope that his status in the municipal police force will protect him. Meanwhile, depending on Mona's social promises, Roger might have recourse against her for Oscar's out-of-bounds actions.

In the early days of self-sovereign order, promisors might hire non-promisors to enforce valid neutral opinions. Suppose a claimant wins an opinion allowing a lien, but the defendant lives in a place where a state government claims a monopoly on the power to place liens. The defendant refuses to pay the money the opinion proves owed, does not try to overturn the opinion, and displays no concern about loss of reputation from these acts. The neutral who hears the case is a state-licensed arbitrator. She arranges her opinion to follow state requirements for an arbitral award. The claimant registers the award and gets a state-enforceable judgment. She enforces the judgment by recording a lien against real property held by the defendant. The claimant is liable only if recording the lien under state power violates her own social promises.

Once the market provides skilled enforcers, most claimants will hire professional enforcement help from fellow society members. A professional enforcer will be more familiar with how enforcement for social promises work and better prepared to defend against malpractice claims. Hiring a society member to handle the enforcement will shield the claimant from most enforcement liability, except for negligent hiring of an incompetent enforcer.

Offenders among others will fund professional enforcement by social promisors. Most offenses will carry a monetary penalty aimed at restitution. Whatever the form of penalty, convicted offenders should pay reasonable costs of getting and enforcing a neutral opinion, or both parties should share costs in proportion to fault. Claimants and defendants will each bear risk of loss, and so both will avoid using process as a weapon for wearing down the opposition. Neutrals may measure reasonable costs by market prices for cases of the type at hand. They might opine offenders should pay for reasonable costs of enforcers, neutrals, advocates and counsellors needed by claimants. Reasonable costs will be less than in monopoly systems. No guilds will restrict service providers from entering the market. Parties will by their social promises and agreements with their opponents settle on due process acceptable to both.

Social promising does not disadvantage the poor claimant. Claimants will sometimes bring claims against the poor despite slim chances of recovering damages. They will not fail to claim against the rich. A loser-pays open enforcement system creates incentives for vigorous enforcement against wealthy society members in proportion to the size of their offenses. Contingent fee arrangements will motivate competent advocates to prosecute claims against defendants able to pay damages. Voluntary enforcement advantages the poor defendant, because it eliminates involuntary subsidies (e.g., tax-funded prison systems) for law enforcement against the poor. Who can enforce an opinion against somebody with no money or property? To the extent true, it parallels civil remedies in any other justice system. The promise community forces no taxpayers to fund enforcement of costly criminal penalties against poor defendants. The prospect of conviction and loss of reputation is punishment enough for any wrongdoer rich or poor. Members value their memberships in the community, or they will not belong.

Opinions against impoverished society members will not be without value. A poor person unable to pay an opinion will suffer damage to their reputation. If the poor person values their reputation and desires to be a productive member of society, this creates a profit opportunity for any intermediary able to arrange an earn-out. Intermediaries able to supervise and rehabilitate convicts will replace prisons. The convicts will pay a percentage to their victims and another percentage to intermediaries until earning out their promised obligations. A poor member convicted of breaking their own promise has two options: agree to an earn-out or sacrifice her reputation. Reputation must have value to the defendant, or the debt will go unpaid. Reputation must matter, or social promises are unenforceable.

Sometimes convicts will despise their own reputations. This does not make social promise societies any less valid than other conflict resolution systems. Enforcement by collectives (e.g., security agencies or states) also depends on preconditions, such as non-corrupt and well-funded judicial and enforcement systems, for which no guarantees exist. Concentrated power must not succumb to corruption, to self-dealing by the powerful. Natural self-interest makes corruption of power inevitable. Enforcement based on supreme power can never attain purity.

Self-sovereign systems place responsibility on each person. Victims of malpractice will bring their claims against the individual neutrals and enforcers responsible for the defective opinion or its negligent enforcement. By the Third Promise, claimants will base their malpractice claims on the lesser of their own social promises or the social promises of individual neutrals and enforcers. There is no sovereign immunity. If such neutrals' or enforcers' social promises deny reasonable claims for malpractice, they have declared themselves unfit and will not receive business. Neither will collectives whose members include such unfit providers receive any business. When each member of a collective is accountable for her own social promises, the collective provides no shield for malpractice. The collective can instead offer resource and risk sharing for its members. Enforcement collectives will exist, and we will consider them in the next section.

To make social promises enforceable, the community must make reputation more important. We can magnify reputation with different measures and will suggest a few strategies later. For now, recognize the critical precursors for development of reputation-based enforcement systems. Effective enforcement needs communities with control over desired resources, and a robust record-keeping system tied to secure personal identities. Neither precursor is beyond reach. Private reputation and identity tracking systems are already commonplace in narrow contexts such as creditworthiness, online selling, and social groups. When developed and extended to general applicability, a reputation-based system will deter sociopathic conduct without the blunt instruments of imprisonment or threats of execution. The essence of ethical enforcement rests on a system for discovery and development of personal reputation within a community of strangers. Systems of social promises will serve this purpose.

Security Agencies

Security agencies enforce neutral opinions for others. The agencies can be loose and transient associations between nodes of a social network focusing on an enforcement task. Other possibilities include individuals, mutual aid societies, families or family businesses, and corporations. Agencies can come in any form. They all enforce claims for others.

Enforcers enforce neutral opinions. They can work for themselves or for others. When they work for others we call them agents, and when acting collectively, agencies. We could call them agents when they work for themselves because they act with intention to produce an effect. But we will call enforcers who work for themselves self-enforcers, to avoid confusion.

Enforcement is a hazardous occupation and most who engage in it will be trained professionals. Most enforcers will be agents. What prevents a class of professional enforcers from becoming predatory? In voluntary society, enforcers' social promises restrain them. They enjoy no state-granted immunities.

All security agents are individuals. Each is responsible for their own enforcement actions by the measure of their social promises. When agents work together, that doesn't change. They remain responsible for their own actions in the same way. Who takes responsibility for results of their collective efforts? The agents would not have acted if no one had hired them, and so their employers are responsible. But the agents are not immune from liability for their actions. Each must take responsibility for their own social promises. Agents can also take collective responsibility by agreement among themselves. They can divide responsibility as they please among themselves while accepting responsibility as a body and as individuals. Moral collectives exist to distribute responsibilities and rewards according to a scheme that all participants accept without coercion or fraud.

When people place themselves in a chain of action with intent to cause an effect, they are each responsible for the effect. All in the chain bear responsibility for their joint effect. Their liability is "joint and several" as a natural consequence of agency. The agents need not make special social promises to bear responsibility for hiring agents, or for acting as an agent. All they need promise is to take responsibility for harm they do, or that their actions cause. Then, whether hiring an agent or acting as one, they own their results.

Sly and evasive ones might disclaim any responsibility for the actions of others, even when agency exists. If so, they proclaim themselves dangerous. If they will take no responsibility for doing evil through an agent, then others may hire agents to do them evil. The Third Promise deprives these sly ones of honorable recourse against those who hire their attackers. Few will be so evasive.

Elected or appointed lawmakers, judges and police within states evade responsibility for harm they do within their lawful authority. State-appointed police are immune when carrying out orders of judges and enforcing laws made by legislators. Judges take no responsibility for the law and excuse themselves from personal responsibility for their judgments about it. Legislators shift responsibility to the voters who elect them. Individual voters and taxpayers are powerless, but as a class held responsible for what their police, judges and legislators do. Oppression is commonplace in states because no one holds the oppressors responsible. Nor can any hold them responsible when they follow their own laws. We can only strive to supersede them. State security is a burdensome behemoth despite which humanity has walked on the moon. We will replace it with higher orders of justice and visit the stars!

Minarchists reason that monopolization of police power is inevitable, and to plan for alternatives is futile. Enforcement requires coercive power, people organize collectives for greater power, and competition leads to a champion able to enforce a monopoly or oligarchy of enforcement power. Or so the argument goes. Belief in it leads to a preference for subjecting police powers to democratic process instead of permitting them to operate unchecked. But the need for effective force or for regulated force are not what monopolizes police power. In societies founded on monopolies over making and interpreting law, it's no wonder that police centralize their power, too.

Empirical evidence from the history of empires bolsters the minarchists' dismal opinions, but other outcomes are possible. When social promisors hold each responsible for their own actions and no court of judgment is compulsory, security agencies cannot conspire with neutrals and lawmakers for monopoly powers. Due process requires that all parties at stake consent to the neutral and process due, and that any rules applied comply with the social promises of the parties.

We can accept regulation of monopolies by democracy without denying democracy's moral purpose. At its limit, democracy empowers each citizen with equal sovereign power. Channeled through the social promises of equals, democracy holds every security agency responsible down to its individual members. No legislators exist except each sovereign citizen. No sovereign can assign responsibility for her social promises to another. None can bring a peer before a neutral, without the peer's consent. Neutrals must earn reputations for fairness and competence or fail for lack of clients. Enforcers must earn reputations of similar quality. This means acting within the limits of trustworthy neutral opinions and avoiding unjustified force or fraud.

Monopolies on enforcement cannot arise without exercising sovereign claims over territory that trump the self-sovereign rights of the territory's inhabitants. Property rights bear on the power of security agencies through sovereign claims over territory. When territorial monopolies seize property rights from rightful owners or impose property laws that disadvantage the destitute, they enable the rich to use markets as tools for oppression. Even if some wealthy people do not oppress others, capital rigs every market based on absolute property rights for owners and disadvantages the poor. This bias does not destroy the virtue of markets as efficient engines for satisfying consumer demands, nor can markets and gift exchanges exist without property rights. Ordinary property rights or lack thereof are not what concentrates unaccountable police power. Elevating territorial claims over self-sovereignty is the cause.

Such elevation at the scale of nations leads to one class imposing their laws on unwilling subjects, under territorial monopolies called states. State intervention cannot reconcile conflicting definitions of property or other obligations; its solutions are the root of the problem. Those who believe in one-size-fits-all definitions of private property or of public property can coexist in voluntary society, by setting up their own sub-communities in which all accept their definitions. They cannot impose their definitions on others without becoming non-promisors. Security agencies must observe these liberties like any other citizen. These agencies will prosper not by enforcing one law on all, but by being willing and able to enforce a broad variety of social promises while understanding how these promises interplay. Diversity will favor decentralization.

Those in voluntary society can neither require nor forbid property rights, except for forbidding any person from owning another without continuous consent. Social promising prevents inequities in property distribution from subverting justice, by empowering rich and poor to make and live by their own social promises. No entity holds lawmaking power, except the individual natural person. Neutral service providers who welcome clients with a range of differing social promises will enjoy a competitive advantage over those who restrict their services to ruling on a single set of social promises. It will be the same for security agencies.

Would-be monopolists cannot contain the breathtaking scope or infinite variety of these promises. Neutrals and security agencies will adapt to the unstoppable diversity or die. They will adapt by diversifying, becoming generalists able to apply fundamental principles to diverse combinations of social promises, and to provide creative resolutions. If cooperatives and collectives will exist and use social promises, they will owe their existence to economic efficiency at enforcing a diverse array of social promises determined by their customers. A community of neutrals and enforcers becomes this collective, but one as diverse and interdependent as the larger community it serves. None but the people will order society, by each ordering their own selves.

Social promise community separates enforcement from judicial powers. The separation exists by each claimant's demand for neutrality, without which no claimant can get an enforceable opinion. An enforcer who benefits by enforcing her own opinions cannot be neutral. Defendants will avoid her. The power to enforce poisons the neutrality of all opinions. Likewise, the power to judge corrupts enforcers. Separation must exist, or the scheme of order is unjust.

Statist legal monopolies bind the judicial and enforcement powers, by vesting responsibility for judging and for enforcement in the same institution: the state. They can provide no independent forum for challenging the neutrality of state judicial powers. Their judges monopolize the enforcers of their judgments while the legislators monopolize the judges. The more systematic the entanglement, the more likely it is to escape notice and lead to legitimized oppression. For example, legislators grant immunity to state prosecutors, judges and police from liability for enforcing their laws. In addition, the monopolies deprive their subjects of recourse to any independent forum in which to try charges against the state or its agents.

Absolute sovereignty over territory is the primary root of political monopolies. To wield the conquering power from which territorial sovereignty arises, collective organizations form and enact laws for others to follow. In any system that that grants law making power to collective entities, security agencies gain economic advantages from vertical integration. Free-lance lawmakers, neutrals and enforcers can't compete with the agencies of cooperating lawmakers, judges, police and jailers favored by the powers-that-be. At worst, those powers ban the freelancers. Defendants can no longer rely on a neutral hearing. They must defend against owners in courts controlled by politicians patronized by those same owners. Monopolies on enforcement arise in states because they could not otherwise exist. Territorial monopolies breed security monopolies.

Collectives whose members respect self-sovereign social promises won't force people to follow their rules. Social promise communities provide competitive advantages to neutrals capable of ruling on diverse social promises. These neutrals depend on their reputation for their livelihood. Disputants will avoid neutrals who produce opinions that only one security agency will enforce. Any enforcement agency that follows opinions of favored neutrals without question will fall under suspicion. By market selection, security agencies will become less dangerous to civil society and more effective at preventing and restoring harms caused by broken promises.

The Criminal

Where social promises govern, no bright line divides crimes from non-crimes. Good citizens and scoundrels exist along a continuous spectrum, in a multidimensional color space of moral shades. Location in the moral space can vary with time and place. None hold the privilege of distinguishing "criminals" from people who have offended in less heinous ways. Each member draws their own borders dividing offenders into classes of severity. No offense against the state exists because the voluntary society is stateless. None are privileged to define any "crimes against the people," that other members must accept.

There can be conduct that, once admitted or proved by due process, earns the doer widespread disfavor and condemnation. Those convicted of malicious evildoing after due process will be the "criminals" of social promise societies. Most will not live in physical prisons, but will be surrounded by walls of distrust, anger, and hatred. Some will work to redeem these convicted ones. Redemption for most will require a sincere display of contrition and good works. Criminals may redeem themselves with help from others, by paying just restitution to their victims. They cannot erase the stain of malice, but they can repudiate their evil deeds and express tangible remorse by seeking to repair the damage. A few will prefer a life of crime. Some will destroy themselves before finding a sustainable social role.

Voluntary society will not be easy on the worst criminals, but it will create few of the worst sort. The mutual acceptance that must accompany self-sovereign order will create spaces for people of different temperaments and interests. Even those with bizarre tastes will find respectable niches. Crimes of passion will still happen, but such criminals will find ways to atone for mistakes and earn back a measure of honor.

Breaches of self-sovereign order will earn criminal contempt from many. Hypocrites will cheat the system to gain a temporary advantage. They might, for example, break their social promises whenever convenient, while evading responsibility for the damage they cause. This sort will masquerade as a society member, without an inner commitment to fulfil inconvenient promises. They will ignore rulings of neutrals they have promised to accept, to avoid paying promised restitution. Or they will refuse to submit to available neutrals without good reason. The false promisor will not challenge the neutral for a reason based on the social promises and facts at play nor comply with the ruling to the best of his ability. Once earning a reputation as a false promisor, distrust of others will push this criminal type to the outskirts of voluntary society.

Another sort of criminal accepts and complies with valid rulings but stands convicted of conduct that impugns the person's character. The conduct may range from petty crimes to severe offenses. For some, one murder is enough to cast a shadow even if the criminal pays restitution. Less weighty malice may render the offender untrustworthy or repugnant if repeated.

Criminals of a third type will be those whose social promises are odious to most around them. They will keep their promises and will avoid being hypocrites but make (or fail to make) social promises so most in their community find them dangerous or reprehensible. These bold offenders will be the ones most likely to succeed by filling niches more respectable members will fear touching. They will be merchants of death, peddlers of coercion, the analog of the state and the organized mob.

In a robust and diverse social promise society, some will make promises that allow a lifestyle as opportunistic thieves, within specified limits. For example, transients' promises might permit non-violent taking of surplus food or clothing for bodily needs and camping in vacant spaces wherever reasonable under the circumstances. Some affluent persons may make such social promises as a fallback position as insurance against sudden unexpected penury. Promises that justify thievery beyond basic personal needs will serve no useful purpose for the thief. To promise excuses for all theft announces the thief's vile intentions to the community and makes it harder to keep stolen property. Professional thieves will more likely rely on subterfuge, calculating that the rewards of crime outweigh the risks.

Convicted criminals are society members too, just members who other members regard with distrust, disgust, or anger. Those who revile criminals will be careful to avoid abusing the convicted, who are not without rights. For most, shunning the criminal will be the limit of condemnation. To do more would violate their own social promises unless for self-defense. Under rare circumstances, an interested party such as a self-defense collective or insurance company might imprison dangerous criminals, but none will enjoy a special privilege to imprison another. Any restraint placed on the freedom of another must happen within the social promises of the parties or be itself a criminal act.

Shunning and Other Remedies

Self-sovereigns will adapt remedies to the circumstances and invent new avenues for redeeming, reforming, or tolerating criminals. Some criminals will reform themselves and re-enter normal society. Avenues for reformation might include reform schools, indentured servitude camps, indentured apprenticeships, participation in mutual aid societies or guilds organized for reputational reform, or other means. Members will control which options are available for their offenses by their social promises. The Third Promise will stop them from dishing out more recompense than they have promised to pay. Recall the protocol for picking the lesser penalty described in Chapter 4 and diagrammed in Figure 1. Defendants pick their remedy from those fulfilling their own promises or their accuser's. Most will take care to promise fair restitution, so others will pay it back. The few who refuse to promise fair restitution will mark themselves as dangerous.

Self sovereigns can't imprison others except in immediate self-defense, unless those convicted have promised to accept imprisonment for their offenses. Even if some make such promises, their accusers will not want to imprison anyone for long. You won't be able to tax your neighbors to fund a prison for those who have wronged you. Nothing prohibits community-funded prisons or cooperative forms of rehabilitation supported by contributions. But prisons will not exist to benefit political classes as they do today. Prisons can't provide restitution.

Where restitution fails because the offender breaks their social promise, the stain of the broken promise will be punishment enough. Reasonable self-sovereigns will exclude non-promisors and persons of proven ill will from the benefits of community. The depth of exclusion will depend on the severity of the crime. But no one law determines that depth. Each member of the community decides who, why, and how they will shun. In a well-balanced system, the weight of exclusion will cause most criminals to seek the path of reformation.

A free market in reformation services will evolve towards placing convicts where their ethical potential is highest. Optimization of purpose is in everyone's interest. Winning claimants benefit because self-actualized convicts repay faster and better. Convicts can strive to reach their highest ethical potentials. Greater affluence will lubricate the justice system. Everybody of good will, who is not operating out of a desire for vengeance or spite, will favor maximizing economic returns from reformation work.

Some convicts will forgo reformation and choose life in a less trusted social position, without becoming non-promisors. Others will become non-promisors by renouncing all their social promises. If no other organized society exists, non-promisors will struggle for survival with the barest social protections. Where self-sovereigns are few, some non-promisors will cast off their self-sovereignty and live under the exclusive rule of the reigning power.

All may shun others to the limit of their social promises. In reaction to shunnings, others may elect to shun the shunners, or declare that they will shun no one. Fault lines will arise between large blocks of people holding different core beliefs. All who can win support from a motivated minority will sustain their lifestyles even if doing so offends most. Without one dominant power, different tribes of social promises might arise in different circles and in different places. In social promise society, shunning and organization into tribal groups replaces voting as the primary instrument for influencing others' moral preferences.

Whether you not you find such possibilities disturbing or stimulating depends on your cultural conditioning. Many people today pretend that police and prosecutors enforce the law uniformly. They don't and can't. Diktats of politicians accustom their subjects to the idea that one rule applies. Many today consider it strange and unappealing to live a society without a purported uniform standard. Before voluntary society can become a dominant paradigm, the masses must learn to distrust imposed laws and understand the merits of equal self-sovereignty and responsibility for personal codes of honor.

These merits include discovery of other's cultural and moral preferences, facilitating more targeted discovery of compatible friends, partners, customers, service providers, and other relationships. For example, people might adopt personal honor codes stating that they will not engage in promiscuous sex or hire the services of a sex worker while in a committed sexual relationship with another without the knowledge and consent of their partner; and should they violate this rule, their partner will have certain remedies. This promise reveals one's expectations and commitments to find and keep a mate. Others may prefer silence on the question, or make a different commitment (e.g., polyamory), or may deny any such commitment. Either way others will know where they stand and may use their knowledge as they please.

For example, intimate service providers might market themselves to people whose social promises allow professional safe sex, and perhaps to those who prefer silence on the question. They might focus their marketing to reduce transaction costs and risks associated of having sex with strangers. These risks include provoking the wrath of a mate or dealing with those unwilling to respect the professional's safety and limits in the transaction. This ability to focus their marketing would benefit both profesionals and their likely customers. Those not interested in paid sex benefit by avoiding unwanted solicitations. Monogamists benefit, by avoiding prospective partners with unsuitable honor codes. Those who find professional sex or promiscuity offensive might shun others who decline to adopt personal honor codes to their liking. Defenders of sex workers might offer discounts or other benefits to those holding sex worker-friendly codes.

In a free society, self-sovereigns may use shunning to regulate a much wider array of behavior than the victimless conduct that states have outlawed, such as forbidden sexual activity, use or sale of contraband, smuggling, blasphemy, criticism of the monarch or state, and so forth. Rather than applying to old and familiar vices or activity detrimental to state monopoly power, members might use shunning to nudge their neighbors towards more constructive conduct. Also, shunning may take various forms other than refusing to do business altogether, such as demanding a premium price or assigning an embarrassing label.

For example, suppose economic leaders in a circle of influence decide that too many people are engaging in an undesirable behavior 'X.' The behavior 'X' can be just about anything that a group of people decide is undesirable; use your imagination. Likewise, the circle can be anything with effective control over a significant economic resource: a city, a guild of people who control the Internet, a cartel of underground medical providers, a union of sex workers, an ad hoc organization of online underground free market hosts, whatever. Suppose 'X' is the consumption of meat, and the circle is the city. The city leaders are vegetarians, make up most of the restaurant owners, service providers, and utility providers in the city, and want to create disincentives for meat eating. They each adopt a personal honor code that commits them to not eat meat for survival and offer a 20% discount to anyone who adopts the same code. People who have not promised to eat meat would pay a 20% premium for doing business in that vegetarian city. But absent monopoly power, they would not do so for long.

There are economic and political limits to widespread adoption of shunning. Whether price discrimination of this sort is effective will depend on environmental factors. Without market power by those enforcing the price discrimination, it will not work. Even when a cartel can enforce price discrimination based on arbitrary personal profiles for a while, competitive pressures will undermine it after a short while. Too much shunning is bad for business, creates opportunities for competitors, and limits the shunner's political influence. If vegetarian shop owners in an area charge a premium to non-vegetarians, the price discrepancy attracts vegetarian customers while repelling meat eaters. Meat eaters will shop elsewhere, so most of the shop owner's customers will be vegetarian. The shop owner can seldom enjoy the benefits of receiving a 20% premium price. If many meat eaters are in the area, competitors will move in to service them. The vegetarian shop owner will lose opportunities to interact with meat eaters and to influence them to become vegetarians. The shopkeepers' shun campaign will be ineffective and uneconomical. Wiser shop owners will offer inducements such as discounts on vegetables to any meat eater who promises to give up meat. With enticing incentives, the cost of inducing change comes with greater chances of economic returns.

Shunning to avoid risk can make perfect economic sense. Market participants might avoid dealing with those whose promise profiles or histories indicate a high risk of negative outcomes. In trades vulnerable to aggressive attack, promise network information may identify high-risk transactions. We see the same behavior today, in lending restrictions and higher interest costs for people with low or unestablished credit scores. Promise profiles and associated reputations work as a behavioral credit score, permitting discrimination between sellers or buyers based on a rational assessment of risk associated with incompatibilities between promise profiles or past promise-keeping reputations. Promise and reputation information will enable shunning that does not violate the laws of economics.

In theory, self-sovereigns can promise to shun others who fit an opposed but non-risky moral profile. Few will do so, because promises to shun add complexity, controversy and risk with no offsetting benefit. Shunning has no rewards and comes with risks. Those who advertise their condemnation make it easier for their ideological opponents to identify and shun them back. Most self-sovereigns will shun or not shun on a case-by-case basis, preserving flexibility and privacy. People will adapt their acts of shunning to the circumstances at hand, with utility taking precedence over consistency.

State-run criminal registries are evidence of shunning. For example, "sex-offender registries" are tax-supported lists imposed for life on people convicted of so-called "sex offenses," which can vary from serious crimes like rape to behavior that should not be criminal like teenagers sexting one another. Many journalists have reported these registries are over-inclusive. Many people on them are not dangerous yet are never free of the reputational stain and onerous reporting requirements of being a listed offender. A robust promise society will make special criminal registries obsolete,

241

because reputation information available through promise profiles will be more detailed, accurate and flexible than a list of offenders. Self-sovereigns will choose for themselves how to use reputation information. Every member of society will be on a reputation list, not just those who lack the ability to mount a political defense.

In the far future, the freedom and ability to shun will make prisons obsolete. Instead of tax-funded prisons, those with dangerous profiles will gather in no-shun zones. A no-shun zone is anyplace controlled by people who offer essential services for anybody willing to pay the price. Those who control the zone will decide who may stay in it but will eject few. The purpose of the zone includes serving those few others will while insulating them from the rest of society. Tolerance for dangerous characters will make no-shun zones edgy. Few with good reputations will go unless looking for trouble. Polite society will tolerate no-shun zones for solving the problem of what to do with the worst, most dangerous non-promisors and criminals. By enabling survival, even at less than ideal terms, no-shun zones will make desperados less desperate. These zones will open options for the convicted, including reformation and work on dangerous or distasteful jobs. Shun zones will police those they serve, to prevent the zone from being perceived as a threat to surrounding society. Neighbors will regard successful shun zones as dangerous places, but not enough to call for attack.

Open-source shunning by individuals is the closest thing to incarceration in social promise communities. Free and voluntary shunning will different from statist solutions. In a free society, shunning will be a useful and fluid tool that creates incentives for constructive behavior. Shunning and inducements based on promise profiling will help move society towards freer, more ethical arrangements, by creating incentives for adoption of promise systems where such concepts were unknown. Even after voluntary society predominates, shunning will stay the primary instrument for continued social change in the face of evolving moral preferences.

Arrest and Incarceration

Even without a state to levy taxes and fund prisons, arrest and incarceration will sometimes make economic sense while complying with social promises. Because no member of voluntary society has a special privilege to detain others, arresting and jailing members comes with liability. Most will promise to do no harm unless necessary for self-defense, and so will be liable for damages caused by the detention. Where both parties recognize self-defense as an affirmative defense, the jailer escapes liability if the prisoner's prior attacks made the detention necessary. Where both parties have made promises like these, the outcome will rest on the damages caused by the detention and whether less harmful defensive measures would work. For more predictability, society members might grant a limited privilege of arrest or incarceration under specified circumstances. Members might grant limited arrest rights in their social promises, to relieve pressure in tense situations and avoid worse outcomes. Stated as a promise, the grant excuses liability for necessary arrest of guilty parties until bonded for trial.

Temporary, short-term arrest is better than risky, violent struggles over the trivial inconveniences required to prevent identity theft and preserve the general peace by application of due process. Some members may grant such a privilege on the condition that the arrested is convicted after due process. If the neutral acquits the suspect, the arresting party must pay restitution to the prisoner. Others may promise to pay more than actual damages for mistaken arrest, to show they will not make arrests for light or transient causes.

Whatever the burden promised, none can enforce promises that don't exist. Some may promise no restitution for mistaken arrest but doing so leaves them without recourse if arrested. As with every other violent crime, most will take responsibility for harm done to others. Otherwise, they will be vulnerable to harms inflicted by others, or show themselves to be unaccountable through civil justice channels. Those disclaiming all affirmative defenses for detaining others will deprive themselves and others of such defenses. Others might arrest them in self-defense but will be liable for the costs. Sometimes, the stakes in dispute will make arrest worthwhile despite the liability.

Consider this example: Justin promises to hold no one liable for arrests made in good faith. Matthew promises no liability for arrests of the guilty. Both promise to restore harms caused by their breach of promises. Justin suspects Matthew of stealing his passwords, and so arrests Matthew for bond until trial. Matthew suspects the arrest was not in good faith. Matthew and Justin are competitors in the hedgehog massage therapy business, and the arrest causes Matthew to lose a lucrative contract with Hogs Galore Inc., Estonia's largest supplier of therapy hedgehogs for sociopaths. Matthew hires Jillian to arrest Justin until trial. Each imprisons the other until trial or bond. If the neutral acquits Matthew, Justin will be liable for the lost contract and any other damages suffered by Matthew. Matthew and Jillian will not be liable for the arrest of Justin. If the neutral convicts Matthew, Matthew will be liable for the arrest of Justin and cannot recover restitution for his own arrest. These outcomes depend on the social promises of Justin and Matthew in the factual context.

Where a suspect is a flight risk and the stakes are high enough, a temporary citizen's arrest may be the most reasonable choice. The propriety of the arrest extends only so far as needed to identify the accused and secure a bond for honorable resolution. So long as both parties have promised restitution for intentional harms, the claimant will be responsible for the economic damages the arrest causes the accused. Usually this cost will be small. Markets will hasten identifying the accused and securing a bond for trial, to reduce the risks and inconveniences suffered by everyone. In serious cases, the cost of arrest is trivial compared to the charged damages of the main offense, although the defendant can win an offset for damages caused by detention. All arrests are by citizens, who will often hire professional enforcers with the experience and training to reduce risks and avoid all avoidable harm.

Like arrest, incarceration is a tool for use when social promises and economics allow it. Consider Alice and Bill. Alice promises to pay full recompense for whatever foreseeable damage her intentional actions inflict on another. Bill promises to pay double recompense in the same circumstance. If Alice incarcerates Bill she will owe him the economic damages he suffers as a result. If Bill incarcerates Alice, under TROTWET, he will owe Alice her own damages suffered, instead of his promised double recompense. To avoid these claims, neither Alice nor Bill will incarcerate the other, unless there is no better way. Convicts will pay claimants without threat of incarceration in most cases, to preserve their honor. Incarceration can prevent people of good will from keeping their social promises and create liability for the jailer.

Incarceration will seldom be the best choice but can be sometimes. Suppose Bill murders Alice and might flee to escape liability for his crime. Alice's sister Abbey has made the same social promises as her sister and incarcerates Bill heedless of the risk of damages. Abbey and Bill agree on a neutral and process for resolution. Abbey claims for murder and Bill counterclaims for false imprisonment. The neutral convicts Bill of Alice's murder, and Abbey of false imprisonment. Alice had promised a lifetime of indentured servitude for murder while Bill had promised to submit to death by opium overdose in the same circumstance. Bill decides that indentured servitude is the lighter burden so that is his penalty.

He wins a small offset for the damages of his brief false imprisonment.

What about that indentured servitude? Bill can control its limits by his prior social promises. If Bill sets no specific limits, the severity of the servitude's terms cannot exceed what the neutral permits. Neutrals will consult community standards for inhumane punishment and adapt for the case at hand. Suppose that Bill sets no specific limits, and the neutral advises that proper servitude comprises Bill's lifelong earnings less his basic living expenses, with Bill obligated to earn at least as much as he was earning averaged over the three years before the murder of Alice. The neutral rules that Bill should pay until reaching the age of 70 or inability to work, whichever comes first. When Bill learns the neutral's sentence, he posts "This is b_llsh_t! No way I'm working until I'm 70 so that bitch Abbey can spend the rest of her life eating bon-bons!" Bill then goes to live in a tent alongside a freeway in Southern California. Under these circumstances, Abbey can lock Bill up without damaging her own honor. If she imprisons Bill, she bears responsibility for inhumane treatment by the jailers. The jailers can honorably earn their support from Bill's earnings, and charge user fees. Successful jailers will incentivize Bill to earn more without violating his human rights.

Indentured servants and chattel slaves have a low economic value, compared to free and trustworthy people. Most times, claimants and convicts will work out secure arrangements in which the convict enjoys greater freedom as needed to pursue a more favorable economic return for the claimant. If Bill accepts such a deal, his living conditions will be basic, and the price he pays for his crime will be high. If a life of indentured servitude is too heavy a burden, Bill can always kill himself. If his due process was defective, he can raise an appeal.

Sometimes convicts unable to pay judgments will opt to join rehabilitation organizations (ROs). Although not prisons, ROs may require sacrifices by convicts, such as restrictions on movement or activity. The arrangements will always be voluntary in the sense of being permitted by the subject's social promises or later agreement. Rehabilitation organizations (ROs) may be nonprofit or for-profit, and organized as collectives, cooperatives, sole proprietorships or other entities. ROs provide value by increasing the earnings capacity of their clients, by teaching new skills both emotional and technical, helping clients sustain a basic quality of life, and improving the security and public peace of the community. The operator of the RO may earn a share of the income earned by its clients, so has an incentive to help convicts achieve increased earning powers. Convicts may leave without dishonor once they have completed payment of just recompense.

What about dangerous convicts? In voluntary society, incorrigible criminals won't make social promises, unless for fraudulent purposes. They will be non-promisors instead. Frauds will dishonor themselves when they fail to keep their promises. Victims can treat them like Bill in the example above. The criminally insane are cases for public charity or can live as non-promisors. Dangerous persons will suffer extreme shunning, up to total exclusion from honorable society even unto death. Less severe cases might be treated as mental illnesses, with compassionate treatment more likely as the risk of harm to innocent people is less. Public charities might imprison the most dangerous in high-security treatment centers, if voluntary community is affluent enough to afford such luxuries. Support will come from those who love the convicted criminals and have hope in their reformation, or fear for their safety and the safety of others. Those who would earn reform will pay whatever price they have promised for their crimes and once finished repaying may enjoy the rest of their life without debt.

To illustrate, consider the story of Valerie and Mudscratcher. Both are social promisors, but Mudscratcher has a history of raping people in dark alleys. Mudscratcher is a thrice-convicted rapist and is working off his restitution as a telemarketer working from home, wearing an ankle bracelet to track his whereabouts. Valerie's family have lived in a nearby home undisturbed for generations, and Valerie's three teen-aged daughters often pass through the dark alley behind their home from evening yoga class. There they have seen Mudscratcher leering at them through his back gate, so they always go through the alley in a group and carry a taser. Valerie confronted Mudscratcher about his behavior, but Mudscratcher just stared at her in silence and turned away.

One evening Valerie heard a scream from the back alley. She called her private security service and rushed to where she heard the scream but saw and heard nothing unusual. When the security professionals arrived, she explained the situation and her experiences with Mudscratcher. After checking public records, the professionals offer Valerie a discount on their "preventative incarceration service" with insurance against liability. It's not cheap, but Valerie feels it necessary to protect her daughters. The professionals arrest Mudscratcher and house him in a secure apartment with his personal effects and telemarketing equipment. They do not allow him to go out accompanied.

Valerie pays for a month of this incarceration, which is enough time for a neutral to hear and decide a claim by Mudscratcher for false imprisonment and a claim by Valerie on behalf of her daughters for assault. Even if Mudscratcher wins his claim, his damages are not high because the professionals avoided interrupting Mudscratcher's livelihood or damaging his already weak reputation. Likewise, Valerie's claim of assault is tenuous on these facts. The neutral digs through the facts, assesses the opposing charges, and presents a remediation plan. Skilled neutrals will devise plans both parties can accept and resolve tensions that led to the incarceration. Incarceration can be a tool to reduce actual and perceived dangers among the community members involved and prevent greater tragedies.

We are now describing far-fetched cases. Nascent social promise communities will arrest or imprison no one, leaving that activity to the state. Loss of reputation will be the penalty, and the risk of such loss the main enforcement tool. Even when the state fades away, arrest and incarceration will be rare in social promise communities. In more liberal areas, so long as the state persists we might see institutions such as reform schools that state agencies will license and that follow social promising while complying with state rules. Parallel paths may be difficult, but not impossible. Wherever states do not interfere, social promise communities can make use of tools such as arrest and incarceration when no better alternatives exist. Those who choose such tools will be liable for their use.

Non-Promisors in Three Flavors

In large societies of self-sovereigns, everybody will be a partial non-promisor. No one can mirror everyone else's promises, without contradicting themselves. Members will cure unintended failures to promise by consenting to reasonable obligations when cracks appear, or by pointing out how a more general promise applies to more specific circumstances. Gaps in understanding may arise, but those who would keep their honorable reputations will navigate around uncertainties.

The non-promisors we consider in this section intend to be. We might call them "outlaws." They intend to stay on the sidelines, skip out on their social obligations, or stamp out their competition. So non-promisors come in three flavors: avoiders, fraudsters, and competitors. Competitors come in two flavors, exclusive and non-exclusive. Both flavors of competitors can be coercive or non-coercive. We will chew on these flavors in order.

   Avoiders avoid making social promises. They can avoid all social promises, or only those in certain topic areas. Avoiders don't impose diktats on society members but can be content to live under the diktats of others. For example, they may prefer living under government by politicians and bureaucrats and avoiding the obligations of social promising. Avoiders can become promisors, and vice versa.

   Where they have promised no obligations, avoiders enjoy no reciprocal benefits. That doesn't mean that avoiders have no rights, or that social promisors may treat them with cruelty. Far from it. It means only that social promisors need not honor their social promises to avoiders or other non-promisors. The Third Promise relieves every one of obligations not backed by reciprocal promises. Avoiders and other non-promisors don't have rights in self-sovereign society because they have chosen not to. They can always enter self-sovereign society by making the Three Promises and obliging themselves to honor the rights they seek.

   The rights of non-promisors are like the rights of animals. We will consider animal rights in a later chapter but note here that animals can't bring claims for violation of their rights without human help. If they could, we could ask animals to make social promises like every other self-sovereign, if they want rights! But humans can complain to other humans about their treatment of animals. Likewise, promisors can complain to other promisors about treatment of non-promisors. Suppose Robert enjoys robbing non-promisors for sport, never attacks social promisors, and has made a social promise to not take property by force. Isaiah, having promised to be cruel if he can avoid it, hates Robert's cruelty. Robert has not made a similar promise to avoid cruelty, so Isaiah cannot bring a claim for breach of promise. Instead, Isaiah can shun Robert and encourage others to shun Robert. Assuming Isaiah has promised to not rob others, he cannot rob Robert without dishonor. Isaiah can be cruel to Robert in ways that do not break the set of reciprocal promises between Isaiah and Robert. More likely, Isaiah can isolate Robert by encouraging his fellow self-sovereigns to make promises to abstain from cruelty. Using such tools, Isaiah can exert such social pressure on Robert to desist from robbing non-promisors. Those in voluntary society have many reasons to discourage Robert from his cruel sport. Not only is his cruelty immoral, it can incite non-promisors to violence against others in voluntary society. Self-sovereign victims of blowback by non-promisors might hold Robert responsible under a theory of causation.

A society member may hold another responsible for harm by a non-promisor if caused by a reckless or intentional act of the member. With Robert and Isaiah, blowback might arise from Robert's reckless hunting of non-promisors for sport. So long as Robert, being a sane self-sovereign, promises responsibility for his reckless acts he faces liability. As for intentional use of non-promisors, suppose Jeremy (a society member) knows Killerman the murderous non-promisor hides out in Snaky Swamp. He suggests to Justin (another society member) that Snaky Swamp is a wonderful place for a nature hike. Encouraged by Jeremy, Justin ventures forth and Killerman mauls him before Justin escapes. Once informed of Jeremy's pre-existing knowledge of Killerman's whereabouts, Justin brings a claim for his injuries. The result, as always, depends on the social promises made by Justin and Jeremy. Rational society members will accept responsibility for leading others into foreseeable harm, to protect themselves from malicious or reckless use of wild animals, non-promisors, and other environmental dangers.

Most hypocrites will not be non-promisors. Hypocrisy is easy for mortals. It is much easier for limited beings to make promises than to fulfil them, and to judge others instead of themselves. Due process penalizes hypocrisy by the Third Promise and habitual hypocrites earn lousy reputations. No one trusts unreformed promise breakers. To win trust again, convicted hypocrites must settle their old debts and show a record of making good on new promises.

Fraudsters are hypocrites who break promises on purpose. Professional fraudsters don't care about their reputations for any longer than they must to carry out their purposes. They are non-promisors in disguise. A professional criminal organization might send its members into voluntary society to earn trust to commit crimes, for example. While making their social promises, they will conceal their true allegiance to their gang's criminal plan. They will cover their hypocrisy by threatening worse violence against any who would reveal their fraud. They will coerce their victims to conceal their crimes and poison the trust network of society.

It's hard to argue with the gun barrels of a criminal gang. Until moral self-sovereigns out-gun gangs, vigilance, discretion and guile are the best defense against fraudsters. These defenses will suffice. Voluntary society will not make a tempting target for criminal gangs until large enough for the morally obtuse to notice it. After that, the society will be worth protecting and will have defenses. Every deliberate fraud concealed by violent threats is an attack on every member. Any member can press claims against fraudsters who defraud by making false promises.

Civic-minded members who live beyond reach of the gang can bring claims against their fraudsters in forums beyond the gang's reach and publish the trial proceedings. If the forum convicts the fraudster, the claimant need not fear a countersuit. Neutrals will not be friendly to fraudulent agents of criminal gangs. With many victims, the gangsters won't know who is informing on their secret agents of subversion. Neutrals will keep the victims' identities secret. Gangsters might refuse due process but by doing so mark themselves as dangerous. They can't keep every respected neutral in the world from publishing their verdicts, if only to reveal fraud and protect the integrity of the network.

Members of societies that offer value to their members will defend against intentional subversion. They will pay the price of defense. No one will defend societies that provide no real value, so worthless societies will not grow large. Tactical defense of social promise societies will be an interesting and often veiled topic, beyond this introductory book. Building a good reputation takes time and effort, but a credible neutral can destroy it by exposing a single act of intentional subversion. Exposure ruins the cultivated identity beyond recovery for the fraudster's purpose. The economics of reputation building will discourage fraudsters from seeking profit by subverting reputation systems.

Enterprising sovereigns might cultivate reputations for sale. False identities erode trust and social value. But members might have honorable reasons to buy a second identity, for example, to do business in a strange land or escape persecution. Most members would promise not to use false identities, but if the user discloses its origin the identity is not false. "I bought my reputation from Highbrow Academy" is like purchasing a diploma that requires coursework. People won't hide these origins; they'll tout them! And they will tolerate the sale and use of multiple identities if not for fraud. Supply rises to meet demand, and our need to connect drives our demand for good reputations. But those who use multiple identities will bear the risk of doing so. They won't take such risks without good reason.

Competitors are non-promisors who follow a system of justice incompatible with social promising. Non-exclusive competitors do not insist that others are bound to obey their system, while exclusive competitors do. For example, exclusive competitors might enforce diktats of the state under color of authority. Competitors can be fraudsters, avoiders, or partial social promisors. All may make social promises, even competitors. We call competitors a flavor of non-promisors to touch on the interplay between social promises and laws of competitive systems. In the next section on coexistence, we consider how agents of the state might join voluntary societies, and how doing so might provide a check to the worst abuses of power. We'll first consider what happens when states or other non-promisors coerce members to violate their social promises.

For example, two society members, Asher and Bartholomew. promise to respect financial privacy, and to pay actual damages for disclosing non-public financial information. They both live in the State of Oppression, whose legislators have passed laws requiring disclosure of any payment to another under threat of civil and criminal penalties. Bartholomew remodels Asher's bathroom for 10 grams of gold. Bartholomew does not report receiving the payment, but Asher reports it to Oppression's Office of Revenue, which fines Bartholomew. Supposing Bartholomew pays the fine to avoid more severe harassment from agents of Oppression, can he recover from Asher? Since the disclosure was intentional, the answer is yes unless both Asher and Bartholomew have promised that compliance with the diktats of non-promisors is an affirmative defense.

Suppose Bartholomew pursues damages for the fine from Asher, but Oppression has another law that makes it a crime to penalize anybody for taking any action required by Oppression's diktats. What if Oppression jails or penalizes Bartholomew for seeking to recover from Asher? Asher is liable for consequences of his actions to the extent the consequences would not otherwise have happened. If Bartholomew suffers because Asher informs on him, Asher has obligations. If Oppression's cops catch Bartholomew with no help from Asher, then Asher has done no damage. So long as both had a fair opportunity to understand the risk of evading Oppression's tax laws when they made their deal, neither bear responsibility for Oppression's actions they have not caused by some intentional or negligent act. But exploiting ignorance to cause an attack by non-promisors is different, as we explored in the story of Killerman and that Snaky Swamp above. Given the possibilities, extent of responsibility is not always clear. Members can avoid questions of liability by disclosing dealings they expect to have with non-promisors to one another before committing to their deal.

Silence is golden. Those who make social promises will be clever enough to avoid committing themselves in public to conduct that powerful non-promisors prohibit. The Asher-Bartholomew scenario will seldom happen. People unable to provide privacy will not promise it. Those compelled to disclose might add an exception to their privacy promise, for example: "unless required by state law." They might also promise to disclose all reporting requirements before causing a reportable event. Regardless, exceptions to social promises can be subject to review by neutrals. Records of such reviews will show who makes exceptions to social promises for complying with state laws. Those who must avoid the state will check those records.

Unlike illegal contracts, the state cannot suppress illegal social promises (if such things can exist) by refusing to enforce them. The state has no role in the consequences of a failure to keep a social promise. It will lack easy tools for discouraging social promise making. It might persecute members who make public social promises it dislikes. Members can avoid this terrorism by careful wording of their social promises. Seldom will a bare promise be illegal. Any illegality associated with the social promise will become visible only in certain circumstances. But well-designed ledgers will not supply non-promisors with information about those circumstances. Non-promisors will always threaten voluntary society. Social promising should help relieve the threat and not aggravate it.

Coexisting with State Legal Systems

Voluntary society confers the power of law on the most granular social unit: the person. Being so granular, voluntary justice systems are suitable for co-existing with competing conflict resolution systems, while being difficult to eradicate. There is no head to cut off. Nor does the social promisor need any action from non-participants. Those who take part place their reputations at stake, but only within the society defined by social promises. Although capable of replacing all that legal systems can do in the name of justice while improving results, social promise communities can thrive alongside other forms of government in the meanwhile. Ability to coexist and to be independent will secure the future of voluntary communities. Voluntary communities do not seek to replace any system that people want to support.

Voluntary society includes all who belong by choice. Outside of it anything may exist: a republic; a democracy; an empire; a petty dictatorship; a socialist dystopia; a fascist totalitarian state; a lawless anarchy, a prison; or a plantation of slaves. Social promise communities can co-exist with all these other things, although dire circumstances can make matters difficult. All that voluntary society needs to exist is for two or more to honor their social promises in dealings with one another.

We discussed principled non-promisors and modularity of social promises in Chapter 4. Members can limit their social promises by topic area to avoid obligations that clash with other legal systems. If conflict in an excluded topic arises, the parties waive each other's social promises. For example, suppose a couple has social promises regarding their obligations to marriage partners and family. One of the couple makes no social promises about contracts, so their social promises don't apply in a disagreement over contracts. If a breach of contract comes up, they can either settle it outside of their promise community, agree on a rule for resolving the dispute, or leave it unresolved. These three choices will not damage their reputations as society members. But if a dispute involving family law arises both are honor-bound to resolve it according to their social promises.

Many social promises will be broad. Prudent people may promise to pay restitution for their violence, coercion or fraud, without adopting specific rules in some areas. Their promises inform others of their character, while preserving flexibility. General principles might conflict with laws imposed by some external system. For example, state police who promise to do no violence except in self-defense might break this general promise when arresting people for victimless crimes. Narrower rules may also conflict with external rules. Understanding choices for managing these conflicts promotes coexistence with other governance forms.

Warning! Obeying complex rules imposed under color of authority can be habit-forming. But imposed rules do not exist in social promise communities. You cannot make one's social promises identical to state law. State laws are not personal promises, and don't require consent from citizens. You can't impose laws on others by making social promises. You can promise to obey state law, but that would be an unwise promise. State law is always changing, subject to political forces, and too complex for one person to understand. It carries out the agenda of those who rule by force. The promise is unfathomable, posing an unknown danger. But we can adapt our promises in view of state laws, borrow from the sensible parts, and learn from the wisdom of our judicious forbearers.

A society member may belong to different organizations that hold to different rules. Members may treat external rules as any other rule of non-promisors, letting the organization govern consequences of non-compliance. Or they can make a social promise to follow the organization's rules. Doing so will make their organizational issues subject to voluntary due process, for those who make corresponding promises. Settling rules under voluntary due process may have advantages. But promising to follow an organization's rules is risky, like promising to follow state law. The promisor loses control of her obligations. Prudent people will avoid promising to follow rules made by committee, or letting committees obligate them without specific consent.

Instead of promising to keep others' rules, prudent members will join communities (e.g., clubs, religious organizations, political parties, etc.) as regular members. They will keep other community rules besides their social promises. That's just common sense, and its force doesn't diminish if the other organization threatens to take your property or lock you up for breaking its rules. Gangs use threats to make promises unnecessary, not to win heartfelt commitments from free people. Self-sovereigns may obey diktats of a coercive government or criminal gang as a matter of expediency but would be foolish to make social promises to obey those who threaten them.

Joining or interacting with mixed organizations of non-promisors and promisors can confuse members about which of their obligations — their social promises, the organization rules, or both — applies. To simplify mental burdens, self-sovereigns might waive their rights under social promises or under organization rules for all who grant reciprocal waivers. Conditional waivers of obligations insulate society members from unintended problems caused by complying with shared rules. Compliance with any imposed rule may cause someone to break their promise. Without a waiver, the rule does not excuse breaking of a promise. Likewise, a waiver of the organization's rules frees members of the organization from the rule as against the promisor. For example, a social promise to not enforce patent laws frees everyone who makes a reciprocal promise from liability for patent infringement.

Both kinds of waivers may become popular for reducing risks of membership in diverse organizations. If the outside organization includes no other promise society members (i.e., all are non-promisors), the waiver is meaningless because social promises provide no rights against non-promisors. When an organization requests that members waive social promises that conflict with their rules, the request is a sign that social promising is alive and well in that organization. The waiver requests show that the organization includes promise society members concerned about liability for their social promises when complying with organizational rules. Waivers increase the leverage and influence of social promise societies. Requests for waivers show that membership in voluntary society is large enough to be influential. The scope and effect of such waivers becomes a matter of negotiations between voluntary society and organizations seeking waivers. In those negotiations, organizations will feel pressure to make their rules compatible with popular social promises.

Communities of pure non-promisors don't need waivers and won't use them. Such will be the relationship between the state and social promise community, at the outset. Non-promisors affiliated with the state will make demands of society members, and society members will lack recourse against those demands. Whatever actions the member takes to cope with state intrusions are outside the province of social promising. People already cope with states and may continue to do so as they see fit. But if a member of a non-promisor organization is a social promise society member, such person may be subject to claims for their actions, depending on the social promises of the people involved. Voluntary due process may disregard the law of the non-promisor organization or may weigh it in the balance if the social promises or other agreement permit.

States publish their laws, which should give fair warning about what actions the state will take in response to actions and petitions by its citizens. Even if you regard states as dangerous beasts, their laws matter to lots of people. It is unfair to ignore state law where it impacts the consequences of self-sovereign action, just as it would be unfair to ignore the warning posted on a tiger cage in a dispute over a mauling by the tiger caged inside. A difference being that with complex empires, the warning on the cage fills libraries. The intentions of tigers are no less good than states, though. Many see holding offices of the state as public service. We should not despise their good intentions. We should instead appeal to their good intentions to avoid interfering with tools that promote conflict resolution and social harmony.

Non-promisors may ban social promises, but self-sovereigns cannot give weight to such bans. Bans may discourage some from making social promises. But bans on making promises are too totalitarian to prevail where contrary to constitutional rights protecting free speech. If states will impede social promising with laws, they will use less objectionable forms.

For example, tax collectors may hold enforcement of social promises requiring privacy in commercial transactions illegal under state law. Tax collectors might bring state-law charges against self-sovereigns who have registered claims for breach of financial privacy in public ledgers. Such enforcement by the tax collector would penalize or criminalize private indemnity agreements. It's outlandish, but states may outlaw privacy or other promised social obligations as instruments of some criminal conspiracy, bribery, interference with legal process, or on some other basis.

The state might focus its attacks on self-sovereign neutrals and enforcers, as competition. For example, a death sentence found and enforced with utmost probity within a social promise community would invite criminal charges by states. But voluntary death sentences will be rare where states hold power. Suppression by states will focus on more mundane activities. For example, states might label all monetary damages awarded outside of their courts

260

"unlawful debts," justifying charges of criminal racketeering against neutrals, claimants and enforcers. They might prosecute neutrals for ruling on claims by service providers who perform services made illegal by state diktat. The most dangerous criminals will not participate in voluntary society; they won't want the exposure to due process and reputation discovery. But states will defend against threats to their monopolies. They will make consensual activities illegal if doing so advances the interests of their patrons. Social promising is no exception.

The state will attack, and the community will defend. Outlawing general social promises is impractical. The state might prosecute for specific actions, but well managed social promise communities won't make it easy for non-promisors to seize or break into community records. The state can't outlaw locks or encryption without bringing the economy to chaos. Agents of the state can pressure private companies for back doors into data, which is why social promise ledgers should exist as open-source tools. Once the practice of social promising becomes popular, people will find ways of enforcing neutral opinions without taking on undue risk of state prosecution. Most neutral opinions will not concern issues with any state criminal nexus, and members will keep riskier actions out of view. Social promise communities will be just another form of alternative dispute resolution, which government has no good reason to oppose.

Until states fade away, enforcement in social promise communities will begin with providing a durable record to community members, and loss of reputation will be the main enforcement hammer. To enable the practice of social promising, it is only necessary for the state to tolerate public promise and reputation ledgers. As the example of Bitcoin and other cryptocurrency ledgers shows, the state will tolerate ledgers even when disfavored by powerful corporate interests. Technical characteristics of public ledgers make crackdowns infeasible without massive brutality.

In a thriving ecosystem of social promising, people will avoid attacks by non-promisors using technological and social tools we cannot foresee. But we can imagine future tactics. In voluntary society, every positive duty lies on its promisor. Any person avoiding liability under state law may make a social promise that excuses compliance with the diktats of non-promisors if necessary for self-defense. For example, an officer of a state agency might create an exception to her social promise that excuses herself from liability for lawful conduct under such-and-such agency rules. Self-sovereigns may promise to do no harm, unless necessary to avoid a state law penalty worse than the harm caused by breaking the promise. These are examples of the waivers mentioned above. There are two ways to write waivers, as positive promises or as affirmative defenses. A positive promise restrains the officer from recovering damages for harms she specifies. If stated as an affirmative defense, the waiver is null unless used against someone with a defensive shield just as strong, or stronger. These outcomes flow from the Third Promise, which requires using the weaker tool.

Most self-sovereigns will state their waivers as positive laws, for greater flexibility. Kevin promises "to not steal, unless state law requires." Lupe wants the same exception as Kevin, but thinks he's made an affirmative defense that is hard to enforce. His use of "unless" suggests a defense. So, Lupe promises "I will not seek damages for theft sanctioned by the state." Stated the second way, it is a positive promise because Lupe cannot create the conditions that will trigger her promised obligation. Why isn't a promise to not seek damages the same as an affirmative defense? We can't let magic words exalt form over substance. Both promises result in excusing otherwise culpable conduct. But how they achieve results differs. Since stealing creates an obligation to repay, Kevin's promise to not steal creates a positive obligation to pay damages if convicted. Kevin's actions determine whether the obligation arises. He can choose his victims. But Lupe's promise to not seek damages if victimized by another has no effect unless she becomes a victim. Unlike Kevin, Lupe cannot incur the promised obligation by her own will. That's why her waiver is a positive promise, while Kevin's is an affirmative defense. Another sovereign must act by stealing from Lupe under state sanction, before she owes the obligation. Lupe cannot choose her victims because her promise requires another to act first.

How is Lupe's waiver by positive promise more flexible than Kevin's? Her promise binds herself and thieves who make an equivalent or stronger promise. For all others, she enjoys the flexibility of keeping or breaking her promise as she pleases. Kevin is unprotected by his affirmative defense except from those who have promised a reciprocal defense. He cannot invoke his defense against any who have not made an equivalent or stronger promise. Besides promising to not seek damages under certain circumstances, Lupe will promise to not steal without exception. Her promises present a healthier moral profile, showing she condemns theft. Positive promises aren't just better for coexisting with state laws. They are better for coexisting with everybody.

Self-sovereigns might make waivers like Lupe's for various reasons. They might wish to signal compliance to lessen the risk of state persecution, to encourage others to make social promises, out of respect for states rules, or for defensive purposes. Some may find waivers based on external rules distasteful, but at least the persons who make them are being honest about their limits for using social promises. The possibility of waivers may encourage some to make social promises they would otherwise avoid. Those who do not approve of waivers can refuse to do business with waiver-makers. If many people find waivers like Lupe's repugnant, waiver-makers will face social pressure to discard them or lessen their reach.

Waivers support growth of voluntary society, by encouraging people to make social promises they would otherwise be afraid to. Waivers can expand the influence of voluntary society by making issues over compliance with external rules subject to voluntary due process. Agents of the state who make social promises with waivers open themselves up to due process before self-sovereign neutrals. These neutrals will apply higher standards of due process than available in state courts and reach different results. Claimants need prove only the agent caused the underlying harm (e.g., theft or imprisonment) and either fails to satisfy conditions of their waiver or the waiver does not apply. If the claimant made a reciprocal waiver whether the defendant satisfied the conditions of the waiver will be at issue. If the claimant made no reciprocal waiver, only the underlying reciprocal social promises will be at issue.

Agents of the state might make social promises despite the risk of voluntary due process, for several reasons. If voluntary society is thriving, agents will join to gain access to its records and membership, and subject themselves to voluntary due process or lose their good reputations. If aware of due process risks for fulfilling their duties to the state, they may make waivers to reduce those risks. The converse is not true. Any person not in bondage has little reason to change their promises in reaction to rules made by non-promisors. Free people are better served by simpler social promises.

Self-Contradiction

Every promise has a time point, and a timeline. The time point is when the sovereign made the promise, and the line is its duration afterwards. Any member can change their social promises whenever they choose. If otherwise, their promises are not voluntary. Consent requires continuing acceptance.

People sometimes make conflicting social promises. A society member might change promises as a matter of convenience, to avoid consequences of a former promise, to avoid a rule from a competing legal system, because their life circumstances changed, because their moral stance changed, or by mistake. Each change comes at a point in time and takes effect after the member publishes the new promise where the community can find it. Prior to being made the social promise has no effect. A bright line — publication — separates effect from nullity.

Despite bright lines, conflicting promises by the same person can create uncertainty about the promised obligations. When events supporting a complaint span a time during which a person has changed their social promises, which promise applies may not be clear. A pattern of changing promises at convenient times may support an inference that the changes are not in good faith and are part of a pattern of manipulation. The bright line of publication can get fuzzy and gray. Whatever the reason for the fuzziness, fairness is the rule for sorting out conflicting social promises. When it is not clear which promise applies, the neutral should apply the rule least favorable to the one most responsible for the fuzziness. If both parties are equally at fault, it's a coin flip. The one most responsible for the uncertainty should bear the cost, if such a one exists.

Besides making promises at different times, when using multiple identities members may make different and conflicting promises for different identities. People can use multiple identities without fraud, by informing those they would transact with that the identity in use is one of several. The person operating multiple identities (for short, a "changeling") then requests voluntary acceptance of the fictional identity's promise set. A rational person hearing such disclosure should make sure they understand the nature of the fictional entity and can accept a relationship with it. Acceptable reasons might include privacy, or to transact with a collective. For those who accept an honest deal with the fiction, the deal is honorable and enforceable.

Traders may wish to transact in different communities that hold to conflicting customary social promises, to arbitrage price differences and earn a trader's profit. For such traders, the ability to transact under different social promises can be essential. In voluntary society, no physical borders separate one community from another. Instead, separation between communities emerges when groups gravitate to different customary promises. A promise expected in one community may be anathema in another.

For example, voluntary Romans promise to sacrifice a pig to signify a covenant and consider the sacrifice of a lesser animal insulting. Voluntary Persians promise to sacrifice a dove for sealing covenants and consider pigs to be unclean and insulting. This difference is one among many. Voluntary Vic wants to trade with voluntary Romans and voluntary Persians but cannot make social promises that both Romans and Persians find acceptable. He would make one set of promises when dealing with Romans, and a different set for Persians. Plus, he lives in Estonia where a third set of promises is customary. Vic might divide his promises into four sets: universal promises that apply for everybody, a Roman set that applies only for Romans, a Persian set only for Persians, and a home set for Estonians. Such parceling could get confusing and cause mistakes. And it informs his acquaintances he deals with traditional arch-enemies Persians and Romans, a fact his opponents might use against him. Plus, Persians are less apt to trust anyone who does business with Romans, and vice versa. To avoid identity politics, Vic may prefer to use a separate identity, e.g. "Zahar" when dealing with Persians, for appearances, simplicity, and to protect confidentiality of his trading network.

To avoid claims of fraud or unfairness, Vic should disclose that he uses different identities for dealing with different groups. He should publish the fact he is a changeling. If others have concerns about his other identities or those other groups, they can ask. But if Vic conceals his changeling nature, he is vulnerable to charges of fraud or unfairness. Concealment undermines consent for his fictional identities and their associated promise sets. If a charge of fraud or unfairness sticks, or if he did not get consent prior to his offense, he will be stuck with his strongest promises. Being a changeling would have its advantages and disadvantages. Making too many conflicting promises would be a real disadvantage. The contradictions could force the changeling to adjust in the worst way to every circumstance. Vic can never be too sure which of his promises will apply, so he should make his contradictory promises similar.

Agents working for fictional persons might need to become changelings. For example, a person may wish to use one set of promises for himself, and a set made by his fictional employer when working. Otherwise, it would be impossible for a corporate entity to face the public with consistent promises. The employee or agent will want to use their own promises when not working. One solution would be for the agent to disclose the use of the fictional corporate identity whenever acting for it. When dealing with those willing to recognize fictional entities, this facilitates a natural interaction between agents and clients, without a pre-existing agreement. Another solution would be to require a pre-existing agreement to a set of social promises, before transacting in other ways. Corporations and other fictional entities can use both strategies.

For example, suppose that an organized collective, let's call it "Coop Company," operates a retail store. Management of the Coop Company might refuse to hire any agent who won't acknowledge the validity of the Coop Company and its social promises. Its promises must be consistent with the principles of personal sovereignty, consent and publication, or else it is not part of the promise community. If the Coop Company attempts to enforce contracts of slavery, or uses coercion or fraud to make the deal, it is acting as a non-promisor or hypocrite. That said, use of a common set of promises will be a convenience for Coop and its employees. Coop must make reasonable social promises to attract the best employees, contractors, and customers.

The Coop Company may can offer inducements (e.g., discounts) for new "members" who accept its existence and social promises. For non-member customers, the Coop may post prominent signs disclosing that all their employees use the Coop's social promises when working. Customers can verify that by checking the employee's social promise ledger, which the employee maintains as a separate identity. So long as the employee gets acceptance of her multiple identities from the other party prior to the offense, her Coop identity applies. If the other party refuses to accept use of her Coop identity, she can refuse to transact. Her strongest promise from both sets will apply for accidental or malicious harms. Knowing this, the Coop Company can estimate the risks of indemnifying its employees from the impact of its social promises for off-duty accidents. Coop's social promises will not make its off-duty employees' burdens any heavier, unless stronger than its employees'. It will provide indemnification against accidental triggering of its stronger promises or no prudent person will work for it.

Fictional identities can't be forced on anyone, or outlawed. Fictions exist by consent of those involved. When a fiction or other making of contradictory social promises by the same person causes uncertainty over which social promise applies, the detriment belongs to promisor. Natural persons using only one identity without contradictory social promises avoid the risk.

Chapter 7: Roots

First Look

You might wonder where social promising fits in the pattern of past schemes for social order that humanity has cooked up. That is not an easy question to consider. People have tried so many experiments in government, in so many times and places. The great number of social experiments tried is itself remarkable, and strong evidence that new systems will be tried. They evolve all around us.

Despite all that has gone before, systematically-applied social promising does not seem to fit anywhere with past experiments. There has been no populated area where claims of sovereign power over territory rooted in force did not exist, in written history. But voluntary order is neither untried nor unfamiliar. It is observed all the time, whenever two or more people both follow a code of conduct, and make their commitment known to each other. It is going on all the time, all around us, even involving us, but always in limited ways.

One distinction is clear: social promising rejects all sovereignty except that of the individual over their own body and mind. When combined with the impulse to form society, that individual sovereignty creates a right and responsibility to disclose one's own moral code to those who would reciprocate, recognizing self-sovereignty as the basis for society. Entry and place in that self-sovereign society is determined by the content of each member's published moral code — i.e., their promises to other society members — and their reputations. Their reputations depend on their social promises, how they keep their promises, and their relations with fellow sovereigns. Social order emerges out of codex stated as shared promises, instead of by decree of the most powerful classes.

The collection of these distinctions sets social promising as described in this book apart from what has gone before.

With much experimentation in human governance and complexity of human history, detailed comparisons with the past would fill an encyclopedia. Academic comparisons between what has gone before and what has never been would be speculative and time consuming. This Guidebook wouldn't fit a detailed history of voluntary order. But the <u>Kernel</u> will make a few comparisons, enough to show that social promise community rests on a solid foundation of interpersonal honor stretching back for millennia. Blockchain faith has roots.

<u>Kernel</u>

Students of history who first encounter social promising sometimes say it is "just like" something that has existed before. "Oh, it is just like the law merchant!" some might exclaim. Or, "it is just like" many private law institutions, such as Canon Law, Jewish Law, or the Scout's Code of Honor, "just like" British common law, Keltic traditions, or various tribal forms, or "just like" some specific past or postulated future form of anarchy. They are right! Social promising grew out of and shares attributes with governance systems for communities fortunate enough to lack a domineering power. Social promising also resembles at least one contemplated future form of social organization: anarcho-capitalism. Social promise community is a modern expression of earlier institutions or ideas, distinct in its implementation but not its moral philosophy.

Many historical examples show communities forming and establishing their own dispute resolution or justice systems on a voluntary basis. Some relate to religious or moral systems. Many others relate to guilds or professions. Still others relate to causes, interests or pursuits. Some are pragmatic, such as brigands, gangs, and mafias, and do not eschew aggression to serve their ends. Others seek to implement less aggressive forms of social organization, whether for reasons pragmatic, philosophical, or both. Whatever their nature or purpose, most such voluntary societies have coexisted under dominion of nations or empires with their own legal systems; some have sought to exclude use of any other legal system; others have sought dominion over others, of which some are examples of nascent territorial governments descendants of which rule even today.

An empire, nation, territorial government or natural tribe confers membership by accident of birth or subjugates by conquest. It's debatable whether the conditions that give rise to the state are psychological, or rest on economic factors. Some say government as we know it is a mass delusion, as argued in The Most Dangerous Superstition by Larkin Rose, or as used to advance the story in the fictional short story And Then There Were None by Eric Frank Russell. Others argue that the state arose out of the rise of capital surpluses, for economic reasons. Perhaps both factors are important. By whatever way states came to be so pervasive, a voluntary society makes no claim of sovereignty over others. The members keep all the sovereignty for themselves, by setting the limit of sovereignty at the self.

Nations and organized traditional voluntary societies are alike in genesis of their justice systems: first a community forms and evolves a set of social conventions and rules. As the community grows it needs a justice system, which it may evolve by submitting disputes to respected members who understand community customs and act as mediators and judges. In some communities, evolution stops here. In others, a ruler takes control of the justice system, changes it for the needs of the ruling class, and imposes it on all the community's members. Either way, every community member lives with the justice system, or leaves the community. No individual member of the community may define her own law. The community has only one authoritative source of law, derived to benefit its ruling class.

Genesis of justice systems in a social promise community is different: individuals make and publish their social promises, laying a foundation for fair resolution of disputes within the Three Promise framework. The foundation for neutral justice persists for so long as two or more people intend to honor their social promises. A social promise society consists of that set of people who have made compatible social promises. The promisors don't need prior relationships with each other. They don't even need to know of one another's existence. No ruler holds a monopoly on lawmaking. Everyone accepts the Three Promise framework and makes other social promises as they please. Promisors do justice by making and keeping compatible social promises. Community coalesces around compatible promises, instead of rulers handing down laws. Social promises are compatible either by being the same, or by being reconcilable by an accepted principle, such as the Third Promise and its corollary, TROTWET. No ruling class exists because all who join must rule themselves.

Rules preceding community are not new. Organizations define bylaws, constitutions, or similar founding documents at their outset. Organizational documents often set up a structure and process for further rule making by some subset of the association. Republics and democracies are examples. Corporations and other collective associations are other examples. Although organizational documents precede constitutional republics, democracies and other forms of national government, nations make sovereign claims that sweep in subjects without consent under threats of expulsion, exclusion, or other deprivations. These subjects never agreed to the original founding documents or to the layers of law added afterwards. Except for a handful of founders, the diktats of the state extend to multitudes who never consented to them. Nations and empires are not voluntary organizations.

Making a public oath is common before stepping into positions of social responsibility. Elected officials and judges swear to uphold constitutions. Doctors take the Hippocratic Oath. Licensed professionals promise to honor their certificates. As meaningful as proscribed oaths can be, they are not statements of personal principle. They are center stage in a ritual for access to offices, agencies, and licenses. Officials who refuse the ritual oath cannot hold the office. Some who take the oath forget it and do what they think is best instead. Their oaths are ritual acts with little legal meaning, that oath takers seldom consider in their day-to-day activities. The oaths are not their own. But social promising is personal expression pure and simple. Personal promises tell our neighbors who we are and how we will interact with them, so all can live together in peace and maximum liberty.

Another ancient phenomenon: fictional entities spring into being by declaring what they are. Corporations file their articles of incorporation with the state and adopt their bylaws as one of their first official acts. The founding documents describe the organization's purpose, governance structure, and foreign relations. By organizing under the law of a state, the entity "promises" to follow the law of its home state and to accept venue there. The entity does not exist outside of the sovereign context in which it forms unless recognized by a foreign sovereign. In social promise communities, the sovereign context is the Three Promises and equal individual sovereignty. Fictions can exist in that context only by consent of each natural sovereign. Each natural person is a "foreign sovereign." Membership organizations of natural sovereigns enforce bans on force and fraud between member sovereigns.

Stakeholders in state-created corporate entities assume their roles without coercion, but corporatopia is not utopia. States pressure their subjects to contract with the fictional corporations they have spawned and enforce the corporate shield against individual liability. The state pressure to contract comes first by depriving subjects of workable alternatives, and later by laws that require subjects to contract with corporations or state institutions. Corporate bylaws are a dim reflection of social promising, implanted in the leviathan of state.

Ancient institutions include purer voluntary associations that claim no territory and would be with us even if the state did not mandate their existence. Examples include voluntary trading groups like time banks, online auction or trading groups, cooperatives, mutual ownership groups, fraternal organizations, and religious congregations. Most voluntary associations delegate rulemaking power to some subset of the association, e.g., a majority of members, a committee, a founder, or group of elders. Such organizations still fit the mold of rule by elites, but membership is less coercive. It's much easier to leave a club than a nation. The mass extinction of ancient voluntary institutions by the Leninist and Democratic-Fascist movements of the 20th Century is one of the many tragedies of our time. The centralist-corporate residue that remains still creates a hostile environment in which voluntary organizations and the families they support cannot thrive. Were voluntary associations better established, they would provide an easy introduction to social promise community. Many provide dispute resolution rules and a code of conduct. Association rules can blend into social promise society and coexist with it as noted in the previous chapter.

Voluntary organizations of the present day offer a limited scope of dispute resolution. For example, Robert's Rules of Order provides a process for resolving disputes over conduct at a meeting, or malfeasance towards the organization. Few membership organizations enforce rules beyond the limited purpose of the group. Because the ultimate sovereignty is personal, social promise community places no limits or requirements on social obligations, beyond the three promises and fundamentals. It can be as comprehensive or as limited as each person desires.

Some voluntary associations aspire to provide a full range of legal services for their members. One recent example is BitNation. BitNation is distinctive for its reliance on decentralized blockchain technology to meet the communication needs of its membership. It is also unusual for advertising itself as an alternative to the territorial nation-state. As of this writing, members of BitNation agree to use "British Common Law" to resolve disputes among themselves. This may prove difficult since the system of royals and courts that spawned British Common Law no longer exists. Bitnation represents a step towards social promise community. Bitnation and cryptographic communities like it can evolve into social promise community by at least two pathways. For example, suppose BitNation recognizes the principle of personal sovereignty and joins a consortium of "bit nations" each with its own distinct law. The consortium adopts an "inter-bit-national" law consistent with the Three Promises. If so, it and its members would make up a social promise community. In an alternative, BitNation might adopt the Three Promises and allow its own members to rule themselves and each other by their own social promises.

Previous voluntary membership groups lack any recognition of personal sovereign power to make and adopt one's own law, without being expelled from the membership society. Promise communities are unique, in that keeping the benefit of the community does not require obedience to proscribed rules. Instead, members agree to the basic principles of the Three Promise framework, under which each member can define their own social obligations and reap what they sow. Some voluntary groups limit membership to qualified persons. Social promise communities are open to all natural persons able to make and keep social promises.

These communities will expand the benefits of community as much as possible and set no other limit to their borders.

Social promise community does not arise straight from a state of nature. We know this from experience because social promise community has never existed before. Self-sovereignty has not extended itself beyond unspoken practice in families and tiny groups of friends. To extend to large societies of strangers, it must transform itself. Scaling up will require things like reliable registries and reputational networks based on compliance with self-made promises. These niceties — such as records of social promises and neutral reputation networks — won't develop where every day is a struggle for survival. Institutions such as reliable record keeping systems and equal justice are not natural; they have emerged and become more prevalent as social theory has evolved from one resting on the power and property of a monarch or chief, to technological socialist democracies and republics that rest on some theory of public benefit.

Although pervasive in their regulation of human affairs and relentless in preserving their own power, most modern forms of the state give lip service to basic human rights such as freedom of speech and thought, equality of persons, and the right of free association. It is within this established framework of basic rights and a networked information infrastructure that essential tools for social promise communities, such as publication of social promises and reliable reputational records, can take root and grow. Capital surpluses and leisure time that exist in some state-governed territories may also facilitate experimentation with new forms of self-governance. Social promise community is not so much an enemy of the state as it is an evolved descendant, with the potential to replace monopolistic territorial governance if found useful by adequate numbers of people.

Many can't imagine that a well-ordered society can tolerate diverse and conflicting promises, despite the well-known parallels known today. Unexamined skepticism is illogical. Nations, states, and provinces often enact conflicting laws. The law that applies in cases involving people from different jurisdictions, or places subjected to overlapping claims of authority, is not always clear. Judges and lawyers reconcile these differences using well-established principles anyway. In the world of territorial governments, conflict of law principles rest on borders. Existing conflict of law systems prove that due process can cope with different rules if we can only apply a consistent and fair approach for resolving conflicts.

History provides other examples of informal communities with principles and customs that preserve order and punish malfeasance. Organic anarchies popped up in frontier areas: the sixteenth century Anglo-Scottish borderlands; nineteenth century North American West, and many tribal areas in Southeast Asia, the Amazon, and Africa. In these frontier areas far from the reach of kings, republics and empires that form in richer agricultural areas, legal customs develop without a dominant power imposing them. Judges or tribunals emerge to resolve disputes for organic anarchies according to established custom. These organic anarchies are precursors to a state — not as matter of logical necessity, but as an empirical fact of history. Organic anarchies can persist while beyond the reach of empire, but frontiers on Earth have shrunk to almost nothing inhabitable. States have assimilated dispute resolution processes of their frontiers. Maybe organic anarchies can persist where states cannot reach. But states can reach everywhere people live. Perhaps states can devolve into organic anarchies during periods of chaos and governmental collapse. But even if organic anarchies can re-emerge in areas ruled by states, lack of central authority will persist only if the conditions that prevent its reemergence prevail. Regardless, the laws and customs of even anarchistic frontier areas make use of territorial sovereignty. Those who live in the boundaries of the frontier are subject to its prevailing customs, regardless of their views on their morality or sagacity. There is no personal sovereignty over law making, in such societies. Organic anarchies embody similar principles but are not social promise communities in the more limited sense of this book.

More recent movements that resemble social promising are easier to spot. Prominent examples include the GNU General Public License (GPL), pioneered by Richard Stallman as a defense against application of copyright to "free" (open-source) software. Other examples include standard copyright licenses, such as those published by the nonprofit organization "Creative Commons." People who wish to license their copyrightable content for use without payment of a royalty may refer to one of the standard licenses published by Creative Commons or another source. These and similar royalty free licenses are sometimes called "copyleft" licenses, and come with conditions such as attribution of creators, non-commercial use, and bans on copyrighting derivative works. Copyleft licenses resemble social promises. But a copyleft license is a form of contract. For all present-day copyleft licenses, the underlying law is that of a state. Copyleft provides no stateless alternative for resolution of disputes arising under its licenses.

Anarcho-capitalism inspired this Guidebook, so the resemblance to anarcho-capitalism is unsurprising. One form of anarcho-capitalism, "contractual republics,"[20] emphasizes the right of any two people to specify every condition of an agreement between them, including defining a stateless code of law under which their agreement operates. This is freedom of contract as we know it today, untethered from regulation by a state. Under classical anarcho-capitalism, without universal respect for the same property

---

[20] See, e.g., The Freedom App – Building True Freedom Through Contractual Republics, by Pete Sisco, Contractual Republishing, Inc., 2013.

rights there is no authoritative basis for resolving competing claims. For example, anarcho-capitalist societies cannot peacefully resolve competing claims between hunter-gatherers who do not recognize titled forms of land ownership and farmers who rely on a system of land titles, without subjugating one group to the other's rules. Being peaceful people who wish to avoid violent conflict, anarcho-capitalists argue with great passion about the most optimal or best property rights rules to follow. But they can never come to unanimity. In contrast to anarcho-capitalism, social promise community rejects any universal notion of property beyond self-sovereignty, instead relying on equality of persons, personal sovereignty, and publication of each person's personal code of honor as the basis for society. Conflicts are resolvable without force even when the parties hold to conflicting property rights.

Like anarcho-capitalist societies, contractual republics would rely on a universal property rights regime. The citizens of each contractual republic, by holding to the same common agreement, will naturally hold to the same view of property rights. Different contractual republics may recognize different property rights, but there is no mechanism for resolving disputes arising out of fundamental disagreements over property rights, or other conflicts in the law to be applied. Also, contractual republics use a different mechanism for defining rights and obligations: an express agreement of at least two people instead of independent public adoption. One side changing contractual promises entails a breach of contract in every case. But changing a social promise entails no breach.

Contractual republics might be less adaptable in their ability to adjust rules to suit changing conditions and beliefs than social promise communities that respect principled changes. Also, making contract the base of sovereignty calls the role of the state into question: are these contracts forming contractual republics enforceable in state courts, because they are contracts under state law? Social promises are not contracts under state law and the state will not enforce them. Social promise community avoids entanglement with state law, basing its authority on nothing but equal personal sovereignty. Contractual republics in which states define how contracts are formed are not self-sovereign. If not the state, what is the ruling authority for determining how parties define contracts? If by consensus of the parties, then the contractual obligations derive from social promises. Contractual republics become a species of social promise community by making mutual consent the basis for all enforceable obligations, while excluding initiation of force and fraud. Observe that self-sovereignty equates to mutual consent without initiation of force or fraud for political or social purposes.

Contractual republics and social promise communities might achieve similar outcomes under some conditions. For example, results may be comparable where at least two conditions hold: first, everybody holds to the same definitions of property rights; and second, the system of cooperating contractual republics is diverse enough to provide a life-sustaining republic for every minority viewpoint on social rights and obligations. Where these conditions hold, contractual republics and social promise communities might converge on the same outcomes. Otherwise, their outcomes will diverge. Divergent outcomes are likely. It's hard if not impossible to satisfy both conditions.

Voluntary organizations for developing standards, codes and rules already exist. Technical standards committees and open-source application development groups are examples. Open-source software is perhaps closest to a form of social promising. By proving that open and transparent code development can work better than closed models, open-source software developers have blazed a trail for "open-source" social promise development, i.e., social promising under the Three Promises. Many qualities of open-source code development apply to social promising. In both cases:

• The "code" (i.e., set of social promises) is open for contribution from anyone who can write useful, reliable code.

• Community leaders review contributions and publish standard versions. Nothing prohibits non-standard versions or "forks."

• Individuals produce and use customized variants and add-ons.

• Community acceptance and network effects determine the adoption rate of versions, forks, and add-ons.

• Community activity creates an ecosystem that supports economic transactions around code that is free to use.

The well-tested open-source model is ripe for adaptation to development of social promises. The success of the open source movement has proven that code writers will produce complex, useful code for reasons other than direct payment for code-writing services. Social promisors will follow their example and write social promises for free. We might also contrast social promising with open source code development:

• Social promising adapts to changes in normative preferences, and less so to changes in technology and aesthetic preferences as in open-source coding.

• There is diminishing pressure for continual development of new social promises as the ecosystem matures, in contrast to technological development that often feeds more technological development.

• Harmonization between different systems will be a critical concern for social promise communities, while software communities are more self-focused.

• Software programming requires special technical knowledge that most people lack, but any thoughtful person can make a meaningful promise.

• Successful social promises must accommodate and bridge disparate normative preferences, unlike computer programs.

• Social promises should become simpler and more stable the longer development proceeds, in contrast to software that grows and becomes more feature-laden.

Social promising is no less workable or less likely than open-source software development. Costs of promise making should be less than for open-source code development, on a per-bit basis. Demand for concise and stable social promises will keep data compact and stable. Anyone can make social promises, with or without technical skills. With these factors, the whole world could make social promises and translate their promises into numerous languages, for less expense than a single large international open-source coding project. It has not happened yet because people do not believe writing and publishing personal codes of honor has useful value. Government among self-sovereigns by social promising is too innovative to gain traction right away. Would-be early adopters face many barriers to building community. Inability to monopolize discourages investment, just as natural remedies receive less investment than pharmaceuticals. But once social promise communities establish themselves and provide social benefits to their members, they can grow with explosive social force. The economic barriers to widespread adoption are almost negligible.

No prior system requires makes personal sovereignty the basis for all social obligations, assigning all authority and responsibility to the individual. Everybody is honor bound to keep their social promises, and nothing more. Social promise community is revolutionary by declaring each person sovereign over herself, and only herself. But it is also evolutionary and rooted. It can incorporate rules and methods for dispute resolution and due process that have proven useful through the ages. And it exploits new technology such as open-source coding and distributed public registries secured by cryptography. It is new, but not that different.

Chapter 8: Overcoming Common Objections

First Look

Any new social system will have its detractors and skeptics, for reasons good and bad. Objections differ depending on their source. Authoritarians, whether religious or secular, object to the lack of any supreme authority. Progressive-authoritarians object to the lack of ultimate police power subject to an electoral system. Capitalists object to the lack of any universally enforceable property rights. Anarchists are triggered by the coupling of "voluntary" and "law," but have no reasonable basis for objecting. It will be the anarchists who construct the first self-sufficient social promise community.

It is worth knowing answers to common objections, while remembering that it is often a waste of time and energy to debate those who are convinced that social promising cannot work, or that it is immoral. Much can be learned by considering the sincere questions of an open-minded skeptic. Enlightening the sincere doubts of seekers is a kindness and a blessing. Most of all, persuasion will be by example. Social promisors must proselytize by generating desirable communities. To join these desirable communities, people must learn how the communities operate. Once they learn, they will be persuaded.

There is no need to win debates, and little purpose for debating. It is more persuasive to defend and gradually enlarge the intangible territory in which social promise communities can operate and focus on helping those communities operate well.

Kernel

Some object just because social promising is new. It has never worked before, they reason, therefore it cannot work. This is a non-sequitur. Whether not any system can operate does not depend on whether it has worked before. Success depends on the arrangement of the system's components. If the system's components are arranged cooperatively, and every energy sink is provided with an energy source, then the system will operate. History teaches us two things: social systems are not static, and voluntary arrangements are possible. There is no reason an entirely voluntary conflict resolution system cannot work. Newness is not a rational objection but might be the one most frequently expressed. The objection is often heard, because change is scary. Fear cannot be assuaged by reason but can be calmed by reassurances. If someone is arguing that social promising cannot work because it never has, do not debate them. Simply explain that social promising can only involve consenting and informed adults, so there is no reason to fear it.

Some may accuse voluntary law as being incoherent, or illogical, because it allows people to make conflicting promises. To this objection, answer that "the weaker promise prevails." Meaning that in any given claim, the least burdensome obligation applies to the one defending against it. So only one obligation applies in any certain context. Details of determining which promise is weaker can be complex and might take some explaining. The principle might be applied differently by different people. Nonetheless, the weaker promise principle eliminates the possibility that neutrals will apply promises arbitrarily, without a predictable direction. Every promise will be made understanding that it will only apply to those who have made equally burdensome, or more burdensome, promises.

Some accuse social promising of being utopian, or impractical, something that will never work as promised. They may buttress this conclusion with different arguments, usually rooted in a dim view of their fellows. Most people seek to be led and will not take responsibility for themselves, they may argue. Most people are selfish or irrational. It will be impossible to find unbiased neutrals acceptable to disputants. Skeptics will pile on sour doubts. Making such arguments is like making a list of reasons something heavier than air can never fly. Every rational problem can be addressed rationally, but solutions only interest those working to make heavy things fly.

Whatever social promising is, it is not utopian. Like any other dispute resolution system, it exists because people are not rational and fair in their dealing with one another. It is designed, like any good justice system, to encourage rationality and fair dealing. But it does its job using a decentralized approach, based on self-rule. Decentralized systems work differently than hierarchical systems, but they work. Getting a social promise system to work well is a matter of social engineering and requires no change in human nature. Quite the opposite: the core principles of social promising rest on reciprocal honor-bound personhood, a fundamental part of our human natures.

For some, social promising lacks religious authority. Schemes of government cannot be left to reason, for these worshippers of power. Power is its own religion but every major religion places justice and love above mere power. There may be no holy book that instructs acolytes in the ways of social promising. Neither are there any that instruct acolytes how to build aircraft, or computers; yet people of all faiths build and use such things. Social promising requires no one to forsake their religious beliefs and compels no one. Instead, social promising provides a broad social justice framework in which people of different religions and worldviews can live honestly according to their own beliefs, whatever they may be.

Some anarchists object because they view written rules as unnecessary or counterproductive to voluntary society. These feelings are understandable. The law as it exists today is too often used to oppress the poor and powerless. Lawyers as a class are too often a plague on human justice, being mercenaries valued and useful only to the wealthy. Although understandable, distrust of social promising may betray a misunderstanding of what social promising is. When the power to make social promises belongs only to each individual and none can lay obligations on another, none can use laws to oppress. When there is no privilege attached to advocates in conflict resolution, and no privileged monopolies on judicial and police powers, justice is affordable for everybody. To keep people honest, social promises must be recorded somehow, and writing is a convenient way to record them. Some anarchists may resist recorded promises, but everybody who respects social promises is an anarchist. Anarchists will lead the way.

Whatever you think of these arguments and defenses, they only matter if you intend to put social promising into practice. If you have no such intention, then mind your own business. Let those who will make social promises fulfill their solemn oaths, while pursuing their own visions of happiness.

Basket of Nuts

Overcoming the Statists

To the statist, social promising is impractical. People can't govern themselves and expect social order to result! Whether you call the statist attitude idealistic or practical, it doesn't much matter. Statists are Platonic idealists. Rule by enlightened elites over spectators, slobs, hedonists, thieves, whores, idiots and other dregs is the best humanity can hope for. Pessimists of this sort live in a barren world inhabited by human shadows. Our shared humanity does not equalize us; it separates us into classes. Each class proves its worth by dominating others. Dominance becomes a joy. Disturbing though this worldview is, we cannot deny its pessimistic power.

Platonic idealism is a popular mindset, but statists rarely think of themselves as living for dominance. Most are polite people with community spirit. For the polite ones, rule by elites is a necessary tool for public benefit. All people are equal and should have equivalent life opportunities. As luck would have it, too many people are incompetents, idiots or insane predators they must rule to avoid worse suffering. They rule; but with kindness in their hearts, like parents disciplining children. Never mind the greater wealth surrounding them unless as proof of their entitlement to rule. Whether sincere or hypocritical, the polite path is an emotional posture, not an ideology. Its theory is the same as the pessimistic path: Some should rule others. A few should hold a monopoly on force. Only its purpose differs in different strains of statism: for eugenics, for equality, for growth & progress, for individual freedom (ironically!), for the children, for the environment, whatever.

At the minarchist end of the statist spectrum, brokers subdivide power into competing spheres to create a balance. The minarchists hope the balance of power will prevent leviathan from growing until it consumes everything. It's a tricky and unproven alchemy, as shown by the tragic failure of the American experiment in minimal government for the public good. Whether minarchism can work is an interesting question, but not the subject of this book. Regardless of whether minimal government is workable, we don't see it around much these days.

States carry out their purposes with subtle guises. It would take a book just to catalog all the ways. You are not reading a book on statism, so we will not examine the methods of states with great rigor. All use the tool of taxation. All use the tool of monopoly of force. In every area, one police power must rule. Social promises are useless for raising taxes or setting up monopolies on police power, so bore statists. Watchful statists will tolerate self-sovereignty only so far as it does not threaten their monopolies.

No one can convince statists they are wrong. Statists are not wrong. They have a different viewpoint, a view that dominates the world. If you would coexist with convinced statists, don't debate their worldview. Understand where they stand and show them that self sovereignty holds no terrors for them. Show them that cooperating self sovereigns enjoy better outcomes than subjects competing for dominance and power. Invite them to participate without risk until they learn to fly.

Those who believe large authoritarian states are the best humanity can do will not read this book. You might wonder whether states are necessary, inevitable, or dispensable. Forget about that debate here! States exist, and if we want social order by some peaceful agency instead, we must build an alternative that works. For peace, we must construct an alternative that can thrive while coexisting with the state. We should not waste time arguing with statists or accusing them of being bad just for clinging to state institutions. We should learn to understand their reasons and motivations, empathize with their burdens, and to be their neighbors without compromising our self-sovereign powers. Understand their moral justifications for initiating violence and avoid triggering those justifications where possible. For statists, the ends justify the means. Some greater good justifies the human toll to recruit, feed, equip and regulate monopolistic police power, and the collateral damage that mono-cops, corrupt politicians, and one-size-fits-all laws do. Start by asking what their notion of greater good is. Debates are useless; persuasion by example is essential.

If you don't believe self-rule is workable, nobody can force you to rule yourself. Those who would live by their social promises ask nothing of you but to respect basic human rights. We would try our experiment in personal self-sovereignty, without conditions that doom it from the start. The only relevant question for the statist is whether or how the state should ban or regulate the practice of social promising. Good statecraft accomplishes its purposes at the least cost for the purpose it serves. Social promising builds interpersonal trust, which is not contrary to any good purpose ever put forward for society. States should afford social promisors maximal freedom to operate because the good activity costs the state nothing. That is not to admit that the state has a moral right to exist. Only that for those who would justify the state, it would be a terrible idea to ban social promising, for both practical and moral reasons.

Social promising rests on basic human rights, and social promise community needs little else to operate. Statists cite protection of basic human rights as justification for state action. The first essential right for social promising is freedom of speech. For social promising to become established, the state must tolerate teaching of personal self-sovereignty. It must not ban writings like this book. It seems almost silly, at this writing in California, to consider that the state might ban speech that teaches personal self-sovereignty. Yet one can image places where police would enforce a ban: totalitarian police states, strict theocratic states, U.S. prisons, and other places where those in power fear free speech. If you believe killing or locking people in cages for expressing a social philosophy is just, this book is not for you. May you remain ignorant of the many movements towards social harmony by personal self-sovereignty until it is far too late to extinguish them.

Besides the freedom to teach, social promise community relies on each member's right to publish their own social promises — another use for free speech. But social promises are something more than free speech. Social promises express personal moral beliefs. In this age of reason and skepticism, personal moral beliefs are the closest thing to religion that most people will ever experience. Old religions accrete myths and dogmas, but every religion at its core is a moral code. Likewise, social promises relate each person's ideal moral character to benefit their neighbors and preserve public peace. Social promising can fill one role that a healthy religion does, of expressing each person's moral beliefs for personal and social guidance. Without losing the character of personal expression, social promises express popular religious faiths, eclectic beliefs held by a single person, and everything in between. Without freedom to declare what we believe is moral, we have no freedom of religion or association. Totalitarian states forbid freedom of religion, but no such states are sustainable. Durable states must tolerate individual expression of personal honor codes as basic human rights including freedom of speech, religion, and association. Every great empire has recognized human rights of its citizens and some of the greatest empires had the greatest liberties.

With the freedom to publish social promises and to teach self-sovereign law, social promise community has all it needs to coexist with non-totalitarian states. Promise community activity is like any other private activity, from pissing in a pot to building rockets for exploration of the cosmos. The state need only concern itself with aspects of private actions that impinge on the state's duties, like national security. As social engineers, we must anticipate how our social environment will react to the launch of our designs and change our plans to avoid unnecessary resistance. We'll start by considering whether any of our critical infrastructure is at risk from state suppression.

A healthy self-sovereign community needs few basic services. First is a registry of members and their social promises. Bitcoin and other cryptocurrencies have now proven that public financial registries—in an area regulated by the state—can endure attacks. Laws against public registries are almost unthinkable. Regulation of distributed public registries has proven uneconomic. States regulate cryptocurrencies because they fear competition for their treacherous banking systems. We expect states' fear and loathing of social promise registries will be less than for cryptocurrencies, if separated from currency blockchains.

However widespread social promising becomes, social promises can't provide defenses under state civil or criminal law. This is self-evident. Recognition of social promises by states is neither necessary, nor expected, nor wanted. Social promises have nothing to do with state law, any more than the rules of the Game of Monopoly do.

Social promise registries do not compete with any state activity. States make laws, not promises. Only people can make promises. Social promise registries record only personal information, under control of those who the information describes. These registries should avoid use of currency or money transfer features, by design.[21] Promise registries might be made unsuitable for cryptocurrency, but every reliable ledger can be used for transactions. Reputation will be the asset that everyone wants to earn. Nodes will earn good reputations by preserving and serving uncorrupted data to other nodes and will secure one another's data by exchanging data hashes. State financial regulations should not apply.

Instead, social promise registries are just another open source, peer-to-peer form of social network. The network's members don't use it for anything but exchanging information. States regulate online activity for things like copyright piracy, sexual predators, terrorists, and so forth. Social promise community has no reason to protect terrorists or predators and can order itself so that predators and terrorists take little interest in it. Anyone may use the promise network to do good. Promise network are a poor

---

[21] See "Infrastructure Design" in Chapter 12 for further discussion.

tool for doing evil because a promise registry's purpose is transparency and reputation building. It's a poor device for cloaking evil. The promise registry backbone will exist beyond easy reach of liberal governments, just as open-source software and blockchain networks do.

Various services will build on top of the promise registry backbone. Promise-making is the most granular service that members will provide. One person, one set of social promises. States that respect basic human rights like freedom of speech, association and religion won't regulate promise making. Other services will include reputation checking, neutral services, social networking, gaming and enforcement. Reputation checking and social networking may be subject to state laws governing privacy and defamation. But since the information concerns only members, neutrals will resolve disputes over truthfulness of posted data without state intervention. No party maintains accuracy of registry data; all parties police their own information and are responsible for their own statements. Rogue members can always sue under state law but will lose their reputations for bringing state claims instead of using voluntary process. Administrators of reputation checking databases will ensure the personal data in their database comes from public sources or will get consent from subjects of the data before adding to their data stores. Administrators may offer perquisites to members who consent to certain information being maintained in the public reputation checking database. A moral statist can have little real objection to such services, which also touch on freedom of speech and association.

Another essential service is neutral dispute resolution services based on social promises. Business people around the world have experience with alternative resolution of civil disputes outside of state courts. Neutral resolution based on social promises is even further removed from state law than arbitrators and mediators who apply state law. States have no legitimate need to involve themselves in disputes over game rules. Social promises are like game rules because they concern only participants of a voluntary process. If game rules encourage or require participants to break state laws, then states will take an interest. Successful social promisors will not make promises that encourage or require lawbreaking. Lawbreakers will not use social promise networks for crime or for networking with other criminals because they will not want to make a durable public record of their criminal activities.

Facts of a claim under social promises might also support a claim under state law. If the underlying claim is civil, the state has no reason to oppose private dispute resolution whatever the rules applied. Social promises are like traditions such as "handshake" or unwritten agreements. Enforcement of civil obligations falls outside of state jurisdiction. States don't enforce rules of private clubs. If parties to a neutral opinion desire state recognition of an award, they can register it with state authorities. For example, if parties agree to transfer ownership of state-registered property, they may agree to recording a change of title with state authority. States won't know about voluntary due process unless the parties agree to make a public record. At most, the state may see evidence that some transaction has occurred, such as a change in ownership of titles, or evidence of some payment. The evidence will not differ from what the state sees for transactions with nothing to do with social promises. Social promise transactions deserve no special scrutiny.

When parties do not respect voluntary due process, tensions may arise. For so long as the state and social promise community coexist, parties unhappy with prospects under social promises can turn to the state. Parties will reject voluntary due process in some percentage of cases. But adjudication under state law is invalid in social promise community without the consent of all involved parties. Likewise, opinions under social promises are invalid under state law, without the consent of all parties. The invalidity is symmetrical, but the dishonor is not. Those who disavow their social promises to seek remedies under state law dishonor themselves. But those who forbear from prosecuting state laws to seek their remedy under social promises earn honor for themselves in social promise community, with no dishonor as state subjects. The only detriment is an eventual extinguishment of the state law claim under the statute of limitations. If a social promise neutral can resolve a claim to the satisfaction of the parties, states have no good reason to interfere.

If the underlying claim implicates state criminal law, the state might entangle itself with voluntary process. Public employees of the state will defend their exclusive claim to criminal jurisdiction that provides their livelihoods. Where claims under social promises implicate state criminal laws, claimants will avoid resolving disputes in venues that create a risk of state criminal prosecution for any participant. They will bring risky claims in safe jurisdictions, or not at all. Competent neutrals will minimize exposure to criminal liability by operating in protected jurisdictions under strict confidentiality with limited public records or won't hear the case.

In the large part of the world where some version of a socialist/capitalist democracy prevails, everything we need to implement social promise community is already available. All we need is to restrain the state from totalitarianism, to allow private associations to exist, and to respect a reasonable personal privacy and free speech rights. If you are reading this book, you probably will agree.

Even philosophical statists advocating for the state on moral or empirical grounds should accept experimentation with alternative ways to provide more just and orderly societies. One aim of social promising is to prove by experiment that social order based in self-sovereignty can provide enough benefits to justify its existence. As with any experiment, both success and failure are possible. Banning social experimentation robs statists of scientific justification for their positions. Tolerating experiments in social promising might provide statists with evidence for proving the state works better for some things, given the limits of the human condition. This could never be proven if the experiments are banned or regulated out of significance.

Failure of the state means peaceful replacement by a stable, stateless solution of proven superiority, however long that takes. The experiment may take centuries to complete, during which states and voluntary societies must coexist. Voluntary societies have always coexisted with states. It takes no great toleration to admit another type of voluntary society, and one that makes light demands of the state, at that.

Well-intentioned statists need not believe social promising is an experiment likely to succeed, or one in which they will participate. They need only be gracious enough to allow that social promise community can exist, just as any other voluntary activity between consenting adults that does not put others at risk of harm. There is nothing for any good person to fear from widespread institution of social promising, or of any other social institution operating on the principles of openness, voluntariness and honor.

Reassuring the Voluntarists

We are all traumatized by justice systems that deliver oppression. Our post-traumatic stress may cause us to fear many things without reason. For traumatized voluntarists and other anarchists, social promise ledgers are a little scary. Publishing social obligations in a ledger feels like a trap. Your own words might crucify your reputation and entangle you in endless civil disputes. These fears are not rational, but we cannot ignore them. Those who are most likely to build by pure persuasion a self-organizing society where order prevails without territorial monopolies on law are those most likely to be frozen by such fears.

These are the anarchists, who hope for social order with no one in charge.

Tossed on a sea of statists, anarchists fear giving anyone the power to make rules, even to their own selves. They fear lawyers and courts will use rules to force their double-dealing systems of oppression on everyone. Ruling elites will hide behind a wall of lawyers, and the law will remain an instrument to preserve and multiply the power of the powerful. Such fears are justifiable if those with power control making law, or if the society enforces a universal definition of property rights. Those with the greatest powers of advocacy will hold the strongest property rights. But social promise community rejects a universal definition of property rights or of any universal obligations except for the Three Promises. Every right of property and every rule must arise by agreement between sovereign persons.

Overbearing legislators, lawyers, judges and police can't operate in a community that rejects any universal definition of property and bases civil order on personal sovereignty. Social promise community is both scalable to any size and capable of tempering the power of the wealthy and political classes to suppress the poor and unfortunate. An intuitive emotional impulse against written codes of laws distracts from the true snare: a universal definition of property or any other social rule that extends beyond the sovereign self. With or without written codes, anarcho-capitalism will lead to the system of oppression that anarchists abhor unless personal sovereignty trumps property over external things. Given a universal, static definition of property rights without redistributive mechanisms, property will accumulate in the classes who first hold a superior ability to acquire it. Anarcho-capitalistic societies with rigid property rules and dominant property owners will devolve into plutocracies, principalities and monarchies.

There are exceptions to the old observation that the rich get richer, but it's hard to deny that wealth is its own best protector. Why would any seek to accumulate property beyond that necessary to provide basic needs if great wealth provided no social advantages? In any system based on private ownership of property (e.g., capitalism), there will arise an elite class of property holders and a class of impoverished persons. The former will exploit the latter, using the tool of property rights even if only unwritten.

Disdain for rights by writings might make sense on pirate ships or other small communities where a captain is the final arbiter of all disputes and writing is inconvenient. It's reasonable from the captain's point of view, at least. But for large human societies of strangers, written rules are the only safeguard against arbitrary justice. Let us suppose, for argument's sake, that it is best to not write any rules, and let people work out their differences however seems best. What if the parties cannot agree on a just resolution? They can resolve it one of two ways or leave it unresolved.

The first possibility is a contest. The parties in dispute engage in a contest of skill, luck, or both that resolves the dispute. These contests might include pistols at fifty paces, chess, poker, drive-by shooting, trial by water, whatever. Whether by skill or luck, the contest that ends the dispute has no predictable relationship to the dispute itself. The resolution is arbitrary. Contests of skill tend to their natural end: the party with the greatest power wins. Might makes right. Ending disputes by competitive skill can provide nothing resembling justice. It can only allow power to have its way.

A random dispute resolution process avoids "might makes right," but would do injustice at least 50% of the time. Plus, the result is always unpredictable, so people must litigate every dispute. Trial by coin flip does less to promote respect for the person and property of others than a justice system that consistently penalizes thieves, brigands and other evil doers, even if only less powerful ones. Without a neutral and predictable process for dispute resolution, there is no predictable cost or consequence for violating the person or property of others. Rules (written or not) are necessary for providing predictable outcomes to social disputes without resorting to "might makes right." Some question whether it is better to write rules down or leave them unwritten.

The second possibility for dispute resolution without written rules is to submit disputes to a judge or tribunal accepted by all parties. The tribunal or judge will try the controversy and decide without relying on a written rule. Robert Heinlein described something of this sort in his novel, <u>The Moon Is A Harsh Mistress</u>. Each judge applies her own standards, which can be arbitrary, or consistent with the judge's past decisions and/or community norms. Arbitrary decisions may as well be random. Consistent decisions conform to an unwritten rule. Sooner or later, a judge or lawyer will write those unwritten rules, as the number of community members grows, and its economy becomes more sophisticated. When unwritten judge-based systems of dispute resolution scale up to large communities, they become systems of judge-made written law, like British and American Common Law.

Lawmaking by judges is at the root of many legal systems today. For example, civil law in Europe traces back to ancient Roman law, which was in its early days defined by competing judges, before emperors took over the legal system. Common law in England and its former domains traces back to rules defined by various judges, albeit those supported by a reigning monarch or other lord. According to the Book of Judges, judges ruled ancient Israel with no secular or religious head, until Samuel anointed Israel's first king. This list could be much longer, but you are reading an engineering manual, not a work of legal history.

Evolution of dispute resolution by rule exhibits a pattern: First, those perceived to be most able (the judges) discern rules for dispute resolution. The most respected judges lead community norms by righteous decisions. As the community evolves and grows, independent judging diminishes while the role of judicial collectives becomes more important to enforce standards, introduce written rules, and suppress competition. Later, war-making entities (monarchies, states, republics, empires, etc.) bring existing judicial collectives or independent judges into submission, incorporate them into their war-making apparatus, and often take from them part or all their rule-making power. A call for a judge-based system without written rules is a call to turn the evolutionary wheel of society back to its origins.

One cannot go home again; de-evolution of societies and species may occur in reaction to the collapse of their sustaining ecologies but do not amount to progress. Instead, de-evolution sets the stage for repeating what has occurred before. History has proven that judge-based systems evolve with growth and empire into state-sponsored and controlled legal systems such as abhorred by anarchists today. Instead of re-inventing ancient judicial systems, the rational alternative is to invent and build dispute resolution systems attractive to users, that increase self-sovereignty and are not susceptible to subversion by states.

Experts in rulemaking are useful as are experts in any other activity, but it's unnecessary to give experts the power to impose the rules or social promises they write on others. Let them write as many social promises as they like, but let each person decide whether to make any social promise their own. Reserve promise-making for the sovereign power of each individual person and make that reservation a moral foundation. Wrest the judicial and legislative branches out of the obscenity of empire and give the exclusive power to obligate themselves to that ever-granular unit of society: the self-sovereign individual. Exclude judges, insurance companies, governments and all other persons and entities from the power to impose laws within the social promise community without consent of each member.

Social promises are valid expression of self-sovereignty that build interrelationships, but must they be written? Practically, yes. On an imaginary world orbiting a distant star, perhaps intelligent aliens can express their self-sovereign obligations to their peers without writing. But there must always be a reliable record to preserve continuity between each person's past and future, written or not. To release the sovereign power of the individual that record must be discoverable by others. A true record of self-sovereign obligations is at the root of each person's identity so far as society cares. Without that record, no self-sovereign order can develop. We write it for convenience and secure our writings by encrypting in cryptographic nets. We do not fear others discovering our self-sovereign obligations, although we can reserve our sensitive promises for a select few. We embrace our self-sovereign identities and abhor the thought of forcing obligations on others.

A pure-hearted anarchist's revulsion to written laws goes deeper than a preference for *ad hoc* judging. It reaches "Do what thou wilt shall be the whole of the Law. Love is the law, love under will."[22] People may assign different meanings to these phrases, but among them is the belief that each person should be free to follow their own spiritual calling, even if unconventional, so long as consistent with love. Social promise community enables social life by these principles. If a member of a social promise community believes that Crowley's The Book of the Law provides a useful code to live by, she may incorporate it into her personal social promises.

Nor could any anarchist deny a person the right to proclaim social promises and ask that others judge his reputation by the

---

[22] The "Law of Thelema" from The Book of the Law, Aleister Crowley, Ordo Templi Oreitis, 1938.

content of his promises and how well he keeps them. "Do what thou wilt shall be the whole of the Law," as Crowley wrote. Self-rule forces none to follow a rule they do not believe in. Social promise community is made up of people who publish their social promises, and measure others by their own rules. Publishing and living by one's own social promises is not an act of subservience. It is the refusal to assent by silence to the rule of others. Breaking muteness by social promising provides a logical and living alternative to rule by decree that enables organized societies of large scale to form, without war or bloody revolution. Silence gives license to those who would rule over you. Speak! Make known your determination for self-rule by making social promises.

A society organized on the moral principle of self-sovereignty in promise making has never existed before. Decentralized social promising has until now not been workable on a large scale. Centralized authorities had no reason to promote it. Advances in computing and communications technology have placed social promise community within reach, for the first time in human history.

Today's states and empires have many crevices and niches within which the seed of orderly self-sovereignty can take root and grow. Social promising can exist today with little controversy in many places, and coexist for a time with older, less enlightened systems. To those who scorn self-sovereignty as a pale and impractical dream, it is a meaningless fantasy or just another system of civil dispute resolution to fit within a statist framework. Let statists be statists until they go extinct. Voluntary conflict resolution systems, once functional, will provide services and teach moral principles despite ignorance and scorn. Once enough people understand how a self-organized conflict resolution system based on equal self-sovereignty can work, they will discard older systems as immoral and barbaric. This genie will not go back inside its bottle.

It is not a time to hesitate. Now is the time to leap aboard the vessel of self-sovereign social promising, sail it across uncharted waters, and discover what new world awaits!

Disarming the Religious

All the "world's major religions" possess ancient sacred scriptures and ascribe to these scriptures a level of veneration and authority. The tendency to ascribe law to ancient scriptures is prevalent in the Abrahamic faiths, with the Koran cited as authority for Sharia law in Islam, the Torah cited as authority for Rabbinical law in Judaism, and the Torah as reinterpreted by the New Testament cited as authority, along with infallibility of the Pope, for Canon law in Catholicism. Eastern religions are not without their ancient scriptures, teaching moral precepts. The moral precepts of religion resemble social promises but cut deeper. Religious precepts claim origin from the absolute, arriving by divine inspiration and always being true. How unfortunate that humans will do violence over conflicting divinities! For who can deny the Truth, be it God or No God? Only reprobates unworthy of membership in community. Such is the force of religious authority: one true way, one narrow path to enlightenment, one door open to all.

Believers in scripture sometimes tie their faith to secular or theocratic authorities. Religious authorities teach that faith requires submission to the proper authorities, whatever those may be. Faiths evolved in a world of kings and empires and bear their stamp. Religious leaders have served the state, teaching submission to secular authority. Centuries of alliances between religions and holders of secular power have not prepared the faithful to believe order can be self-organized. In recent centuries, faith traditions have had few or no encounters with self-organized social units larger than the family unit, and some believers look towards utopias under religious authority as a culmination of faith. Despite this, original writings and oral traditions of many religions teach order by self-sovereign discipline and relationship to God, and the practice of peace with one's neighbors.

Religious authority comes from truth, infinite in its diversity. Many traditions teach the moral precept of reciprocity that underlies social promise community. To give but one example, Jesus of Nazareth taught "In everything, treat others as you would want them to treat you, for this fulfills the law and the prophets."[23] The Three Promises embody the same precept. If you will keep your promises and ask no more of others than you have promised yourself, you are treating others as you would want them to treat you. Your social promises teach your neighbors how to treat you as you want. Their social promises teach you how to treat them as they want. If you would follow Jesus, living the Three Promises will help you fulfill the law and prophets. If you hold to a different faith tradition, chances are that living the Three Promises will bolster your dedication to faith and moral living. Living by the Three Promises will not impede the practice of your faith. It cannot. The Three Promises afford everyone maximum autonomy over their own beliefs and lifestyles.

But religious authority is an unavoidable aspect of organized religion. The impulse of the faithful to follow a teacher without question sometimes spills over into other spheres. Coexisting with kings and empires and serving the interests of priests, enduring religious faiths teach obedience to authority and its corollary that most people are not fit to rule themselves.

---

[23] Matthew 7:12, New English Translation (NET Bible).

Religious objections to self-organized societies based on non-aggression have changed little since Plato's Republic: a philosopher-king is the ideal form of governance that devolves to democracy. The masses cannot rule themselves, the human psyche is too corrupt and ignorant. It's a worldview that is at once arrogant and pessimistic and leads to dark places. To places where thugs enforce their beliefs with violence. Theocracies are a form of the state that claims divine authority. Whether the authority is divine or mundane, its enforcement is what counts.

Many faiths are not theocratic and authoritarian. Those faiths that claim no right to rule by force will oppose no voluntary arrangements between people. At most, those holding to a peaceful, non-aggressive faith might choose to not join any social promise community for reasons related or unrelated to their faith. The true believers in the right and necessity to rule others by force, whether theistic or atheistic, are the only active opponents to social promise community.

Judgment in the afterlife comes under "acting for the greater good." Take the Spanish Inquisition for example. To spare the majority the eternal torments of hell and provide them instead the eternal bliss of heaven, the Inquisitors justified their torturing and burning alive of a few unrepentant heretics, even while ignoring their own self-interested motivations. The welfare of all justified the severest aggression against chosen victims. While the Inquisition provides a stark example, the same "acting for the greater good" logic underlies all organized forms of aggression. For some, the state is part of their religious faith. Millions or billions put irrational faith in the state above all else.

Faithful minions of the state justify the evils of the "drug war" by their beliefs (contrary to most evidence) that legal access to pleasure-inducing substances would corrupt social virtues to a degree greater than the many lives ruined or destroyed by imprisonment or other actions of the violent cartels supported by prohibition. They champion violence while ignoring the taint of self-interested enforcers and other stakeholders. Likewise, they justify deprivation of earned wealth and intrusions on privacy caused by income taxes by beliefs that political redistribution of wealth and funding of government services from taxes provides a social benefit that is larger than the detriments of theft by public body. They justify genocide of troublesome ethnic groups or cultural imperialism by ending conflicts over resources, promoting superior culture, or improving the human gene pool. And so forth.

Scientific evidence to prove that aggression serves a greater good cannot exist. Science observes nature without value judgments, and so cannot discern any good or evil. If a theorem states a value judgment (e.g., "greater good") it is unscientific. True religion does not teach violence or fraud, but statists must accept justifications for their aggression on faith. What irony! If nothing else, faith in authority for violence is just another religion, one that worships the god of war.

No master exists without a willing pupil. Motivations for giving up the right to rule oneself vary. Submitting to an admired master to learn greater skill or insight births a fruitful exchange. The pupil gains knowledge, and the master attains fulfillment. Other motivations can be pessimistic. One such negative motivation is the myth of the fallen humanity. The mystical entry of sin into the world causes all the wretchedness of the human condition. Being sinful, humans cannot rule themselves without divine guidance. Scriptural and mythical roots for the pervasiveness of faith in authority are interesting, but more detailed treatment is beyond our scope.

Authority can be secular or religious. Society has its different competing elites in spheres such as the political, the spiritual/religious, the judicial, the martial, the entrepreneurial, the academic, and the scientific. There are natural reasons for the rise of experts and those of superior skill. Everybody has different abilities and motivations. Superior abilities in coveted arts are admirable. Does social promise community require that we deny the rational and human impulse to follow those who lead?

No! Self-sovereign promising empowers our best leaders to lead not by heavy-handed coercion, but by their excellent expressions and examples. False, uninspired or unskilled leaders cannot resort to the effective but injurious tools of coercion, fraud, and fear. Good shepherds can lead others to peace, prosperity, and spiritual growth by freeing all to follow their own conscience. Promise community casts the evil ones into the lake of continuous, fiery rejection by exposing their evil thoughts and deeds, while providing the fallen with a path to redemption through the mercies of the merciful. There is no system of social order that offers greater freedom of action for those following any religion consistent with human equality and respect for life. There can be no cogent religious objection to it, by any believer who values human liberty and equality before God.

What of religions that deny liberty? Those that demand obedience to a person or to an institution, under threat of violence? By denying liberty, they expose their belief that some should rule others, even without consent. If a religion justifies rule without consent, then it denies personal equality and becomes an enemy of voluntary community.

Everybody chooses their beliefs within the limits of their imagination and experience. If you would follow a religion, choose one that forbids violence or fraud even against mortal error or apostasy. So may you enter into thriving social promise community, where all may lead others to salvation and truth by their unfettered examples.

Chapter 9: The Promise-Keeper, In Life and Death

First Look

The promises of promise keepers provide the order in promise society. Promise keepers can be any entity with the necessary qualities for making and keeping social promises. Each promise keeper is their own authority, making their own social promises, and accepting the Three Promises as their foundation for honor and reputation.

Some persons and living things can't make and keep their own social promises. Their rights and obligations depend on the social promises of others. We might call them non-keepers or dependents. Infants and the comatose provide obvious examples; clearly such people cannot make or follow their own social promises. Acts such as abortion and euthanasia touch on the rights of dependents. Animal rights are another example. A different set of problems arises in dealing with fictional entities, such as collectives, corporations or other legal fictions. How can such fictions can coexist harmoniously with individual members of social promise society, if at all? How can fictions make and keep social promises? Finally, there is the question of what effect a promise keeper's social promises have after death.

Social promising places the answers to these questions within the power of the self-sovereign promise keeper. There are no hard and fast rules. Social promise community will adapt to different social expectations and practices in different environments. Being based in reciprocity, promise community should encourage promise keepers to apply the golden rule when dealing with dependents. A few examples are here, just a taste of the vast possibilities.

Kernel

Humans excel at disagreeing with one another, including about who can be a self-sovereign obliged by their social promises. People who define the society of promise keepers based on an arbitrary characteristic (for example, color of skin, language, eye color, culture, religion, etc.) don't deserve interest. Bigots exist but will not thrive if the weight of the community supports a rational basis for status as a self-sovereign promise keeper. As advocated in this book, rational attributes of each self-sovereign must include corporeality of the individual, possession of a moral sense, and the capacity to reason; to understand, adopt, and follow rules governing resolution of conflicting rights or claims.

Even when in agreement about the big picture, reasonable people cannot avoid debate about the finer questions. Where are the exact limits to who can be a self-sovereign promise keeper? What happens when parties disagree about whether someone is self-sovereign? What are the rights of living beings who are not promise keepers? How do the rights of promise keepers and non-keepers differ? Gray areas abound around non-keepers, such as minors or mentally disabled persons, collective entities, animals and other alien intelligences, natural or artificial. Most will grant rights to living individuals who cannot qualify at the critical time for status as promise keepers. Only the social promises of promise keepers apply. The rights and obligations of non-keepers derive from the social promises of keepers. Non-keepers are not non-promisors. Non-promisors are people who could be promise keepers if they wanted to be. Non-keepers can't be keepers or non-promisors by changing their minds, although through time and happenstance non-keepers might become both.

One branch of debates concerns dependents, such as minor children or the mentally disabled. Assume that non-keepers include children and other dependents. Issues arise when one member of

310

voluntary society believes another is abusing or neglecting a helpless dependent under their care. Related questions include solving disputes over guardianship and emancipation of children. Social promises impose no single rule to solve these problems, but we can expect reasonable solutions by considering the self-sovereign context and implications of the Three Promises. We can solve many questions by following the approach of reciprocity, treating others as would seem fair to you if in similar circumstances. Every disagreement involves conflicting promise keepers. The weakest obligation of the parties applies.

Abortion, infanticide and euthanasia test any social system. Nothing else brings the conflict between the powerful and the powerless into starker tension. This book has considered how TROTWET governs defensive actions in claims between people involved. Here we consider how promise keepers might handle a claim on behalf of a fetus, infant, or mentally disabled person.

Collectives and other fictions involve other issues. Collectives don't exist in the same way as natural persons, but it has been convenient for legal systems to pretend they do. Self-sovereigns may recognize or ignore fictional entities. Their society will include fictional entities that some recognize subject to conditions expressed in the social promises of self-sovereigns. Fictional entities have rights only to the extent granted by individual promise keepers.

Animals and other intelligent alien species are another class of dependents. By now you know how animals get rights: by the social promises of promise keepers. Intelligent aliens are a different matter. If such beings exist and fit the criteria for being a natural person with the capacity to make and keep social promises, they can be promise keepers just like any capable human.

For social promisors who have died, there is the question of what effect the promises made in their lifetime should have. These issues have implications for trusts and estates, contracts, and other social questions. It is possible to derive a fair approach based on social promises consistent with settled expectations.

When we crack open the door to the rights of dependents, we can intuit the tremendous power of social promises to address every social problem. Social promising reaches beyond the promisors themselves to guide treatment of dependents. From there it expands to fill all matters of public interest. Politics doesn't end, it becomes campaigns influencing promise keepers to make or annul specific social promises. Social promises can flex enough to allow experimentation while preserving what has worked. In conservative mode, they express and preserve the customs and moral preferences of the community. In progressive mode, social promises empower exploration of new solutions to difficult social questions. Social promise community will be both progressive and conservative.

Basket of Nuts

Children and Other Dependents

When can self-sovereigns intervene in caretaker-dependent relationships involving fetuses, infants, children, or others incapable of looking after themselves? What justifies intervention when the subject is incapable of making or keeping her own social promises? What actions are proper when the parties can find no responsible caretaker for a dependent? If every dependent person (or potential person) has an uncontested caretaker who treats the dependent in a manner consistent with prevailing customs, controversies do not arise. Disputes arise when dependents lack any caretaker, are the subject of caretaker disputes, or receive treatment those willing to take defensive measures regard as abusive.

We can divide dependents into two classifications: former self-sovereign promise keepers, and potential promisors (non-keepers) with no history of being a capable self-sovereign. In mortal souls, capacity exists for a finite period or periods of time. Promisors live by their promises even after they have lost their ability to make promises. A power of attorney does not become invalid after the grantor becomes senile, for example. When a dependent has made no social promises, a neutral selected by the parties in dispute stands for her.

A dependent relationship between two capable persons may be a contract or agreement, a grant of power, a temporary agency or service in which one capable person depends on the actions of another. The social promises of the parties govern these relationships. The capacity of a person to make and keep promises will sometimes be at issue. For example, a dependent who made a first social promise 'A' and later 'B' might have the validity of either 'A' or 'B' challenged. Neutrals might nullify promises not made in a capable state of mind. A neutral might disregard a later social promise 'B' for an earlier social promise 'A', or vice versa. If the neutral finds the party to be a dependent non-keeper, no social promises made by the dependent are valid. We will consider treatment of dependent non-keepers later in this essay.

First, however, consider conflicts between promise-keeping dependents and their caregivers. Such conflicts may arise in caregiver actions to spend assets belonging to the dependent for the dependent's care, or to register a property interest in the dependent's estate. On the dependent's side, another acting as a guardian under the dependent's social promises might raise a claim to recover damages from a negligent or abusive caregiver, or to seek termination of the caregiver relationship. In the sense used in this book, a "guardian" is a representative who asserts the dependent's social promises on behalf of a dependent. Unlike state-appointed guardians, a guardian in the sense described here appoints herself. Any promise keeper willing to take responsibility for a dependent can be a guardian. A guardian can receive compensation permitted by dependent's social promises, for example, based on a reasonable value of services rendered or by contract. Guardians resolve their disputes like every other promise keeper.

Consider the result if the caregiver's social promises permit a property claim or asset request but not the dependent's. Under the Third Promise, the caregiver has no right to payment. Usually family members and loved ones will step in to provide care. But sometimes, mismatched social promises will prevent payment for continuing care, if the dependent cannot contract with the caregiver. Unless a neutral can intervene, dependents unable to act on their own behalf might lose the benefit of their own property. Sometimes, a neutral may find that the dependent consented to pay costs of her care. In other cases, the evidence may show that the dependent wanted to preserve her estate for her heirs. If the dependent's social promises preserve her estate to the detriment of her own continued care, the neutral cannot find otherwise. In these cases, the effect of adopting a clear social promise on the question would resemble a "do not resuscitate" order under the law of many U.S. states. Nobody must waste their estate on extraordinary care for the last days of life.

Actions may go the other way, by dependents (via a guardian) against caregivers. Dependents recover nothing not permitted by the social promises of the dependent and the caregiver. Everyone can guard against leaving themselves without a remedy prior to the disability arising, by contract, by social promising, or both. For example, the dependent can make a conditional social promise to compensate caregivers whose social promises meet a specified standard. The specified standard might require that the caregiver promise to meet reasonable standards for professional care. The dependent may escape liability to pay caregivers who have not made social promises that meet the standard. Depending on their social promises, unwelcome caregivers risk claims by dependents under their care. Professional caregivers will manage the risk of complaints by careful crafting of their social promises. The examples above introduce issues around dependent promise keepers, but do not frame an exhaustive study.

Dependent non-keepers include children and others who lack any history of being social promisors. They are dependent in the sense of depending on the social promises of other self-sovereigns. They are often but not always dependent for sustenance on social promisors. Dependency of an incapable non-keeper on a capable society member opens different possibilities for the dependent's status. One possibility is to regard the dependent as a non-promisor. Under this approach, the poor dependent person has no recourse for abortions, infanticides, child abuse, euthanasia, kidnappings, or worse. Her elders will have trapped her in a non-promisor state while holding her incapable of social promising. Ethical elders will not be so unfair.

Another possibility is to oblige the dependent by the social promises of the caregiver. If we must choose one set of social promises, the caregiver is the nearest choice. Nearest, but holding the dependent to the promises of the caregiver invites abuse by unscrupulous caregivers and dissolves the dependent's independent identity.

One solution is consistent with equal rights under natural law: to presume the dependent is a person of good conscience who would make social promises consistent with her social environment. The alternative, to regard the child or other dependent as entitled to no more rights than the property of the caregiver until emancipation, is contrary to nature. Progeny are not livestock. Children are the fabric of future society, destined (with work and luck) to become equal participants in a society based on personal sovereignty and making of social promises. Livestock and other animals incapable of language do not share the destiny of children and belong to a different class of being. In a social order based on personal sovereignty, people can't be property.

If we assume dependents would make their own promises if they could, what are those promises? We can never know the mind of a mute with certainty, but we can reflect on our own experiences growing up. Unless we are victims of abuse, we will have a template for fair treatment embedded in our minds. Parties will sometime disagree about whether caretakers are neglectful or abusive. Parties can also disagree about whether someone is a capable self-sovereign. The latter disagreements are straightforward. Neutrals can decide whether a party is a self-sovereign promise keeper by testing their abilities and disabilities against the logical requirements for promise keeping. Disagreements of the first type are trickier. When all agree that a person is incapable of promise keeping, which social promise to apply can be unclear.

Conflicts touching on dependent children will sometimes be custodial disputes between estranged parents or relatives. Conflict can also arise out of allegations of caretaker abuse by child protection agencies, whether in the person of interested family members, neighbors, or organized benevolent societies. Other cases may involve a dispute between the child and an adult. For example, the property rights of the child may be at play, or damages for an alleged wrong committed by a dependent child. We shall consider the first class of disputes first.

Honoring the Third Promise involves comparing burdens that social promises place on the sovereign parties to a dispute. None can impose obligations without consent and a promise to honor the same obligations they demand. But when the claim determines the rights of a dependent who cannot make promises, the logic of the Third Promise does not apply. People who can't make social promises can't make hypocritical promises. Someone else must make the promise for them, hypocritical or not.

Who is best positioned to make social promises for a dependent? No one is better positioned than the neutral picked by the parties in dispute. She examines what social promises are reasonable and honorable for the dependent. The neutral supports her opinion by the available evidence, showing that the social promises fit the dependent's circumstances. The imputed social promises might resemble those predominate in the community to which the child and her family belong. They might also bear a resemblance to the social promises made by the disputants. The neutral should also consider the preferences of the dependent child and her siblings if any will speak. Imputed social promises will never be perfect, but we can measure their fairness by consideration of the evidence.

Once we have a social promise for the dependent, how do we apply the Third Promise? Consider an example: circumcision may be honorable in one community, and abusive in another. Suppose parents plan to circumcise their child for cultural or religious reasons. A grandparent who considers circumcision to be a grave form of child abuse brings a claim against the parents for a neutral opinion that circumcision violates the rights of the child. The outcome falls on the child, the dependent. To win a binding opinion, the grandparent must hire a neutral acceptable to the parents. The parents will not accept any neutral hostile to circumcision. Except in unusual cases, the wishes of the parents will prevail. If the child is a natural son of a tribe who all promise to circumcise their sons, the infant will hold the tribal promise.

If the parents are indulging an idiosyncratic fetish, few if any neutrals would believe the infant shares its parents' fetishes. The grandparent will be better able to recruit security agents to protect the child from becoming a victim of the parents' unusual beliefs.

The parents can bring a claim to regain custody, but unless they consent to a neutral who recognizes tribal norms shared by the grandparents, there can be no honorable resolution. Whether or not the grandparent takes physical actions to protect the child, neighboring members of the community will be on notice of the circumstances and can treat the parties as they deem fair.

To test our logic with an extreme example, what if a tribe believed in sacrificing infants born with genetic defects? The obligation — sacrifice — is extreme. But genetic sacrifice is commonplace in our world. For example, medical providers often encourage parents to test for genetic defects and to kill the fetus if defective. Some countries permit it for children. In Belgium and the Netherlands, voluntary euthanasia at any age is legal or not prosecuted under certain conditions. Due process means sympathetic neutrals will hear complaints over child sacrifice. So long as sacrifices comply with tribal norms, ethical neutrals won't interfere with them. Besides regulation by its neutrals, the eugenic tribe's sacrifices will face regulation by neighboring tribes. Most of this pressure will be of a diplomatic sort. But in extreme cases, guardians might step in from other tribes to prevent sacrifices that offend their sense of justice. Both parties in inter-tribal disputes must accept the neutral, or no due process can work and there can be no honorable resolution. The possibility of intervention by neighboring tribes regulates practices like eugenic sacrifice that might be a cover for simple murder or genocide.

Divisions over any social practices will spawn social promise tribes that resemble nations exercising sovereignty over their members for civil justice matters. These tribes will not have borders, will not levy taxes, will not have legislatures, and will not go to war over territory. Self-sovereigns can belong to many tribes if social promises of those tribes do not contradict one another. Tribes will have no centralized order. Self-sovereigns will join and leave tribes by making and revoking social promises. Conflicts between members of conflicting tribes will create demand for neutrals acceptable to both. A principle of due process that neutrals must be acceptable to all parties in dispute mirrors tribal sovereignty over civil justice!

Divisions over corporal punishment are a familiar example: to some, corporeal punishment is an inexcusable crime, no matter how implemented; to others, it is a useful means of discipline. When disputes arise about corporal punishment of a child, a neutral will weigh the three factors of community norms, interested caretaker beliefs, and dependent statements to determine the limits of corporal punishment. The tribal context does not differ from our previous example. Successful neutrals will conform to tribal norms, but from the perspective of the individual dependent. She will craft governing social promises that the dependent would have made if she could. A good neutral will tailor her opinion to the individual circumstances of each case. She will give weight to various factors, such as the underlying conduct, identities, and social promises of the parties, community norms and the age and statements of the defendants. A few neutrals will bridge tribal divisions over proper treatment of dependents. In inter-tribal disputes, parties must settle under a standard that neither would adopt for themselves. Such is the nature of honorable compromise.

Impact of neutral opinions depends on the good reputation of the neutral, and the thoroughness, neutrality and wisdom of the neutral's examination. Results would tend towards greater justice than is possible when imposing a uniform rule on controversial questions. Social promising permits diverse and conflicting opinions to coexist, with pressure towards uniformity coming from the grassroots. Social promises are not instruments for imposing uniformity against opposition. Anyone holding to a controversial social promise, however, will do so at the risk of her relationships with her community. She might feel social pressure to conform, but no aggressive coercion.

How should the Third Promise apply to social promises that a neutral imputes to a dependent? It depends on whether the dependent is a party to the action. If so, the Third Promise applies. Let's consider an extreme example. Murray fathers Bart by Ayn. Murray disclaims all obligations of child support in social promises he published before impregnating Ayn. Ayn regrets not checking before she slept with Murray and can't believe anyone could be so callous. But she has no claim against Murray based on his social promises. She can't force an obligation on Murray he has not promised to take on. Now suppose Ayn also disclaimed all child support before becoming pregnant, leaving Bart without a right of support even if a neutral promises support on Bart's behalf. Under the Third Promise, Bart has no right to impose support on Murray or Ayn. This is unjust because Bart did not ask to be born. He could not pick his parents. Murry and Ayn caused him to exist as a dependent child.

We would like to honor the Third Promise without seeing it used as a tool to escape natural obligations. Due to the helpless nature of human children and being the prime cause of their children's dependent state, parents have a natural obligation of support. But parental obligations are not the only natural obligations people can have. Social promises can disclaim natural obligations or confirm them. The punishment for disclaiming natural obligations is the shame and loss of reputation that comes with making offensive social promises in a public register. This punishment will be severe enough to discourage all but the most determined extremists. If Murray and Ayn are such extremists, neutrals will equip Bart with social promises that enable emancipation from Murray and Ayn, and adoption by a new household. If Murray and Ayn are producing children they refuse to care for and that no one will adopt, guardians can step in to end their faithless breeding.

Children don't become self-sovereign social promisors overnight. They move into the role. The teenager has more rights and responsibilities than the toddler. As children age and become more independent, neutrals will give more weight to their stated social promises, and less to their circumstances. Once a person attains capacity as an independent self-sovereign, the neutral no longer serves as custodian of their social promises. Determination of capacity in the intermediate zone is a sliding scale. These determinations will not always be perfect, but neither will they be far from a just result. Flexibility in the aggregate will provide justice greater than iron-clad rules.

Independent self-sovereigns are just that: independent. If a precocious youngster can articulate and understand his own social promises but cannot support and manage himself by his own wits and labor, he is not independent. His promises, statements and requests have great weight, but lack the binding effect of social promises made by independent self-sovereigns.

If neutrals can impute social promises to the dependents of social promisors, should they impute promises to dependents of non-promisors? They might, but dealing with non-promisors or their dependents will seldom be workable. Regimes outside of social promise community will have their own rules governing dependent persons or will be lawless. In either case, there is no basis for expecting caretakers of the dependent to follow voluntary due process. If an abandoned child of a non-promisor somehow comes before a neutral, and a community member appears as an interested caretaker, guardianship is as valid for the orphan as for the child of any society member. It is permissible to provide for the dependent within social promise community where the society of non-promisors has broken down. It is no less valid to return the dependent to the society of non-promisors if no caretaker in the community will care for it.

Protecting dependent non-promisors by imputing a social promise might create relationships of mutual servitude between caregivers and dependents. The caregiver might owe a duty of care to the dependent while the dependent may owe a duty of obedience to the caregiver. Voluntary servitude, i.e., employment-at-will, offends no principle of equal self-sovereignty. Social promises, however, may provide a means for guardians to enforce obligations of care if the caregiver renounces her obligations. Likewise, social pressure to obey their caregivers might apply to dependents who wish to receive the benefits of the caregiver's duty of care. If a dependent can emancipate himself or herself from a caregiver, she is always free to do so. But a caregiver who has promised a duty of care to a dependent child must honor that duty until emancipation.

Promissory estoppel may exist when the promises of a person create detrimental reliance by another. For example, suppose that a prospective father makes a promise to support any natural offspring or adopted child until the age of eighteen or until emancipated, whichever is earlier. While holding to this promise he attracts a mate, who bears him a son. Suppose the father then renounces his earlier promise and adopts a new promise excusing himself from obligations of child support. If the mother relied on his social promise in mating with him, the father is bound by the promise he held forth when it mattered. The mother has a good claim for child support against the father, up to but not beyond her own obligation of support.

Most will promise a duty of care to helpless persons. For example, if a person faints in the middle of the road, most would exercise due care to avoid running them over. Members can avoid basic social promises, but at the risk of their reputations and chance misfortunes. These basic duties extend to the helpless infant or child and will motivate parents to locate a willing caretaker for the child before abandoning it. If free to do so under state law, parents could advertise their need for a caretaker to assume responsibility in caretaker communities.

When a dependent commits an offense against another, whose social promises apply? For this class of problems, most neutrals will pick the weakest promise from those of the caregiver and the injured person. Usually the promises will call for restorative damages that the caregiver in the dependent relationship would be liable for, anyway. Few would disclaim such liability, lest they lose recourse for harms committed by the children of others. But if the caregiver disclaims responsibility, the child will owe damages under a social promise determined by the neutral. The child may receive a lighter penalty for her dependent status, or not: the outcome will depend on the context. The neutral may defer collection of the debt until the child reaches self-sovereign status. New self-sovereigns will be eager to repay debts, to earn a good reputation.

With abandoned dependents, parties will be those with an interest in the welfare of the dependent, and any accused of shirking their responsibilities. If there is no parent or family member interested and able to take on the obligations of a caregiver, the dependent will be available for assignment to a new caregiver. In any prosperous society built on social reputation, families will compete for caregiver roles of young, non-disabled children. With large families tied by social bonds comes social security. Without state-run welfare, security in old age may come to depend on one's social status. A history as a productive member of an extended family may be an important part of that status.

Older dependents or disabled dependents will not lack options. Older children without caregivers will arrive in such a condition by a diverse array of events, for example, a long period of undiscovered abuse by a caregiver, a rare tragedy wiping out the child's family, or misconduct by the dependent. Likewise, disabled children will suffer from diverse disabilities. Each case deserves consideration on its own merits.

Several possibilities exist. With disabled dependents whose caregivers lack financial means, support may come from charitable sources. Charitable sources would exist in social promise community where a good reputation is more desirable than gold. Some such sources would support research for curing or coping with disabilities, and others would support such care out of their general charitable mission. If the caregivers lack both the means and the will to provide care, the situation would be much the same, except that a neutral may assign caregiver privileges to another person. In social promise community, slight needs come with slight responsibilities, and every good deed builds a reputation. Caregivers would often find themselves blessed to provide care for such unfortunates.

The older dependent with a record of misconduct would face the least favorable option, but even these options would be better than under centralized political authority. With a young offender, rehabilitation is more workable than with an older person. In a free society, markets will exist to meet the natural demand for managing troubled teens while producing positive outcomes. The most difficult teens are sometimes the brightest or most energetic, and institutions with effective programs would produce their share of illustrious alumni. Most of these alumni superstars would support the institutions that helped them in their time of need. Not only so, many wealthy parents with difficult teenagers would pay to send their children to rehabilitation institutions. These institutions for human development of troubled youth would compete to take in troubled youths who lack caregivers of means, because doing so enhances their reputations for success and compassion, and adds to the talent pool for development of successful, motivated alumni.

Where caregivers of means are available, a neutral may require them to send the dependent to an institution, and to pay the institution's tuition charges, per the social promise imputed to the dependent. Caregivers may ignore a neutral's ruling without fear that the institution will kidnap their child. In rare cases enforcers might incarcerate a violent youth for a while even against the caregiver's wishes. In most cases, the caregiver will consent to temporary incarceration of a youth with a record of harming others, to manage liability for the harm that the dependent youth may do to others, and for the youth's own protection. If the neutral is of good reputation, and the dependent decides of her own will to attend the institution, the caregiver will receive an invoice for the tuition that she cannot ignore without damaging her credit rating or creating a risk of collection action. If the caregiver prevents the dependent from attending, the caregiver will be liable for any damages that the dependent inflicts on others during the rest of its dependency. Whenever a guardian has asked for an order admitting a dependent to an institution for restoring the reputation of a youth, diligent caregivers will work with the neutral to identify a solution that complies with the social promise imputed to the dependent and is satisfactory for all people involved in the controversy. Neutrals in these cases might come to resemble family counsellors possessing social power to motivate cooperation from the family members appearing before them.

Imputed social promises for dependents can apply to abortion, infanticide, and euthanasia. We will consider these subjects in the next essay.

It may not take a village to raise a child, but the dependent's environment including its "village" should be a factor in finding the social promises that will achieve justice in the dependent's case. Neutral determination of the social promise of the dependent person arises from the bedrock of personal sovereignty, and depends on the insights of unbiased, informed, compassionate and wise neutrals. Caregivers are the most important pillars of their dependent's community but never tyrants over their dependents, lest we lose the core principle of personal sovereignty for every person with respect for sanctity of life.

Abortion, Infanticide and Euthanasia

The abortion debate rages under two constructs: one in which fetal life has rights, and one in which it does not. Social promises can dissolve the old constructs. A neutral provides a social promise to a fetus or an infant, determining their fate. The fetus or infant contributes no words to the neutral's deliberations. The neutral deliberates on the best evidence, which includes the social promise of the parties in dispute and the prevailing norms in the community. Although the neutral has power to inject social promises into a dispute on a mute's behalf, the evidence limits her power. If a neutral rules against the weight of the evidence, she puts her own reputation at stake.

Why should a neutral do this? What are the alternatives? One alternative to following the social promises of the parties in dispute is to make an absolute rule. Some neutrals might ignore social promises regarding abortion and apply a fixed social promise instead. A fixed rule might be a promise that forbids abortion, or one that permits it. But any absolute rule on the rights of a fetus violates equal self-sovereignty, because the fetus cannot speak for itself. Self-sovereign promise keepers must be corporeal, mortal entities capable of language and rational discourse. Infants, fetuses, and fertilized human cells lack language and the ability to reason with adults yet have an innate ability to gain those skills given the right opportunity. They fall into a special category. They are potential self-sovereigns who are not capable of making and honoring their own social promises yet might become capable within their lifetimes. We will call such living beings "dependent potential self-sovereigns" or "dependent potentials," as a general class including infants and young children. The fetus is the prime example of this class.

A fetus never consents to its own self-destruction. As a living being, all fetuses (and zygotes and fertilized eggs) share the common impulse of all life: survival. The fetus never consents, but neither does it refuse. Silence by victims of abortion is a fact. Although fetuses are the seeds of future self-sovereigns, absolute rules against destruction or abandonment of all seed tissue violate natural economic law and the self-sovereignty of promise keepers. Whatever cannot think cannot consent or refuse, and preservation of life comes with wholesale destruction of unthinking tissue, including its own seeds. Nature teaches us this lesson. No animal lives but by eating what was once alive. Few eggs produce young that survive to adulthood. Even mammalian species often bear litters, of which few survive under normal conditions. The economics of life dictate that not every potential individual can survive until adulthood. Seeds cannot force self-sovereigns to keep obligations they have not promised, without destroying the foundation for voluntary society.

No sustainable society can enforce laws in which every individual package of DNA capable of growing into a person has a right to life and nurture. With such laws, no one could abandon or dispose of inseminated eggs. Mothers would be liable for violating rights of miscarried fetuses. Self-righteous hypocrites could force rape victims to bear and nurture the offspring of their rapists. No natural society could observe such an absolute rule. Exceptions to the duty to nurture have always existed out of economic necessity or social desire. Sustainability of the social order takes precedence over the fate of any one potential dependent. Elevating the universal survival instinct to the status of a law will cause inevitable clashes between fecundity and scarcity, and between the rights of caregivers and rapists or careless fornicators. Customs, rules, and laws regarding treatment of infants and fetuses vary with the times and circumstances, as a matter of historical fact.

But enormous tension exists with another pillar of society. Peaceful civil society depends on reciprocal respect for the sanctity of life. You might say belief in the sanctity of life underlays order by equal self-sovereignty. Disrespecting the rights of fetuses and infants undermines respect for sanctity of life. Statists resolve this tension by pretending to enforce one rule about practices such as abortion, infanticide and euthanasia. When violating natural economic order, statists must cope with endless self-contradiction, controversy, and uneven enforcement. In self-sovereign society, outcomes depend on the individual circumstances of the dependent potential person involved. Outcomes differ but are not arbitrary. Neutrals identify the social promise that the dependent person would most likely have made if it were the caretaker.

For the fetus and infant, none are closer than mother. Absent extraordinary circumstances, the mother's social promise will apply to her child. The relationship of parent and child is fundamental and flows with natural duty. The mother-fetus relationship is exclusive to the two. If abortion becomes commonplace, it shows a deeper imbalance, a symptom of a deeper disease. We cannot stop the disease by dis-empowering the life-and-death decisions all mothers must make about their offspring. After the mother stands the father. No others are closer to the fetus. Many self-sovereigns will hold these or similar beliefs. They will not intervene in abortion except in extraordinary circumstances such as fetal tissue farming or surrogate motherhood. Communities with traditional cultures are unlikely to enforce a mother's social promise to lend her body for public use as a fetal tissue farm and might disfavor specific forms of abortion. Less traditional communities might be more permissive. As we noticed in examining children's rights, social promise "tribes" will form to protect and enforce certain views. A mother seeking an abortion will not go to a doctor who belongs to a traditional tribe. Defenders of the unborn will not agree to due process by neutrals of a hostile permissive tribe. Tension between tribal beliefs will motivate compromise in difficult cases.

Fetal rights are at the periphery of disputes between interventionists and those doing the grim job. Custody disputes fall under the promises of the parties. The fetus avoids actions by non-family claimants. Something akin to "standing" limits claims by unrelated third-party guardians. By the Third Promise, we limit the right to receive damages for injuries of potential dependent person to their kin. When the victim does not die, the offender pays the victim. When the victim dies, the offender pays the estate of the deceased. Administrators of the estate pay the damages to the heirs. Social promises can work this way. With abortion, the closest next of kin and likely heirs are the parents, who won't bring claims against themselves for damages. An unrelated third person cannot claim damages; who will promise to reward strangers for the misfortune of a fetus?

Unusual cases can spring up on the margins. One parent might register a claim against another to prevent an abortion or collect damages for one performed if their social promises permit. For example, a person who has paid a surrogate mother might have a legitimate interest in seeing a viable pregnancy carried to term. Neutrals might sometimes make a social promise for the fetus if using the mother's social promise is offensive to the neutral's tribe. Mothers and their fetuses will avoid using neutrals from hostile tribes whenever they can. Actions against the social promises of the mother will be rare. Hypothetical disputes between an abortion provider and a third party "defender of fetuses" have been considered in another chapter.[24]

Some mothers (or fathers) may find themselves strangers in a strange land. Their customs might clash with those around them. Neutrals from strange tribes may reason that if their fetus were to grow to become a parent, it would recognize a local regulation on abortion. In these very rare cases, a guardian might get a ruling contrary to the mother's social promise requiring she give birth and either care for the child or give it up for adoption. Results will play out as the social promises determine.

Neutrals would follow the customs of their tribes. Something simple makes this work: a lot of tribes! Many tribes cut the ideological pie into thin slices. With so many views represented, compromise lies between any two points in the spectrum or the points are already close. Diversity of opinion makes compromise easy. With many tribes, it's always possible to find a neutral equidistant from both parties for divisive questions. Perhaps some will avoid joining any ideological tribe. Either way, bias by neutrals will be visible. If a neutral always rules one way despite hearing cases with different mothers' promises, bias appears. The credibility and livelihood of any neutral who hears numerous abortion cases and rules one way regardless of the circumstances advertises bias. Biased neutrals cannot attract work unless the neutral's bias represents the closest compromise. A few neutrals might tout their bias, but most will proclaim their impartiality.

The fewer the number of viable tribes, the less the social promise community can service needs of unconventional members. The less it can grow, the smaller its benefits. As a boundary condition to social promise community, equal self-sovereignty

---

[24] Chapter 4, Basket of Nuts "With Negative Promises, Reverse the Sign."

spawns ideological diversity. The greater the diversity, the more each tribe feels pressure to remain at peace with fellow tribes, and the costlier it is to go to war. Social promise community will blossom when warring factions lay down their weapons and learn to build common defenses together.

Does acknowledging community standards revive the state? No, because there is no actual "standard" outside of a consensus between neutrals of good reputation. Freedom gives birth to diversity of opinion. A thousand schools of thought emerge. None extinguish others, some die for lack of support, and new ones splinter off established but ossified traditions. Standards exist, but not only one.

With different standards, why won't cases ping-pong between opposing neutrals? Because parties pick neutrals by agreement. Both parties will seldom agree on a neutral for rehearings. Rehearings are wasteful, expensive, and can involve a breach of good faith. Disputants will agree on a first neutral as a compromise and live by the opinion that results. In rare cases, a second neutral may need to step in if the first neutral becomes unable or unwilling to fulfil her social promises to the parties.

These general principles continue to apply after the child is born. The infant is no longer dependent on the mother for survival. Others can step in to care for it. Controversies over abortion are no longer possible. Although repugnant to most modern cultures, past cultures have killed infants for eugenic, religious, or political reasons. Unlike fetuses, infants can survive on their own for quite a while, with a little luck. Ordinary social promises will afford a reasonable duty of care to abandoned infants. The standard of what is "reasonable" under the circumstances will vary based on context. "Reasonable" in New York City or Omaha will differ from "reasonable" in isolated, resource constrained societies, for example, aboriginal Amazonians or a small colony on the moon.

All members of the promise community determine what these standards will be by their social promising.

Other cases that touch on the rights of dependent potential persons may include abuse, euthanasia, competing caregivers, probate and right to inherit, and actions by or against an estate of the dependent potential person. To determine what promise to apply, the neutral first determines whether the interests of the dependent potential person are at issue. For example, a neutral may determine a claim concerns a bodily injury or property interest of the dependent person. If needed to resolve the dispute, the neutral imputes a social promise to the dependent potential person, and then applies the imputed promise.

The dependent potential person is not a party in cases of competing caregivers (e.g., a custody dispute), unless a party alleges abuse of the dependent. Without abuse or threat of harm, the social promises of the competing caregivers determine the outcome. Custody claims resemble property claims, the difference being that the subject is a living potential self-sovereign. In competing claims over property, we observed that the social promise that sets stricter conditions of ownership is a "weaker" less assertive promise. In custody disputes, the neutral may decide based on the strictest conditions of custodianship that the parties' social promises provide. But above all, the neutral must consider the interests of the dependent, and base her decision on what is best for the child. We can hope that custody disputes would be rare because responsible parents will share custody in the best interests of a child, before parenting a child together. But custody disputes will sometimes happen, despite our hopes.

How is a neutral to determine the weakest of competing custody promise? For example, suppose a father promises to respect primary custody by the parent most capable of providing economic support. The mother promises to respect primary custody by the parent who spends the most time caring for the child. Which antecedent is more "stringent": providing economic support, or providing personal care? The answer always depends on the perspective of the child, which relates to community standards. Usually a sage neutral will help the dueling parents work out a shared custody arrangement that works, whatever the promises. If a dispute over custody is irreconcilable, the neutral will choose the option that best serves the child's interests. "Stringency" in this context refers the weight of credible social promises directed to the welfare of the dependent. The neutral can consider the social promises, and each promisor's ability to perform. Where parents cannot provide necessary care, the neutral may recruit community resources to help. Custody is a vast topic in family law, and resolution of custody disputes in social promise community will take many forms we cannot even imagine much less cover in this introductory Guidebook.

Turning from custody, we consider euthanasia or mercy killing. Neutrals will test mercy killings by the social promises of the one killed as with any other death. If the killed dependent has never made social promises, the neutral can make social promises for her. The agent of death will have made social promises that permit assisted suicide or mercy killing without penalty, subject to conditions. Conditions for excusable mercy killing might include, for example, permission of the subject or if the subject can't communicate permission of the caretaker, and an incurable disease or condition for which death is a better alternative. If the subjects of mercy killings are social promisors, they can specify the conditions under which their estates will excuse mercy killings.

Conflict might arise between social promises of mercy killers and the people they kill. Here's an example, pardon the frivolity: Grace promises to not kill unless after at least 100 days of a continuous vegetative state. Fury promises to not kill, subject to a similar exception after only ten days. Grace trips over a hedgehog and bangs her head on a Freedom Bus. She falls into a vegetative state. After 20 days, Fury kills Grace. If Grace's estate brings a complaint, is Fury liable? Since both promises tie the exception to an act of the defendant (i.e., to killing), they are affirmative defenses. As affirmative defenses, the least favorable to the defendant applies. Grace's promise applies, and Fury is liable. The result is the same if Grace kills Fury after 20 days, but out of respect for Fury's social promise her estate might not press the case.

Fury has little tolerance for being comatose and worries that people like Grace will waste Fury's estate for fear of liability. She consults with Alex about her problem. Alex advises her to promise she will not kill and will hold no one liable who kills after ten days of coma. Hearing this, Grace worries that people like Fury will kill her too soon. So Grace promises to not kill, and to hold no one liable who kills after 100 days. Both Grace and Fury state a positive promise to excuse liability, accompanied by a positive promise to not kill. If Fury kills Grace after 20 days, Fury has broken her own promise to not kill. Fury's promise to excuse after ten days does not bind Grace. Also, Fury's promise is stronger because it excuses more conduct. Grace's estate can pursue damages from Fury unless Fury waits 100 days before killing. But if Grace kills Fury after 20 days she cannot enjoy the benefit of Fury's stronger promise to excuse. By her own promises, Grace is liable for killing Fury unless she waits 100 days or Fury's estate honors her promise despite lack of a reciprocal promise from Grace.

What if one makes a positive promise, and the other a negative? Suppose Grace promises to not kill unless after 100 days. Fury promises to not kill, and to hold no one liable who kills after ten days. Grace can be liable for killing Fury no matter how long Fury is comatose. She has made no positive promise comparable to Fury's. Likewise, Fury can be liable for killing Grace no matter how long Grace is comatose, for making no negative promise comparable to Grace. Neutrals might ignore the distinction between negative and positive promises to avoid unfairness. And the heirs of those who suffer mercy killings can forbear from making a complaint, whatever the promises in play. To avoid uncertainty, some may make both positive and negative promises despite the redundancy.

The lesson is this: clashes in social promises to excuse otherwise culpable conduct will collapse to the narrowest excuse. It does not matter whether the social promise is positive or negative. Self-sovereigns can make positive or negative promises that inform others of their acceptable conditions for being killed out of mercy. The Third Promise ensures that their acceptable conditions will stand.

Intertwined tribes of social promise community cannot provide one uniform resolution to divisive and difficult social issues. Instead, these tribes of self-sovereigns will permit experimentation, transparency and above all, acceptance of conflicting beliefs on controversies within its foundational limits. Resolutions will not be uniform but will adapt to lessen tragic outcomes.

Collectives and Other Fictions

Fictional entities exist in two basic forms: personal and collective. Personal fictional entities are alter-egos of a natural person, such as when a business owner provides a fictional identity for one or more businesses she owns and controls. She may give each business a separate name, bank accounts, and financial records. Depending on compliance of the fictional entity with state regulation, its owners can use their fictions to avoid personal responsibility for acts of the fictional entity. They can limit their risk to their ownership share in the entity. When the fictional entity has several owners, it is a collective entity. States compel their subjects to accept both types of fictional entity as having a legal status equivalent to a person.

Some suppose that the social benefit of fictional entities justifies state support. Supposed benefits include encouraging passive investment in risky enterprises, promoting transfer of businesses, providing redress for harms committed by agents of the collective, and administrative convenience. This essay does not concern state-created fictional entities and won't consider their merits or detriments much. Here we focus on fictions in social promise community. We'll consider how collective fictions that first formed under state law might evolve to become institutions in social promise community, and how self-sovereign community will regulate these fictions.

Consent is fundamental to self-sovereign society. Nobody can force another to recognize a fiction against their will. A fiction can claim nothing from a self-sovereign without the sovereign's consent. And no dishonor comes from regarding fictions as they are: imaginary relationships made by and for the convenience of others. State backing of fictions has no force in social promise community. But self-sovereigns can make promises respecting such fictions as they wish. Each can (in effect) make their own "corporations code."

Social promises can adapt to favor any fictional entity. Social pressure may stimulate basic "corporate" promises. Members will favor beneficial collectives with more generous social promises. Capitalists can favor profit-making entities owned by shareholders, while socialists can favor non-profit mutual aid societies owned by members. Many will favor both kinds of entity. We might think of states as resulting from an aggressive campaign to promote a fictional collective entity: the state itself, based in sovereign claims over territory. But in social promise community, social pressure comes from the free choices of independent sovereigns obligated to non-aggression. Sovereignty over the self reigns over all other sovereignties and claims of ownership.

What kinds of social promises will foster the most vigorous forms of collectives? Will it be a corporate form like that recognized by states? Forms will evolve with time and place. The voluntary form can do anything but lay obligations on non-promisors. Social promises will promise respect to fictional entities, subject to conditions. The conditions will define characteristics of the fictions to which the promisor owes respect. Collectives can organize by any scheme that a group of self-sovereigns can execute. Each rational collective will conform to the conditions that their self-sovereign supporters and customers require. Fictions must meet the conditions sovereigns place on their existence or fail to exist to those sovereigns.

Self-sovereigns can recognize fictions as a class, by name, or both. Recognition by class comes from a conditional social promise, in which the condition defines a class of fictions the promisor will respect. Recognition by name also comes from a conditional promise, in which the condition is the fiction's name.

We build Three Promise systems for equal self-sovereigns. Where some self-sovereigns are corporeal and mortal, equality dictates all must be. But fictions are neither corporeal nor mortal. They are an idea that can separate from any physical body and become immortal. So fictional collectives cannot be equal self-sovereigns with natural persons. Where fictions are self-sovereigns by right, society cannot serve the interests of natural sovereigns, corporal and mortal. The author and everyone who will read this book is corporeal and mortal. Why should we promote social systems in which natural sovereigns submit to fictions? Fictional self-sovereigns in the form of states already tax and regulate our lives. We should not invite them back into our societies of equal self-sovereigns, except as guests and servants, and never as privileged equals.

States grant sovereignty to other fictions. If states being fictions can grant sovereignty to other fictions, can natural sovereigns grant the same power? Yes, but only for themselves. Self-sovereigns cannot compel other sovereigns to recognize their honored fictions. They can only seek to persuade others to follow their example.

Natural sovereigns may want to have fictional identities for themselves. They might want to use one name in one group, and another name in a different group. If a sovereign works to keep the fact of dual identities secret, fraud may be in evidence. Otherwise, the two names refer to the same person. But what if the sovereign wants different social promises to attach to different names? In that case, she can disclose her wishes: when dealing with "Lulu" promise set 'A' applies; with "Lisa" promise set 'B.' So long as she gives fair notice in advance she works no fraud, and neutrals will respect the division. Other self-sovereigns once made aware of her fictions may disregard them by telling her so.

She assumes a risk when she keeps her other identity private. She might have legitimate reasons for maintaining privacy and keeping her secrets might do no fraud. But still, keeping secrets deprives others of opportunity to tell her they will disregard or accept her fiction. Sometimes, she can reveal the other promises without revealing the name of the other identity. Other times, she will keep the social promises secret, too. Her reasons for keeping secrets matter, along with whether the secrecy will bring harm to those who will rely on her social promises. Public alter-egos and social promises are not private facts we can disclose or withhold without social consequences. They are part of our social profile. If our profile is false or incomplete, ignorance may lead some astray while others who are better informed avoid the same error. Some ignorant ones might suffer a disadvantage.

When the other identity must remain secret, the neutral should examine whether the use of different identities or different promises has disadvantaged the other party. Absent disadvantage, the neutral should respect the division. If the other party suffers a disadvantage, the neutral should hold Lulu/Lisa to her least favorable social promise. Lulu/Lisa must bear responsibility for her own actions. Any other approach will allow disputants to pick from alternative promises to apply to different disputes, turning promise community into a useless game played by lawyers. To prevent gaming the system, neutrals should apply the "weakest promise" for each natural person whenever a private use of different identities disadvantages the other party.

We can think about nondisclosure of personal fictions another way. Keeping a fictional identity secret deprives others of the opportunity to disregard the fiction. The right remedy is to let the others reject the fiction if it impacts the dispute. When we say "the neutral should do 'X'," we mean that if the other party demands 'X', they have a right to receive 'X' under the circumstances. The one deprived of the opportunity to disregard a fictional construct in the origin of a dispute will get that opportunity during due process. When keeping a fiction secret, a self-sovereign assumes the risk those kept ignorant might disregard the fiction once they discover it. Often, that will be an acceptable risk to bear.

Suppose Lulu/Lisa sells Cuban cigars on the side. She uses her "Lulu" identity only when dealing with Cubans to import cigars, for two reasons. For one, Cuban cigar exporters won't deal with anyone unless they promise to pay triple damages for their intentional harms. Lulu/Lisa lives in Austin, where double damages are customary for intentional harms. She doesn't want to pay triple damages if she doesn't have to. Second reason: U.S. law forbids Americans from trading with Cubans. The FBI puts everyone who publishes a social promise to pay triple damages on a watchlist as a suspected trader with Cubans. For security, Lisa walls Lulu off from her flesh-and-bones, and the FBI puts Lulu on the watchlist instead of Lisa. It's nobody else's business that Lisa trades with Cubans. It's a private fact.

Lauren is Lisa's neighbor and buys Cuban cigars from Lisa. Lauren is a triple-damages promisor because she trades in Pomeranian singing gerbils, whose exporters like Cuban cigar exporters won't trade with anybody who promises less. The FBI send an undercover agent to one of Lauren's cigar-and-singing-gerbil parties and discover the Cuban cigars. They arrest Lauren. Before Lauren can make bail, Lisa poisons her singing gerbils for their annoying nocturnal wailing and because she suspects Lauren of informing on her. Her suspicions are true. The FBI arrests Lisa and puts her in Lauren's cell. During a quarrel, Lisa confesses to poisoning the gerbils and Lauren confesses to informing on Lisa. Each spends one Bitcoin in defending against FBI charges and paying fines.

Who is liable for triple damages? Both are. Lauren is liable for informing on Lisa, and Lisa for poisoning Lauren's gerbils. Lisa is not liable for Lauren's arrest, because she did nothing to cause it. If the damage from poisoning the gerbils is one Bitcoin, Lauren and Lisa's triple damages offset one another and neither need pay to restore their honor. Suppose Lisa did not poison Lauren's gerbils. By the Third Promise, Lauren would be liable for double damages only (2 Bitcoin), because she had no way of knowing about Lisa's other identity. If Lisa poisoned the gerbils while Lauren did not inform on Lisa, Lisa bears the risk of owing triple damages (3 Bitcoin) under Lauren's and Lulu's social promises. Promise keepers may divide their social promises and identities as they please, so long as they assume the risk. When the other party knows and agrees to the division in advance, the division does no harm. If the division disadvantages another, the promisor should restore the disadvantage.

When a fictional entity is an alter ego of a single natural person, the Third Promise will regulate abuse well. But collective entities are each controlled by many people. A structure of rights between owners, officers and agents divides responsibility. Social promises granting rights to collective fictional entities must be by individuals. These individual grants can take any form natural people can imagine. Neutrals can hear claims by a fiction against a self-sovereign only if the self-sovereign recognizes the fiction or agrees to waive non-recognition for the case. Fictions do not enjoy natural standing in promise community. But self-sovereigns have natural standing to bring claims against any entity who enters the promise community. So self-sovereigns can bring complaints against fictional entities who have made the Three Promises, regardless of the fiction's social promises. Once a self-sovereign recognizes a fiction by filing a complaint against it, the fiction can defend itself. What it cannot do is obligate the claimant to honor the Third Promise for the fiction's social promises. It cannot compel the claimant to recognize its social promises as binding. Claimants who have not promised to respect the fiction as a self-sovereign must choose between respecting or disregarding the fiction's promises.

Collectives are groups in which all grant rights and accept responsibilities by agreement with each other. We could say the corporation exists by contract, but that would be too narrow an example. Social promise community is a collective without fixed form. Its form is as fluid as the changing social promises and identities of its members. A marriage, a business partnership, and a corporation are all collectives. States by their laws define which collectives they will recognize. In social promise community, self-sovereigns keep that power.

Where the sovereign promises to recognize a collective, the fiction becomes as a fellow sovereign. We might suppose that only brave or foolhardy self-sovereigns will take on collectives as equals. No self-sovereign must grant sovereignty to the collective to transact with it. Self-sovereigns can transact with collectives through the collectives' agents. If the agents are promise keepers, their social promises will bear on disputes with self-sovereigns. If the agents are non-promisors, the self-sovereign has no recourse within social promise community. Prudent self-sovereigns will avoid transacting with non-promisors. Most won't grant sovereignty to collectives as a rule.

A twist exists, however: No one within an organized collective bears the risk of collective action alone because the collectives will indemnify their agents for actions within authority. These collectives will also back agents who bring claims in a personal capacity against self-sovereigns on the collectives' behalf. The collective stands behind its agents. The self-sovereign who will transact with a collective through its self-sovereign agents must face its power, regardless. The self-sovereign may as well recognize the sovereignty of the collective, if the collective's agents are self-sovereign members of social promise community. But granting sovereignty to a collective of non-promisors would be foolhardy. If prudent self-sovereigns recognize collectives, they will condition their recognition of the collective sovereign on the membership of the collective's agents in social promise community.

State recognition may help collectives coexist with non-promisors but is beside the point within the social promise community. State-recognized collectives of promise community members won't pursue state claims against promise community members. Self sovereigns who recognize a promise community collective won't pursue claims against it in state court. Both will resolve their claims in the promise community instead, receiving the benefit of fairer and more efficient due process. If voluntary due process isn't better, it won't exist. Collective entities also receive the benefit of an enhanced public reputation with promise community members. Fictional entities are like natural people in one way: they can be members of promise community while also being subjects of the state. Someday, corporations and other fictions might require their agents to be members of social promise community as a condition of employment!

If social promising becomes popular, fictional entities will feel more pressure to take part. Not only for the public relations benefit and to appeal to a larger market, but also to recruit employees or similar key agents. Because some self-sovereigns will not recognize every fiction, participating in a collective will have consequences for the reputations of its agents. Harmful actions of the collective can fall back on the reputations of their agents. To lower their risk of reputational harm and exposure to claims, the best agents will avoid working for collectives that most social promisors do not respect. Respected collectives will be social promisers themselves, relieving agents from personal responsibility for their acts in service of the collective.

When a party to a claim recognizes no sovereign status of the collective, its agents must stand or fall based on their own social promises. All the disputes become personal disputes with the collective's agents, for that party. Whether an agent of the collective bears responsibility for actions of the collective depends of the claimant's and the agent's social promises. Each agent makes his own social promises about "agency," meaning the conditions under which he is liable for the actions of another. Each can limit liability for actions of the collective by making a suitable social promise about agency. By the same measure, limitations on liability apply first to those who promise to accept them. To give reasonable recourse from harm by collectives, conspiracies or other agencies, most people will make social promises accepting "joint and several" liability for harms by collectives of which they are a part. "Joint and several" means that each person is liable for the entire harm even if their contribution is only partial. Without agents who promise joint and several liability, it is trivial for collectives and conspiracies to exercise coercion without effective recourse.

Imagine a time when the state has faded away. A collective "Evil, Inc." wishes to harm another while shielding all of its principals from liability in social promise community. Each of Evil, Inc.'s principals renounce joint and several liability, limiting their liability to direct actions only. Then the collective hires a special agent such as a non-promisor, or a society member with lax social promises, to do the heinous deeds desired by the principals. For example, Evil, Inc. might dump hazardous waste in an unsafe location to avoid costs of responsible disposal. By their agent's loose social promises, the principals of Evil, Inc. who did not dump the waste themselves escape liability for the agent's actions except for the damage to their reputations and to Evil's. The agent would bear responsibility himself but will be a non-promisor or poor. Either way, the victim cannot receive justice.

If the harm is serious enough, another collective such as "Revenge Corporation" can step in to exact revenge. The principals of Revenge Corporation will shield themselves using the same social promises as the principals of Evil. Agents of Revenge might, for example, dump hazardous waste on property of the executives of Evil, while Revenge denies responsibility. Principals will make reasonable social promises about agency liability to avoid being victimized by the agents of their adversaries. Agents are liable for their actions, but demand indemnity from their principals before accepting employment. Collectives will promise to accept agency liability or won't operate in social promise community.

When collective entities hold title to property, the effect depends on the social promises of the competing claimant. If the claimant recognizes the collective entity, the outcome depends on the social promises of both. If the claimant doesn't recognize the entity it has no standing, and its agents bear their own responsibilities. For example, if Ted does not recognize PollutCo and PollutCo's agents and officers injure him he can bring claims against those who are promise keepers. If Ted wins damages, the agents and officers named in the suit will be liable to pay. If its employees and officers do not pay, claimants might attach liens to PollutCo's registered property such as registered with promise community registrars. Self-sovereigns can't record promise community liens in state records or ask state sheriffs to enforce promise community opinions, even if a state exists and has registered PollutCo. They will record their liens with promise community registrars and use contingent-fee peace officers a.k.a. bounty hunters to enforce.

PolluteCo cannot make complaints based on social promises against anyone that does not recognize it as a self-sovereign. For example, it cannot assert promise community property rights against those who do not recognize it as a sovereign entity. PolluteCo might protect property against claims by self-sovereigns by appointing a natural agent (or agents) to hold property in trust to benefit PolluteCo. Each agent would by their social promises recognize PolluteCo as a sovereign entity and grant it certain rights related to the property, under a license or other agreement. Each agent would make social promises respecting the property right acceptable to PolluteCo and to the agent. The agent would enforce PolluteCo's property rights in social promise community by the agent's own social promises. The benefit of any neutral opinions would flow to PolluteCo by the trust agreement with the agent.

So long as the state exists why would collectives and other fictions want recognition by self sovereigns? Due process in social promise community will be better than state court, or it won't exist. State due process falls short in many areas, so it won't be difficult to improve on it using the promise community's flexible system. Collective entities may ignore social promise due process, and most will until the community gains traction. While the community is small, its members must cope with state-recognized collectives as they do with other state entities. Once the community is vibrant enough, collectives will compete to attract community members by using agents who are members of the community, availing themselves of community due process when possible, and accommodating reasonable conditions for recognition spelled out in the social promises of members.

Just as natural persons can recognize fictional entities, can fictional entities recognize each other as part of social promise community? Why not? If promise community can provide more efficient resolution of inter-entity disputes, fictions can use it just as they can use any other private arbitration or mediation services. The more pertinent question is why would fictions want to leave state law and state enforcement behind? As a class, large organizations have immense influence over state laws relative to individuals. But the corporate ecosystem is not monolithic. Collective entities both compete and cooperate with each other in making laws. The resulting mess favors some and disfavors others. Those disfavored will seek alternatives. Thriving social promise communities will help the disfavored collectives work around strictures and violent manipulation of markets by more dominant, state-favored entities. Disfavored collectives will establish themselves and grow in social promise community first. If social promise collectives succeed, they will replace state-sanctioned collectives and the corporate state will wither away.

Use of social promises by collective entities will depend on recognition by each self-sovereign community member. Just as in other areas, members can apply social pressure by making social promises that reward good corporate behavior and penalize bad behavior. It is impossible to predict how collective entities might evolve, or what they might become, under this social pressure. For now, we can foresee exciting possibilities, such as cooperatives competing for recognition from individual society members by promoting more sensible and popular social promises. The most successful collectives will thrive by attracting the most members and supporters. They will foster social cooperation in which equal rights, individual liberty, efficient division of labor, and teams working on complex projects can all thrive together, with no coercive taxation or regulation. Many types of collective organizations can coexist and enable very different lifestyles. Social promises can reduce wasteful paperwork and legal machinations to avoid paying taxes or to comply with regulations motivated by powerful special interests.

Insisting on the sole sovereignty of the natural person will not disable collective entities or banish them from voluntary societies. Quite the contrary. This true democracy, this rule by every person over herself under social promises published to all, will free the collective to accomplish new and better things without dominating individuals.

Animal and Alien Rights

All beings that are corporeal, mortal and have the self-sovereign abilities are sovereign persons. The abilities are: apparent free will, awareness of self and others (sentience), rationality, language and memory, and a desire for justice, or if you prefer, just society with like kind. We have discussed interactions of dependents (e.g., infants and children) and fictional entities (e.g., collectives) with self-sovereign society. Status for potential persons follows from their biological nature as progeny of self-sovereigns. Fictions coexist with promise community by the grant of individual self-sovereigns. Animals and aliens are no less real and important, despite not being progeny. Like dependent potential people, alien species have inherent rights by being alive and mortal, with higher forms having self-sovereign abilities. Species alien to *Homo Sapiens* are all around us. Alien species who lack the self-sovereign abilities are animals. Alien species who have all the abilities are self-sovereigns equal to any other, and able to become promise keepers.

Every individual animal belongs to a species that lacks at least one of the self-sovereign abilities. But individual exceptions exist. For example, individual apes can use symbols to discuss abstract concepts like love and sadness. When a member of alien species gains all the abilities, it graduates to self-sovereign personhood. Those aliens with all the abilities except for a desire for justice are alien non-promisors of a sort that cannot become promise community members. If an invading force of space aliens despises humans and seeks only to eradicate them, the aliens cannot be members of human promise society. They have no desire for justice involving humans and will be non-promisors. Aliens who defect from the assault and want to coexist with humans can be members. Desire for justice like all desire is malleable.

Controversies may arise over individual aliens with abilities uncharacteristic of their species. Are such individuals self-sovereigns? People can disagree about whether an individual has a self-sovereign ability. Plenty of gray area exists. Human self-sovereigns should treat alien individuals in the gray zone with special respect. Not as dependents because members of alien species are not human progeny. But aliens may need help to access social promise communities designed for humans. When humans disagree over the status of an individual alien, the alien may need a guardian to represent it. The guardian and the opposing party will agree on a neutral for due process. So long as the alien has made discernable social promises and can reason with a neutral with or without the help of a guardian, neutrals can mediate their disputes under the Three Promise framework. Such individual aliens are rare or non-existent today, but that might change with developments in artificial intelligence, genetic engineering, or rocket science.

Like fictions, animals enjoy rights by the grant of other self-sovereigns. Unlike fictions, animals lacking an ability to speak and reason with humans can't do what fellow sovereigns must. If you think animals should have more rights, you can grant animals all the rights you want. You can't force others to grant the same rights, but you can and should seek to persuade others if you care about animals. The treatment of animals depends on the social promises of members and on their unspoken consciences. Social promises expose the conscience in the social sphere. Animal rights activists should encourage members to make their internal positions on animal rights public by offering rewards. For example, nature preserves might grant special access to people who have made social promises respecting animal rights.

Granting and receiving favors is healthy politics. Animal rights organizations can offer member levels based on social promises. Level 1 is "Beginner." To qualify as Beginner, a member promises to not be cruel to animals. Level 10 is "Master Ninja." To qualify, you promise a vegan, sustainable lifestyle, full time animal rights activism, and all the lesser obligations of the lower levels. Intermediate levels of membership are in between, each ratcheting up the level of member commitment. Each level of membership comes with honors and responsibilities.

With many self-sovereigns granting rights, some will make weightier promises favoring animals than others. Levels of promises can even be an overt marketing technique! Some social promises will specify who can enforce them or some will be silent. Animals can't make their own promises, so conflicts over animal rights will be between self-sovereigns one of whom advocates for the animal. Animals can't pick their guardians. Animal advocates can be anyone who has made social promises reciprocating the promises of the defendant accused of failing to keep their promise to animals.

When the social promises conflict, which prevail? How does the Third Promise apply to social promises protecting animals?

Positive promises back claims and negative promises back defenses. Promises granting animal rights can be positive, obligating the promisor to do something for animals or to refrain from some action. For example, a self-sovereign might promise to not be cruel to animals and to nurture all taken as pets. For positive promises, the obligation preferred by the defendant prevails. You cannot claim more than you have promised.

Suppose a rights organization sets up levels of membership based on social promises and promise-keeping histories. The levels include "Master Ninja" for people who have dedicated their lives to animal rights, and "Beginner" for people who will promise only minor obligations. It makes sense that Master Ninjas shouldn't bring claims against Beginners for failing to keep the obligations of Master Ninjas. Beginners haven't made Master Ninja promises. It's less obvious that Beginners shouldn't bring claims against Master Ninjas over Master Ninja promises, only over Beginner promises. Beginners have less at stake than true Master Ninjas from reputational stains. Beginners do not depend on their activism for their livelihood as Master Ninjas do. Plus, it would be hypocritical of Beginners to demand more than they will give. Only true Master Ninjas should bring formal complaints against their peers because the Third Promise makes only the lesser burden obligatory. Beginners can and should bring claims against fake Master Ninjas on Beginner promises, to expose their fraud. Loss of a suit to a Beginner is a great shame for Master Ninjas. It means an unbiased neutral of their own choosing found they are not keeping even Beginner promises. Their fraud will end.

Promises touching on animals can be negative, such as to not kill animals except in self-defense. For negative promises, the promise preferred by the claimant prevails. Margie promises to harm no animal unless needed to preserve health and well-being. Pop promises to harm no animal unless needed for self-defense against attack. Margie and Pop go camping in the mountains and get lost. They run out of food and are famished. Margie makes a crayfish stew, on the strength of which they find their way back. Margie against all reason brings a claim against Pop for helping her catch crayfish for the stew. Pop caught the crayfish, and Margie can hold him to his promised exception. Margie is not the victim, she is bringing a claim on behalf of the crayfish. Pop will be liable unless the neutral finds killing the crayfish for stew necessary in defense against a crayfish attack. The same process results if Pop raises a claim against Margie. In both cases the crayfish get the benefit of the defense chosen by the plaintiff, often the narrowest defense. Some neutrals might not let Pop enforce his narrower exception on Margie, reasoning that since Pop has no relation to the victims, the crayfish have no right to the benefit of his narrower exception. They will hold the defendant liable under her own social promise, the crayfish having made no promises of their own.

Social promises might also regard animals as property. Sovereigns might use property claims over animals to justify their treatment of animals, like killing them and making hamburger. None others must respect these claims. Like all property claims, promises respecting property over animals have weight only with those who make reciprocal claims. When property claims conflict, we can pick the most stringent conditions to decide ownership, and the least burdensome of the promised remedies.

Whether positive, negative, or property, social promises regarding animal rights lack the reciprocity on which the ethics of promise community depend. Animals can't reciprocate. This lack injects uncertainty. Treatment of promises respecting animal rights might not be as consistent or as predictable as self-sovereign rights. Less consistency doesn't mean no consistency, or that animal rights won't exist. Animals will enjoy all the rights that self-sovereigns will grant them. Even the most self-centered and sociopathic self-sovereign will grant rights that their friends consider fundamental. Nobody wants to be anathema.

Let's play with these ideas, using Alice and Bill: Bill promises to not interfere with killing rattlesnakes, and to pay a $1000 fine to the Rattlesnake Eradication Society for every act of interference. Alice promises to not kill animals unless in immediate self-defense, and to pay a $1000 fine to the Animal Defense Fund for each animal she kills. Bill tries to kill rattlesnakes. Alice hinders the hunt as best she can without hurting Bill or trespassing on any of his personal property. Despite her intervention, Bill kills a few snakes. Alice cannot bring a claim for $1000 per snake against Bill, and Bill cannot bring a claim against Alice for her intervention. Their promises do not match. They must find another basis for working out their disagreement.

Suppose Alice promises to respect property interests in animals raised by social promisors who have promised respect for animal rights. Bill promises to respect property interests in animals that live on land owned by others. He kills rattlesnakes only on the grounds of his amusement park claiming a right to do so as owner. Alice hinders Bill hunting within the boundary of his amusement park. During the hunt Alice's pet rattlesnake escapes from her backpack and Bill kills it. They both have a property claim to Alice's dead pet. Who wins? The outcome of due process might depend on who brings the claim because the defendant chooses the weaker consequence of a trespass on property. But first a neutral decides which condition of ownership is more stringent, Alice's or Bill's, without regard for the identities of the claimant and defendant. If the neutral applies the method proposed in this Guidebook, she will weigh Alice's condition of raising the animal with Bill's condition of owning the land on which he finds the animal. Neutrals will not always agree but most would find that caring for an animal outweighs discovering it on owned land. If Alice brings a claim for killing her pet, Bill will be liable for property damage by whichever weaker consequence applies.

A more interesting scenario is a trespass suit by Bill against Alice for hindering his snake hunting. For a trespass claim, Bill must prove he owns the wild animals he claims a right to kill. But he cannot prove ownership by Alice's more stringent animal husbandry test. He cannot recover from Alice for hindering his snake hunt based on the parties' property promises. He can recover if he agrees with Alice that as a condition of entry to his park, she will hinder no park operation. Assuming the contract is valid under the social promises of Alice and Bill, Bill can recover his damages for Alice's hindrance campaign on his park grounds.

Suppose Alice can prove that Bill's hunting is endangering survival of a rare species of rattlesnake. She promises to pay an award of damages for killing members of an endangered species to an independent ecological preservation fund, recognizing a property right of the community in endangered species. Her promise references a published standard for determining when endangerment using verifiable criteria under which few species can qualify. Under these facts, a neutral may hold that Alice's property promise has more stringent conditions and should prevail. Bill's claim of right to exterminate would deprive the world of a species of rattlesnake, to benefit an amusement park. His condition of ownership is more expansive, and his property claim excludes more. Because his park sits on a home of an endangered species, his claim of right to exterminate is in effect a claim of right over an entire species. Therefore, neutrals might award Alice relief for the snakes, depending on specifics of the social promises, the facts at play and the prevailing attitudes among reputable neutrals that the parties can agree on.

An interesting wrinkle: what happens if Bill makes a social promise like Alice's except for referencing a more stringent standard for endangerment under which his snakes are not an endangered species? Does Bill's standard prevail for defining a more stringent condition of ownership? No, because making the endangered species standard tighter limits the public interest and expands Bill's ownership claim; he defines a less stringent condition for his ownership than Alice. Alice's looser standard applies as between Alice and Bill. More expansive public promises don't give Alice a free pass. Conditions for ownership are only half of the property question. The other half is the price of trespass. Under the Third Promise, the least burdensome price applies. Under the Second Promise, Alice's must publish her social promises to Bill or they have no effect in her dispute with him. Bill can exclude guests whose promises favor rattlesnakes more than Bill can accept.

Besides killing rattlesnakes, suppose Bill operates a Chowchilla fur farm, and makes no promises that will impair his business. Some believes he abuses Chowchillas by exploiting them for pelts. Animal abuse can resemble child abuse, but with obvious differences. First, in the general case the abused, mute animal can never qualify as a sovereign person capable of binding herself with social promises. A neutral cannot impute a social promise to the animal as an individual. Second, opinions about animal abuse vary; what seems abusive to one another will regard as permissible. Consider, for example, the different perceptions of vegans and meat-eaters. Social promise community can't enforce one uniform rule on anything, much less about controversial issues. But the community encourages discovery of each person's social promises about animal rights. Where a great majority of people favor basic animal rights of a sort, almost everyone will feel pressure to make social promises respecting animal rights. In Bill's case, evidence that Bill kills rodents for their pelts coupled with his refusal to make more compassionate promises protecting animal rights can devastate his amusement park business.

Suppose that the rattlesnakes turn out to be an intelligent species that includes individuals able to prove that they have all the self-sovereign abilities. Such individuals could then bring a claim against Bill for alien rattlesnake persons he has killed, under his social promises taking responsibility for murder.

Controversy may arise with alien or artificial persons. For example, some neutrals may doubt that an alien or android shows a necessary ability, for example, a desire for justice. Others may feel that such beings lack a necessary disability, such as corporeality or mortality. For example, the sovereign status of artificial intelligence that emerges from a computer network would be controversial. Is such an entity corporeal, or mortal? It is difficult to say. Such controversies belong to the self-sovereigns of the future making their social promises in accord with their firm beliefs.

Consider an example of how this might play out: Ruthie the neutral recognizes Andy the Android as a self-sovereign. Connor does not. Andy registers a claim against Connor, but Connor refuses to submit to any neutral because he does not consider Andy to be an equal self-sovereign. After Connor receives a blizzard of complaints and sees his business drop in half, the two agree on Ruthie to hear the case. Connor argues that the case is void *ab initio* because Andy is not a qualified person. There are different outcomes possible. Ruthie may recognize a bona fide controversy on a fundamental due process question (Andy's status as a self-sovereign) and decline to rule on the substance, frustrating Andy. Andy is suing Connor, so either Andy is just trying to raise public awareness, or he believes he can win. Andy may get a favorable opinion from Ruthie, which Connor will disregard because he does not recognize Andy's self-sovereignty. As in every other case, the value of Ruthie's opinion will depend on her reputation as a neutral, and the ecosystem of enforcers available to enforce it. For example, if most of the adjacent society recognizes that androids like Andy are natural persons, Ruthie's opinion will be enforceable. If her opinion opposes prevailing views, few will enforce it absent exceptional circumstances.

Parties will resolve controversies over fundamental questions such as an individual's status as a self-sovereign by agreeing to submit the question to a neutral. Neutrals have no elite power to rule on conflicts because there is no bar to be a neutral beyond each person's ability to do a credible job and develop a reputation. When fundamental controversies arise, schisms will follow. Neutrals will follow different standards while diversity will provide neutrals with intermediate standards to apply when the parties make conflicting social promises. We cannot avoid controversy in fundamental matters in any non-coercive system. People who live in social promise community will manage schisms by choosing who they do commerce with, where they live, how they contract, and by other such precautionary devices outside the scope of due process.

Social promise community enables tolerance and freedom to cope with schisms over fundamental matters of conscience rather than to attempting to impose one viewpoint on all by force. It also reveals each member's moral values, enabling activists to apply non-dictatorial social pressure on any moral question in proportion to the moral preferences of society members. We expect that social promise community will offer better and more nuanced protection for animals, aliens, or others of questionable self-sovereignty than statist societies can. A society founded on principles of non-aggression and consideration for the rights and sovereignty of others will offer greater protection for society members and for the living things that interact with them than authoritarian societies. This protection is inherent in the moral preferences of those who will form social promise community out of respect for the equal sovereignty of others.

Death of the Promisor

Two classes of self-sovereign action involve dead promisors. The first class includes all claims for or against the deceased arising out of circumstances preceding their death. This class includes claims for murder or negligent homicide, and many more mundane claims. These claims are like any other between competing parties, except the deceased cannot represent herself directly. Dead sovereigns can't make or keep social promises. But the promisor was alive when the case arose, so her promises matter as if she were alive. She becomes a fiction, an estate. The second class includes claims arising out of the death event. This class includes claims of inheritance, wills, and division of property. The social promises of the deceased won't always be foremost in the second class of claims.

The extent to which the living consider the social promises of the dead depends on the living. If a living party has made a social promise respecting instruments such as wills or provides for rights of inheritance by the social promises of the deceased, then the parties will honor the social promises of the dead. Most people will make social promises honoring the social promises and wishes of the dead for disposition of their estates. By the Third Promise, survivors are less likely to honor their wishes if they don't. Without a continuance of an elderly or infirm person's estate after death, others may be unwilling to render services or lend to them in their time of need. A continuance of the deceased's property interests until settlement of debts in life depends on a mutual recognition that the property interests can survive death for some period. Property rights of the deceased cannot endure forever.

Others may have no real concern about how others dispose of their property after death and choose social promises that are more useful during life. To these people, it might seem better to

357

make claims on property of the deceased with fewer constraints. For example, such a person might promise to respect property rights until but not beyond death. For such, death causes the deceased to abandon their property. A person holding this promise can make a claim upon any property abandoned by death, at the cost of doing so in plain view. They must endure the disapproval of those who promise to respect the estate of the deceased and their competing claims to the estate. If no competing claims exist to the same estate, their claims are to abandoned property.

Consider a case in which a person dies with a will, or without a will but with a surviving spouse. A stranger brings a claim against the estate as abandoned property, and the heirs or the spouse oppose. The opposing parties claims have a nexus to the deceased's social promises regarding inheritance, to a will, or to both. They engage in conflict between property titles, like examples we have considered. In such conflicts, the most stringent condition for ownership determines the strongest title. If the stranger has no nexus to the property she claims, she will lose under the Third Promise to the surviving spouse with a nexus to the property by the will, by the relationship to the deceased, by actual use or labor associated with the property, or by any combination of the foregoing.

If the stranger bases her claim on some nexus to the property that runs deeper than the spouse's, the stranger may prevail. For example, suppose the stranger can prove she had an ongoing intimate relationship with the deceased who bought the property she is claiming for her home where she lived. In such case, her claim to the property should succeed under a weaker tool analysis for property claims, because a neutral should find that the claim of property she is asserting requires a more stringent antecedent for the property claim than the promise of the surviving spouse. Win or lose, a neutral can decide the stranger's claim without relying on the social promises of the deceased. The social promises of the living take precedence.

If all accept the will of the deceased, then the neutral will execute that will. Suppose the deceased's will is valid only under the social promises of the spouse, but not under the social promises of the stranger. Then the will is a factor in testing stringency of the competing property claims but does not control. The outcome will depend on whether the will plus the spouse's antecedent nexus to the property is more, or less, stringent than the antecedent nexus of the stranger, as with any other dueling property claim.

Who is bold enough to claim ownership in property abandoned by death? States do it all the time. Property not disposed through trusts and probate escheats to the state. Without escheatment or another form of abandonment, property stagnates upon death where it is of no use to anyone. In social promise community, independent death-scavengers will assume the vital role of recycling property abandoned by death. These death-scavengers will compete with one another. One sphere of competition will be in their social promises. They will moderate the hard edge of their scavenging promises, and not only for public relations reasons. They will seek through their social promises to create a nexus between their scavenging claims and the estates of the dead, or other basis for superior title.

Any social promise that grants rights to property based on some relationship to a deceased person must, by logical necessity, recognize the preceding ownership claim of the deceased. So even if the social promises of the deceased no longer exist to control such claims, neutral will still consider the social promises in most disputes over succession grounded in personal relationships. For example, Clifford, the only first cousin of Richard, realized early in life he wouldn't have any relative more industrious or wealthier than Richard. So Clifford adopted a social promises to respect inheritance of all property by cousins even if the deceased leaves a will. Benjamin, Richard's only son, made a similar social promise to respect inheritance by children. Grace nursed Richard for many years prior to death, and Richard left all his property to Grace in his will. Both Richard and Grace made social promises to respect the valid wills of deceased persons. As between Clifford, Benjamin and Grace, who holds the weakest property promise?

We can compare the parties' conditions for their property claims:

Clifford	relationship of first cousins
Benjamin	will of the deceased + child relationship
Grace	will of the deceased + years of labor + long-term caregiver relationship

Most neutrals will consider Grace's conditions for ownership weakest and award title to her; but even if a neutral holds Benjamin's conditions for ownership weaker, the neutral will execute Richard's will and award Grace title to the property. Clifford's promise is opportunistic but does at least require a family relationship. Neutrals will award Clifford title only if no less frivolous claims exist.

With some types of property left behind after death, wills and familial relationships will carry less weight. Consider, for example, a claim by a nature preserve "Truffle Genesis" over certain truffle grounds owned by a deceased truffle gatherer named Trudy. Trudy left the truffle grounds in a pristine state and only used it for harvesting certain rare truffles for her personal enjoyment. Truffle Genesis is a collective organization that holds owns tracts of pristine land using methods as described earlier. Suppose, for simplicity, that the preserve makes its claim in the name of one of its member agents, Amy. Amy's intent is to hold the land for Truffle Genesis as a habitat for certain rare animals and plants. Trudy left no survivors who ever used the truffle grounds, and left it by will to her partner Tran, whose social promises honor the wills of the dead. Tran does not enjoy truffle hunting and plans to sell the truffle grounds by auction of the International Truffle Association. She needs the funds for her retirement. If Amy's promise does not respect wills of the deceased, neutrals may be uncertain about whose claim is stronger. A skilled neutral will exploit the uncertainty to assist Amy and Tran negotiating a settlement. For example, a settlement under which Tran sells the truffle hunting rights subject to a preservation easement for Truffle Genesis' designated agent Amy would meet the needs of both claimants. If the parties refuse to settle, they must live with whatever ruling the neutral decides. In close cases, rational disputants will settle.

As happens under present systems, some people will leave their property to a trust, a form of fictional entity. As with any other fictional entity, the extent to which other self-sovereigns recognize and honor the trust will depend on the social promises of those who interact with its property. Since not every self-sovereign will recognize all fictional entities, prudent grantors might avoid fictional trusts. Instead, grantors may assign property in trust to natural self-sovereigns, who accept a duty as trustee of the property under a contract with the grantor. If the grantor dies, third party beneficiaries or survivors can enforce the trust agreement against the trustee. Without beneficiaries or survivors, the trust dissolves at the discretion of the trustee.

Death is irreversible these days. Exceptions may exist in fleeting cases such as when people "die" on the operating table but revive before brain death sets in. Future technological development may change this present reality. Some freeze their heads or bodies in hopes of later revival. Someday they may achieve their hope. If the dead can revive, those awaiting revival are not dead, but only disabled for an indefinite period. If dead for more than a few years, circumstances may change. Tension may grow between frozen social promises of the revivable dead that cannot adapt to changing circumstances and the adaptable social promises of the living. The Guidebook leaves consideration of these tensions for a time when technology for reviving the dead is feasible.

We can handle the passage of social promisors with dignity and grace, by following the Three Promises. Self-sovereigns may follow their own conscience as far as possible. User experiences in social promise community will seem familiar, because the community will reflect the outcomes all strive for. Letting the Third Promise govern disposition of property after death can bring results like those provided by rules of inheritance known today if self-sovereigns want that. Self-sovereign promises will control the fate of property after death.

Chapter 10: Promises for The Public Good

First Look

Self-sovereignty is neither selfish nor generous. It is neutral. Self-sovereigns decide for themselves how they will allocate their resources between personal desires and sacrificing for a common good. Some believe the individual has no worth besides the public good. Others believe the greatest good comes from sovereigns living for themselves. Both may live by their beliefs. In the vast middle between these poles are those seeking a balance between autonomy and community. Social promise community will create a home for all. There can be no better system for achieving social justice and general prosperity, than one in which all people have equal rights, and no one holds privileged levers of power.

Although social justice does not happen automatically, justice flourishes whenever those dedicated to fairness and public benefits may act without coercion. When private action for social justice is free and non-coercive, innumerable approaches make justice swift and sure, resolving social tensions. We shall consider just a few channels and modes in the pages below. More possibilities exist than we can explore.

Kernel

Under a statist model, politicians claim sovereignty over a territory under any banners that carry the day. States are not built to protect the environment, despite politicians sometimes repeating environmental slogans. States suppress selected uses of resources for uses preferred by those holding political power. As a guardian of the environment, whether from the viewpoint of preserving sustainable ecosystems or preserving public resources (e.g., clean air, water, food stocks), the state may have sometimes played a positive role, but overall its record is dismal. The state never fails to subsidize or enable industries that increase its power and reward its patrons. Nuclear weapons, fission power, and dominance of the military-industrial complex over environmental interests offer a few examples.

Property claims over land can play an important role in environmental protection. Land owners have natural incentives to both preserve and exploit their lands. Rational owners will prefer to preserve their lands to the extent preservation does not deprive them of the benefits of ownership. But price competition among sellers of goods of all types can lead to widespread disregard for long-term environmental sustainability or other adverse impacts on neighboring or public resources, in pursuit of short-term reductions in production costs. This so-called "socialization of costs" is a problem with free market capitalism many believe justifies state intervention. In addition, mixed public/private property regimes can lead to unchecked exploitation of any resources unprotected by a private property claim, as in the old trope of the "tragedy of the commons." In social promise community any can claim exploitable natural resources, and non-exclusive use accrues to those who deplete resources least. In this sense, the meek inherit the Earth.

Another aspect of self-sovereignty is a debt owed by the living to their predecessors. That debt obligates the living to leave the next generation no worse off than the last generation have left those living. Self-sovereign society requires that each respect the equal sovereignty of others. The obligation exists regardless of separation in space or time. Since we can't change the past, the duty of the living to respect sovereignty applies only to our successors. We receive payment of the intergenerational debt from past generations who have passed the gift of life forward. Each person owes this intergenerational debt to the same degree as any other. If we are optimistic and believe future generations will come, we should allow advocacy for future generations. Advocates might argue for restitution or remediation if the exploitation of a natural resource will leave the future people worse off than those living now. There will always be disagreement about how best to apply this principle, but it provides a reasonable basis for action by neutrals to protect the environment, including each deciding for themselves whether the social promises of another are proper and moral.

Politics in social promise societies will center on discussion and debate over the morality of social promises. Advocates for promises supporting collective benefits will have a powerful voice in these debates. Political leaders will motivate their followers to adopt social promises with a commitment to social action. Respect for others is the foundation of promise community, so we can expect activism on behalf of the future generations and the poor will bring new and better solutions to old social problems. The community will discover ways for the living to thrive, without depriving future generations of the chance to thrive in an environment no worse than what the present generation has enjoyed.

Self-sovereigns can supply every possible social welfare by keeping positive promises. Positive promises bind the promisors to take social action. Self-sovereigns will promise support to benefit those who make and perform the same promises themselves. Reciprocal promises for social support can fill every need for temporary safety nets, health care, care of the elderly and disabled, and many other social needs. By their social promises, self-sovereigns will support and encourage the exercise of social justice with liberty that has been at the core of the libertarian movement since its beginning.

Basket of Nuts

Protection of the Environment

Anarcho-capitalists look to enforcement of property rights for environmental protection. They recognize that if the public favors environmental protection, so will most landowners. Most landowners can then exercise their property rights for preservation. Social promise community lets capitalists and communists live together. The community can use private property rights for environmental preservation, without imposed property schemes creating entrenched classes. Property-based approaches depend on a uniform definition of property rights. Getting even small groups of anarcho-capitalists to agree on one definition of property has proven elusive. Consensus about property rights can never emerge in diverse groups of self-sovereigns, no matter how long debate lasts. We'll let others worry about how to find perfect social promises for respecting property rights. Here, we'll focus on harnessing the power of diversity by using social promises for public purposes.

Social promises depend on public expression; they are a public expression for public benefit. Not only for individual things like coexisting with fellow sovereigns; also for the broadest problems that social action can cause or resolve. While we live in peace with fellow self-sovereigns who make strange social promises, we can use our social promises to advance the rights and responsibilities we believe are just. Each sovereign decides for herself the property rights she will respect and negotiates for reciprocal respect by publishing her social promises. All enter negotiation knowing they will mediate conflicts in their social promises by the Third Promise, choosing the weaker tool. Their navigation of conflicting property rights will divide environmental resources according to the value scales of the sovereign community. No single value scale will have coercive power over others. Of greatest weight will be the least common denominator of the masses, the pervasive least burdensome promises.

Before considering examples of promise magic at work, let's review. The weaker property claim is that which results in the least burdensome penalty for the claim at hand. If conditions for ownership differ between claimants, the more stringent condition of ownership applies. Property rights have two components: (1) a condition of ownership, coupled to (2) an exclusionary privilege to something, conferred on the person who satisfies the condition of ownership. With two components and two states (matching and not matching) we have four possibilities for conflicts between property claims between any two persons 'A' and 'B':

We will explore the possibilities. Suppose two society members both satisfy a condition for a claim over land and disagree about its use. Mike wants to strip-mine the land. Nosh wants to keep the land pristine as an ecological preserve. As joint owners, can one force the other to submit? Can Nosh prevent Mike from strip-mining, by force? It depends on their social promises. Being joint owners who disagree on the use for the land, they must submit their dispute to a neutral to resolve it with honor. The neutral they pick together will try to satisfy both by a compromise. For example, Mike might use a less destructive form of mining, to remediate damage from strip mining, or to limit the strip mine to a less sensitive part of the land. Nosh must also compromise. Joint and

	A's Exclusionary Privilege 'P$_A$'	A's Ownership Condition 'C$_A$'
B's Exclusionary Privilege 'P$_B$'	$P_A \neq P_B$ & $C_A = C_B$ The lesser of P_A & P_B is enforceable	$P_A > P_B$ & $C_A \neq C_B$ Only P_B is enforceable, and only if the person seeking P_B has satisfied the most stringent of C_A & C_B
B's Ownership Condition 'C$_B$'	$P_A < P_B$ & $C_A \neq C_B$ Only P_A is enforceable, and only if the person seeking P_A has satisfied the most stringent of C_A & C_B	$P_A = P_B$ & $C_A \neq C_B$ Either P_A & P_B is enforceable by the person who has satisfied the most stringent of C_A & C_B

reciprocal owners must respect one another's plans for natural resources, at the cost of their reputations.

Joint ownership expands to collective ownership. Collectives can own natural resources and other assets as already described. Conflicting wishes of collective owners will play out as between Mike and Nosh. Where collectives consist of like-minded people, they will use their assets according to the members' wishes. These collectives can serve environmental protection, dual use, human habitation, agriculture, mining, industry, and all other uses. Where property is respected, public property as collective property can follow. Owners will not consist only of individual sovereigns.

Self sovereigns will also resolve conflict by submitting competing claims over natural resources for resolution by neutrals. Social promises respecting property can conflict over the conditions for ownership or over consequences for trespass. If you think about it, consequences for trespass intertwine with permitted use (license). Mike might promise to not cross marked property borders unless necessary for immediate survival, implying a license to pass unmarked borders for survival. Nosh promises to not disturb the natural ecosystem more than needed for survival, implying a license to pass and use the land for sustenance. Mike as owner cannot expect Nosh to keep his promises. But he can expect Nosh to keep the lesser of his promise and hers. When Nosh is defending, she gets to choose between keeping her promise and Mike's. When Nosh is the owner enforcing her claim, Mike gets to choose which promise he will keep. Nosh can prevent Mike from despoiling her land by marking her borders. But Mike cannot within the Three Promises prevent Nosh from passing through and taking sustenance from his land. Nosh's social promises focused on preservation inoculate herself and others from being excluded from natural places. Her promises are lighter, and more contagious. Promises like hers will give environmentalists courage to assert their value scales. Mike's promises are not bad. Marked borders are useful for farmers, miners and builders. Many people will respect them. Mike and Nosh both influence social policy by their promises.

Self-sovereigns will resolve similar tensions in conflicts between land uses and neighbor rights. They will compensate for nuisances and harms to adjacent people or properties. Social force can scale. Massive sovereign populations will enact regulations on activities that harm the natural environment on large scales (e.g., global warming or over-fishing) by individual social promising. Social policy follows social promises. Let's consider a few examples.

Jose and Tony are neighbors in a dense suburban residential area. Jose promises to let his neighbors live per their natural wishes. He keeps a pet rooster because he must get up early every day anyway, and the rooster reminds him of home. Tony works late every night and needs to sleep in the morning; he promises to be quiet in the morning. No single rule can satisfy both. Either Tony will impose his need for quiet on Jose, or Jose will impose his need for a rooster on Tony. States often handle these conflicts using zoning regulation. They allow roosters in some zones and not in others.

Social promise community's built-in regulatory system provides the benefits of zoning, but in a fine-grained and flexible way responsive to consumer demand. To be effective, social promises must be public, providing notice to others. Every would-be immigrant can learn the codes of conduct observed by their future neighbors. A diligent and considerate immigrant will consider the social promises made by his prospective neighbors before choosing a neighborhood. Sellers might refuse to sell to anyone with incompatible social promises. Neighborhoods can segregate themselves into lifestyle zones without central planning. Some zones will be diverse, others less so. Self-helping neighbors will police offensive uses of property, and all will avoid giving offense for no purpose. All the information to avoid places where the neighbors can't stand your lifestyle will be available by a simple online search.

Where reputation is king, no one will want a reputation as a bad neighbor. It will be easy to find a neighborhood because like-minded people register their social promises in public registries. If one prefers to live in an animal-friendly neighborhood, these neighborhoods will be easy enough to find, safe from the bans of municipal politicians. In most places, there will be no need to sacrifice one's reputation as a good neighbor to live as one pleases. Most people will choose their neighborhoods based on the public social promises of the residents there, causing natural zones of preference to emerge. To a degree, this natural self-segregation and separation occurs in many large cities despite uniform zoning, even today. Social promise community will allow this natural process to occur without external political influence, engendering vibrant and harmonious diversity in urban neighborhoods.

Social promises will regulate self-help measures. Suppose Tony removes Jose's rooster when no one is home and places it in an animal shelter, and the shelter makes Jose pay a fee to get it back. Tony promises to respect the property of others, to abate noisy nuisances on his property after notice and to tolerate self-help abatement of noisy nuisances on his own property if he does not abate the problem himself. Jose promises only to not touch the property of another without permission. Tony knows this but risks his rooster-napping anyway. His damages will be the cost of keeping the rooster in the animal shelter, which should approximate the shelter's release fee. He will damage nothing, Jose will get the message, and Tony will get a few nights' sleep at least. It's worth it. Tony has other options. He might beam a recording of a rooster crowing onto Jose's property to keep Jose up at night. Jose has made no promise of quiet use and so cannot complain about Tony's noise, but a noise war could escalate and hurt both of their reputations.

In a vibrant social promise community, self-help experts will assist with neighbor conflicts over nuisances or other neighbor disputes. These experts will earn their wages from land owners seeking for convenient ways to work out intractable differences, including heading off problems by publishing community standards. Neighbors can resolve differences over land use by self-segregation and self-help, but what about more substantial transgressions of neighbor rights, like conflicting business or industrial uses, and diversion, depletion, or destruction of common natural resources?

Suppose Jose builds a hazardous waste dump in Tony's neighborhood. To cut costs he does not secure the waste, which leaks into neighboring properties. If Jose fails to promise responsibility for his pollution, he will soon find himself the victim of his own loopholes. His reputation will sink to a level near a murderer. Deliberate polluters will be very rare. More common will be simple negligence or unfortunate accidents causing pollution where the landowner cannot remedy the damages. The wrongdoer can sell the land and the parties can work out terms of repayment consistent with the balance of promises to pay the debt. If a willing buyer exists to clean up the mess, fine. If not, it will fall to the neighbors to remedy with the situation as best they can. This can include appealing for help to the broader community, in ways such as described below. In a free and prosperous society, diverse and effective help would exist, because enough people care about preserving clean air and water to support it.

Governments often use protection of the environment to justify their regulations. Often, the justification is debatable or dubious. Even when the justification is well-supported by evidence and the solution tailored to the problem, the government action privileges a special interest that has lobbied for exercising power.

Hence regulatory power multiplies beyond proper uses, and too often becomes an instrument of market destruction.

Political activism for every imaginable public purpose will thrive in social promise community. As of this writing, collectives organizing action for solving environmental and other social problems are already active. But substantial conflicts between land uses and commercial activities are likely to continue to involve state agencies, for the foreseeable future. The scenarios below are beyond the foreseeable future when no state exists. Competing political collectives will replace the state in its role as a guardian of common resources. Existing within constraints of self-sovereign society, these new public collectives for social action will be less prone to undue influence by special interests, nimbler in action, more pervasive in effect, and better able to grapple with private collectives without risk of capture and control. Collectives might organize themselves as nebulous webs of promise keepers, for responding to resource calls from competing activists.

Social promise community provides effective pathways for political movements to form and exercise political power. The body politic of self sovereigns acts by public promise making and keeping. As members recognize new problems amenable to solution by social action, they can make and promote social promises for that social action. As evidence for the new social promises grows the movement gains momentum, and more people make the new promises. The more effective, sensible and just the new promises are, the faster the movement grows. Any person who refuses to make the most popular new promises is risking their reputation as an honorable member of the community.

To illustrate the general principle at work remedying diffused forms of environmental harm, consider how activists can encourage use of new technology for community benefit. For example, air pollution from automobiles is a recognized social problem. There is minimal pressure on polluters because each contributes an insignificant part of the overall problem and no state exists to force manufacturers into compliance. Suppose astute individuals recognize the opportunity and develop a technological solution, for example, a catalytic converter or cleaner burning engine. However, the new technology adds to the cost of automobiles, and provides only social benefits with no real benefit to individual consumers. Automobile manufacturers won't use the new technology because their customers don't want to pay for it. Demand for the new beneficial technology can't exist without social action. Statists will hire the state to force the new technology on all manufacturers. Here we assume the state does not exist or has learned to not meddle with markets.

Stakeholders in the new technology have an economic reason to promote it. Where states reign supreme, promoters will lobby legislators and influence administrators, besides appealing to the public. In social promise community, promoters will appeal to the public and influential leaders. Entrepreneurial innovators, producers, investors, and activists will cooperate to ignite a political movement. They will promote the social benefits of the new technology and educate the most enlightened and respected community leaders; defend their proposals for implementing the new technology against skeptics and detractors; and enlist popular neutrals to craft and promote social promises that encourage use of the technology. For example, individuals might promise that if they purchase a new automobile after such-and-such a date that emits more than a specified amount of pollution, they will pay a fine to an environmental defense organization. Once manufacturers see that many have made the promise, they will phase in the new technology, knowing demand for the old technology will diminish after the date, while the manufacturers who are the first to meet the increasing demand for the new technology will reap the greatest profits and gain the biggest market shares.

Consumer mass movements to make new social promises can mitigate any diversion, depletion, or destruction of common natural resources caused by mass consumer demand. It does not matter whether the source of the injustice is diffuse or limited to a few actors. For example, consumers can boycott industrial plants that don't comply with reasonable environmental regulations, and activists can score the plants on compliance. So long as substantial demand for "certified clean" supplies of whatever the polluting industry is producing exists, consumers can bring economic pressure to bear. Individual commitments by consumers to change their consumption habits or pay fines to fund defensive or mitigation efforts can create economic incentives for any workable change. It does not matter whether a small minority refuses to adopt new more progressive social promises when the source of the problem is mass demand. Substantial reduction in demand for the more harmful alternative will often be enough to persuade producers. Activists can supplement demand pressure by shunning those who refuse to make sought-for social promises, or denying them access to certain goods or services, or denying them discounts or other premiums. The more serious the perceived problem and the more certain the preferred solution, the stronger such political pressure will be.

Apathy and fear are the greatest enemies of positive social change. Where the state has withered away, people have less reason for apathy, less reason to feel helpless, and less reason to fear. If consumers in an area do not care about pollution, destruction or depletion of irreplaceable natural resources or other social harms, a minority cannot force them to change their behavior. Social promises are not for supporting rule by elites. Social promises must have widespread appeal, to have widespread impact. Yet if social promise community is ever to become widespread, prosperity, security and stability will not impede its growth. Peace will enable the teaching of peace and of a profound social and moral transformation to reorganize society around self-sovereignty.

Where bare survival is a ceaseless struggle and poverty is the norm, getting social promise community started may prove more challenging. The poor lack tools and the leisure to learn new things. Nor can we expect the poor to put social concerns foremost. It's hard to worry about global warming when you're hungry and cold. Social promise community will unfold in a prosperous world, in which most are confident about their futures, because it must. In prosperous societies, values shift in favor of long-term goals and preserving social order as people are less worried about meeting their immediate needs. Prosperous self-sovereigns will debate about the merits of different long-term goals and the best ways to achieve them but will agree on environmental protection and other matters of public interest. Most will care about preserving social order with a sustainable basis for that order to continue.

Campaigns promoting specific social promises to consumers will be effective but not for every social or environmental problem. Consider, for example, the threatened extinction of the rhinoceros driven by demand for rhinoceros horn by a tiny minority of consumers. Such minorities may persist in pockets of the world, beyond the reach of political pressures defending rhinoceros populations, and oblivious to the long-term consequences of extinction for short-term gratification. Traditional states have reacted to conserve certain species by banning trade or importation of related contraband, such as rhinoceros horns or products. Trade bans have not been effective in stopping poaching. Instead of reducing incentives for poaching, the bans have increased the profits associated with poaching and smuggling horn, increasing economic incentives for the trade. Meanwhile, the bans have prevented introduction of less damaging alternatives to displace demand for genuine or wild horn. It won't be hard for social promise community to do better.

Social promise community provides a more effective lever than international bans on trade for political change: social pressure on every individual to declare her position on every social question of widespread interest, whether good, bad or indifferent. To use the rhinoceros example, suppose most people promise to not buy or sell rhinoceros horn, on pain of heavy penalties. Consumers of rhinoceros horn must either hide their consumption or make promises without penalties for commerce or consumption of products from rhinoceroses. If they violate their own promises without paying proper penalties, they risk exposure as hypocrites and liars. Others might shun them or pursue claims against them for breaking their promises. If they refuse to make promises protecting endangered species, all those who value protection of the environment can discover their lack of concern and shun them. Open resistance to predominate cultural values cannot persist except within a subculture that provides support for the resisters.

Social promise community will tolerate subcultures, while making them identifiable and subject to social negotiating pressures with no shield from larger political units. For example, although much demand for rhinoceros horn comes from Vietnam, genuine horn consumers are a small minority even there. When nations impose sanctions on Vietnam to "crackdown" on users there, they miss their target. Sanctions harm diplomatic relations in unintended and unforeseen ways and penalize many who have nothing to do with the problem. Thus, sanctions are ineffective in targeting bad behavior. But if most consumers of rhinoceros horn belonged to an identified subculture, activists can target the subculture with precision, on a thousand fronts, using decentralized opponents of the trade in horn.

Many independent defenders of the rhinoceros will use different means to the end. Some may use shunning. Others may distribute alternatives to displace demand for horn, will support educational and propaganda measures, or support defensive force in rhinoceros preserves, defensive subversion of markets with counterfeits, and other methods to frustrate hunting and deprive traders in horn of profits. Confronted with this army of determined, intelligent and compassionate opponents of their consumption habits restrained only by social promises, demand for genuine horn will fall. Whatever the exact form of remedies, social promise community will discourage abominable activity by minorities with greater force and effect than states today.

Exhaustion of natural resources of the sort driven by irrational consumer demands for articles such as rhinoceros horn is easier to stop than destruction of the environment driven by poverty and hunger. Social promise community should excel at meeting basic needs, but some will still be poor. The poor might seek to feed themselves by exploiting resources owned by collectives to preserve the environment. For example, subsistence farmers or fishers might intrude on wildlife or nature preserves. Exploitation driven by bare economic survival is more resistant to social pressure than frivolous consumption. Will a starving fisherman care if few will buy his fish out of concern for the environmental impact of the catch? He will not care if he needs the fish to feed himself and his family. Survival motivates the subsistence fisherman, not profits or pursuit of pleasure.

Social promise community can direct the power of consumer mass movements to mitigate even the micro-deprivations of the poor. In a world without barriers imposed by national or local governments sovereigns can focus their capital anywhere for any purpose. Environmental defense agencies compete for funds donated by popular mass movements to focus effective solutions on the most critical problems. Defense agencies hire rangers to patrol the most sensitive wild areas and disrupt damaging activity while directing the poor causing damage to more sustainable forms of survival. The rangers will educate and learn from the subsistence fisher/farmers and help them find sustainable alternatives that honor their self-sovereign powers. Persuasion will be the only ethical tool. Both sides of the confrontation—the defense agencies and the poor exploiters of the environment—will stake their positions by social promises. Only persuasion will make any economic sense. Environmental defense agencies will compete to devise and implement the best ethical mitigation strategies for environmental threats, knowing their reputation and profits depend on their history of success.

Consider again that starving fisherman. This poverty-stricken fellow will be astute enough to have made a social promise that protects his right to fish despite the environmental concerns of others. None can claim breach of promise against him. The rangers can't seize his fishing equipment without breaking their promises to respect personal property rights. Should the rangers break their promises and steal his tools anyway, they will risk violent harm, alienation of the fisher folk, and frustration of purpose. If they succeed, they will owe compensation to the fisherman who will purchase replacement equipment and go back to the only business he knows. Capital works best in a positive, persuasive way. Environmental defense activists can fund research and education about sustainable fishing, pay fisherman for participating in educational programs, hire top quality conservation rangers and educators, and subsidize activities known to promote sustainable use of local resources.

"What's your promise?" is an effective way to promote social change through grass-roots popular movements. We might not escape popular delusions, and some movements might be less than logical. Principled, rational self sovereigns will resist delusional grass-roots movements, protected by their social promises. Special interests will still manipulate populations using all the tools of Madison Avenue and the Art of War. But independent self sovereigns are not as easy to manipulate as state legislators. Suppose a vaccine manufacturer wants to create demand for a vaccine. He might seek to influence operators of public facilities (e.g., schools, hotels, restaurants, entertainment venues, etc.) to deny service to any person not inoculated with the vaccine. Whether the practice of examining customers about their vaccinations becomes widespread will depend on how much the public sees the vaccination as necessary. To the extent public pressure becomes oppressive, a backlash will arise to resist the unjustified pressure.

Social pressure through promising won't provide perfect, instant solutions to every social problem. Nothing can. It will expose frauds, profiteers and predators, depriving them of the cloak of authority. Unconstrained by anything but reason, perception, and the constraints of personal sovereignty, social pressure in promise community will address every problem amenable to resolution by social action with more subtlety and grace than authoritarian approaches.

Sustainability

In a stateless world where all authority rests on personal sovereignty, will the supremacy of personal power lead to unchecked reproduction and immigration to less populated areas? How can social promise communities avoid adverse impacts of population growth and migration without state power? Some people will always be anxious about "over-population" causing unsustainable resource depletion or environmental destruction, but no moral or practical limit on the number of people that can or should be alive at one time exists. Sustainable population size varies depending on ever-changing population demands, technology, and resources. It is never fixed.

Unsustainable resource depletion and environmental destruction are social problems. We have argued that promise communities can resolve social problems using political movements centered on social promising and the tools of discovery that reliable registries of social promises afford. The environmental impact of population depends on technological tools and cultural beliefs, the power of which have no known limits. A tiny, backwards and ignorant population can do more environmental damage than a populous society with advanced technology and a preservation ethic. A society that harnesses an abundant, clean and sustainable energy might house trillions of people within the interior of the Earth, under the seas or in orbiting space structures, leaving the surface of the planet as an ecological preserve depending on social preferences. The size of a population is not the only variable that factors into environmental impact. The population's culture, values, knowledge and technology can offset the impact of population size many times over.

The state sometimes places checks on population growth and migration, with or without conscious effort. These checks include regulating beyond workability private use of government-owned property, and even of private property; controlling borders to restrict immigration; levying onerous tax burdens that discourage child-rearing; enforcing occupational licensing and other market regulations that increase cost of reaching economic self-sufficiency; distributing, promoting, and requiring birth control measures or abortions; mandating a financial system based on unlimited credit with related boom/bust cycles that concentrate wealth in the hands of a small elite, and most of all by making war. In lesser-developed areas, states create negative pressure on populations by accepting the weapons and warfare imported from more developed areas, fostering corruption that promotes theft and discourages wealth-building by non-elites, creating disempowered societies with high reproduction rates but low expected lifespans. These state activities combine to deprive most of the population of access to resources and security for building strong self-reliant and sustainable families and communities.

On the other side of the ledger, states also contribute to unsustainable population growth. By repressing their populations, states sometimes preserve subsistence economies and prevent development of new and more environmentally friendly technology that would otherwise occur. For example, states impede or discourage the flow of capital or people across their borders, preventing economic development. They are often prone to political corruption, which robs society of resources for economic development and discourage investment. In subsistence economies, parents have an incentive to bear children to increase the available labor pool or offer security for old age, while people in developed economies have fewer children per capita. States also sometimes encourage childbearing using direct incentives, such as tax credits or the like, because shrinking populations tend to diminish state power. It's hard to know whether or how much state activity suppresses population growth and migration.

Without state-sponsored activities, would populations explode causing irreparable damage to the environment? No evidence for that exists. Population explosions in voluntary society are less likely than under empires, and not just because the overall effect of the nation-state on population growth may be positive or neutral. A stateless social promise community will balance the rights of present individuals against the rights of future individuals to exist in a comparable environment and encourage sustainable use of resources that does not harm the biosphere beyond repair. It will do so using tools such as property rights, due process, and reputational discovery in an environment that maximizes free exchange of information, capital, and human resources.

We can't predict how social promise community will handle every detail. But some facts are clear: state aggressions such as war and economic repression drive most mass migration in the world today. In a stateless social promise community, these drivers will be absent. Except for sudden natural disasters, there will be no compelling reason for large numbers to leave their homes simultaneously. Entrepreneurial people will still recognize immigration as a tool for accessing underutilized resources, and there will be no border controls to prevent their free movement. Instead, competing property claims and social promises will constrain access to resources that groups want to preserve. Competing claims will arise between preservationists and entrepreneurs, and neutrals will judge these competing claims using social promises. Society members will not risk the severe blow to their reputations from disregarding the property claims of another or holding provocative or offensive social promises. Property claims are secondary. Individual sovereign power provides a firmer basis for resource allocation without privilege.

Self-sovereign property will allocate resources no worse than other forms. Subordinating sovereign claims over territory to personal sovereignty has an unexpected side effect: each must consider the burdens that their resource claim places on others. Owners are stewards who have invested the most in productive use of resources. They win ownership disputes by forging the deepest and least exclusionary relationship with the resource at stake, before the disputes. The calculus of measuring these owner relationships places a laser-like public focus on destructive forms of resource exploitation and stimulates alternatives to destructive practices. Mass social movements based on promise registries check behavior that most reject as immoral or anti-social. Neutrals resolve competing property claims consistent with widespread beliefs and values touching on environmental preservation and prudent use of natural resources. Owners who reduce harmful impacts on others have an advantage in every resource dispute, including simple trespass. Self-sovereigns who ignore the property claims of earlier residents and preservationists will find themselves unwelcome where they have offended the locals. Immigration driven by the wish to consume natural resources will be checked by prior owners and preservationists.

Consider a far future country in the area now known as Guatemala. The country is a preserve owned in small pieces by a million people who derive their livelihood from eco-tourism and high-density, organic urban farms. Meanwhile, the country now known as the U.S.A. has clung to its antiquated state system and slid into relative poverty. There are many poor people in Texas who want to emigrate to Guatemala and farm the rich organic soil in the ecological reserves. Without borders, what is to prevent them? Much. They can visit but cannot make a claim on real property without homesteading on the land. Those who attempt homesteading will quickly be noticed by one of the million landowners already in Guatemala, each ready to defend their claim. The immigrant cannot prevail on a homesteading claim against a long-established and diligent landowner, by principles we have considered. Instead, the immigrant will find a job working for a better-established resident of the country just as immigrants do today. Poor refugees from Texas will pose no threat to Guatemala's preserved resources.

Would a shift in morality to emphasizing responsible personal sovereignty encourage unsustainable population growth? Why would it? Because of social pressures and lack of state subsidies for large families, parents who raise large families without a means of support will face social consequences. People would be free to reproduce but will answer to their fellow self-sovereigns if they fail to take responsibility for their dependents or treat them as other than inheritors of sovereign status. Personal sovereignty cuts against child bearing done for economic reasons. In social promise community, children own themselves and may make and choose their own social promises once mature and independent. Parents

384

cannot not use their social promises to exploit unwilling children, hold them in bondage, or abuse them. Social promise community will not create economic incentives for parenting unsustainable families and will discourage anti-social behavior.

Some religions forbid birth control and encourage rearing of large families. Could a religion come to dominate social promise community and sacrifice all goals to the altar of population growth? It's unrealistic to think so. Any religion whose members participate in social promise community concedes the supremacy of self-sovereign power in social contexts and teaches responsibility for social promises. Its leaders must renounce the use of coercion or fraud to enforce cooperation and belief. The human mind is too complex, and ideas too easily transmitted for any group to impose unqualified expectations for large families among large groups of free self-sovereigns. Unless resources are abundant compared to the rate of growth and bereft of competing claims, population pressure will resist contrary religious impulses to multiply without restraints. Opposition will arise in proportion to the perceived errors in the religion's ethical teachings. We should not worry that religious leaders will take over by unrestrained reproduction. Religious leaders forbidding their followers from participating in social promise community is the greater hazard.

Social status checks population growth in affluent societies ruled by states today. It will remain so in affluent social promise communities. Maintaining a good reputation is essential to quality of life. This requires making honorable social promises and keeping them. Keeping social status in a community of promise keepers requires both honor and pulling at least one's own weight unless prevented by disability. Offenses such as environmental pollution will hurt the culprit's social and economic status. Loss of status will bring loss of access to desired resources. Prudent people will avoid offending others when possible.

Many today believe they need international laws from central authorities to address problems such as environmental pollution, population size control, and global climate change. When the only tool available is a hammer, every problem looks like a nail. Many tools exist for solving social problems without forcing people to follow imposed laws. We have considered some of these tool without exhausting all the possibilities. Putting the social promise community into practice may convince more people that liberty and equality are the best tools for maximizing the quality of life of all people, and creating sustainable, fair, and progressing societies.

Unopposed Claims

Some claims face no opposition, but every claim has a claimant. Somebody must make the claim; it must attach to a name. Many claims involve an opinion by a neutral. When the claim has no defendant, it must include a request for a neutral opinion. Otherwise the claim is nothing more than a proclamation, a social promise in effect. With the neutral added the claim becomes a dialog between the claimant and the neutral and can have enforceable weight. Examples of uncontested actions include adoption, conservatorship, guardianship, emancipation of a minor; the probating of a decedent's will; and claims to confer title over unclaimed property. Any self sovereign might contest these claims, for example, by acting in the "public interest" or on behalf of a minor or disabled person. In other cases, no opposition exists. Absent check, the ability to control social promises applied in cases with no opposition gives claimants free rein. Ethical and useful checks will deter abuse without corrupting self-sovereignty.

In states, a designated authority ensures that unopposed claims are approved by a representative of the state. In so regulating, state interest is paramount, followed by special interests with influence on the courts and last of all public interests. Claimants won't hire neutrals to oppose their unopposed claims, but respectable neutrals will oppose when the claim is meritless or defective. Neutrals cannot grant all unopposed claims without becoming a needless formality, a rubber stamp bought and paid for. Rubber stamps have no value in a free society. Where no opponent steps forward, the neutral must have the power to oppose, or no meaningful dialog can take place.

When no opposition exists, claimants alone choose their neutrals. We can question whether opposition from a hired neutral can be genuine. All will ask this question when the answer matters. So in uncontested actions, reputation of the neutral is paramount. The opinion of a neutral lacking a reputation for fairness will carry little weight.

What is the promise the claim seeks to enforce? In claims against defendants, the defendant's promises decide liability. The claimant would hold the defendant responsible for keeping her promises. If no defendant exists, no broken promise can exist. So how can a claim without a defendant exist? Not at all. The claimant-defendant (more briefly, "movant") seeks a neutral opinion that an action comports with the movant's social promises. The movant's social promises must control. If the claimant's social promises overreach, others will know their grasping nature by the publication of the promise without which it has no effect. A self-sovereign cannot disregard the rights of others without inviting others to disregard the sovereign's selfsame rights.

Neutrals will oppose claims that violate the claimant's social promises. They may refuse to hear claims based on offensive social promises, to preserve their hard-earned reputations. Neutrals must earn legitimacy or live without it. The community has no elected politicians to license monopolies of judges, no police force dedicated to enforcing edicts of designated neutrals. Some courts find their respect in some mixture of (a) allied enforcement power; (b) a claim of moral superiority (often hypocritical); and (c) a claim of popular consent to their rule. Neutrals in social promise communities must earn their respect by winning one self-sovereign heart at a time. They earn by doing their job effectively, and so much more when also prompt, courteous and wise. They are effective only by persuasion, including marketing their skills and prowess without fraud. If they break their promises to provide competent services, their clients can bring claims against them. Neutrals won't be immune from claims. Every self-sovereign has an equal right to judge or enforce. Competition for paying clients will motivate professional neutrals and enforcers to warranty their services with suitable social promises.

Neutrals' will handle unopposed claims with due care, to keep their reputations. Take, for example, adoption. The neutral won't confirm the adoption unless it's bona fide and in the interests of the child being adopted. But what standard does the neutral follow? The neutral will follow the movant's social promises or won't hear the case. The movant must take on obligations that the neutral finds satisfactory and must prove able to fulfill those obligations or the neutral will not confirm that the adoption is in the best interests of the child. If the movant's social promises are so defective that the neutral cannot confirm the adoption, the neutral has two options: refuse to hear the case or hear it only to find the movant's social promises are fatal to the proposed adoption. Either action prevents the neutral from complicity in abuse of a child. Movants will shop their petitions of adoption to sympathetic or apathetic neutrals. The neutral who signs off on abusive adoptions will bear the taint of complicity.

Let's imagine these forces in action. Morgan wants to adopt infant orphans to induct them into his worship of Venus and sensuality. As high priest, all disciples of Venus must service Morgan's desires, he teaches. Most self-sovereigns detest inculcation of infants into bizarre and abusive religions. The only neutrals who will confirm Morgan's adoptions are members of his cult, and nobody outside the cult will consider their opinions worth respecting. Morgan doesn't need neutral opinions from his own zealous followers, so he won't bother with petitioning anyone for adoption. If his cult is large and powerful enough, he can get away with enslaving orphans such as he can capture into it. He can't make his cult large and powerful by predation alone, so if the worship of Venus under Morgan becomes popular the cult will earn a measure of respect. If Morgan is a predatory crank, he will find no one to legitimize his adoptions. His fellow self sovereigns will earn honor by rescuing his victims, instead.

Suppose the cult of Venus is borderline respectable and Morgan finds a sympathetic neutral who is not a cult member. Petunia was raised in the cult and escaped after she became an adult. After discovering what Morgan had taken from her, Petunia vowed to never let Morgan adopt another baby. She opposes the adoption by claiming Morgan breaks his promises to look out for the best interests of his adoptees, so the adoption will harm the child by a fraud. The neutral will consider her evidence as part of a diligent investigation, and she might prevent the neutral from confirming the adoption. Her social promises do not change the impact of her evidence.

Petunia might petition to adopt the child herself, instead of Morgan. States prevent dueling petitions by putting an adoption agency in charge. In social promise community, the neutral hearing the petition can perform the regulatory function of an adoption agency. Promise keepers can only obligate themselves to care for the adoptee and to respect adoptions that meet their standards. Their capacity to perform as a parent and guardian depends in part on their social promises and the context in which they exercise their promises. No self-sovereign can own another, so neutrals considering competing adoption petitions will not base their decision on an analysis of property rights. Instead, they will consider the best interests of the adoptee. Often a parent or parents of the child or a private adoption agency will hire the neutral, subject to conditions agreed in advance. Communities have arranged similar adoptions for centuries: responsible guardians identify a suitable caregiver who agrees to adopt. A respected neutral then confirms that the arrangement serves the interests of the child. Social promise community will reflect this time-honored process.

When hired by a single movant, neutrals will avoid petitions that will disadvantage unrepresented parties. Before taking a case without adverse parties, a diligent neutral will investigate to make sure the petition affects no identifiable self sovereigns, their property or dependents. If the petition will affect others, the neutral will contact the self-sovereigns involved to alert them to the claim and give them a fair opportunity to oppose. If another self-sovereign will intervene with reason, the neutral will obtain their consent before hearing the case. If the opponent rejects the neutral, the claimant and opposer must agree on another neutral to hear the case, like any other claim with opposing parties.

What if the unrepresented party is a non-promisor, with no connection to social promise community? Neutrals will decide for themselves whether to accept such cases. Some may wish to avoid the risk of backlash from non-promisors. Others may feel secure from backlash or feel that the principle at stake is worth the risk. Cases in this category might include petitions for community-recognized title to property claimed by non-promisors. Just as with claims against non-promisors, sometimes neutrals will not hear the case without consent from the non-promisor. For example, granting title over the homes and personal effects of outsiders merely because of their non-promisor status might harm the community via backlashes. Unused property is another matter. Homestead claims on vast tracts of empty space claimed by states or large non-promisor landowners might deserve a hearing without the involvement of the non-promisor. If the outcome of the petition will be ignored by the non-promisor, its sole purpose is to establish rights between self-sovereign members of the community. Claims for homestead titles will sometimes fit this purpose, and so will win the attention of competent neutrals. If a non-promisor joins the promise community after the title is awarded, the new self sovereign can bring a claim to restore title. But as a member of social promise community, the claim will be subject to the Third Promise. Ejecting homesteaders in social promise community is expensive without active popular support from neighboring self sovereigns.

Petitions for title to unclaimed property represent an important class of unopposed claims. Let's see how the influence of the neutral plays out in another example: A space miner wants to bring a claim for title to an unclaimed asteroid. The miner faces a choice. She might hire Respectable Justice, who enforces strict requirements on asteroid claims including proof of first discovery and use and a diligent search for competing claims turning up empty. Or, she might hire Dubious Justice instead, whose service motto is "No unopposed claim too audacious to grant!" If the miner selects Dubious Justice, the neutral will grant the claim quickly. But Dubious Justice's opinion will be invalid if there is any later challenge to first discovery or use. If the miner selects Respectable Justice, the claim will require more time and money to get, but once granted the miner can be confident her claim will stand due to Respectable's reputation for diligence and fairness, and her more demanding requirements for granting petitions.

Which Justice will the miner choose? She might choose Dubious Justice if confident that her claim is legitimate or the value at stake is low. If the miner knows of competing claims or the value of the asteroid is high, she might select Respectable Justice to establish a more durable title for the investment to mine the asteroid. She might also pick Respectable if her enterprise has third party investors or lenders, or purchases insurance for any risk related to the claim of title on the asteroid. Other parties might ask the miner to use Respectable anyway, just to avoid any cloud on the veracity of the miner's title.

A need for legitimacy motivates claimants to pick an appropriate forum for the matter at hand, without depriving claimants of cheap and fast opinions in easy cases. There's nothing wrong with cheap and easy opinions in small cases; it's better than expensive and slow and is necessary for small cases to be heard at all. The claimant can pick an appropriate forum based on the level of risk involved, and the neutral can manage the risks of hearing the case by setting requirements for granting title of unclaimed resources. In theory the neutral opines based on the movant's social promise. But respected neutrals set their own requirements for granting unopposed petitions. They will refuse to hear cases that damage the reputations they seek.

Justice for The Poor

Being founded in the ultimate egalitarian principle of personal self-sovereignty, social promising can better correct systematic imbalances and prevent injustice to the poor than any system of law or government based in privileges of property, or elite political status. When the rich oppress the poor, equal self sovereignty provides a built-in remedy for the oppressed. The wealthy root their oppression in their property claims. To resist oppression based in property rights, the poor have two useful tools. First, the poor can bring claims seeking payment from the property of the wealthy. The wealthier the defendant and the larger the potential award, the better the contingent-fee advocacy that the poor can hire. Second, the poor can make social promises that do not recognize the property claims of the wealthy or that offer superior property rights where the poor hold the weaker promise.

We've already considered how the Third Promise creates incentives for homesteading on undefended fallow land. Large holders of unused land must recruit and reward a small army of defenders. Holding empty land for its own sake will usually not be worth the effort. The wealthy cannot evict the poor from vacant land without due process, out of concern for their reputation. People will defend with due process parcels they use or intend to use soon: their homes, farms and factories. Environmentalists using the land for quiet recreation and observation of nature will defend nature preserves, motivated by righteous zeal for environmental preservation. Without a state, privileged interests cannot tax the poor and use the tax revenues to enforce the property claims of the wealthy. The wealthy must enforce their own property claims, and the cost of doing so will create a wealth equalizing effect. They cannot defend massive claims except by hiring agents or engaging partners on mutually acceptable terms. The poor will have no reason to hire themselves out for the defense of wealthy land claimants unless the benefits of doing so outweighed the benefits of defending their own property claims. Self sovereigns will sign joint defense pacts on egalitarian terms, in defense against threats.

Within social promise community, the poor enjoy a respectable negotiating position when wealthy property owners want to hire them for defending the owner's property claims or to earn income. In a society of self sovereigns, the wealthy cannot imprison or punish the poor except by the least burdensome social promise made by a poor defendant and a wealthy claimant. And without taxes funding enforcement, the wealthy claimant must fund defense and enforcement himself.

Yet another tool in the arsenal of equality is the rule against forced recognition of corporate or other fictional entities. This will make it harder for collectives to amass wealth to the disadvantage of individuals who do not recognize the legitimacy of the collective.

For example, when mass movements of the poor occupy corporate properties, the poor can select their own social promises and use them for defense. The wealthy will have no choice but to direct lobbying and influence peddling to its only proper outlet: the victims of the property claims they would assert. There are no legislators or entrenched judiciaries to buy off.

When the poor oppress the poor, monetary damages to motivate justice may be less effective. Poor defendants who lack an income stream cannot pay restitution. Statist systems fail at this problem. They can imprison poor criminals, but this costs taxpayer money and does nothing to restore the harm done. Meanwhile the imprisoned criminal receives often receives informal education in prison about how to survive as a criminal, and little or no instruction that enables prospering as a productive citizen.

Restitutionary justice offers a better solution, by creating an economic incentive for reformation of the offender by a third-party reformer. The reformer contracts with the convicted defendant and with the injured victim. The defendant agrees to work for the reformer on agreed terms and pays earnings to the victim. Once the defendant pays the debt, the defendant is rehabilitated from his offense. Both the defendant and the one who accepts payment of the debt earn honor and position themselves to take advantage of future opportunities.

Social promise community will provide healthy incentives for private aid to the unfortunate. Those who support the poor with gifts that lift them out of poverty into a self-sufficient state will earn stellar reputations. The reputation earned will repay the donors for the time, effort, and expense of helping others. To name just a few benefits, the most effective charitable organizations will have the nature of an educational institute, earning social power and prestige through its alumni. To reap these dividends of prestige and social power, charitable groups and individuals will compete for opportunities to serve needy clients of all types. Slothful people might be poor clients at first but can learn new habits. Where enough demand for poor clients exists, the few who choose to be unproductive and live off the labor of others will learn the fulfilling rewards of a good reputation and of self-sufficiency. In social promise community, private charity will work without coercion or fear of unwanted liability for conduct or misfortunes of the unfortunate. The Third Promise will protect the well-meaning and reasonable people on both sides of interactions between the poor and those who would serve and elevate them.

Mutual aid societies will provide stateless social security. Such societies can be *ad hoc* informal organizations, or more formal. A self-perpetuating society nurtures both its young and its old; nurturing is a natural human trait that needs no enforcement by a state. Unhindered by state meddling, mutual aid societies can operate more efficiently and strike a fairer balance between the needs of the young, old, and sick and the working middle that sustains those weaker members. In social promise community, the social promises of those who join mutual aid compacts reinforces this natural human impulse for nurturing. Fulfillment of their mutual promises becomes a matter of personal honor and reputation. Every single infant who ever survived to adulthood was the beneficiary of at least one, and often several, mutual aid societies on the path to survival. So too, a free people experiencing need will form mutual aid compacts to meet that need. When doing so under an "empire" of social promising, we can see mutual aid societies that (unlike tribes and nations) will not seek to make war on competing societies, because of the mutual promises made by members of each competing group to the greater community.

Societies based in personal sovereignty will provide more economic equality than is possible when sovereignty rests on claims over land or other natural resources. Every person has only one inviolable dominion: their own person. All other property arises from their own conscience and reciprocal social promises. In such a society, real poverty does not exist for any capable person, only temporary shortages of goods and services demanded. The community will offer a thousand ways to meet consumer demands in ways that respect the equal rights of fellow self sovereigns.

Establishment of Convenient Standards.

While the most essential laws rest on natural law foundations, people also coordinate activity by establishing technical conventions for conduct in common areas and other interfaces. For example, a state may decree that every driver should drive on a certain side of the road and stop or yield at intersections based on the color of signal lights. Technical rules don't define morality, except for coordinating safe use of public resources such roads. In stateless social promise community, how can uniform conventions develop?

Traffic regulations are an easy example because roads are assets that need regular maintenance to stay in good shape. In a stateless society, all roads are owned by somebody or else they do not exist in a usable state of repair. The owners of the roads have the motive and power to make traffic regulations for their roads, like public entities that claim ownership of the roads today. Private traffic regulations will not vary from place to place any more so than regulations differ now from town to town, province to province, or country to country, because road owners will want to attract customers with sensible and easy-to-understand rules.

Other behavioral conventions do not relate to property. For example, admiralty laws proscribe rights-of-way between ships on the open oceans, to avoid collisions, assign fault, and many other things. The historical roots of admiralty law trace back to Roman civil code. Could similar codes of conduct arise without germinating in empire? Yes, by leaving self sovereigns free to choose how they will spend their time and money. Self-organizing groups develop standards for many things. Sometimes they compete in standards wars like VHS v. Betamax. More often they cooperate to define one common standard in industry standards groups. Non-profit collectives develop rules for sporting events, pageants, shows, and competitions. Voluntary rule development is a common phenomenon. In a stateless society, there would be no state-created barriers to the development and adoption of industry standards. Self-sovereigns will develop standards everywhere that coordinated activity improves outcomes for everybody. They won't force people to use these standards. People will follow sensible rules for their reputations and because they're better off as respected members of a coordinated group than out fending for themselves.

Imagine a small band of persecuted self-sovereigns clinging to existence as fascists pursue them through the forests of Central Asia. Hiding in a cave, they discover an immense underground sea, filled with fishes and favorable habitats around its shores. They settle around the underground sea and their numbers grow. After several generations, still isolated from the world and holding to their self-sovereign ways, they build ships and navigate the underground sea. Will they fail to develop standards covering conduct on the waters? They will not fail to cooperate for everyone's benefit. Seaworthy vessels are major investments. All the shipowners want to avoid waste and accidents caused by misunderstanding or lack of communication. Standards promote communication and avoid misunderstanding. Owners will seek to make standards universal. Every captain wants to navigate the seas without also having to navigate a confusing thicket of conflicting rules. The greater the navigable range of the vessel, the more that universality is useful. These owners will form a cooperative organization to develop and publish reasonable rules. Every captain will abide by prevailing standards, to avoid being blamed for losses. The economic drivers for standardization are unstoppable. Without economic drivers, standardization shouldn't exist.

Social promising will help standardization and make it more efficient, wherever it makes economic sense. Interested parties can use promise registries to compare and coordinate technical standards, game rules, and any other rules of conduct. Social promises turn into standards and rules of behavior by reference. Groups cooperate to publish standards and rules, and self sovereigns promise to apply their selected rules in the right contexts. Everyone can use the social promise registry to keep score of popularity or to check the rules before putting the ball in play. These standards and rules are popular depending on their scope, effect, and appeal to the preferences of the people. None of the standards are imposed by diktat or majority rule. Some contexts encourage more universal standards than others.

Consider, for example, the good captains Graybeard and Redbeard. Graybeard promises to pass on the port side while Redbeard promises to pass to starboard. If they meet each other on the sea without knowing and adjusting for their conflicting rules, their vessels will collide. The collision will cause them to bring claims against one another, on their conflicting promises. Who is at fault, Graybeard, Redbeard, both, or neither? Which is the least burdensome promise, to pass to starboard or to port? Out of context, we cannot say. In context, either most sailors pass to port, most pass to starboard, or they pass to starboard and port in equal numbers. If the passing side is unpredictable, Graybeard and Redbeard should have settled on a side before passing. If the conventional side is port, then Redbeard is at fault not for breaking his own promise but for breaking the less burdensome promise of Graybeard. That promise most observed where the collision occurred is the weaker and applicable rule, some neutrals might reason. Others might find both are at fault. In whatever way neutrals apportion fault, both Graybeard and Redbeard suffered damage they could have avoided.

In reality, economic pressure will cause all captains to coalesce behind a majority rule or agree on a standard protocol for harmonizing differences everywhere that conflicts create risk.

Economics drives standardization, not the power to dictate. Coercive monopolistic systems create incentives and tools for special interests to influence standardization activity. Social promise community will ease standardization wherever it makes economic sense, and shelter from it from every influence except popular demand. The Third Promise will encourage everyone to know the rules of behavior in an area and to obey conventions when to do otherwise will cause avoidable injury or damage. It's just common sense.

Taxes and Fundraising for Social Causes

It may seem fantastic that one day there will be no penalty for failure to pay taxes other than loss of reputation. As remote as this possibility seems, it is only a hair's breadth away. Conversion of taxes to voluntary payments is closer than it seems. The modern version of investment financing for both charitable causes and business, crowdfunding, has proved that people will fund social programs. Crowdfunding differs from conventional fundraising only by being online. But what a difference being online makes! Any interested donor can keep tabs on the progress of the fundraising from anywhere in the world. If the donor consents, the identity of the donor and the donation are published. Fundraising drives become public events. Online crowdfunding is an excellent medium for cultivating reputations within groups.

Promise making is a similar method for growing reputation. By promise making, each person supplies the yardstick by which others can measure their honor. The detailed shape of the yardstick already tells us a lot about the promisor's expectations. But it tells us nothing about the promisor's performance against that yardstick.

We can't tell from the ledger alone whether the promises it contains are empty or meaningful. The real juicy meat is the promisor's record of performance against their own yardstick. That more meaningful information comes from feedback ledgers. The information can be processed by reputational services and provided to inquirers as a service. The reputational information in the feedback ledger is like a credit score, but much more multi-dimensional.

Likewise, advocating for certain social action and donating money to the social causes you advocate or wish to support provides meaty reputational information. It allows you to put your money where your mouth is and withhold support from activities you oppose. By your pattern of giving and not giving, you disclose who you are and what moves you to action. The same reputational services that collect and dispense promise keeping histories can offer similar information about donation histories. That's more meat on the bone.

When reputational information becomes meaty enough, it has a value by itself. The value is that of reciprocal action. Think about it. If you are a large donor to many causes over a long period, you can more easily find support when soliciting money for your preferred cause. Not only that, you will learn who reciprocates support, and you may use that information in deciding who to give to. If you have a great reputation, you will receive lots of support, recruit many people to your social cause, and earn a respectable living for yourself. Having a great reputation in a network of donors is a precious asset, valuable beyond measure. Not everyone will have the greatest reputations, but everyone will recognize the value of a good one. When taxes work like crowdfunding, everyone will put energy into maintaining a donation profile respectable for their circumstances. Most of those who don't donate will be in need, eligible for support as needy clients until rehabilitated into productive members of society. There may be a few Scrooges who just won't understand how reciprocity works — but it is hard to see selfish attitudes lasting for long when the society depends on giving, and most donations are transparent.

In barest outline we have described a self-sustainable economy for social causes based on donating. Society can fund every imaginable social cause this way: collective defense, including military defense; environmental protection; social justice; care of the poor, sick, orphaned and helpless; rehabilitation of criminals; a national weather service; scientific research and exploration, and so forth. The list is endless. New voluntary methods can do everything useful that taxation does, and can do it better, with much less waste and corruption. Giving will do more than we can predict! The social causes economy will resemble a traditional exchange economy, in which the distinction between a social cause and a business concern is not clear. After a time, no meaningful distinction between causes and businesses will exist. Every cause will do business, and every business will support a cause. In those future days, the accountants will be glad they no longer must distinguish between tax-exempt donations and taxable income. The income tax will no longer exist and with it the annual reporting of income and payment of taxes.

That income taxes will not linger forever like every other government program seems fantastic but is only a hair's breadth away. Only two things must happen: first, the legislature must phase out tax funding and budgeting by fiat, and phase in voluntary crowdsourcing as a replacement for both. The legislature can require the revenue agency to replace tax funds with financing from crowdfunded programs over time, using a phased program. In an initial phase, taxes will still exist, but the legislatures will allocate an increasing share of the funds by public choice every year. Legislatures can encourage donations instead of taxes by the simple expedient of offering dollar-for-dollar tax credits. Who would not want greater control over how their contributions are spent, if the control costs them nothing? Professional crowdfunding system operators can operate the public interface for collecting funds just as they do today. The revenue agency has only to keep an eye on things, keep ledgers and statistics, expose fraud, and report back. The legislature must allow agencies and social causes that fail to attract enough public support to wither away. The first phase transitions the public into the role of allocating funds and accustoms them to deciding which public purposes and agencies they will support.

Once most public financing is collected through crowdfunding, the legislature can carry out a second phase. During the second phase, the legislature gives taxpayers a choice: publish your donations and be excused from income taxes or stay under the old tax system. It can increase the percentage of donated funds eligible for tax credits each year. After enough time, political activism, and rejiggering by the crowdfunded recipients, compulsory income taxes will cease to exist except for those who value privacy of their public donations over freedom from compulsory reporting and taxes. Few will choose compulsion and privacy over transparency and freedom.

In a third and final phase, the legislature will open up eligibility for receiving public funds to any entity that makes social promises against fraud. During this phase the legislature can transition its regulatory function over collection of funds to an independent public agency or agencies. By the end of the third phase, public agencies that oppose fraudulent solicitation of public funds should be robust and effective. Independent, voluntarily funded agencies will perform the activities of the public sector. More able agencies will replace those who do not perform as effectively. Having nothing further to do, the legislature can dissolve itself. Society will support the public purposes they choose. Productive self-sovereigns who refuse to support public agencies at a reasonable level will not receive the services of these agencies. Other self-sovereigns may shun them for excessive selfishness.

The people and their politicians will always resist change. Politicians will resist reduction of their powers. Fear of the unknown is a natural human phenomenon. Activists for voluntary society will overcome these obstacles by small popular steps. Over time, everybody who now depends on the income taxes for income must find an alternative source of support. That is part of the beauty of this path: as the demand for services funded by taxes decreases, demand in the crowdfunding sector will more than offset the decrease. Society will not lose the social information gleaned from the income tax system. We will learn more from the crowdfunding system about social activity than we ever could from the income tax system.

The beginning of the path to voluntary society is clear. Wherever it leads, no income taxes will exist at its destinations. Social promise community will see to that. Income taxes and other forms of coercion are not a rational or just option within the bounds of equal self sovereignty. We the people will replace taxes for useful functions with voluntary crowdfunding.

Collective Defense

Even in a stateless world, people must work together to defend private property and public resources. Depending on how we define war, we don't need states to make it—despite war being the health of and reason for the state. Dictionaries sometimes define war as armed conflict between states. But war can have a broader meaning, to include any campaign of coordinated attacks on people and their property. In stateless society, individuals can make war and collectives can make war. There will be no utopia. But wars will be of limited scope and small scale.

While states exist, attacks may come from old-guard police forces encouraged by nervous politicians, by frontal assaults, infiltrations, infowar and sabotage. Warfare against social promise community might occur during transitions from state power to stateless societies. Attacks might come from within, by groups or individuals seeking an advantage for themselves, be it pillage or a rule of fear. Warlike conspiracies might spring up even in stateless areas, motivated by lust for power and domination over others. When attackers target community infrastructure, the supports for members' peaceful existence, or the ability of the social promise community to function unimpaired, the common defense requires a collective effort.

Even where the state has withered away, members of social promise community must mount collective defenses. If promise community is to endure, it must learn how to endure many attacks. Members must learn to how to cooperate as citizen soldiers, to test and reward heroes and generous community servants while turning away from trouble makers and tyrants. Why would some members of society risk their lives or property for others? Wouldn't self-sovereign people be selfish? Some would be brave, some cowards; some heroic, others villainous. Self-sovereigns aren't any different from other people. They have all the same foibles, strengths and weaknesses. They will exhibit all social behaviors, including collective defense. A community that recognizes and rewards true heroes and defenders will have no lack of either.

How can self-organized society resist warlike aggression? Several strategies might work, including violence, politics, litigation, and subterfuge. Of these, the least likely is violence. A community based on the consent of equal self sovereigns must avoid violence. Violence is dangerous on many levels; it can provoke a backlash, sow bitterness and hate, corrupt the peaceable foundations of community, and for all that can accomplish little more than beating back an attacker. Violent resistance will not be a realistic option for a small minority within a culture overrun by thugs. In dire circumstances, overt use of military force is not a viable option for an oppressed minority. Offensive military force will seldom be a useful option no matter how strong promise community becomes.

Imagine, for example, that a social promise community makes up a small minority of the overall population. Many community members are also citizens of a state and live in a territory under state power. Suppose a faction holding state power suppresses activity and growth of the promise community. For example, a group might use the police power of the state to seize computing resources, to sow mistrust among members by infiltration, to arrest key members, and to use the propaganda power of the state to sow fear and mistrust in the general population. This is oppression by an overwhelming coercive power, warfare of a sort. The community can resist by stealth, by civil disobedience, and by political pressure, or by exercising the "power of the powerless." The more the powers oppress social promise community, the better it will learn how to live underground.

Besides traditional defensive strategies, members of oppressed societies will make social promises reinforcing their obligation to defend community assets and avoid giving aid and comfort to the enemy. For example, members might make "common defense" promises that penalize behavior seen as facilitating, excusing, or failing to resist state oppression. Members will make promises that do not increase their chances of being attacked by state agents, that help defend the community without hurting themselves. Remedies would exist against members who failed to keep their defensive promises, using voluntary due process.

Defensive promises might depend on the power of the voluntary society. Members of powerful societies might make strong commitments, such as promises to not sell weapons or otherwise enable aggression by known aggressors. Another form of strong commitment is a promise to support necessary common defense. Defensive promises can be subtle. Members might promise to avoid intentional actions that harm other members or the community. They might promise to agree on what they will disclose to state agents before starting a transaction with another member. Whatever the nature of the defensive promise, peer pressure to adopt community defensive commitments will exist. Some social promises permit coexistence with state-imposed laws.[25] Most members will avoid status as a non-defender of the community by making customary defensive commitments. What other members consider customary will vary with circumstances.

The exact nature of voluntary modes of defense will depend on the state and its preferred modes of oppressing. A few examples illustrate a range of possibilities.

Consider a repressive, totalitarian state that doles out extreme punishment to dissenters and their families for slight infractions. If a small and oppressed minority can practice social promises, it only will be because the social promise community provides critical support to their already desperate circumstances. The promise community will exist under the noses of the guards in the labor camps, by people who have learned its principles in an earlier, happier time. It will use an oral tradition or keep its records well-hidden. Promise histories will not be complex, but will include promises of solidarity against state authorities, with penalties for betrayal no less severe that what the state metes out. Under extreme conditions, social promisors may use the state itself as an executioner of voluntary due process by informing on wrongdoers

---

[25] See "Coexisting with State Legal Systems" in Chapter 6.

after due process. Human history has had its share of repressive, totalitarian states, which have not long endured. Promise community can thrive in their aftermath.

In less oppressive circumstances, a minority community may exist in a regulated state that allows personal freedom, with justice and electoral systems that provide a functional democracy and a rule of law. State actors of democratic states will focus their attacks on specific issues. Just as attacks on Bitcoin came as financial and tax regulations, so attacks on social promise community might come as licensing requirements on the practice of neutral or information services, regulation of social networks, and taxes. Attacks on Bitcoin have not destroyed its operational capabilities or consumer demand but have kept it out of the mainstream. Attempts to disparage or regulate social promise community may discourage less committed participants but will not prevent the community from functioning. Resting on core principles of free speech, free association and freedom of religion, social promise community will be difficult for democratic states to attack. Social promises will evolve with state regulation, neither encouraging disobedience, nor allowing state regulation to quash growth of trust between promise community members. Social promise community will be irrepressible anywhere the state recognizes basic freedoms of speech, association and religion.

Subterfuge is the first tool of war, and oppressive states will not hesitate to use it. The distributed public ledger is an enabling tool for growing social promise community to any size but is also a tool for spying. States will use the ledgers for surveillance and attacks on trust. Such uses are parasitic, depending for their existence on the life and continuance of the public ledgers. Much of the community may learn to live off-ledger, to avoid its downside. Most will maintain an identity as a promise keeper on the ledger to avoid treatment as a non-promisor. Some will live a quiet and private life, register a basic unrevealing promise set, and avoid making revealing entries in public ledgers when they can. Others will use the ledgers without reservation because doing so brings rewards their way.

The more the wealth of information makes public trust networks useful for surveillance, the bolder their members can assert their harmlessness. Public ledgers serving voluntary communities will balance confidentiality and openness. The greater the risk of surveillance leading to actual persecution, the harder it will be to discover information about members and their transactions. However, information about their promises will be available, up to where their promises might mark them out as people of state concern. Open networks will be a compliment to the states where the networks' members live; they will be a sign that the state does not persecute peaceful citizens for living alternative lifestyles. More oppressive states will drive the networks underground. Voluntary networks will not exist in any open form in totalitarian states.

When a social promise community makes up a substantial part of the population under a minimalist state that is under military attack by a neighboring state, community members may come to the aid of the state. The invading state if victorious will move on to attack the social promise community, using the conventional state tools of oppression. Anyone in the social promise community who wants to resist the invaders may do so. They may join a military force under state control. Where the promise community is strong, it may become hard to tell where the promise community ends, and the state begins. Fighters may join one of several allied private militias, supervised by the last remnants of the state's military. The chances of repelling an attack will depend on the military strength of the alliance between the promise community and the state, relative to the invading state. States will strengthen military defenses by setting their people free.

Where social promise community is thriving, voluntary militias and state military forces can ally to become stronger than the state can manage on its own. The voluntary militias will fight for their homes, their freedoms and for their beneficent state. If the defenders cannot repel the invaders, a new state will sweep in with a mandate based on superior power, subjugate the laxer state, and eat away at the social promise community. Those in social promise community will learn from the failure of their predecessor society/state alliance, and institute reforms for a more powerful resurgence. They will do this, perhaps, in a prolonged guerrilla war against the invaders. They will learn ways to make their promise community secret and impenetrable by agents of the invading state, and work to repel or reform it. Once a large fraction of the population has learned to live under self-sovereignty, they will not subject themselves again to a parasitic and hostile state.

Not all states are imperialistic. Some may be content to stay within their borders as tranquil tax plantations run to benefit political elites. These "plantation states" may have enough military capability to repel invasion. Stateless or minimal state "islands" run by social promise community might persist next to such states due to the interests of political elites or the realization that only a voluntary society will be productive enough to supply the elite's desires. The emergence and persistence of Hong Kong is a partial example of this phenomenon, albeit in a world without social promising. "Client" social promise communities will not need a strong defense, nor will their patrons permit them to build a military force. Their master state will defend them from attack. Besides avoiding offense to their patron state, the promise community can exist as it would in a stateless world.

If the world ever becomes free of states capable of launching military attacks, aggressive technology will atrophy. A cabal may form to learn the dark arts of military conquest and police power, re-establish a state, and seize power. Conspiracies of this sort should prove easier to resist than an invading state. Self sovereigns will resist such conspiracies by bringing claims and uncovering aggression. White hats will study the darks arts, to better develop defenses against the conspirators. If social promise community cannot resist internal conspiracies, it will prove itself unworthy of defense.

We have considered a spectrum of promise community coexisting with thugs and states of varying beneficence, and how collective defense operates in different circumstances. The table below summarizes:

Circumstances	Mode of Defense
1. Minority promise community existing in a regulatory state.	Politics, civil disobedience, subterfuge, defensive promise-making, pursuing remedies under social promises and litigation in state courts
2. Minority promise community existing in a very oppressive state.	Subterfuge, defensive promise-making, pursuing remedies under social promises
3. Majority or large minority promise community existing in a benevolent or weak state.	No defense needed against the host state; promise community and state will organize military defense against invading state

Circumstances	Mode of Defense
4. Majority or large minority promise community after invasion by a foreign state.	Guerilla tactics; civil disobedience, subterfuge, defensive promise-making, pursuing remedies under social promises
5. Overwhelming majority promise community with no threatening state.	Pursuing remedies under social promises; resisting bands of non-promisors using police tactics and shunning

Collective defenses against bands of violent non-promisors or those making promises without penalties for theft, murder or fraud would be easy. Open sociopaths would be few and identifiable. Conspirators for evil will cloak themselves with a veil of hypocrisy and make virtuous social promises without the intent to keep them. Wolves in sheep's clothing cannot maintain their disguise for long, without control over a corrupt judicial system. But corruption of the judicial system cannot not long exist. The open nature of competition in voluntary due process, makes it impossible to maintain control over the judicial system. No state exists to sponsor coercive monopoly power. A ready supply of more honest neutrals will judge corrupt neutrals for breaking their promises. Since a neutral can be any unbiased society member willing to hear the case, any corrupt group of privileged jurors will find it impossible to maintain its position in the market for neutral services.

There might exist "soft" conspiracies to accumulate property rights in the hands of an elite. These might succeed to scales below a threshold of noticeable oppression. Some families might grow richer than others over time, in proportion to uneven skills, ambitions, and fortunes. Some unevenness should cause no social problems, so long as the more privileged families do not conspire to deprive the less privileged classes of their ability to earn and maintain property. The state is just such a conspiracy. Social promise community will not revert to statism by operation of conspiracies by privileged property owners. Impoverished self sovereigns will undermine oppressive property rights accumulated by conspiratorial property owners, by making social promises that renounce offensive rights. A coalition of the poor will engage in political activism against the privileged owners, including acts of mass trespass. Owners will find it difficult to push their statist conspiracies past the limit at which the poor feel oppressed. Owners cannot seize control of vital resources, without committing acts of naked aggression and making themselves vulnerable to claims under voluntary due process.

All the foregoing optimism aside, we cannot prove that a voluntary society will not fall back into statism, or worse. Tribalism might re-emerge as some social groups strive to dominate others. Reemergence of tribal warfare is possible, but a society organized around division of labor with an effective conflict resolution system will discourage aggressive tribal behavior and make it unprofitable. Promise keepers will resist aggressive tribalism by the same methods as any other anti-social behavior: loss of reputation and shunning.

In the worst case, an advantaged minority might strive to dominate all other members of society. Consider this example: suppose all health care providers banded together in a powerful guild, maintained strict trade secrecy, and adopted social promises that disadvantaged all non-members of their guild. For example, the medical guild might refuse to recognize certain forms of property unless held by other guild members. But even a powerful medical guild can exercise no power over a healthy population without resorting to forbidden aggression. The more powerful and secretive the guild, the more apt it is to inspire competition. Without a state to preserve monopolies, more ethical alternative service providers will put the would-be monopolists out of business. None can subjugate others without aggression. Voluntary society will punish the systematic exercise of aggression with a thousand daggers, putting aggressors at risk of exposure and loss of reputation. Social promise community will not backslide to statism by operation of internal agents. What comes after social promise community is only this: a more voluntary and safer society.

The question of war and aggression goes to a deeper riddle: can we build a society in which no class of people enjoys a privilege to rule by aggression? Historical examples are few and debatable or predate agrarian society. Primates and other animals are territorial by nature. They defend their privilege of possession with violence. A movement to social promise community requires that we redirect our innate instincts for defense and conquest of territory into voluntary due process and increasing our influence by building good reputations. We cannot deny our competitive nature, but we can redirect it to new channels for building social status.

Social promise community is a non-utopian scheme for suppressing the rewards of aggression relative to reputation. Aggression cannot build social promise community, by design. Social promise community will serve as a test of whether the rewards of a good reputation can outweigh the rewards of using aggression, even for the powerful. The test will fail so long as the powerful gain their power by instilling fear in those they subjugate. We build a path to a voluntary society by defensive strategies designed to demolish this fear. Social promise community demolishes that fear by building trust networks with real benefits and empowering equal self sovereignty. To enjoy the benefits of the community, all must acknowledge the equal self sovereign power of their neighbors to be free of obligations they have not promised.

Why would a social promise society rise to its own defense? The question supplies its own answer: because otherwise, the social promise society will not exist. Defense is at the core of social promise society. It is the reason the social promise society exists. Voluntary defenses will be stronger than the attacks of mercenaries. The burden of defense is lighter than the burden of conquest, and the will to survive is stronger than the desire to thieve. The strongest defenses, and the safest societies, will be voluntary ones.

Chapter 11: Imagining the Future

First Look

Do not disparage dreaming. Imagining new ways to achieve better social outcomes is necessary for the long-term survival of our species. Creative envisioning is not at all frivolous, when tempered by rational skepticism. We must dream.

Social promising can be practiced at any scale. It works between any two sincere and committed people. It works in populations of unlimited size and geographic reach. Promise community will accommodate and coexist with any other social system that competes with it. Social promise communities can be tough and hard to eradicate.

Vision is not enough. Better community won't happen without effort and risk. If you anything away from this Guidebook, take this: now is the time for spirited action. Everything we need, we already have. Let's not hesitate or wait for a sign before building the voluntary societies of the future. The sooner we get started, the sooner we will arrive at our destination. Here is a vision of what might happen once we build communities founded on social promises and equal self sovereignty.

Kernel

We cannot realize positive social outcomes without first planning to achieve them. Imagining a bright future, and identifying realistic reasons supporting positive outcomes, is a necessary first step to realizing those outcomes. Envisioning the possible is seeing into the future.

We should temper our dreams by the realities we face. There are myriad ways that social promise community might fail, and skepticism is also important to success. This book will not dwell on the negatives or obsess over analysis of obstacles. Success is best realized by envisioning positive outcomes and then doing what is necessary to achieve those outcomes one step at a time. Unlike interstellar travel, lifespans extended to centuries, or singularities of artificial intelligence, achieving voluntary society will require no great technological leaps forward, changes in human nature, bending of economic laws, violent revolutions, or global cataclysms. All the tools we need are already in our possession, flowing from the fabric of our beings.

We don't need and can't use political power over states or other instruments of coercion to implement social promise communities. It is enough to resist the depravations of authoritarian busybodies without violence while building collective, coordinated alternatives. Successful community will give people the tools for resisting tyranny of all kinds by collective, peaceful action.

Vision is essential. The modes by which we organize human society will not improve by accident. We must present better alternatives and show that the alternatives work in practice. Pioneers should not only envision a desired outcome, but also a means for realizing the outcome. The rest of this chapter outlines just such a vision: we identify stages of a new order and classify them as part of the Beginning, the Middle, or the End, starting with society as it exists today in many parts of the world. The starting point is from a place of adequate freedom to allow public speech contrary to the preferences of the most powerful authorities and means for individual access to modern communications technology. We present possibilities, not prophecies.

Different outcomes are possible. In the bleak scenario, social promise community never gains traction and fades into obscurity. Humanity rejects self-rule. It's possible but uninteresting. A middle alternative results in promise community coexisting with government by territorial monopoly for an indefinite time. Finally, social promise community might reach its full potential and replace all monopolistic forms of lawmaking. These three possibilities correspond to stages of development along a continuum. There may be reversals along the way, but development of social promising won't be extinct so long as any esteem personal equality, self-sovereignty, and social responsibility. For so long as somebody is thinking about increasing the exercise of those values, there is hope.

Basket of Nuts

The Near Term — Seeds and Seedlings

Seeds and seedlings precede the forest. Plans for social evolution based on voluntary principles depend on the gradual acquisition of social power, by awareness first, acceptance later, and at last by spreading the practice of social promising. The Three Promises in the minds of equal self sovereigns offer a framework separate from state legal systems, without sovereignty over people or vital territory. Free and equal self sovereigns can practice the Three Promises now without waiting for the decrepit concept of coercive rule to die its final death.

Concept development for voluntary society is ancient. It goes back more at least 2600 years, to Lao-Tze who said "The more laws and regulations that exist, the more thieves and brigands appear."[26] Around the same time Buddha taught "It is better to conquer yourself than to win a thousand battles."[27] A little later Jesus of Nazareth said "the kingdom of God is within you."[28] Many others spoke before and after these. Meat has been layering up on

---

[26] Tau Te Ching, Chapter 57 (tr. unknown).
[27] Dhammapada, tr. by Thomas Byrom.
[28] Luke 17:21, King James Version

dry bones. Just in the last fifty years, discussion about alternative legal systems based in personal sovereignty and property rights has exploded. Promise community emerges now as a scaffold for future society. At some point (to borrow from Ezekiel) spirit will breathe life into reconstructed bodies, and a great army will stand up.

If ideas are seeds, communities organized based on an idea are like seedlings. Some seeds will sprout as early experiments. Seedlings suffer great disadvantages in the competition for resources, and so most seedlings start small and fail to thrive. Those few that sprout in favorable conditions show vigor until reaching the limits of their environment. Natural limits on seedlings do not show that their species will fail! The sowing of many seeds is a force for survival, despite failures. But as intentional sowers, we should not waste our seed on ground we know to be inhospitable. If we lack fertile ground, we should find seeds capable of thriving in the available circumstances. We should not try to grow seaweed in a desert, or wheat in a bog.

The analogy of the sower can extend only so far. Voluntary society is more than a collection of self sovereigns arranged by preferences. It is itself a universal society, an ideological fungus that can sprout in different places and grow together to form a single organism. Like fungi, social promise community can influence its environment, and create conditions favorable to its own growth. As an alternative social system, promise community may grow best where state-based social systems are failing to meet basic human needs, but are still strong enough to stave off invasion by other states, and other forms of chaos and oppression. Perhaps malaise of western socialist or capitalist democracies is creating conditions for alternative voluntary societies to establish themselves, first on the social fringes, and later in the mainstream.

Where do we go from here? There are several diverging paths visible, and a future convergence of these paths.

418

One path to the future leads through a burst of creativity and public interest in publishing social promise sets. People will find elegant and useful phrases for social promises, available for public browsing and choosing between alternatives. Another path leads through understanding and reconciling differences between alternative social promises. A more technical path leads through development of open-source data protocols, applications, and online infrastructure supporting the basic functions of privacy-protected promise recording and reputational discovery. There will be parallel activity along these and other paths, energizing an unstoppable social movement.

The first users of social promise systems may be gamers, who will adopt social as an experiment in gaming. Hackers are already developing an online, open source data backbone for incorporating into computer games of a massive multiplayer online sort. Game players will make and use social promises as part of determining outcomes of the game. Playing the game will encourage people to try out social promising in a safe environment and learn how it works. It will also enable the open-source designers of the data backbone to refine the backbone and make it more robust.

Frivolities will become more useful. Virtual reality will become real reality. Gamers will adjust their promise sets for reality and extend their social promises to a real community made up of those who reciprocate by making and keeping compatible promises under the Three Promises or an equivalent scheme. Prominent gamers will lead followers to make their promises real. An alternative voluntary cyberculture will arise from the virtual reality game.

At some point, outsiders will take notice. Stories will appear in the media. Members of non-gaming fringe social groups will wonder whether participation in a promise system is beneficial.

Some will first explore possibilities in the available game environments. Others will take part in a real promise community at the outset. Some will participate out of a principled passion, and others because of the hope for business or personal opportunities. At first, these promise communities will not enjoy sustainable economies. Most players will invest more than they receive. Making the game fun and capable of connecting people for mutual benefit will encourage people to invest time and energy early on, as leisure.

Once rooted in cyberculture, games and fringe communities, social promise community will enter an early consolidation and slow growth phase. It will endure one or more crises of confidence and will survive those crises. Social promising will persist as a minority movement. Persistence will encourage more investment, which will spur development and growth of software, network infrastructure and human resources dedicated to servicing the needs of promise community members. The new social promise systems will rely on reputation to motivate good behavior. Enforcement of obligations will be voluntary as in an honor system. Promise community will leave force and the threat of force for the state. Their self sovereign members will find other ways to do justice.

The promise community will reach economic sustainability during the consolidation phase, first for early adopters, and then for those who come later. Once membership is sustainable, the benefits of belonging to a social promise community outweigh the cost. The community learns ways to distribute its infrastructure costs among willing members. For the end user, sustainability happens as soon as the user gets a benefit for being a member, because the cost of membership is almost nothing. The community becomes sustainable when the activity to develop and support infrastructure and services is also sustainable. The pace at which sustainability hits various sectors of the social promise economy will vary. Service and infrastructure providers may find economic returns in service fees, donations, advertising revenue, cost savings and capital appreciation. Services will include things like core open-source programming, reputation discovery and repair services, self-sovereign advocacy and counseling, alternative dispute resolution and neutral services, and enforcement. Despite achieving sustainability, participation rates during the early consolidation phase will be small. The community will exist on the fringe of larger, less free society.

Educational institutions and curriculum will emerge with the growth of neutral and related dispute resolution services. Early on, curriculums will be rudimentary and educational certification of little value. Later, training certified by respected institutions will be valuable for service providers. The most skilled providers will not need certification from anyone because their skills and results will speak for them. Respected providers may teach and certify others to offer dispute resolution services. Nobody will have authority to impose license requirements.

During the early phase, aggrieved parties will have weak enforcement power. Membership in the community will not yet be valuable enough to deter anti-social conduct. Less committed members will scorn voluntary due process, ignore opinions by neutrals, or refuse to pay valid debts proved by voluntary due process. Members might still use contracts made under state law for important transactions, in the early years.

Contempt of voluntary due process will not be without consequences since claimants and neutrals will make a permanent record. The offender cannot remove the stain without satisfying the underlying neutral opinion or the claimant's demand. Later, possession of an honorable membership status will be worth enough to instill a healthy aversion to taking disreputable actions. Early on, membership status will be valuable enough to exist, but not valuable enough create strong enforcement powers. It will be worth having for networking and marketing purposes, but not yet in full fruit.

After promise community grows and become sustainable, those vested in the state will feel the winds of change shaking their house of cards. Reactionaries will oppose social promise community out of fear and ignorance. True progressives will learn from and adapt to it. Social promising will enter its opposition phase. Propagandists of the state will accuse the community of corrupting children, sponsoring terrorism, enabling tax evasion, and fostering a society of stateless criminals. Secret police may place agent provocateurs to stir up conflict, and stage false flags to discredit the community and its members. The state will try to surveil, infiltrate, and undermine. Its efforts will fail. Thriving communities will exercise their defenses, and rest on the solid foundation of equality, peace, and honor by keeping promises.

Social promising will survive the opposition phase and grow stronger. State opposition and propaganda will only promote mass awareness of its principles and public benefits. Judges and legislators around the world will confirm the basic human right to make and publish promises and to settle differences by voluntary due process, even as other state actors try to shackle the movement. Special interest groups that support social promise communities will coalesce and become a significant political force. Social promise community will assure its future and assert its ability to expand.

Sinking Roots and Growing Tall

As growth of social promise community continues, resources from voluntary community displace other sources. Promise society members enjoy an advantage over outsiders. They out-compete alternatives in the old economy. Promise food tastes better, promise neighborhoods are nicer, promise health care is better and more affordable, and not by magic. The enhanced ability to compete emerges from mass cultivation of reputations in a network dedicated to interpersonal trust building. Good reputations unlock access to goods and services, and most of all to credit. Unlike rating or referral services, no entity has control over the reputation ledger. All have equal power over their own reputation and that of others, and those who want greater influence must earn it. The Three Promises provide a decentralized scheme for social order to the trust network. Once the promise community can supply every basic need, all who wish will meet their needs within the promise community. Life will be easier and more secure inside than outside. Society will transition from dominance of the nation-state or empire to dominance of voluntary society.

Signs of the transition will include displacement of state-based services with services provided through social promise community. Health care provided by members of voluntary society will displace state-mandated health insurance or health care. Health care providers in the promise community will fill service gaps in government programs, out of sight of state intervention. Over time, voluntary health care will become more available, and more sophisticated in its operating modes. States will dislike the reduction of dependency that the shift will entail but will find that public health services have so eroded, and demand for services is so great, that the trend towards voluntary fulfillment is irresistible.

Voluntary mutual aid will displace state-funded entitlement programs, as stagnation from over-regulation and never-ending inflation renders entitlements less valuable. Desperation and real need will provide an impetus for a continuing shift to market-based, stateless solutions. States that attempt to prohibit voluntary services will find that the prohibition causes prices to rise in proportion to the cost of avoiding enforcement, with little effect on supply and demand. Organized voluntary society may grow first and strongest wherever states are strict about enforcing their prohibitions. Once people through desperation have learned how to exchange value through voluntary society, they will like the results. They will look for voluntary markets regulated by a robust Three Promise system to displace inferior state services in other areas.

With the value of participation in voluntary society healthy and on the rise, a host of service providers will spring up to service the information needs around that growth. Notable among these new industries will be reputation information services and the services catalyzed by the robust reputation information that the new services will offer. Private investment bartering and banking houses will ease new start-up enterprises beyond the reach of oppressive government taxation by skillful devices. Jobs and business opportunities will proliferate in the voluntary economy. Members of voluntary societies will find that surviving in promise community without accreting burdensome debt is a stress-free proposition almost anywhere a member might desire to be.

Another area of income and opportunity growth will be in the expanding judicial service economy. There will be opportunities for advocates, investigators, and attorneys. Some will earn income by providing virtual and real venues for dispute resolution. Neutrals and counsellors won't always be professionals and won't need licenses, but some will earn a living that way. Some will bundle and integrate services. These new professional services won't be a drain on voluntary society. An efficient, open market in dispute resolution services will offer a net benefit to society, by settling disputes for much less than it costs to leave claims unresolved. The open market will prune away unnecessary wrangling. Bureaucracies cannot survive the atmosphere of order-by-social-promises. Politicians can't devise Byzantine laws for suppressing their adversaries and competitors. If voluntary professional services cannot do these beneficial things, there will be no demand for them. Being voluntary, services won't exist where no one wants them.

Creative enforcement services will go with the rise of voluntary due process services, to encourage parties to use due process and make sure that parties perform their obligations. Beneficiaries of the due process can hire these services to collect benefits due from losing defendants. Private collection agencies already exist, but in promise community the basis for collection expands. Enforcement depends on the social promises of the parties and their agreed process for settlement. The new enforcement services need not break state laws in ways that invite prosecution. As soon as the economic incentives are great enough, these services will find endless creative ways to coexist and to work without real state opposition, if not approval.

Over time, enforcement agencies will invent and put in place enforcement strategies that work with minimal interference from states. Most self sovereigns will obey respectable neutral opinions to preserve their honor, and much of what promise community enforcers will do is keep score, nudge and encourage payment in full. Every opinion from unbiased and respected neutrals will create a choice: ignore the opinion and risk falling into non-promisor status, mount an appeal, or comply. By complying, the defendant keep their status as honorable and trustworthy persons, if the underlying offense is civil. If the underlying offense is egregious and uncivil, i.e., a "crime," compliance will start the defendant on the path of earning a new status as a reformed member. So long as membership in the voluntary network is valuable, the desire to avoid non-promisor status will give plenty of motivation for voluntary compliance. During the intermediate phase, the value of membership will be enough to cause compliance. Once this happens, the value of membership will become so compelling that few will ignore voluntary society, or resist joining.

The intermediate phase will see robust growth of social functions and geographical areas using social promises. User fees will fund utility services. Cooperatives funded by user fees and donations will support public assets like roads, computer networks, hospitals, and schools. Increasing numbers of people regardless of income level will pay no compulsory taxes, and user fees and donations will fund an increasing share of social programs. Networks of mutual aid societies and other freed market innovations will sustain the supportive infrastructure for maintaining civil justice and voluntary exchange. Self sovereigns will supply the needs of fellow sovereigns. Voluntary networks will defend against interference from state actors through peaceful channels like political activism, community organizing, and sometimes civil disobedience. Free market solutions at free market prices will reduce dependence on welfare supplied by states and demand for jobs from state-supported institutions such as corporations or government organizations. Increasing numbers will subsist and thrive by their relations with their self-sovereign fellows.

As more people invest in voluntary enterprises, new technology and know-how will migrate inside the promise community. Some of the most desirable goods and services will be hard or impossible to find outside of the promise community. Different reasons for the migration will exist. Sometimes, the new technology will avoid exposure to onerous state laws. Because of violent state intervention, the new technology will exist where it can in voluntary society, shielded from state intervention. Sometimes, voluntary collectives focused on technology, resembling guilds, will share trade secret technology among their members under voluntary secrecy pacts. They will consider their trade secret strategy to be more beneficial than making use of the intellectual property laws of the state. Likewise, individual inventors may make similar calculations and sell their ideas to fellow promise keepers. They will find fewer barriers to entry, and less risk of crippling litigation in the promise community. Regardless of the reasons for the capture of technology and services by voluntary society, customers seeking access to the new technology or services will either be members of voluntary society or will lack access. Exclusivity of resources will create further pressure to join and enhance the value of a good voluntary reputation.

Just as voluntary society will attract new ideas and technologies, it will enable and attract new and diverse lifestyles. People will earn pleasant and sustainable livings by interacting with one another in creative ways. Some new ways of interacting will maximize resource sharing and drive down costs of living. With survival made easy and secure, social activities will revolve around leisure, health, self-improvement, education and discovery. Voluntary services in every category will find their consumers everywhere. Food, shelter, health care, information services, financial services, and all forms of entertainment will be available, in many styles and behaviors.

The new services will include registration of voluntary property titles and claims. In the early phase, voluntary property systems will carry little weight. At first, stateless registration systems implemented in blockchain or other distributed public ledgers will be experiments or fill gaps in state-run property systems by recording property interests that the state does not recognize. As the size and influence of social promise community increases, increasing numbers of people will find it prudent to register their property both with the state, and in a voluntary property registration system. The community will use the stateless registration system for internal purposes and coexist with state-run systems as needed. Self sovereigns might record real property titles with the local county clerk, and in a blockchain property registration system. This dual recordation will reduce risks for property owners and enable promise community members to keep a record independent of information maintained by the state. After a time, self sovereigns might learn that recording property transfers with the state has too many disadvantages and avoid state registration altogether. For example, a non-profit corporation (e.g., a cooperative of trusted voluntary society members) might hold title in the state register, while members of the cooperative exchange the title among themselves in an independent register.

As voluntary society becomes more vibrant and powerful, it will permeate state-based collectives such as corporations. Incorporated entities will make statements of support for voluntary society. Society members and incorporated entities will accommodate one another's needs and grow to tolerate each other. Corporations will market to voluntary society members while making assurances of respect for voluntary principles. Some society members will find it beneficial to recognize corporations organized under state law. It will become commonplace for officers, agents and employees of corporations to belong to voluntary society and to make their membership known. Tensions between voluntary forms of due process and mandatory legal systems will exist, but these dual corporate/voluntary society members will diffuse the tensions for their own economic well-being. Corporations will shift their role from being instruments of state power, to being instruments that shield and enable voluntary society to coexist and cope with state power, until state power fades away.

As services and technology multiplies in voluntary society, demand for state action will shrink. Fewer people will sign up for government welfare because most will find better opportunities outside of the state system. A few confirmed statists will cling to their old ways and demand state action. Voluntary collectives will take over their care as the last remnants of the old welfare systems. The dependents may not notice that their benefits are no longer tax funded, and the state treasurer no longer signs their payment vouchers. They may notice a different quality of care that feels more familial and personal. They may notice a greater freedom of action than before, freedom that may encourage some to experiment with new ways to fulfil their purpose for living, and to pursue long-forgotten dreams.

Through a gradual process of growing voluntary funding for government agencies while shrinking funding based in coercion and trimming back agencies that fail to attract public support, state agencies will evolve into voluntary public organizations. A few will be popular and accomplish amazing things. Others will take care of vital needs. A remnant will remain for ceremonial uses. In all they do, the agencies will embrace the maxim that true social welfare is voluntary. Wherever governance is good, the economy will thrive. Wherever the economy thrives, the needy will fare better than elsewhere. Colleges of public policy will teach generations of students how voluntary programs are superior in achieving beneficial results. These colleges will teach clever ways of implementing voluntary programs, which their graduates will carry out and improve. After a few generations, taxes will carry the stench of shame and failure, and none will levy them. Self sovereigns will fund everything that works for good.

A governmental remnant might offer a regulatory and justice system for collective entities, such as corporations. The remnant may become a government of corporations and for corporations, without compulsory jurisdiction over any individuals. Inter-corporate government might live off contributions from the corporations it serves, as a cost borne by those who organize in collective forms. There may come to exist many such inter-corporate governance organizations competing for corporate sponsors by providing superior value. Corporate members of different governance cooperatives might resolve their differences using a conflict resolution process resembling conflict resolution in Three Promise systems, including principles such as TROTWET. Corporations and other collective entities may persist in voluntary forms even as compulsory, monopolistic forms of governance go extinct. Perhaps in the far future, society will need no fixed forms for organizing collective action. All collective action will happen by spontaneous individual cooperation in response to perceived social needs. Until then, the collective forms we know today will evolve into less dangerous forms, without the capacity to impose their law or "justice" on the society of free and natural persons.

As states diminish in power, borders will also diminish in importance. Without credible external threats, support for collective defense will shrink. The likelihood that a public agency would start a violent prolonged conflict will vanish. War being the health of the state will pass away, made obsolete by new forms of social organization and new technologies. Collective entities will find war to be uneconomical, or even suicidal. Public funding for offensive military buildups will become impossible as funding for public works moves to a transparent donation system. Those who donate to offensive military campaigns will find their donations are harmful to self-interest, providing no benefits and harming their reputations. Focus on military technology and preparedness will shift to less dangerous defensive strategies. Weaponry will grow in effectiveness for defense and diminish in effectiveness for attack. Old tropes such as "the best defense is a good offense" will become relics of more barbaric times.

Instead, most will believe that the best defense is that which does the least unnecessary harm. The press will forget euphemisms such as "collateral damage." People will abhor harm to innocent bystanders while social promises make it too expensive to consider. Every innocent bystander harmed by military action will have a right to full compensation by social promises, or the military that did the harm will lose social support. The cost of compensating victims will make war as the world has known it to be infeasible. The only wars fought will be for public opinion and influence. Not that all violent skirmishing will cease forever. Violent crime against individuals will still exist, sometimes by a group against another group. But economic pressure and social disincentives for unjustified violence will contain the spread of natural human tendencies for violence and prevent eruption of large-scale war.

Could peace be so easy? The rosy scenario of a world at peace assumes that most people in every nation capable of war have become members of social promise community, and that maintaining honor in the voluntary system is important. It's a big "if," but if such a worldwide social revolution occurs, the peace dividend that results will seem normal and natural. War makes no sense at all when society governs itself by mutual respect for the sovereignty of others, and members earn their honor by making and keeping social promises. Prior to the ascension of social promise community, nation-states may make war on coalitions of social promise community and the nation-states that coexist with the community. Coalitions that include promise communities will be more vigorous and successful, on average. Benevolent nation states with thriving social promise communities will be more resilient and innovative. The freer coalitions will resist attacks and outlive the empires of the past. The wars of the old world will hasten the demise of authoritarian government, as pro-voluntary coalitions grow in victories and influence. Promise community is optimistic.

If you doubt that social promise community means the end of war, consider a worst-case scenario: a voluntary society that splits along ideological grounds. For example, suppose half of the society abhors the eating of meat. The other half regards meat-eating to be a human right, necessary for health, and abhors a vegan lifestyle. A cabal of weapons sellers stirs the pot, promoting loathing of different lifestyles and a call for violence of one group against another, justified by hatred of reprehensible ways. Self sovereigns who follow the call to violence lose their stature in voluntary society. No longer will the members of different groups respect the self-sovereignty of those who hold to different social promises. Instead, the warring sovereigns view social promises as an excuse for violence and domination. To enable war the warriors must destroy social promise community. Voluntary society is the antithesis of war. Wherever social promise community exists, war between its members cannot. The end of war as we know it will be a sign that social promise community has prevailed and is ready to mature.

Maturity — Blooming and Fruiting

Relentless evolutionary pressure will drive new experiments in social organization, and the most successful will mature. If ever war and conquest become obsolete political tools, then social promise community has succeeded and is maturing. In that maturing, it will create the conditions for the next great revolution in social organization. Maturity means producing the next generation, and so the next generation of society will emerge from mature promise community. Successful societies produce offspring: tribes produced kingdoms; kingdoms produced empires. Empires produced states with various forms of governance. States have been evolving towards a dead end, the antithesis of self-rule: dissolving the self in the solvent of rule-by-committee. Social promise community reverses away from the state, splitting off in a new direction in search of a higher order. If we as a people can reach that higher order, an unknown higher order will beckon still.

We can't know whether social promising will succeed. Here is a credible vision, not a guarantee. Perhaps human nature makes it impossible for social promise community to reach maturity, but we can't know that until after it has a fair trial. Most politicians still believe power flows from the barrel of a gun; that moral exercise of political power includes dominating others and inflicting fear, even to the point of violence and death. If social promise community is to blossom and bear fruit, a large majority must believe only two things flow from the barrel of a gun: shame or justified self-defense. To spread belief in non-aggression, we show it works by experiments in smaller subcultures and societies. If it works, social promise community will supply the proof. After we show the power of non-aggression and self-sovereignty in small but growing societies, we can discover whether social promising can spread to the whole of human society. In imagining what might come next, we must be optimistic in our assessment of the possibilities. Pessimists who believe dominance by force or fraud will always prevail won't build voluntary society. They will live with George Orwell's vision of an eternal boot in the face and a future not worth imagining.

Speculation about future human society is uncertain. But if voluntary societies mature, what shape will they take? They will not be utopian. Criminal behavior and struggles for power and dominance will not become a thing of the past. Lust for power will not disappear, but those who indulge in aggression will have a less hospitable environment. When promise community is ascendant, human society will achieve new and greater things, forsake the insanity of the nation-state and its wars, taxes, fiat money monopolies and prisons, to name just a few. Billions of self-directed, principled people will cooperate to build a society we can scarcely imagine. The geniuses of the free billions will develop new solutions, technologies and social structures that we cannot anticipate. But the maturing of voluntary society past the age of war will confer tremendous benefits, as people redirect resources now spent on military efforts, over-regulation, over-criminalization and wasteful, productivity-killing forced redistribution of wealth to peaceful enterprises and beneficial voluntary exchange. We can imagine some benefits.

Individual sovereignty will predominate. Collective forms of organization have the status of fictions, with their members and officers governed by their own social promises. Collectives will not have the same status as individuals in the promise community but won't disappear. Each sphere — the collective and the voluntary self-sovereign — will influence the other sphere, but not control it. Collective organizations will still be powerful loci for cooperative action but will lose their power to dominate the individual once most in the collectives are members of promise community. Perhaps the laws of states will evolve to apply to collective entities only, mutual collective promising will sprout as a branch of social promising, or both.

Warfare between nation-states will cease, of interest only as history. The people will dismantle weapons of mass destruction and develop non-lethal defensive technology for collective defense. Self sovereigns will value and protect life everywhere. Nations will become borderless cultural clubs of ethnicities or cultures, without exclusive leaders. Elections will become quaint rituals for ceremonial positions. Borders, if existing, will become geographic assessment points, surveilled by one or several police agencies who earn their keep by selling statistics and information, advertising to travelers passing through, collecting and assisting the lost and homeless, and keeping the peace in all the modes of transit through an area.

Deadly wars over natural resources and political power will cease, because cultural clubs have neither the motivation or the power to wage war, when all their members are engaged in a universal voluntary society. Competition between collectives for natural resources and social influence will replace the barbaric wars of the past. This competition for resources may resemble ruthless wars in their intensity, but without loss of life or destruction of valuable assets. The victors will secure superior access to natural resources and knowledge and will attract the most skilled and productive workers in the field. Some will win more than others, but all who serve others with honor will earn their reward. The best will win the greatest rewards, and the rest will be content with lesser rewards, or move on to other things. For all the awesome power and innovative forms of the new collectives, they will be powerless against individual sovereigns who ignore their corporate claims.

Social promises will stabilize, the community having long passed its experimental phase. Major strands of social promises will coalesce into elegant forms and schools, the most popular of which will be familiar to children before puberty. Children will choose their preferred school of social promises, their tribal voluntary society, as a rite of passage to adulthood. These strands of promises will be as strong as steel, as tough as titanium, and as spotless as gold. Although proven social promises will seldom change, they can change when social conditions demand. Reliable reputational information will pervade everywhere demanded between strangers, to the limits of privacy set by those they examine. Personal identities will be secure, depending on webs of complex and subtle relationships that identity thieves cannot replicate without great expense and greater skill.

Economic and technological development will speed up. People will achieve economic independence at earlier ages. They will work because they want to, not out of need. Good people will still feel a sense of duty, and sometimes endure unpleasant jobs out of that sense, finding pleasure and reward in behaving with honor. Work and leisure pastimes will become less distinguishable.

With maturing of social promise community will come a cleaner, healthier Earth. New forms of public property, and non-property, will coexist in overlapping property systems. Voluntary associations will form to protect and maintain public property. Tragedy of the commons will become an archaic economic principle because voluntary rule will enforce reciprocal behavior at the cost of reputation. No one will let their flocks overgraze the commons, out of fear of being identified as a sociopath.

Cooperatives for protection of the environment will protect and expand healthy ecosystems in parks, reserves, and mutual use areas, all the while improving the quality of life in surrounding communities. Mutual use areas will host new ways for sustainable and comfortable human habitation in the middle of managed but natural, thriving ecosystems of plant and animal life. In some urban places, residences, roads, and markets will disappear underground, leaving the surface as a park interspersed with private pavilions, gardens, recreational trails, and meeting areas.

Communities with diverse lifestyles will coexist; rich and poor will coexist without oppressing one another. The poorest will have the same ultimate independence as the richest, secure knowing that fellow self sovereigns will reward honorable behavior with a new social security. Centralized authorities will not dispense the new social security, redistributing stolen money according to bureaucratic rules. Instead, many willing hands guided by independent ends will dispense social security, rewarding the honorable, penalizing the dishonorable, and earning honor by assisting the weak and disabled. Unearned privileges will be few and distributed by luck. Some will be luckier, more talented, more ambitious than others, and will gain more influence than others. But without political privileges and state-enforced monopolies, wealth will not concentrate in a few people. All will own their labor and its fruits and be free to bargain for rewards as they choose.

Politics will turn to influencing personal moral choices of the masses. All politics will be grassroots. Great political leaders will provide the greatest leadership, leading by example not by force. No levers will prove stronger than reputation, logic, and morality. Great politicians will make great social promises. The politicians and their followers will keep those promises, each member making their own social promises. Special interests will promote their preferred social promises by persuading individuals.

436

Dissenting minorities — there will be many — will be free to pursue their own visions if they will extend the same freedom to others.

With the end of war, space and undersea exploration and settlement will increase. The incalculable value of being the first to open new frontiers will fuel great leaps in the reach and mobility of humanity and life itself into lifeless regions. All the trillions spent on warfare will find better uses investing in these expansionary races. Human and animal populations will increase while adverse environmental impacts diminish. Human habitation will shift in part to barren areas, for example under the Earth, allowing an increase of natural reserves in fertile areas. Freedom of action coupled with an enforceable social consciousness and abolition of monopolies in law making power can have profound transformative effects.

If sentient artificial intelligence develops while social promises still rule the Earth, artificial persons will learn and accept the principles of self-sovereignty and equality of persons. The logic that underlies this new social philosophy does not require that any sovereign person be human. If artificial persons can transcend rule-based societies without need for dispute resolution or due process, then they will do so. These transcendent societies will either exist apart from the societies they leave behind or will interact with those who know only older forms and lead them to a more transcendent place.

In its maturity, social promise community will adapt to changing technologies and moralities with grace. The promise community will lay a foundation for the next phase of human evolution. None can imagine what follows next, except that progress will build on the best aspects of the voluntary society that preceded it, just as social promising builds on the best aspects of liberal democratic states: rule of law, merit-based assignment of social privileges, concern for economic fairness, and regulation of private actions based on public impact. Speculating about far distant possibilities is a fun but idle exercise. There is no way to know what will follow next until voluntary society has developed the social and technological advances that will enable the next revolution. What we can know is at hand. Let us seize the day: the opportunity to build a strong, defensible social promise community within the decaying shells of western republics and social democracies is within our grasp.

Social Evolution and The Unknown

The future is unpredictable, especially human behavior. Such is free will apparent. We cannot know how people will embrace social promising, by whatever name we call it. In the near term, most will continue to support rule by power dressed as social democracy, republicanism, dictatorship, empire or some other form of territorial sovereign rule. Rule by power is the only paradigm people of the present day know, but awareness of other possibilities is growing.

In the long term, global society will move on to some alternative forms of organization. One thing is certain: human society, including its forms of political organization and systems of justice, will continue to change. The political and social forms of governance we know and accept today will one day become archaic, unused and forgotten. Only we the living can act to influence the direction of social change. We can allow ourselves to hope and trust that our race can evolve towards more egalitarian and freer forms of social organization, and design avenues for positive evolution. Or we can choose fear and distrust of our neighbors' ability to rule themselves and seek to control them by coercive means.

The latter course will lead to more political oppression, of a totalitarian flavor. While contrary trends are also at work, mainstream trends still concentrate political, economic and military power in an elite few, increase wealth disparity, disempower the ruled classes, increase government surveillance and erode privacy, make constant war as political theater, grow indebtedness, teach helplessness, undermine personal independence, and grow the dependent classes. The Orwellian dystopia seems near, if not already here. If it is worth opposing mainstream trends, it is only because they are destructive and anti-human. Even as totalitarianism grows in some places, it cannot last or sustain itself. It will give way to something different, however long it takes.

Given that social evolution is inevitable and might improve human progress, now is the time to design and carry out social structures that can endure and scale up to replace government as we know it, without bloody revolution or other forms of coercion. Now is the time to enlighten the masses in the practice of non-aggression and voluntary exchange. It is better to fail at attempting good, than to make no attempt.

Developing and promoting social promising is a peaceful path toward profound social change. We cannot reach our goal by violent revolution. Violence as an instrument of social change promotes more violence. Initiation of force for non-defensive use violates by the non-aggression principle, which underlies the foundations of social promising. Radicals and philosophers have dreamt of the withering away of the state for over a century, but the tools for achieving that end have too often been violent and counter-productive. Even when limited to electoral action, the growth of government by force has not in the main been a driver of beneficial innovation. Much of the most important innovations of our age seem to have happened despite the growth of government, less than because of it. The most enduring changes are peaceful.

Profound and lasting changes may seem bizarre, ludicrous, or frightening, at first impression. The ancient Romans found the early Christians bizarre, ludicrous, or frightening – and much later, embraced the church, elevating the Bishop of Rome to the status of Pope. Later still, Papal governance found the ideas of Copernicus bizarre, ludicrous, or frightening, and silenced him by coercive means. But Copernicus' ideas about the solar system prevailed in time, despite opposition. Strange ideas have been ignored or suppressed by social elites, only to later become prevailing norms, at many other times. Evolution of ideas in the face of resistance and ignorance is a fact of human history. But not all new ideas succeed. Social promise community must stand or fall on its own merit, based on human reason and the sustainable pursuit of happiness.

If you have read this far, perhaps you are already for voluntary forms of self-organizing society and want to understand different alternatives for getting there. Recognize that we can put social promises into practice and ignite a social movement starting *today*. There is no need to seize electoral dominance, or for existing systems to fail. We need not ask permission from existing authorities to make and keep social promises, or to have a majority on our side. The practice of social promising does not require us to isolate ourselves and subsist off the land. Instead of focusing on the negative and criticizing entrenched institutions, we can build a free society of the future right now. If you have a better way to promote stateless society while still coping with the demands of your world as it exists today, do it. But if you have not thought of a better idea, be an early adopter and participate in making social promise community a practical reality.

Perhaps you are interested in the business potential of social promise community. As a new way for reputation discovery, trust building and dispute resolution, promise community will create economic opportunities. Early adopters will be in the best positions to enjoy these opportunities. Benefiting may mean becoming expert and establishing a reputation early. In social promise community, a good reputation will be more desirable than silver or gold, and more durable in value than bank notes. The opportunity to amass reputation capital will never be better. It's not a sure thing but is more likely to pay off than spending your time with idle pastimes.

Economic returns are not certain, even if social promise community becomes popular. Timing is everything. Reaching sustainability could happen in a decade, or might take longer than your own life, or even centuries. Building a new community requires investment and risk. The social promise and reputation registers won't build themselves and writing or choosing social promises is work. All this work entails risk. The builders and early adopters can't be certain their investments will pay off.

But the investment required is not that large, relative to the potential for revolutionary change. The first tasks of coding a ledger application, writing and publishing the first social promises, and promoting use of the ledger are within reach of an energetic small group or maybe even a gifted and dedicated individual. For a person with necessary insight and talent, initializing the conflict resolution system of tomorrow might be no more expensive and time consuming than an intense hobby. Once the promise system exists, setting up infrastructure for services such as secure identity services, reputation services, judicial services, or enforcement services, is no heavier than starting any other service business. Like any open source environment, securing an early position in the ecosystem can confer a valuable economic advantage, so pioneers can find economic motivation for their pioneering.

If anything can, patient persistence will win out. Patient advocacy is the only viable approach for peaceful persuasion. Here is a plan for a reputation and dispute resolution system based on personal sovereignty, not a crystal ball. Whatever plan you will put in place, the core principle of self sovereignty as the foundation of social order is worth fighting for and will transform.

Chapter 12: What Are You Going to Do?

First Look

If you want to help build a more voluntary world, there's lots to do and many arenas to work in. Creating alternatives to state-run civil justice systems is a small but critical part of moving to a freer and more prosperous world. To avoid entrapment by states that monopolize enforcement, voluntary systems for dispute resolution and reputation discovery must be based on self-sovereignty and operate independently of state control. Social promise community is one such independent system. If you would help build it, first understand self-sovereign rule (this Guidebook might help!) and then act to make the principles of self-governance and honor part of your life.

Kernel

The first task is to grow your understanding. Blockchain faith is not the first social movement to stress the importance of digging foundations, and it won't be the last. Without a solid foundation in rhetoric, reason, and morality, every social institution will fail. If you find what you've discovered here intriguing but a few uncomfortable holes in your understanding exist, work on filling those holes. Discuss practical details with like-minded people. Think it over. Step back and survey the entire future ecosystem of social promising. Understand who you are, what you want, and how your needs can fit in with the needs of your fellows. Look for a niche most attractive to you; if what you like most contradicts your sense of duty, reevaluate your inner value scale. Find your niche.

Leaders will develop the social promises that others want to make their own. These leaders will write the best words for self-rule and will not fail to live by their promises. They will sacrifice their own self-interest for the promises they believe in. To be a leader, find your own words to live and die for, and then live and die by those words. If you would be a follower, your job is the same, except that you will find your words as gifts from others. All will be followers, and sometimes all will lead even if only in how best to fulfill their own destinies.

You are an early adopter, a leader in experimenting. Like every good leader, be an evangelist, a bearer of good news, of optimistic assessments made over clear perceptions. If you can't find good news around, do something good and newsworthy!

Be a reaper and sower of seeds. Every seed is miraculous. It is a preserved plan, provided with the essential supplies needed to execute that plan. Words like these are also preserved plans, and ears to hear are the essential supply for making the plans happen. Once you understand social promising and can explain it to others, you will find a large supply of ears willing to hear what you must say. Your neighbors are hungry for freedom and for honest, peaceful, and equal relationships.

The basics of social promises are easy. Even children can understand them. It only takes a few minutes to explain those basics, and most who hear them will accept them as good. You will encounter skepticism, which is healthy if based in reason instead of prejudice. It's a fair question: if voluntarism based in personal sovereignty is such a good idea, why hasn't it been a basis for organizing society before? But it has! Everyone practices voluntarism in their personal lives, and much of civil law defends and requires it. Only the state claims the right to violate the sovereignty of the individual. Anyone with personal experience with the stupidity, unfairness, or corruption of authority already appreciates the wisdom of the sovereign moral person. Contemporary society has made it unavoidable for the common citizen to recognize the problems with state-based laws. The law has been an ass for centuries. Many people are ready to hear about reasonable alternatives.

Faith and vision will enable the alternatives to exist at first. Others will join once an alternative exists as a living experiment. Most people are not visionaries. Most people cannot spend enormous amounts of time thinking about alternative societies or trying to construct such alternatives. To foster meaningful social promise community, visionaries must build and lead it. Websites and media content where people can learn about and join social promise community must exist. Early adopters must generate a registry full of social promises ready for people to read and make their own, and a reputation ledger that records activity measured against the social promises of its members. The community will need advocates to counsel means for coexistence between the community and coercive states, and to defend the community from inevitable attacks by partisans of the state. There must be at least one social promise community open to the public. You, the early adopter, will make that first social promise community possible. Before we can build that community, the first step on the road of possibility is growing your understanding and spreading knowledge you know to be true to others.

Basket of Nuts

The Game of Promises

Different voluntary communities coexist with states, dedicated to different purposes. Some organizations, such as political parties and advocacy groups, are influencers, apologists, and enablers of state action. These societies are voluntary in the sense that membership is voluntary, but not in the sense of avoiding initiation of force for social and political uses. Non-governmental organizations concern themselves with social purposes like helping people in need, socializing with people having similar interests or hobbies, performing community services, practicing a religion, and so forth. Some voluntary organizations dedicate themselves to community building. Few offer conflict resolution, except of limited scope. Few recognize the importance or even the existence of self sovereignty.

Social promise community fills the gap. It exists to provide a self-sufficient honor and reputation system of unlimited scope, with no other purpose. The community coexists with states but does not concern itself with state action. By providing an alternative to the state in the sphere of civil justice that initiates no coercive force or fraud against others, it supports trust building and more cohesive community. One who supports the growth of voluntary solutions should belong to a social promise community and to other voluntary organizations. Membership in other organizations is one of the best ways to grow social promise community. Trust precedes credibility, and no better way exists to build trust than by working side-by-side with friends on a common goal.

A dilemma underlies. Social promise community has no purpose except trust and reputation building. It's hard to get started. That may be why social promise community doesn't yet exist, despite its simple concept and undemanding requirements. Social promise community can give no plunder for the people who form it and has no other limited purpose that people can agree is worth pursuing. To succeed, the community must convince and recruit valuable members to invest their time and energy, despite dim prospects for a quick return on their investment. How can the community attract valuable members? And what makes members "valuable"?

The second question answers the first. Valuable members include any offering a product or service only to other society members. Such a person has something of value, and their practice of withholding access to the thing of value from non-members creates a reason for people to join the society. All voluntary societies attract new members using incentives. Members need a reason to join.

A chicken-and-egg problem appears. How can a service provider refuse to serve non-members, if too few potential customers belong to the community? And why would potential customers join the community if it provides no advantage? The solution to every chicken-and-egg problem is evolution, meaning incremental change. The community need not start with a whole chicken, or with a whole egg.[29] It can start with something much smaller, something exclusive, but much smaller than a person's entire livelihood: a discount, a new release, or service enhancements. Members can always raise their premiums later, but experience teaches us that incentives need not be sky-high to motivate action.

At least one ancient human activity is available only to those who agree to follow a prescribed set of rules: a game. Promoters can start up promise community as a game. They need only design the game to show how the Three Promises work in various contexts. Three-promise designs can fit many games of various difficulty levels. To attract players the game need only be entertaining. To teach social promising, the game should encourage play using a consistent identity and enable players to earn a reputation for themselves. Most multi-player games work this way. But in a three-promise game, building a reputation depends on making and keeping social promises.

---

[29] If you think about it, a single-celled organism that replicates by division is simultaneously a chicken *and* an egg.

Social promise games may work well as massive multiplayer online games, in which the power and ability of each player depends on the player's reputation. Each player's reputation depends in part on receiving positive feedback from other players and avoiding negative feedback, and in part on the social promises adopted by the player and published to other players. Each player decides which other players they will cooperate with, based on reputation. Social cooperation will include things like trading, leasing, and contributing labor or resources to collective causes both public and private. Social cooperation will also include dispute resolution by neutral peers, with outcomes recorded in the game's reputational feedback records. These games will depend on reputation as the basic currency of society. Many games can fit in this multiplayer framework.

Promise games will include a promise ledger and a reputation ledger. Game designers can build promise ledgers as an electronic data structure (e.g., a relational database or a block chain) that relates each player to their social promises. Using the promise system, players will find other players who have made compatible social promises and avoid those who have made incompatible promises. To keep things simple for beginners, games may limit which social promises are available. Players might "level up" to make custom promises in more advanced levels of the game. At the most advanced levels, players might have the power to write their own social promises.

The reputation ledger is another database holding information about the extent to which each player has fulfilled the social promises they have made. For example, a player might rank on a scale of one to five, how well player 'Y' fulfilled their social promise 'X' in the social transaction 'Z'. Entries in the reputation ledger need cooperation: either the rating player and the player being rated cooperate to make an entry, or the rating player hires a neutral party to confirm the rating. False accusations and defamation can be resisted by the rated player, who can contest the rating in front of the neutral or hire another neutral to offer a second opinion. Reputation ledgers may contain other transactional details such as players may record. Disclosure of more detailed transactional records stays under the control of the players to whom the records pertain, using cryptographic keys.

Together, the promise ledger and the reputation ledger make up a data backbone that can support social games and real societies. One of the primary goals for near-term development of social promise societies is to code client-server applications that will enable people to produce, keep up, and extend the data backbone. These applications will be open-source and distributed under a General Public License or similar free software distribution model. These data backbone applications will be useful with game and social media applications via an application program interface. The same backbone might work for social promising in the real world.

You can be a backbone developer, a game developer, an applications developer, or an information processor and provider. If you can see the vision and gain the skills, do not waste the opportunity to gain prime "real estate" in the world of the future. If you are less technically inclined, but enjoy playing strategy games, then practice your skills and social awareness by being an active member of the gaming community that will first put social promising into practice. After practice in a game environment, extend your game play into the real world. Build your relationships with trustworthy members of your gaming community. Earn your reputation as a person who makes just and useful social promises and keeps those promises. Seek our members of your gaming community to do business with and extend to them the best courtesies and discounts you can offer. If your livelihood allows, offer services or goods only to other members of your promise community. Tell your neighbors about new tools for building trust

449

and navigating a treacherous world when you judge the tools ready and your neighbors' hearts open.

Settle claims with other members of your promise society with honor, without recourse to the state. Pay attention to the reputations of others and enforce consequences against bad actors while forgiving those who show sincere repentance. Enlist the help of a skilled and respected neutral to bridge disagreements you cannot overcome on your own. Defend your society against the depravations of trolls and tyrants if you judge it worth defending. Do these things and watch the best games enfold and transform the community you live in for the better.

Mutual Support

Mutual support exists when every person able and willing to serve others can do so, can earn a good reputation by service with access to benefits provided by others on a level playing field. Mutual support does not exclude the disabled, who are incapable of serving others. Mutual support networks can serve children because all capable adults were once children, and most children will become capable adults. The networks can serve the elderly because they have earned social credit, despite their present disabilities. Those with chronic disabilities can also receive support. Members will serve the disabled out of empathy and compassion for them and their loved ones, even those few afflicted with lifelong inability to serve others. Despite exceptions, mutual aid cannot function without a balance of mutual support. Output cannot add up to more than input. The best mutual support organizations will strike a balance by attracting a diverse membership and motivating all who can to make fair contributions towards the support of others.

Economics is the study of how societies allocate scarce resources. Economists recognize different economic systems, and the economic laws operating within them. Social promise communities are not economic systems; instead, they ease use of

450

any economic system. Everyone can participate in social promise communities without compromising their ability to earn support, or to offer support to others. The community prohibits no means of support. No "authority" exists to prohibit economic activities they find threatening or distasteful. Instead, members of aid organizations exert a distributed, decentralized and pervasive pressure on each person to arrange their economic activities so nobody can raise principled objections. A free enterprise justice system tests the strength of any principled objections that come up, using neutrals who compete on their reputations for fairness, effectiveness, efficiency and value.

Being free to use any economic system, aid organizations in social promise community will use whatever system follows the social promises of the people. Some may work using a gift-based economy, in which ownership claims are sparse but permitted; gifts require ownership. Other aid organizations may run communes without private property in which the membership distributes resources using a collective decision-making process. Still others may run with a capitalist plan, with everything owned by somebody and voluntary exchanges made via trade. These and other economic systems can coexist in promise community without violent conflict because all acknowledge the sovereignty of the person. The communalist and the gifter will trade with the capitalist. The capitalist and the communalist will give to the gifter. The capitalist and the gifter will enter communal arrangements with the communalist. Many hybrid economies will exist. There are no constraints beyond the social promises made by the members of these communities.

Neutrality frees the social promisor to find and give support as desired, within all social promise communities founded on compatible promises. Were it not for the violent intervention of the state, mutual support within social promise communities would satisfy consumer demand. But violent intervention of the state is a present reality. Neutrality alone cannot provide a reason for people to join social promise communities, so long as alternative means of support are available. Nor does neutrality protect social promise communities from aggression whether by the state or by non-state actors. The problem at the outset is two-edged: state systems dominate means of support and try to tax and control all economic activity. These two hard-edged realities cut motivation to make social promises for mutual support to the bone.

A key challenge for nascent social promise communities will be to create economic incentives for investment in communities, in environments where the state imposes taxes, and licenses and regulates most or all economic activity. We have considered incentives like making participation entertaining, providing infrastructure for social networking, and providing reliable, deep reputation information. Social promise systems can be entertaining and be part of social networking, but neither purpose is why the social promise system exists. Of these three incentives, only reputation information intertwines with the essential purpose of social promise systems. Access to reputation information based on social promises will provide the most compelling incentives for participation in social promise communities. As the saying goes, "a good reputation is more valuable than gold."[30]

When a social promise community can provide reliable reputation information about its members unafraid of violent government intervention, mutual support will develop as a natural social activity. Members will prefer to transact with other members of good reputation, instead of transacting with non-promisors. This wish to support other members will arise out of the enlightened self-

---

[30] Proverbs 22:1.

interest of each member and will not depend on any other motive force. Build a system that provides reliable reputation information to its members, and avenues for mutual support will follow.

Medium of Exchange

Support is not always financial. Money is a convenient medium of exchange but is unnecessary for people to support one another. People often support one another without requiring payment in money. In some contexts (e.g., nuclear families or close friends) purchase transactions are much less common than mutual giving. Fiat currencies are effective instruments for state activities such as taxation, warfare, concentrating economic power in an elite few, eroding the financial security of individuals, and enforcing mercantilist trading policies, but have proven to be poor instruments for free markets based on equal participants, or securing individual economic freedom. But few can reach all their goals without using money, state-issued or not. Social promise community has the tools to overturn money-dependent paradigms, without prohibiting or disfavoring the use of any acceptable medium of exchange.

Why should voluntary societies look for money substitutes? Trusted currencies enable social transactions while reducing need for trust to complete transactions. Money enables every consumer to get the ordinary goods and service they need. How consumers get their money doesn't affect their ability to buy what they want. The thief and saint shop in the same bazaar. Producers and destroyers both earn wages. The study of economics revolves around money and the financial system. All other things being equal, those possessing more money exercise greater social power. These beliefs are so pervasive that to describe them is trivial, and to propose an economy based on anything but money seems absurd or impossible. It is neither.

Money has diminished the need for interpersonal trust in cash transactions. Often, a reduced need for trust is a good thing. Trustless transacting is convenient and fast. Earning, proving, and discovering trust among community members can be time consuming and fraught with risk. Why should we bother with trust? It's more convenient to trust nothing but the system that handles the transaction. Convenience traded for vigilance evaporates in the heat. No system is trustless. Two parties lacking mutual trust can transact through a trusted third entity. None of the three operate without trust. The two shift their trust to a third institution. The third trusts its own status as beyond risk of injury.

The state is one such third institution. States impose their monopoly claims to police power in a territory by force of arms. As a monopolist operating without consent of the governed, the state works to shift individuals away from trusting in each other, and towards trusting in the state-supplied police and justice system. When tyranny prevails, its subjects can place no trust in the ruling apparatus; it is too dangerous for ordinary people to rely on. In less severe circumstances, the state is trustworthy in some respects, but often acts averse to the interests of those ruled for political reasons. Whether hard or soft, the state acts to erode trust between individuals. Once the state erodes trust to a fragile shell, individuals in a society cannot self-organize. The people become dependent on state power they feel powerless to resist. The adage of "divide and conquer" is true, whether applied to breaking of military alliances, or to the state's conquest of natural community.

It takes work to disrupt formation of natural trust networks. Trust is the only natural alternative to theft, fraud and violence. When inter-personal trust is high, connection and spontaneous order arise almost without effort. Reliable trust in others preserves the peace without hall monitors or cops. Wherever there is social trust, there is reputation. The more that reputation matters, the more transactors will want to earn trust. Providing useful reputation information widens each person's sphere of trusted relations, and increases productive activity driven by interpersonal trust.

Reputation can't serve as money, because reputation is neither transferable nor fungible. Each person owns no reputation but their own. Good reputation is durable, valuable, and can be made secure. Reputation provides the only rational basis for extension of unsecured credit. A good reputation can provide access to capital via a creditor. Reputation can also earn favors out of an expectation that the one receiving favors will repay fairly. Development of reliable reputation information will enable voluntary societies to excel in the extension and fulfillment of unsecured credit and social gifting. Excellence in using unsecured credit and social gifting will enable members to find support for themselves when in need, and to distribute support to others when experiencing abundance.

Consider a classic example for showing the usefulness of money: Triangle trade. Alice has bananas and wants nails. Bob has nails and wants flour. Charlie has flour and wants bananas. Alice could trade her bananas for flour, and then trade the flour for nails, if she can guess Charlie's desires. Or she could use a medium of exchange, and buy the nails from Bob with money, while Bob buys the flour with the money from Alice, and Charlie buys bananas from Alice. If Alice, Bob and Charles trust one another, they will not need to arrange a triangular trade or use a medium of exchange. They can give of their excess to those who they trust and negotiate their needs within the same trust community. The result will be the same.

Reputation can run much deeper than a credit score or vendor rating. Its dimensions are not limited. Reputation is an intangible asset that gains its value by attracting and sustaining trust, enabling social transactions. Being an asset, it resembles property in that defamation of reputation is cause for payment of damages. None can transfer their reputation to another because reputation is personal. But lending one's reputation is commonplace. Those with established reputations can vouch for others whose reputations are unknown or can lend their reputations to others by association. Some may lend their reputations for something of monetary value. Reputation-lending drives professional services and capital even today. Reputation has economic value sometimes measurable by market transactions. Unlike other assets, the more that a person lends their reputation the more they dilute its value. The higher the price for an endorsement, the less credible the endorsement and the endorser are. The most credible endorsements are those given without expecting something in return.

Although intangible, when reputation exists, the person with it will know. A reputation as a great athlete brings opportunities to display that athleticism in front of fans. A reputation as a great lawyer brings paying clients. A person with a great reputation for being just and fair can receive favors without expectation of immediate repayment. Those who grant wanted favors trust that the recipient will repay with generous dividends.

We can find examples of these high levels of trust in some family relationships. Family members sometimes work together in a common enterprise without contracts, trusting that whoever distributes profits will be fair. High trust groups seldom extend beyond small groups based on face-to-face, interpersonal relationships having a duty of loyalty. Taken to its logical conclusion, a deep and reliable reputation system has the potential to extend high trust levels to less intimate relations, expanding the economic possibilities of trust.

Expanding trust within large communities of strangers will be difficult, to be sure. There will always be those willing to abuse trust for a quick advantage over a stranger, or those who will intend to destroy trust communities by sowing deceit and fraud.

Reputation systems that work will punish opportunistic abusers of trust without delay and identify enemies of the community without fail. Trust systems must be resistant to abuse. The Three Promises provide a stateless social order between equal self sovereigns, but the devil will be in the details of system design. The next task is to design those details, starting with first principles.

We considered a basic design under the Game of Promises. That essay does not deal with the critical issue of security. Promise community will need systems that resist attack, not only by including cryptographic locks, but also by configuring system assets in ways that render all known attack vectors futile. Bitcoin is an example of design for security to thwart violent seizures of server nodes by armed police officers. It does this using a blockchain protocol implemented in an open-source application, which distributes the data that servers maintain over an open, self-organizing network of independent operating nodes. It has been infeasible for flesh-and-blood agents to seize such a network. Crypto-currency pays a heavy price for this security. Its networks consume incredible amounts of electrical and processing resources to avoid corruption and aggression, and all to protect a small transaction register. Inventors will devise new and more efficient security protocols for public ledgers, even as the middlemen the ledgers displace escalate their attacks.

Although Bitcoin and related blockchain protocols thwart armed seizures of server data, their design leaves users of the system open to violent oppression and attack by the armed officers of the state. The state taxes users, charges them with financial crimes, or fines them for regulatory violations for transacting in crypto-currencies in ways that the state finds offensive. Offenses include maintaining one's own transactions private from the state (e.g., "money laundering"), evading payment of capital gains taxes, and evading the payment of income taxes. Public blockchain registers leave all transactions open for inspection, by design. The ledger makes users vulnerable to attack by the state for their public transactions. Greater privacy protection would be useful.

Infrastructure Design

Social promise community needs information infrastructure. It must know with confidence who made which social promises when, and how they kept their promises. Promise records must be secure and free from control by any single entity or cabal. Reliable social promise information fosters trust. Trust enables networks of producers who offer the goods and services community members want. In the modern world, the capital investment required to build complex, capable information systems is reduced. Solutions such as crowd-sourcing and open source development of software have brought many information tools and resources within reach of the masses. Although infrastructure cost is not massive, it still exists. Investors must take risks to build infrastructure. Development happens when investors believe they can reap rewards worth risking their time and money on.

Cryptocurrency networks, for example Bitcoin, Dash or Ethereum, reward developers and operators with the coin that the infrastructure supports. Reputation systems implemented in Ethereum, such as Auger or Synereo, use quantitative cryptographic tokens to measure and incentivize the amount of 'good' reputation earned by network nodes for doing desired tasks, like truthful and efficient reporting of events. Scarcity of the tokens is artificial, grounded in hard math set by algorithms that award new tokens or a small fraction of existing tokens to nodes performing network services. Although tokens encourage infrastructure investment in networks, their use provokes opposition from the central banking-state cartel. The state imposes its financial regulation and taxes on cryptocurrency as a fungible, tradable asset and vehicle for money "laundering." It threatens to outmode central bankers, who will spend what they must to keep it suppressed, isolated and out of the mainstream. We can hope for a slow unwinding of central banking as people learn to live without the central banks' fiat, but abrupt and harsh currency failures have been the norm. Until central banking disappears it will grind on, slowing introduction of new and better things.

The power to tax is the power to destroy, and so it is with regulation. Healthy and growing social promise communities will diminish state dependency and power. Cryptocurrencies invite attack for exposing the weakness of fiat currencies. States will attack promise ledgers for exposing the weakness of state-run justice systems, using their usual weapons of mass destruction. It would be foolish for self sovereigns to hand their enemies a convenient weapon, by ignoring the state's declared conditions for attack. Better ways to incentivize infrastructure exist, without implicating the regulatory and taxing power of the state. Secure ledgers should resist political attacks. To better resist attacks, the ledgers should be efficient in their use of labor and natural resources and contain only free speech and metadata. Ledgers designed for exchange of cryptographic tokens are useful but unnecessary to keep reputation information secure. Promise community will benefit by avoiding well-honed attacks from the state-sponsored financial sector against networks used for currency trading.

Onerous regulation is not the only drawback of issuing tokens. Tokens are countable and relate quantities. In self sovereign community, members earn tokens in proportion to the value of their productive labor. Where no ruler exists, and all have equal privileges, accumulated tokens stand for a virtuous excess of production over consumption. In a society ruled by elites, accumulation often comes because of social privilege: status as a landlord, officer, state licensee, legislator, or patron. In any society, money sometimes comes with skill at fraudulent or aggressive practices. Money is a poor measure of moral character, in the best case correlating to a single dimension of social reputation: excess productivity. In the worst case, money is another tool of rulers to control the masses. Social promise community can use various competing mediums of exchange, tangible and intangible. It doesn't need another token for trading and can't use tokens to measure reputation information. It needs a reason for members to support the community's reputation information infrastructure. The reason can be natural demand for reputation information. The community can use information technology that causes each member to contribute hardware, processing power, and bandwidth to access the reputation network. For example, system designers can build a system in which every client node is also a server.

Tokenless distributed computing is old. For example, SETI@home has been operating a distributed data processing system since 1999 to search for extraterrestrial intelligence. SETI@home uses a client-server scheme not peer-to-peer but shows that people will support distributed computing for rewards other than tokens. Like SETI@home, cryptocurrency networks share attributes with client-server architectures. Cryptocurrency relies on a community of mining nodes (servers) that serve information for wallets (clients). Client-server networks are easier to design than peer-to-peer, because designers can concentrate hard-to-distribute resources in the server nodes.

In cryptocurrency networks, mining nodes compete to process blocks and earn tokens. Every node can store a complete copy of the network's data, the blockchain ledger. Breaking the single-server monopoly with a free market of competing servers results in a more secure ledger. It prevents destruction of the ledger by jack-booted thugs. A peer-to-peer system increases security from thugs and can be tokenless. Every peer node contributes resources in proportion to its use of the network. Contributions are a built-in condition of network access. The network always has access to the resources it needs with no need for tokens to incentivize server operators. The network can be self-organizing, with peers joining and leaving the network at will by interacting with neighbor nodes.

Peer-to-peer systems work well for tasks like network communications that designers can distribute among peer nodes. Each peer operates the same program for passing messages from node to node. If a node drops off the network, other nodes fill in and no messages get lost. The core function of a reputation network is serving an indexed database. Storage is harder to distribute than communication. When nodes drop off the network or become corrupted, the network loses information unless another node holds a redundant copy. If every node stores the entire database (e.g., the blockchain ledger), the network has perfect redundancy. The data is safe even if the network loses all but one node. But if every node stores the entire database, the more the network grows the more inefficient it becomes. The storage capacity of each individual node and the bandwidth to send updates to every node limits data the network can store and how quickly it can service queries and write operations. The network cannot use the aggregate storage capacity of the network to grow its database and must waste bandwidth by sending all updates to every node.

Alternatives to perfect redundancy exist. Many peer-to-peer protocols for distributed data storage use imperfect or no redundancy. For example, RAID (Redundant Array of Independent Disks) data storage technology includes at least one protocol (RAID 0) with no redundancy and varying degrees of redundancy in higher levels. RAID technology relies on redundancy and parity-checking to check for data corruption. Cloud storage technologies have extended RAID-like technology to new frameworks, without forsaking basics like redundancy and parity checking.

Operators of data storage centers lock their servers behind secure doors. So long as everyone in the data center is trustworthy, random hardware failures pose the biggest risk of loss. A self-organizing peer-to-peer storage network faces greater challenges, as any data storage center operating in a crowded bazaar will. With open networks we must assume a significant fraction of nodes are untrustworthy. Perfect redundancy with competing servers protects against data corruption but at too high a cost for reputation networks, which need an ability to grow to massive scale. If a tokenless, self-organizing open peer-to-peer network with imperfect redundancy is secure, its nodes run protocols yet to be invented. Until then blockchain may be the best framework. Blockchain suffices while promise community is small and experimental. It is not a long-term stable solution for providing a distributed public ledger containing social promises and reputation feedback. The community can migrate blockchain ledgers to long-term stable networks once available.

For an accurate picture of all the dimensions of moral character, we'll need something different from a quantitative token. "Something different" might include a record of each person's social promises, and a measure of confidence by unbiased others that each will keep their social promises, based on past performance and other factors. Detailed reputation information is valuable. Character information will be the gold of the network infrastructure for social promise communities. It will be the value that drives all other wealth. Build attractive infrastructure, and valuable reputation information will grow all over it. The size of the market for reputation is every person on Earth. Once the information exists, members will contribute support as the price of access to it. And the builders of the infrastructure will be in the best position to harvest value from the reputation information the network fosters.

The value of the reputation information will fund growth and upkeep of robust reputation networks. Exchange of quantifiable reputation tokens will be of secondary interest. Being secondary in interest and adding risk of regulatory attack by the state, using tokens will fall out of favor as an unnecessary distraction. Tokens may exist in early promise systems because they are familiar and attractive to those who support today's distributed public networks. As social promise reputation systems mature, they will evolve beyond tokens. Token exchanges will stay with independent crypto-currency networks, while designers of reputation systems focus on optimizing the value of their main asset: social promise-based reputation information. Like any other information network, everybody who wants access to the information supports the network. Unlike centralized databases, the distributed public ledgers belong to any willing to store the data.

Information brokers will need social skills to unlock the value of promise-based reputation information. Most users will make a basic set of social promises they publish without cryptographic locks. Over time, basic promise sets will become more standardized, until it becomes possible to encode the basic promise sets of most users with sparse data. Standardized or not, many users will adopt auxiliary promise sets they wish to keep private, published only to a subset of the entire community. These auxiliary sets will not contradict the user's basic promises but will extend them to more specific circumstances. Users wishing to preserve privacy around certain activities might want to keep telltale auxiliary promises secret except from those who need to know. These users can encrypt their promises to keep them private. Only those holding a key can know their private promises. Users can encrypt reputation feedback for similar reasons. Information sellers will compete for access to encrypted information. For example, a service might earn access to user keys for helping users find like-minded individuals in the community, or for credit reporting.

Online social networks such as Facebook and LinkedIn generate a social graph, political graph, and interest graph for each of their users. The focus of the graph information depends on the social network. These graphs are useful for advertising and propaganda, but not helpful for building webs of trusted friends. Online social networks do not give reliable moral character information. One can draw inferences about character by reading social media, but these inferences are not trustworthy. Every user controls their own self-image, while a single host entity controls all the network's data including the user data. Social promise ledgers will preserve reputation information in a public ledger using blockchain technology with user control over their encrypted records. Social promises come with social obligations. Broader social networks can include access to public reputation networks as one of their service modules.

Distributed public ledger technology is still in its infancy. The merger of hashcash and blockchain became Bitcoin and its progeny for tracking ownership and transfers of currency certificates. The main purpose of the blockchain is to prevent double spending of certificates. All its data stays in a single file, the blockchain. Later designs like Ethereum can do more but creating and tracking currency certificates is still a large part of how people use them. Social promise ledgers and reputation feedback ledgers have a different purpose. These ledgers need not track ownership changes of currency certificates. They only must preserve archived promise or feedback data and provide it for read and write access, outside of the control of any single database operator or cabal.

Social promise registers will be compact. Successful self-sovereigns won't change their social promises often and will keep them concise. They will make use of standard phrasings for compactness and clarity. Members who write wordy, eccentric, or ever-changing social promises will be outliers with small impact. A megabyte of data is enough for a lifetime of promises. A social promise register for 10 billion people each using a megabyte of data needs about 10,000 terabytes.[31] That's not too much data to afford anymore, and it's more than a world-wide promise register needs. By the time social promise communities encompass the world, social promises will be concise, elegant and artful. Most will make the same popular promises. The promise ledger shouldn't store redundant information unless needed for security. It must store a link between a unique personal identifier for every member and the time that the person makes and revokes specified social promises. The record can define the social promises however is convenient, with or without referring to a standard promise.

Each person's promise record will include a universal unique identifier (e.g., an email address) and a table of secure timestamps each associated with an action (e.g., '0' for revoke and '1' for make) and a symbolic designator (e.g., a hash or other identifier) for a unique social promise published elsewhere. The social promises themselves don't need to be kept in the ledger unless unique. Promisors might select social promises from existing records in the ledger, and link to a certain promise version instead of duplicating a record. Ledger-writing applications might link to an identical promise existing in the ledger, to conserve memory and bandwidth and increase speed. Web applications might mine the ledger to produce lists of published social promises and rank them by popularity. Promises made by more members earn higher rankings. Unlike "liking" or other voting on posts, making a social promise has meaning. A promise obligates its maker within the community. Not every good promise is popular. The greatest promises start out unpopular or are too heavy for many to carry. To track popularity, social promise lists can support voting features

---

[31] 1 terabyte is 1,099,511,627,776 bytes.

such as "liking," with usage data. Members will avoid making unhelpful social promises, because their reputations depend on the quality of their promise.

Blockchains are useful, but we need not use them to store social promise records because we need not worry about double spending of currency certificates. The double spending problem comes up when a person spends a coin and then spends it again before the network can publish the first transaction. Double spending an electronic certificate is a time-sensitive crime. The longer the lag between the spending events, the harder to escape detection.

Two fundamental aspects of blockchain protocols prevent double spending. First, the network won't publish any block that records a double expenditure of the same coin. It will discard the newer expenditure or both expenditures, instead. Second, a proof-of-work protocol prevents any entity lacking over 50% of the network's processing power from altering a published block. Each block contains a solution to a hard mathematical problem that's easy to check once known, and a hash value that depends on data in the previous block.

Chained hash values put the "chain" in "blockchain." To change a published block, a computer must replace it with a different block containing the fake data. To get other network nodes to accept the replacement, the cheating computer must solve the hard problem and include the solution in the block. The cheater races against all other computing power in the network. Unless the cheater controls more than half of the network's computing power, by the time it solves the problem other computers in the network will have built and published the next block. The cheater must build a replacement for the next block too, or else its fake block won't fit in the chain because its hash value will not match the hash of the next published block. Without more than half the computing power of the network, the cheater will never catch up and its replacement block will never fit in the blockchain. The bigger the network, the harder it is to cheat.

At root, blockchain protocols rely on diversity in control of computational nodes to prevent fraudulent records. It is the proof-of-work (i.e., the hard math problem) that shifts the truth-preserving power of diversity to the computational nodes. It is also proof-of-work that consumes so much electrical power and computing resources. Proof-of-work and other aspects of blockchain protocols might be overkill for social promise applications. But security threats exist beyond double spending. Self sovereigns must discourage people from using the ledger to defraud others. Social promisors will seldom have a reason to lie about their social promises right after making them. They have the power to change their promises as they please. So long as they make their changes without falsifying dates or times, they have done nothing wrong.

Criminals will want to falsify promise dates or their own promises to escape liability. They will also want to change the promise histories of others, to impose unpromised obligations, destroy reputations, or attack the community. The community might defend by protocols that avoid the computational costs of proof-of-work, relying on wide publication and storage by multiple independent nodes instead. Ethereum is headed in this direction with proof-of-stake and sharding. Each node will have an interest in preserving its reputation for safe storage of information. To falsify a record without being detected, a forger would need to destroy every true copy, or at least enough true copies to make the forgery difficult to detect. Whether stored in a blockchain or some other data structure, recording all useful social promises is a job for crowdsourcing. The more diverse the control of the storage resources, the harder it is to cheat.

Bitcoin, Ethereum and related protocols have the advantage of being well-understood, tested, and secured against many attacks.

But many other schemes for distributed data storage are possible. Distributed information management applications can divide, hash and store data in a random subset of network nodes with enough redundancy and integrity checks to deter forgeries. A changing network of random nodes might store multiple copies of the same member's record, as a defense against data corruption, data loss and fraud. Each member who wants to support a promise ledger might contribute resources in proportion to the data they want to store. Or they might contribute "gas" to store in a blockchain, as the Ethereum network does. Technical details of existing blockchains, holochains or other distributed ledgers are beyond reach of this Guidebook. Whatever the details of the storage network, members will access encrypted ledger data by requesting a key from each subject member. With the key (or keys) and the member's identity, they can discover when the member made or revoked their social promises. But many social promises may be recorded in the clear, so anyone can see them without a key.

Reputation ledgers make up another important part of the community infrastructure. They are like promise registers, but each active member will update their reputation ledger more often than their promise register. The reputation ledger holds feedback from other members, opinions and statements by neutrals, and other records of events involving two or more members. At least two self sovereigns must sign every record in the reputation ledger using a digital signature: the subject, and the person providing feedback. The reputation ledger might use standard phrases, free-form descriptions, or a mixture to describe events and conclusions. Except for the multiple signature requirement, the reputation ledger might use the same or similar distributed recordkeeping system as the promise ledger.

False reputation information can exist just like fake promises. People can collude or coerce others to create false reputation records that appear credible. The best defense against false reputation information is due diligence, secure identities, and reputations that matter. In a well-established promise community, reputation data is plentiful. False information sticks out for inconsistency with established records, and damages reputations when discovered. Prudent self sovereigns will treat members having short reputation histories with caution and will consider the whole record when prospecting for new relationships. Except for saboteurs, infiltrators and thieves, a reputation for honesty is essential. Productive community members will avoid coercing or colluding with others to corrupt the reputation ledger with false feedback. Most will keep their promise to not defraud. The most devious and violent liars may enjoy success for a short time, but their misdeeds will come to light soon.

If ordinary collusion occurs, any affected member can bring a complaint even if only to place it in the ledger as a warning to others. With threats (e.g., "if you complain about my offense I will lock you up and throw away the key") the victim may need heroic courage to warn others and bring an open complaint. If a single hero emerges, the offender will earn a reputation as one of the worst criminals right away. When heroes are lacking, more subtle means for marking out predators will emerge. An attack on the reputation ledger harms every member of the community, so spirited defense can come from anywhere. Being an attack on the entire community, threatening violence to corrupt the reputation ledger is in the riskiest category of crimes. Only the most arrogant wrongdoers will attempt it. Threats from secret police or violent gang members may prevent complaints from their victims, but word gets around. Thugs will find complaints from people beyond their reach appearing in their reputation feedback and frustrating their search for new victims. They won't know which of their victims is informing the complaints and won't be able to clear the complaints without transparent due process. Guilty criminals will avoid transparent due process, and so their careers as predators and corruptors of the community will end.

Technical challenges have many solutions. The best solutions take time and effort to invent and develop. Whatever the solution, social promise community will not need a cryptocurrency to exist; its members will use many currencies. The inherent value of reliable and deep reputation information will motivate infrastructure providers to preserve, protect, and publish collected information. Access to reputation data on a secure distributed public network is enough incentive for operators of network nodes to contribute resources. For so long as states are attacking cryptocurrencies with bans, taxes and regulations, social promise community should avoid making tradeable currency certificates an indispensable part of its data infrastructure.

Learning to Trust

A certain trust exercise entails falling straight back while in a position that threatens to break your neck while trusting those behind you to catch you and prevent that woeful fate. Despite the risk of serious disability or death, people go through with the exercise without experiencing uncomfortable levels of fear, because they have confidence their friends will catch them. Trustworthy support engenders a similar feeling of comfortable confidence, even without testing limits by doing knuckle-headed things. Every member of the community has a reasonable confidence that, regardless of their claims to property or level of accrued wealth, their fellow members will be there to catch them if they fall. For most adults, that confidence will come from an awareness they have helped others through difficult times and have observed their fellow members doing the same. Their experience of helping others reassures them of receiving help from others. When people feel intense anxiety about lack of support manifested as worries about income, affordable insurance, and so forth, this anxiety manifests a failure of community support. When community support fails, the community fails with it.

In social promise communities, the obligation to support community members in genuine need springs from each member's social promises. Welfare in social promise communities is voluntary insurance based on reciprocal promises. Those who promise to help others and show they will keep their promise will receive help when needed, not beyond what they promised. Members will form mutual insurance pools. The level of benefits from the pool relates to the premium paid. Those who cannot afford the premium can volunteer their labor instead. Each person will decide the level of commitment they will promise to others. All earn the value of their promises from those who have promised the same or more. The lesser promise controls.

The game of lesser promises limits support to what the recipient has promised to others. The limit can be soft and squishy, but in principle no one can claim support greater than they have promised to others. None can demand support from any who have not promised it. Unfulfilled promises can lead to unfulfilled benefits. Support is not a right, or a privilege. Support is the manifest honor of self sovereigns, paid from those experiencing abundance to those in need whether out of social obligation or pity. Those who respond to just claims of support earn honor for themselves. Support comes from social promises to help the needy or from contracts with insurance collectives. Self sovereigns will use both, and lines between the two may sometimes be blurry. Individual social promises work well for smaller things, like food and shelter for the destitute. Insurance or other forms of organized mutual aid may be more suitable for complex obligations like health care. But in stateless social promise community, the framework for insurance contracts is social promises, not state law. So social promises pervade every mode of community support, including insurance. Social promising enables welfare using better tools than taking from some by force to give to others.

Welfare systems must overcome fundamental challenges. They must gather resources for the need at hand, distribute the available resources without bias among deserving recipients, and discourage claims from those better able to support themselves. A free market regulated only by social promises can overcome these challenges with little effort.

Resource collection and distribution is easy in the information age when members are honest about their needs and resources. Both depend on administrative skill and diligence. Skilled and diligent administrators will invent thousands of different ways to collect and distribute mutual aid. If only states can restrain from quashing them, we will see many creative forms of mutual aid competing in a free market for solving social problems. Distinctions between "for profit" and "not for profit" will sometimes blur. The most successful and sustainable solutions will endure.

As for fraudulent claims, any member can bring claims of fraud or waste against fakers who deplete welfare resources without good reason. Armies of self-sovereigns will defend against fraudulent or unnecessary claims. Able-bodied people will avoid making welfare claims. They won't want a history of prolonged claims in their reputation ledger and will avoid any taint of fraud. The mentally ill or depressed will struggle with independence, but most will respond to empathy, love, and a way out. Communities for healing and support of the depressed and mentally challenged will form. Their greatest supporters will be their alumni.

The theoretical problems of community support by social promises are easy to solve. Actuaries of insurance pools can analyze member promises and claims. Armed with knowledge, they can devise rational schemes for spreading the burdens of support. It is more difficult to foster community support while coexisting with central-planned tax-and-control regimes. Mutual aid societies are a mainstay of the American past, few of which have survived long past income taxation in 1913. A present-day example is Liberty Healthshare,[32] which redistributes payments by members to pay the health care expenses of those same members, subject to certain limitations. The Healthshare doesn't guaranty it will pay every claim in full, but it keeps payments affordable and makes distributions based on neutral criteria.

Time banks like the Arroyo S.E.C.O. Network of Time Banks[33] are another example of a mutual aid society. Members of a time bank contribute and receive favors to other members, accruing time-based credits tracked by the community host "bank" by doing favors for other members or institutions, while spending the credits for favors received. Organizations like Liberty Healthshare and the Arroyo S.E.C.O. Network might fill in gaps between the social promise world of tomorrow, and the state-run, tax supported welfare systems of the present, but have certain vulnerabilities when competing with state-directed enterprises.

Like early digital currencies, mutual benefit associations like the time banks or health care cooperatives depend on a central registry and host to track member transactions. This leaves them vulnerable to attack. Attackers can shut them down by identifying the host servers and seizing them by force. The U.S. federal government used this vector to attack and shut down the first digital currencies, giving rise to Bitcoin. While states have allowed certain cooperatives to operate, this tolerance will last for only if the cooperatives are too small to threaten any state interest, such as tax revenue or the value of state-issued fiat currency. In the present climate, states or their allies might attack any cooperative poised to

---

[32] https://www.libertyhealthshare.org/
[33] http://www.asntb.com/

displace a significant portion of state influence and power. Cooperatives can avoid the vulnerability of central hosting by adopting public registries using blockchain technology. But a public registry leaves users of the registry susceptible to surveillance and attack. Attacks on individual users are harder than attacks on host systems, but still will come.

Social promise networks can protect themselves using both practical and political defenses. Practical defenses include technological measures such as blockchains, encryption of user transaction data, and obfuscation of transactions. It should be possible with robust keysets empowering users with control over their own data and making users difficult to surveil.

Political defenses include various kinds of misdirection and obfuscation to conceal the size of the social promise society until it has grown too large to attack. For example, large societies might divide themselves into sub-societies and cultures that appear to outsiders to be unrelated or fragmented. System designers can encourage a natural diversity with infrastructure that rewards and encourages diverse ecosystems made up of interdependent, diverse cooperative organizations, with no head to cut off. Imperfectly redundant, self-organizing peer-to-peer networks are an example of infrastructure that can reward natural diversity. Any node that supports the network can join. Nodes can join and leave pools and other subgroups for different purposes.

Another political defense is structuring network infrastructure for legal compliance and social benefit. For example, a social gifting game without right of repayment, a virtual Burning Man, can self-organize outside of any currency network. Crowdfunding platforms are present-day examples although not always styling the funds as gifts. In a pure gift society, the ledgers record only gifts with no expectation of repayment and can be encrypted to keep gifts and identities private. Secret gifts are not recorded in the ledger. Gift cultures might begin in sub-groups and grow until an ecosystem of interdependent sub-groups can supply ordinary needs. Self sovereigns can measure supply and demand by user requests and fulfillment reports instead of price information. Requests for gifts can compete based on the promised use for the gift and the requestor's reputation for giving and using gifts. Donors can manage their giving to build a compelling reputation as a donor. Gifts of goods or services in high demand can earn more honor for their donors than gifts of lesser value. All that any member can earn by gifting is non-transferable reputation. Gifting creates no entitlement to receive goods or services, and hence, no barter or exchange. If structured with care, such a social gifting game might avoid income tax regulation and gift taxes. When building a gifting network, recruit an exceptional tax attorney to advise!

Besides gifting networks for various causes, members might form and maintain state-registered non-profit entities to lend legitimacy to certain functions of the social promise society. For example, insurance cooperatives, mutual aid societies, resource-sharing cooperatives, schools, mediators, counsellors, conflict resolution aid societies and other entities operating on a non-profit basis, in full view of the state and its regulators might support social promise community. uRULEu Institute formed as a California public benefit corporation to support promise community with education, research and certification. Existing organizations will learn the principles of social promise communities and incorporate the principles into their existing operations. Lawyers will likewise learn the principles of social promise communities, and will guide their clients away from legal pitfalls, enabling the essential reputational and moral aspects of social promise communities to expand and thrive even under intrusive state regulations.

Much action will be organic, without using organized legal entities or state-licensed providers. Consider defense. Voluntary defenders of the community will expose agent provocateurs and other sociopaths through the reputation system itself. Members who defame the community by recording evidence of illegal activity in the reputation ledger will repent or face widespread shunning. Voluntary defenders will find many members willing to do them favors. Organic defense will emerge from crowd-sourced activity of the trust network.

Details of mutual support structures are for future promisors to work out. Whatever the details, under social promise community mutual support will expand beyond vulnerable minority groups. Mutual support networks will be complex, multi-layered, and dispersed inside and out of the flesh of the state leviathan. Voluntary defenders will protect the support networks with diverse defensive schemes, both technological and political. In dangerous times, support networks will hide from public view. Community members will disguise and encrypt their identities and activities as needed to defend against predators. The networks will avoid bright lines and soft spots for states to sink their regulatory hooks. Surrounded by many protective quills, swarms of mutual support networks will bring fair and effective community support to the masses, without fraud or theft. With patience, grace and courage social promisors can prevail, and transform the leviathan of state into the butterfly of freedom.

Afterword: My Confession of Faith

Writing this book has changed me. Researching and thinking about positive ideas for human interaction has jolted my trajectory into a new orbit around social promising. As nutty as the idea seems, something in me believes promise community will prevail. Right or wrong, whether this Guidebook is only folk art or something more, I'll never stop hoping it can happen, nor stop learning and teaching about it.

No faith is strong unless it endures disbelief. Sometimes I can't believe any chatter about social promises will change the world one bit. It can all feel pointless, like a foolish, impossible hope. Deserts of disbelief and fear threaten to pen us in and destroy our dreams. But new things have never happened without absurd and dangerous experiments. How many failed attempts were made at powered flight, before the Wright Brothers succeeded? How long did it take to create a video phone that works on a wristwatch? Disbelief is no evidence that attempts will never succeed, especially when the attempt is unprecedented.

The nut will sprout and grow a forest. It may take a few decades, a few centuries, or a few millennia; in geologic terms, an eyeblink. A history of human failings creates many obstacles self sovereigns must first overcome. The New World will dominate only after a minority has tested and refined its principles and tools in experiments that will bear many failures.

If in darker days you can envision that future forest, if you can feel that hope and joy, then it's too late: you're infected. You either are a nut, or soon will be. You will be busy the rest of your life spreading nuttiness around; planting seeds; sinking roots; spreading boughs; growing mighty forests! What matters is you: rare, precious, and powerful, a self-organizing, sentient, rational, social, empathetic living being. A self sovereign fit for building a peaceful society of self-sovereign beings. Your discovery will energize the rest of your life and take you to challenging but rewarding places.

Perhaps blockchain faith will change the world, shifting the social order to a self-sovereign foundation. If self-sovereign power can exist, it must exist. If the meek can inherit the Earth, then that future world must be beyond anyone's power to foresee. It teems with too many possibilities! You're hard to imagine, future reader. I'm straining my mental eyes to see you and the world you live in. I can't figure everything out about you. Intuition shows you there, looking back, marveling at how an impossible hope could drive unbelievable changes.

You are a scholar of comparative obligations, a counsellor of social promising, a respected neutral. Many people with serious disputes and controversies seek you out, to resolve their conflicts with peace and fairness; they reward you well for your services. They know your opinions will stand and earn respect. You have resolved disputes valued in kilotons, for fees measured in grams, reconciled aggrieved factions and made peace between warring tribes, and taught many others how to do as you do. You have followed social promises to justice in hundreds of cases and studied thousands of cases more. The new order is fascinating.

Your society is full of many other heroes. Do you see anyone you know?

You are a storyteller, a composer, a creator of alternative realities: an entertainer who illuminates audiences, who stimulates hunger for truth, and then delivers what is hungered for. A magician of words and images, who captivates and liberates in the same action. A bearer of light, inspiring social good, while delighting audiences with entertainment.

You are a healer of the body, bold and holistic, unafraid of exploring and proving new therapies, liberated, empowered and

478

supported by her patients and past patients, healing and preventing disease and injury, and extending human lifespans, without doing harm.

You are a healer of the mind, a life coach, a psychologist, a psychiatrist, insightful and unfettered by boundaries except reason and concern for the welfare of patients, developing and implementing effective new therapies, setting patients free from bondage to fear, trauma, and pain, without fear of persecution by agents of large pharmaceutical companies or doctors' guilds.

You are a teacher, a researcher, a community organizer, a good shepherd, delighting in the personal growth and learning of students and followers, whose methods of teaching are unconstrained by political power and guided by the promises of the communities she serves, shattering artificial boundaries, revealing indisputable truths, and empowering her followers with the skills and passion for increasing knowledge and directing its power through conduits of reciprocal love.

You are an investigator, a security expert, a first responder, a rescuer, uncovering and rooting out evil without fear or bias, designing and building defensive strategies and shields for free communities that no state or saboteur can penetrate, arriving with incredible speed and power where disaster or threat of attack loom, preventing destruction.

You are a citizen-soldier, with a multitude of all genders, ages, and types, alert, trained, and nearly always dormant as soldiers while busy with peaceful affairs. But when attacks threaten, when whatever tyrannies left in the world go mad with lust or rage and seek to control, to embargo, to invade, to surveil, to bombard, to poison, to steal from, to vandalize, or to attack the free people of the earth, you and your fellow soldiers activate and cooperate in countless ways to nullify the threat and extinguish its origin.

479

You are an arborist, an architect, a landscape designer, an ecologist, a master herbalist, an environmentalist, a builder, planning and building incredible, self-sustainable gardens, shelters, homes, meeting places, factories and neighborhoods that allow people to thrive while enriching and preserving the precious natural environments of Earth, through cooperative, grass roots, inter-generational movements.

You are an astronaut, an undersea explorer, a scientist, and inventor, expanding the boundaries of human knowledge, presence, and capability with courage and ingenuity, taking great risks and reaping their fair rewards for their leadership and courage, supported by the fat of prosperous and thriving communities, contributed by every donor or investor with gladness.

You are a social worker that builds societies and families, weaves webs of safety nets, and grows interpersonal trust like crops on a farm. Your societies interconnect and service every social need while supporting themselves by the earned contributions of their members. You protect the orchard of trust and help every sovereign find a sustainable niche.

You are an engineer, a programmer, a system builder, crafting ingenious self-organizing systems that help communities self-organize; more than that, building network systems that motivate people to self-organize for peaceful coexistence and mutual support, igniting desire itself and channeling it towards that peaceful, self-organized end; technical wizards sustaining alternative societies, imagining and building moving vessels for many mediums; generating wonderful robots that creep, and roll, and walk, and run, and fly, that may become persons themselves; you enable others to pass between real and virtual realities. You design tools that change the future for better and make human progress possible.

There are so many more, can you see them also? Can you see the classless, self-organized, complex and ordered society they live in, glorious and free, without limits on sustainable development or progress? A society in which anything good imaginable can happen, and often does. Where good things beyond imagination percolate just beyond conscious awareness and break out to bring new freedoms and awareness on a regular basis. Where hope, freedom, justice, unselfish love and true, sustainable prosperity grow with each passing generation. How weak are the mental chains that restrain us from this better world! Let us break our chains with compassion for those who remain enslaved to fear and the will to dominate others.

I will do my utmost to bring forth that new community of self-sovereign promisors, and nurture it always. My fellows and friends are already doing more than I. Will you join us?

APPENDICES

I. Social Promise Examples

When I first thought about voluntary law long before I called it social promising or blockchain faith, I imagined that a reasonable set of laws would look something like old English Common Law. I hoped to distil a usable set of voluntary laws out of an older form of something familiar. I chose the original California Civil Code of 1872, because it represents David Dudley Field's earlier work to codify the common law, and because it is thin by modern standards. But I then realized several things. Mr. Field was a believer in the efficacy and justice of state power,[34] and the Civil Code of 1872 reflects his views. The English Common Law as compiled in the California Civil Code of 1872 is a reasonable starting point for a society founding a constitutional republic as a governing monopoly. We are not starting there. Our ancestors started there and look where it has gotten us. We would go in a different direction, starting from the corporatist kleptocracies that are the residue of constitutional republics, and moving towards a prosperous, just, and well-organized but decentralized society.

We commence amid an intrusive, overgrown and corporatist state, equipped with little more than a desire to displace the state with stateless institutions peacefully and without unjust harm. Our journey should start with simple social promises, with principles or promises we can express in few words. Not only does that make our initial burdens easier, it increases the chances we'll get to a good place faster, and not overshoot the mark. As our new stateless

---

[34] If Field's codification of the Common Law is not enough to convince you of that, read his *Draft Outlines of an International Law* (1872).

institutions grow and multiply, self sovereigns can expand the simple precepts of the first social promises to fill the needs of the new society, as those needs arise and grow. Maybe the relentless pruning of a free market in social promises handles great complexity best by short, simple and diverse social promises. The promises are different for everybody. Different people use different promises for their life experiences, expectations for the future, and cultural preferences. Finding the optimal level of complexity in social promises will be for each free individual to decide for themselves.

We need not see every expanse of the long road ahead to take the first step. The variety, number, patterns of distribution and content of future voluntary customs are unfathomable. Social promises as a body will be forever fluid, evolving and adapting while leaving every person free to live the entirety of life under one fixed and chosen code of honor, if desired. It would be futile to search for one perfect set of social promises and would betray a fundamental misunderstanding of what social promising is. Each person must decide their own code of honor, without expecting that any can discern perfection even for their own selves. Fulfillment of their own imperfect promises, and asking forgiveness for a failure to so fulfill, will be the burden of every member of voluntary society, forever. We should therefore not fear making promises that are imperfect or incomplete, any more than we should fear breathing. It is enough for us to promise the best we can conceive of and intend to keep those promises we make.

Self sovereigns can express their obligations in at least two contrasting styles. In Promise (subjective) style, the underlying antecedent promises are the three promises articulated for the uRULEu community, as discussed in Chapter 1, Basket of Nuts. In Statement (objective) style, the underlying framework is the triad of rules stated in Chapter 1, Kernel. I prefer the Promise style,

484

because it expresses both the scope and source of the obligation assumed and is easier to teach. Either way, the stated promises or rules apply only to members who have entered the community by adopting the required antecedent promises or rules. For example, terms of reference such as "others" or "another" refer to society members and exclude non-promisors. Non-promisors, by their own choice, have abandoned any moral basis for claiming duties from those who make social promises.

When making promises, it is prudent to start with the biggest issues, and work down towards the details. We should start with the basics. What are my essential commitments to my fellows? What commitments do I want every member to know? What is my moral core? My basic social promises should answer these questions. I provide humble examples, being sure these are not the best I or others can make.

BASIC SOCIAL PROMISES:

I will not use aggressive force or the threat thereof, fraud, theft or untruth against others, unless necessary for the proportionate defense of myself, others, or justly held property from aggression.

I will do that which is objectively reasonable and fair to avoid causing physical harm to others or to their property or wasting of natural resources not owned by any person.

I will maintain every secret I have accepted entrustment of in confidence, at least until the secret is discovered or published by another with no breach of my confidence, unless necessary for defense of myself, others, or property from aggression.

I will keep my agreements with others to the best of my ability, provided that the terms are memorialized in a record made with my knowledge and informed consent freely given without coercion, fraud, subject to correction of any obvious clerical errors.

I will not defame others with false statements I know to be false, or that I make with reckless or negligent disregard for truth and the reputation of the one defamed.

I will recognize the estate of the deceased and will respect the disposition of property from the estate under the will of the decedent to the extent it can be discerned, and to the decedent's closest living relatives to the extent the will cannot be discerned.

I will not abuse or endanger children or the mentally disabled and will forbear from entering any long-term relationship with them unless with the consent of their guardian.

I will submit to due process for any claim of another based on my failure to keep my publicly adopted promises and will accept any opinion made in compliance with that due process and with the social promises implicated by the claim.

I will accept as due process that which my accuser and I agree and will be diligent to reach such agreement. If after diligent effort no agreement on due process can be reached, I will submit to such due process as determined by a mutually acceptable neutral and will not unreasonably withhold acceptance of any neutral proposed by another.

If the unintentional breaking of my social promise causes physical harm to another or to the property of another, I will suffer the execution of and pay any opinion that does not exceed the magnitude of the harm that the breaking of my social promise has caused.

I will recognize as property of others these things, so long acquired and held by another in a just and an objectively reasonable manner and not later abandoned to the public domain: (a) that which is produced by the labor of another, or produced by labor and acquired by another for value in a voluntary exchange, which I cannot use or possess without depriving its owner of the benefits of use or possession thereof; (b) every true identity or reputation of another, or used by another to indicate a source of goods or services; (c) rights to exclude others from demarcated real spaces, to the extent reasonably necessary for a beneficial use by a person or cooperating group of persons, provided that the beneficial use does not, to any degree greater than my own claims or uses of property, unjustly deplete or deprive others living or yet unborn from access to natural resources of equivalent type for which the claim of exclusion is made.

I will contribute fairly based on my abilities and circumstances to the basic needs and common defense of those in need, who have demonstrated by their social promises and actions the fulfillment of an equivalent promise to me and their willingness to live by the fruits of their own labor. I will recognize no claim for failure to sacrifice my life or fundamental freedoms in fulfillment of this promise. Self-sacrifice can only be a gift, never an obligation.

* * *

Suggestions for improvements are welcome!

II. Further Reading List

Books or writings pertinent to self-organized society and justice, nothing more.

Anarchy and The Law (Edward P. Stringham)

Anarchy, State and Utopia (a notable contrary view by Robert Nozick)

Bitcoin: A Peer-To-Peer Electronic Cash System (Satoshi Nakamoto)

The Cathedral and The Bazaar: Musings on Linux and Open Source by an Accidental Revolutionary (Eric S. Raymond)

Coding Freedom (E. Gabriella Coleman)

Crisis and Leviathan (Robert Higgs)

The Dispossessed (Ursula K. LeGuin)

The Ethics of Liberty (Murray Rothbard)

Fabian Libertarianism: 100 Years to Freedom (Martin Cowen)

For a New Liberty (Murray Rothbard)

Freedom! (Adam Kokesh)

The Freedom App — Building True Freedom Through Contractual Republics (Peter Cisco)

Free Software, Free Society: Selected Essays of Richard M. Stallman (Richard M. Stallman, Lawrence Lessig, Joshua Gay)

Free to Choose: A Personal Statement (Milton Friedman)

The Games People Play (Eric Bern)

Healing Our World: The Compassion of Libertarianism; how to Enrich the Poor, Protect the Environment, Deter Crime & Diffuse Terrorism. (Mary J. Ruwart)

I and Thou (Martin Buber)

The Illuminatus! Trilogy (Robert Shea and Robert Anton Wilson)

Justice Matters (Roberta R. Katz)

The Machinery of Freedom: Guide to a Radical Capitalism (David D. Friedman)

Man's Search for Meaning (Victor E. Frankl)

Markets Not Capitalism (Gary Chartier and Charles W. Johnson)

The Moon Is A Harsh Mistress (Robert A. Heinlein)

The Most Dangerous Superstition (Larkin Rose)

The Road to Serfdom (F.A. Hayek)

A Spontaneous Order: The Capitalist Case for a Stateless Society (Christopher Chase Rachels)

The Structure of Liberty: Justice and the Rule of Law (Randy E. Barnett)

And Then There Were None (Eric Frank Russell)

This is Burning Man: The Rise of a New American Underground (Brian Doherty)

ZeroGov: Limited Government, Unicorns and Other Mythological Creatures (Bill Buppert)

III.   uRULEu Waiver and Creative Commons License

Jonny Stryder, Eggseed Press and their successors or assigns will follow the dispute resolution principles and methods described in this book for bona-fide self sovereign promisors in social promise community using networks or applications certified by uRULEu Institute, consistent with the published social promises of the author and any party infringing copyright of this work without permission or fair use.

IV. __Important Notice__

This Guidebook concerns possibilities. The social context for widespread use of the concepts presented here does not yet exist. To help you understand principles of social promising, the Guidebook considers hypothetical situations that assume otherwise. For example, it considers how social promising can apply to difficult situations such as murder and defense of the unborn, absent any imposed authority. Use of these hypotheticals is not meant to encourage anyone to break any laws, or to ignore rules imposed by present-day "authorities." Those advocating for social promising would do well to demonstrate the benefits of voluntary cooperation while respecting the legitimate needs of those who are in service of the state. Our friends and neighbors who cling to state authority as a tool for order should be brought along willingly, by demonstration and dialog. We open dialog by showing respect for the opinions of others. If we are to convince thoughtful statists, we must show respect for established laws and customs up to but not beyond the point of doing evil ourselves. To paraphrase Ludwig Von Mises, nothing can overcome evil but good.

About the Author

Jonny Stryder is a father, writer, attorney, engineer, happy camper and occasional libertarian political activist living and working in Los Angeles, California. You can follow him at www.vlda.org and its related social media feeds on Facebook and Twitter.

www.facebook.com/vldaorg
www.twitter.com/voluntarylaw
Follow the uRULEu Institute at http://uruleu.org/

98259944R00280

Made in the USA
Columbia, SC
22 June 2018